Carolyn Zerbes Enns, PhD

Feminist Theories and Feminist Psychotherapies
Origins, Themes, and Variations

*Pre-publication
REVIEWS,
COMMENTARIES,
EVALUATIONS . . .*

"**T**his book is an atlas of the many roadways that feminist therapists and counselors have laid through the terrain of psychotherapy over the last thirty years.

Bracketing the usual question of what is feminist about feminist therapy, Carolyn Enns asks instead 'What feminisms are at play in the rich array of feminist clinical theories and practices?' Her answer is at once a valuable guide to the 200-year history of feminist thought and a celebration of the vitality of present-day endeavors.

Feminist therapy is an enduring landmark of second-wave feminism. This compelling and generous compendium of feminist therapies will be of interest to practitioners, scholars, and students alike."

Jeanne Maracek
*Professor of Psychology,
Swarthmore College*

"**C**arolyn Zerbe Enns has once again produced a very readable, fascinating work on a current, important topic. Anyone with any interest in feminist theory and/or feminist therapy will find this book a necessary and basic addition to their library. Certainly all those who work with women in psychotherapy should consider this book a must read. Finally, we are provided with an excellent, informative examination of prominent, influential feminist themes and theories, including historical roots from relevant disciplines, along with specifics about applying theories to practice in feminist psychotherapies. This thorough exploration and integration of feminist theories and therapies, plus distinctions and diversities among beliefs and styles, is long overdue. This book effectively bridges a major gap in feminist psychological thought and literature. Clinicians, teachers, students, and clients will all benefit. Reading this work will make everyone, including those who call themselves feminist therapists, reexamine their beliefs and practices. An invaluable book for all."

Mary S. Gilbert, PhD
Psychologist,
Olivet College,
Olivet, MI

"**F**eminist Theories and Feminist Psychotherapies* is an important book for clinicians in training and seasoned professionals alike. Whether one is being newly introduced to the idea of feminist therapy, or is looking for ways to answer the personal question, 'What do I mean when I call myself a feminist therapist?', this book provides an intelligent articulation of the theoretical roots of feminist therapy. The text is scholarly and well written. Dr. Enns does not shy away from exploring the complexity and diversity of feminist thought that has informed current clinical practice.

This text should be read by all clinicians and academics regardless of their theoretical orientation. The insightful overview of feminist therapies and the underlying theories will provoke practicing clinicians to question their approaches to working with female and male clients alike."

Cheryl L. McNeilly, PhD
Clinical Psychologist,
Mid-Eastern Iowa
Mental Health Center

More pre-publication
REVIEWS, COMMENTARIES, EVALUATIONS . . .

The Harrington Park Press
An Imprint of The Haworth Press, Inc.

Feminist Theories
and Feminist Psychotherapies
Origins, Themes, and Variations

HAWORTH Innovations in Feminist Studies

Esther Rothblum, PhD and Ellen Cole, PhD
Senior Co-Editors

New, Recent, and Forthcoming Titles:

Feminist Theories and Feminist Psychotherapies
Origins, Themes, and Variations

Carolyn Zerbe Enns, PhD

The Harrington Park Press
An Imprint of The Haworth Press, Inc.
New York • London

Published by

The Harrington Park Press, an imprint of The Haworth Press, Inc., 10 Alice Street, Binghamton, NY 13904-1580.

The Haworth Press, Inc., 10 Alice Street, Binghamton, NY 13904-1580.

Cover design by Marylouise E. Doyle.

Library of Congress Cataloging-in-Publication Data

Enns, Carolyn Zerbe.
    Feminist theories and feminist psychotherapies : origins, themes, and variations / Carolyn Zerbe Enns.
        p.   cm.
    Includes bibliographical references and index.
    ISBN 1-56023-873-9 (alk. paper)
    1. Feminist therapy. 2. Feminist theory. I. Title.
RC489.F45E56 1997
616.89′14′082—dc21   97-1571
                                                                                      CIP

CONTENTS

Acknowledgments

Thanks to Cornell College for providing the sabbatical year that supported my work on the first stages of this project. Thanks to Gail Hackett for being the graduate school mentor who first encouraged me to write for publication and who first exposed me to the literatures on feminist theory and feminist psychotherapy. Thanks to the many students, colleagues, and clients who have helped share my thinking. Thanks to my family—Larissa, Jessica, and Richard—for being a steadying influence, providing a source of healthy distraction, and keeping me grounded in reality. Thanks to my Cornell support group—Diane, Jayne, Jan, Sue, Alison, Ellen, Gayle, and Diane—for emotional and practical help, the willingness to listen to complaints, and great advice.

ABOUT THE AUTHOR

Carolyn Zerbe Enns, PhD, is Associate Professor of Psychology at Cornell College in Mt. Vernon, Iowa and Senior Staff Psychologist for the University of Iowa Counseling Service. A frequent presenter at conferences and workshops, Dr. Enns has also written over 20 journal articles on feminist therapy and counseling and sexual abuse. She is an editorial board member for *The Counseling Psychologist* and a former editorial board member for the *Journal of Counseling and Development*. Dr. Enns is a member of the Association for Women in Psychology (AWP), and Divisions 2 (Teaching of Psychology), 17 (Counseling Psychology), and 35 (Psychology of Women) of the American Psychological Association. She has also been Chair of the Division 17 Committee on Women Task Force on Memories of Childhood Sexual Abuse.

Introduction

This book has been in process for over a decade. It emerges from my efforts to integrate the literatures on feminist philosophy and feminist therapy. I first identified myself as a feminist therapist while I was completing my doctoral degree in counseling psychology. During my first term of study, I was fortunate to be exposed to the classic feminist statements on feminist therapy. These commentaries shaped all other aspects of my graduate education. They affirmed my life experiences, influenced my research interests, and played an orienting function throughout my graduate training and subsequent work.

To expand my frame of reference, I read various writings in feminist philosophy. I was surprised at the absence of cross-referencing and integration between the two literatures of feminist theory and therapy. I was also impressed with the diversity of feminist thought and the conflicting ideas within feminist theory about causes of oppression, goals of feminism, and solutions to women's problems. Although authors who discussed feminist therapy noted that their work was informed by feminist philosophy, they rarely discussed which writers influenced their thinking and what specific philosophies informed their practice. Ellyn Kaschak's (1981) review of the first decade of feminist therapy was one of the few documents to explicitly note the differences between nonsexist therapy, liberal feminist therapy, grassroots feminist therapy, and radical feminist therapy. However, this article did not connect these distinctions to theoretical writings that clarified differences between theoretical and political approaches to feminism.

As I became more immersed in the feminist therapy and theory literatures, the reasons for the absence of integrated statements on feminist therapy and philosophy became more apparent. Some feminists resisted defining feminist therapy or connecting it to theory because these activities were seen as "fetishizing a merely intellectual distinction" at a time when "feminist therapy does not need definition so much as decision" (Chase, 1977, p. 22). Feminist therapy was typically described in terms of how it was different from traditional therapy rather than as a unique approach in and of itself (Thomas, 1977). Consistent with many feminist therapists' goals of participating in social change, early work focused less on "what feminist therapy is but what happens in it" (Lerman, 1976, p. 378). A second issue that persists into the present is that feminist therapists and feminist theorists often use different vocabularies to communicate their ideas. Many feminist theorists have been trained in the humanities while many feminist therapists are more comfortable with the methodologies and vocabularies associated with the social sciences. As a result, writings on feminist theory are not easily digested, and feminist therapists sometimes remain unfamiliar with many major theoretical and philosophical perspectives on feminism. Furthermore, there are few opportunities during counselor and psychotherapy training programs to participate in interdisciplinary exploration of feminist thought. In a typical graduate training program in counseling or clinical psychology, required coursework and practicum experiences are so extensive that it is difficult to find the time or opportunity to read widely about feminism across disciplines. Becoming fully informed about the intersections of feminist theory and therapy requires significant personal commitment and effort.

After exploring some of the implications of the different feminist theories for feminist therapy, I wrote a short article titled "Toward Integrating Feminist Psychotherapy and Feminist Philosophy" (Enns, 1992a). While writing the article, I realized that I was only dealing with important distinctions in a cursory manner. The idea for this book was born at that time. Readers may wonder why it is important for feminist therapists to be informed about feminist theoretical perspectives. Laura Brown's (1994) thoughts about this matter are especially informative. She states the following:

> Why is it important to understand the various models of feminism and the therapy theories that they reflect? It is, I would argue, because the models and theories by which any psychotherapy is practiced inform reality for the therapist and the client. Those constructs that a particular model names and

defines become real, present, and observable in the psychotherapy process of practitioners who use that model. (p. 48)

A feminist therapist's theoretical notions about psychotherapy
represent deeply held, complex convictions about the nature of human
functioning (Mark, 1990). These personal ties to a theory lead to the
powerful expression of one's identity in therapy and lend authenticity,
power, and effectiveness to interventions. Likewise, one's orientation
to feminist theory may have a profound impact on one's worldview
and the nature of feminist therapy that one practices. As a result,
feminist therapists should examine their personal assumptions in
light of feminist theory to ensure that their practices are anchored in
coherent and consistent frameworks (Enns, 1992a, 1993).

If feminist therapists mistakenly assume that feminist philosophy
is a monolithic entity, they are likely to draw erroneous conclusions
or overgeneralizations about the nature of feminist psychotherapy.
Alternatively, if therapists do not systematically explore the intersection between feminist theory, psychotherapy theory, and feminist
therapy, they risk the possibility of putting together a mishmash of
theories that are subjectively appealing but that have no clear rationale. Mismatches between interventions and assumptions may
result in blind spots and diminished effectiveness on the part of the
feminist therapist. The unsystematic combination of approaches and
theories may also result in confusion on the part of the therapist or
client or at worst, unethical behavior (Enns, 1992a; Lazarus, 1981).
For example, if the feminist therapist does not have a clear theoretical understanding of the principle of egalitarianism, she or he may
engage in inappropriate boundary violations. Feminist therapists
who work with gender role issues run the risk of practicing without
clear frameworks unless they are exposed to various feminist perspectives and integrate their beliefs about feminism with their
theoretical orientations to psychotherapy.

As many psychologists and social workers prefer an eclectic
approach to psychotherapy, feminist therapists may also prefer an
eclectic approach to feminist philosophy that combines elements of
different theories in a personally relevant fashion. It is important,
however, to distinguish between technical eclecticism and theoretical eclecticism. Whereas theoretical eclecticism is often problem-

atic because the practitioner attempts to integrate assumptions that may be in conflict, technical eclecticism involves the adoption of diverse techniques within a consistent theoretical framework. As noted by Arnold Lazarus (1981), "technical eclecticism implies using many techniques drawn from different sources without also adhering to the theories or disciplines that spawned them" (p. 5). A fully informed technically eclectic framework is only feasible, however, if one is fully aware of the theoretical values and assumptions that inform one's work. The feminist therapist who desires to operate from a coherent theoretical framework while also being technically eclectic will benefit greatly by increasing her or his knowledge about varied feminist approaches.

I encourage readers to use this book in combination with other recent books on feminist psychotherapy such as Laura Brown's (1994) *Subversive Dialogues: Theory in Feminist Therapy*, Ellyn Kaschak's (1992) *Engendered Lives: A New Psychology of Women's Experiences*, Judith Worell and Pam Remer's (1992) book titled *Feminist Perspectives in Therapy: An Empowerment Model for Women*, and Laura Brown and Mary Ballou's (1992) edited volume titled *Personality in Psychopathology: Feminist Reappraisals*. Each of these books present a rich theoretical base and practical information about the implementation of feminist psychotherapy principles. In contrast to other volumes, this book draws extensively on interdisciplinary scholarship. It focuses on the evolution of feminist therapy and how historical and current feminist practice interconnects with feminist theoretical and political thought. It is not a book about how to implement feminist techniques, which are discussed in many other sources, but represents an effort to provide a brief introduction to feminist thought and to discuss the compatibilities of psychological theories and feminist therapy techniques with various feminist theories. It also traces the evolution of feminist thought and feminist therapy so that practicing feminist therapists can better understand the relationship of their work to previous efforts. After reading this book, I hope that feminist therapists will read many of the original works that are briefly summarized in the following chapters.

Chapter 1 describes consensus values of feminist therapy. Although these values and practices are interpreted in diverse ways, this elaboration of shared principles is important as a foundation for later chapters. I have also integrated research findings about potential clients' reactions to various types of feminist therapy within this chapter. Chapters 2 and 3 summarize the major assumptions and contributions of liberal feminism, radical feminism, socialist feminism, cultural feminism, the feminisms of women of color, and feminist epistemologies. I have chosen to use the phrase feminisms of color in order to reflect the rich and varied views of women of color and to avoid suggesting an artificial and false dichotomy between white and nonwhite perspectives on feminism. Chapters 1, 2, and 3 also include short self-assessment questionnaires that readers may use to reflect on their own orientations to feminist therapy and feminist theory. Following these brief overviews of feminist thought, Chapter 4 focuses on the contributions of liberal feminism to feminist therapy, Chapter 5 describes the contributions of radical and socialist feminisms to feminist therapy, Chapter 6 elaborates on the connections between cultural feminism and feminist therapy, and Chapter 7 describes the contributions of women of color to feminist psychotherapy. The book concludes with a brief chapter that compares main features of the feminist therapies and identifies possibilities for combining and integrating feminist theories. It also comments on practical strategies for developing a personal approach to feminist therapy.

It is important to note that the boundaries between the various feminist theories are not rigid, but fluid and continually changing. It is somewhat artificial to divide the various feminisms into the categories and chapters that I use in this book. However, for the purpose of entertaining an organized consideration of significant issues, I have used categories that have historical and practical value. I also used a "best fit" approach, and embedded the discussion of some psychotherapy approaches at points where the linkages seemed most logical. Another author with a different set of assumptions and life experiences may organize these connections in a different manner. For example, some of the psychotherapy techniques that I discuss in the chapter on liberal feminism and feminist therapy may be relevant to other chapters and integrative approaches to theory and therapy. I encourage readers to maintain a flexible and open frame of reference as they think about the most useful intersections between feminist theory and feminist therapy that can inform their work.

Chapter 1

Basic Principles of Feminist Therapy

WHAT IS FEMINIST THERAPY?

Self-Assessment Questionnaire

For all questionnaires in this chapter, indicate your level of agreement for each item by using the following scale:

do not agree at all	slightly agree	moderately agree	strongly agree	completely agree
1	2	3	4	5

As a counselor, I:

_____ 1. encourage my clients to become financially independent.

_____ 2. encourage my clients to become involved in social and political actions.

_____ 3. encourage my clients to use counseling as a process to understand themselves better.

_____ 4. encourage my clients to engage in traditional gender roles in intimate relationships or marriage.

_____ 5. am flexible in helping my clients find ways to solve their problems.

_____ 6. view women's problems as largely caused by external social, cultural, and political forces.

_____ 7. focus on my clients' "inner worlds" in order to help them understand themselves.

_____ 8. encourage my clients to adjust to their social situations and to the demands of others.

_____ 9. do not ask my clients to do anything in counseling that they do not agree with.
_____10. encourage my clients to put their own needs before those of others.

How Are Feminist Therapists Different from Other Psychotherapists?

The self-assessment questionnaire is a modified version of an instrument that has been used in studies examining college students' reactions to descriptions of traditional and feminist counselors (Enns and Hackett, 1993; Epperson and Lewis, 1987; Hackett, Enns, and Zetzer, 1992; Lewis, Epperson, and Foley, 1989). Items 1, 2, 4, 6, 8, and 10 are based on the classic description of feminist therapy authored by Edna Rawlings and Diane Carter (1977). The scores for items 4 and 8 should be reversed in order to reflect agreement with a feminist position. The remaining items (3, 5, 7, and 9) represent consensus values of counselors who practice according to most mainstream and humanistic approaches to counseling. The "feminist" and "traditional" sets of items do not represent mutually exclusive attitudes or behaviors, and your scores may reflect a high endorsement of all ten items.

In order to allow you to compare your reactions to those of research participants, this section will summarize how respondents in two research studies rated three types of therapists: (1) a nonsexist-humanistic counselor, (2) a liberal feminist counselor, and (3) a radical feminist counselor (Enns and Hackett, 1993; Hackett, Enns, and Zetzer, 1992). One of these studies (Enns and Hackett, 1993) used ten-minute videotapes to depict typical counseling sessions. In the second study (Hackett, Enns, and Zetzer, 1992), nonsexist, liberal feminist, and radical feminist counseling approaches were represented via (1) videotapes, (2) written transcripts of sessions, or (3) written descriptions of each therapist and her approach. The client and her portrayal of problems remained the same across all counseling situations. She was depicted as a senior in college who was considering complex issues in her life including personal dilemmas, career choices, and how early socialization experiences influenced her decision making.

The nonsexist/humanistic therapist used open-ended questions, reflection, and clarification to help the client sort out dilemmas. The counselor emphasized personal choice and growth issues, and did not focus explicitly on gender issues or external factors that had influenced her concerns. The liberal feminist therapist acted in accordance with values of liberal feminism, which will be described in detail in subsequent chapters. In addition to using the basic communication tools of the nonsexist/humanistic counselor, the liberal feminist therapist encouraged the client to consider how socialization had influenced her choices, to expand her options for the future, and to change traditional gender role definitions if alterations were consistent with her personal goals. The radical feminist counselor applied feminist principles in a manner that was most consistent with radical and socialist feminist values (see later chapters). The term "radical" was used to reflect the counselor's belief that in order for women's psychological health and status to improve substantially, society must be changed at its roots. In keeping with the liberal feminist therapist's approach, the radical feminist counselor explored how socialization and gender role injunctions had influenced the client. However, she also explicitly communicated her belief about the importance of equality in human relationships, encouraged the client to become aware of the common issues that influence women, and suggested some methods that would help her client actively influence her environment. The counselor suggested that the client could join a consciousness-raising group or become involved in women's issues on campus, thus encouraging the client to consider becoming involved in social change activities (Enns and Hackett, 1990, 1993; Hackett, Enns, and Zetzer, 1992).

Summary of Reactions to Feminist Therapy Items

A summary of reactions of respondents to items associated with feminist counseling goals follows. These results emerged in two studies unless the text specifies otherwise (Enns and Hackett, 1993; Hackett, Enns, and Zetzer, 1992).

  (a) *encouraging the client to put personal needs before those of others (#10)*

Both liberal and radical feminist counselors were seen as more likely to convey this attitude than the nonsexist counselor.

(b) *encouraging financial independence (#1), viewing women's problems as influenced by external factors (#6), and suggesting that the client become involved in social action (#2)*

The radical feminist counselor was seen as more likely to emphasize these principles than the liberal feminist counselor; the liberal feminist counselor was seen as more likely to focus on these goals than the nonsexist counselor.

(c) *encouraging the client to adjust to her situation and others' needs (#8)*

In one study, both liberal and radical feminist counselors were viewed as less likely than the nonsexist counselor to convey this attitude (Hackett et al., 1992); in the second study, no differences emerged (Enns and Hackett, 1993).

(d) *encouraging traditional roles in intimate relationships (#4)*

No differences between counselors were found in the first study (Hackett, Enns, and Zetzer, 1992); in the second study, both feminist counselors were viewed as less likely to encourage this outcome than the nonsexist counselor (Enns and Hackett, 1993). Although statistically significant differences were found, 1.54 was the highest rating given (nonsexist counselor) on a scale in which "1" signified low levels of endorsement and "5" signified strong endorsement.

Summary of Reactions to Mainstream Therapy Values

(a) *viewing counseling as a process to gain self-understanding (#3), and flexibility in helping the client solve problems (#5)*

Both the nonsexist/humanistic and liberal feminist counselors were viewed as more likely to emphasize these goals than the radical feminist counselor.

(b) *focusing on the client's inner world (#7)*
The nonsexist/humanistic counselor was viewed as more likely to focus on this goal than the liberal feminist counselor, who was seen as more likely to emphasize this goal than the radical feminist counselor.

(c) *not doing anything in counseling that the client does not agree with (#9)*
In the first study, participants perceived no differences between the various counselors (Hackett, Enns, and Zetzer, 1992); in the second study, the nonsexist counselor was viewed a less likely than either of the feminist counselors to do anything the client did not agree with (Enns and Hackett, 1993).

Research participants generally rated the two types of feminist counselors as emphasizing the same goals, but viewed the radical feminist therapist as communicating these goals more strongly than the liberal feminist therapist. This suggests that counselors who identify their approaches as feminist tend to hold many common values, but prioritize and communicate them in different ways. Given the variation across nonsexist and feminist approaches, it is important for counselors to engage in careful self-assessment as an important step in identifying themselves as feminist counselors (Enns, 1992a). The remainder of this chapter will define consensus values of feminist therapy and how feminist counselors view the problems that individuals bring to counseling. Later chapters will describe the variations of feminist theory and therapy and how these variations influence how consensus values are interpreted.

The Complexity and Variations of Feminist Therapy

Feminist therapy has existed as an approach to psychotherapy since the early 1970s. Despite its twenty-year history, feminist therapy is often described as difficult to define (e.g., Ballou and Gabalac, 1985; Juntunen et al., 1994; Waterhouse, 1993). Some of the complexities of defining feminist therapy are associated with the reality that feminist psychotherapy was not founded by or connected to any specific person, theoretical position, or set of techniques (Brown and Brodsky, 1992), and that feminist therapists integrate complex bodies of knowledge about social structures, counseling methods, feminism, and the diversity of men's and women's lives (Enns, 1992a).

At its most basic level, feminist therapy represents a conceptual framework for organizing assumptions about psychotherapy (Ballou and Gabalac, 1985; Johnson, 1976; Kaschak, 1981). It is closely connected to the term *feminist*, which is defined as

> a person, female or male, whose worldview places the female in the center of life and society, and/or who is not prejudiced based on gender or sexual preference. Also, anyone in a male-dominated or patriarchal society who works toward the political, economic, spiritual, sexual, and social equality of women. (*The Wise Woman*, 1982, cited in Kramarae and Treichler, 1985, p. 161)

As noted by bell hooks (1981), a fully inclusive definition views feminism as a commitment to eliminating all forms of oppression, including racism, sexism, heterosexism, and classism. A feminist therapist is a person who is self-identified as a feminist and who chooses an approach to psychotherapy that is compatible with the value system of feminism.

Throughout this book, I use pronouns that refer to women more frequently than men. I have made this choice because feminist approaches were initially developed by and for women, and continue to be especially relevant to the experiences of women. Feminist therapists hold divergent views about whether men can serve as effective feminist therapists, and these differences will become apparent in subsequent chapters (see also Enns, 1992a). Regardless of their views about the gender of the therapist, however, feminist therapists with divergent views about feminism agree that the principles of feminist therapy can be useful for working with men.

Definitions of feminist therapy indicate that a wide variety of personality and counseling theories can be incorporated within a feminist approach (Dutton-Douglas and Walker, 1988; Rawlings and Carter, 1977). The only tools eschewed by feminist therapists are techniques that are immersed in sexist theory or that encourage women and men to think in narrow, restricted ways about themselves and their options (Lerman, 1986; Rawlings and Carter,

1977). Thus, multiple forms of feminist counseling exist and are based on the unique combination of the counselor's feminist orientation and counseling approach (Dutton-Douglas and Walker, 1988; Enns, 1992a; Worell and Remer, 1992). Although all theories of feminism focus on the importance of equality, beliefs about how equality can be achieved vary substantially. As noted in the first section of this chapter, the therapist's personal view of feminism will have a significant impact on how feminist counseling is interpreted and conducted (Enns, 1992a; Kaschak, 1981). This book traces the development of the diverse feminist philosophies and seeks to explain some of the ways in which a therapist's orientation to specific feminist theories may influence her interpretation of what feminist therapy is and should be.

The competent feminist counselor understands that effective feminist therapy is based on ongoing and continuous examination of personal values (Feminist Therapy Institute (FTI), 1990; Kaschak, 1981), intentional creation of an approach that demonstrates consistency between one's theoretical orientation to feminism and theoretical approach to psychotherapy, and an understanding of how intersections of gender, race, class, economic status, and sexual orientation influence women's and men's lives (Brown and Brodsky, 1992; Kaschak, 1981; Reid and Comas-Díaz, 1990). The feminist counselor must not naively assume that bias exists solely in specific theories or techniques, but that therapists may use any theory, including nonsexist theories, to inadvertently support and reinforce stereotypes about gender, class, race, or sexual orientation (Cammaert and Larsen, 1988).

In order to develop a fully integrated feminist therapy approach, the counselor must have working knowledge of a variety of complex fields. These disciplines include but are not limited to the following: the psychology of women; psychotherapy theory; sociological perspectives on gender, race, and class; political science and social change strategies; and multicultural issues. Furthermore, an explosion of knowledge, research, and new theoretical work continues to occur within each of the fields that deal with gender issues; the task of staying informed about new developments is an ongoing challenge for persons who integrate feminism with counseling.

Laura Brown's (1994) recent definition of feminist therapy efficiently summarizes its complexity as follows:

> Feminist therapy is the practice of therapy informed by feminist political philosophy and analysis, grounded in multicultural feminist scholarship on the psychology of women and gender, which leads both therapist and client toward strategies and solutions advancing feminist resistance, transformation, and social change in daily personal life, and in relationships with the social, emotional, and political environment. (pp. 21-22)

The remainder of this chapter is divided into three sections. The first section will describe the feminist therapist's conceptual framework for understanding problems, the second will discuss the therapeutic relationship, and the third will describe basic goals of feminist therapy. The second and third sections also include brief self-assessment sections that precede the discussion of specific principles. It is important to note that the interpretation and implementation of these basic principles, which are shared by individuals who define themselves as feminist therapists, varies depending on the type of feminist theoretical framework that the therapist employs. These theoretical frameworks will be discussed extensively in later chapters.

A FEMINIST APPROACH TO UNDERSTANDING PROBLEMS

Feminist therapists hold several distinctive beliefs about women's problems. The first emphasizes how the external realities of women's lives influence women's problems, how the personal is the political. The second perspective examines how women's problems or symptoms can be understood as methods of coping and surviving rather than as signs of dysfunction.

The Personal Is Political

The *personal is political* reflects the belief that the personal problems women encounter are connected to the political and social climate in which they live. These problems are influenced by and reflected in the external realities of men's and women's lives. Many feminist counselors prefer to use the phrase *problems in living* rather than the term *pathology* in order to convey the feminist view that counseling issues are inextricably connected to the social, political, economic, and institutional factors that shape personal choices (Butler, 1985; Gilbert, 1980; Sturdivant, 1980).

Intrapsychic explanations of problems and most diagnostic labels based within a medical model tend to decontextualize problems, support gender bias, or promote victim blaming. When counselors and therapists rely solely on traditional diagnostic labels, they are more likely to define problems as a set of internal characteristics and to emphasize goals that focus on overhauling internal deficiencies rather than promoting healthy change and the alteration of oppressive environmental conditions (Greenspan, 1983; Rawlings and Carter, 1977). When clients are encouraged to look exclusively inside themselves for the source of a problem, they are inclined to blame themselves for the entire problem, and "adjust" to the circumstances around them (Greenspan, 1983).

Although examination of external factors that contribute to women's problems is crucial, feminist therapists also should attend to physiological or intrapsychic factors that interact with external forces (Brown and Brodsky, 1992). For example, the American Psychological Association (APA) Task Force on Women and Depression recommended a biopsychosocial approach to working with depressed women (McGrath et al., 1990). Through feminist analysis, clients learn to distinguish between internal/psychological and external/social aspects of the issues they are dealing with, and to identify both personal change and social change strategies that can be used to deal with these respective areas (Gilbert, 1980).

In their work with major issues such as depression, traditional therapists often deal primarily with internal cognitive and emotional patterns that reinforce depression; their primary training often prepares them to focus primarily on the psychology of the individual. However, feminist therapists recognize that women who are especially vulnerable to depression include women who have experienced sexual and physical abuse, live in poverty, work in lower-status positions, or are mothers of young children (McGrath et al.,

1990). Some of these factors cannot be influenced through individual means alone; individual choice and initiative must be accompanied by legal and social change. These connections between internal and external worlds illustrate that the personal is clearly political; the internal cognitive, emotional, and behavioral changes that women make must be matched with institutional changes.

Symptoms As Communication or Coping Tools

Feminist therapists view clients as individuals coping with life events to the best of their ability. Many symptoms represent "normal" reactions to a restrictive environment (Greenspan, 1983; Kaschak, 1981). Marjorie Klein (1976) noted the following: "Not all symptoms are neurotic. Pain in response to a bad situation is adaptive, not pathological" (p. 90). Feminist therapists highlight the communication function of symptoms by defining them as behaviors that arise out of efforts to influence an environment that is constricting or oppressive. For example, symptoms may emerge from conflicting nontraditional and traditional demands associated with multiple roles (Sturdivant, 1980). Alternatively, symptoms often reflect influential strategies that were taught or modeled, such as by parents, peers, the media, schools, and intimate others. At one time, these behaviors were functional or had survival value, and may still be reinforced by the environment. However, these coping methods often become less successful over time and contribute to the person's distress as the client attempts to meet life tasks that require different or new skills (Greenspan, 1983). For example, a woman who used dissociation successfully as a child in order to psychologically survive sexual abuse may find that the coping mechanism of dissociation may contribute to her potential revictimization as an adult (Brown, 1994; Zilber, 1993).

In traditional approaches to therapy, symptoms are presumed to be aspects of problems that need to be eradicated (Halleck, 1971). If the focus of counseling is to label a symptom and remove a symptom without understanding the past context that shaped it and the current context in which it is reinforced, clients may be deprived of the indirect influence of symptoms, such as "dependency" or depression. They may, in fact, feel even less powerful after therapy than before counseling (Halleck, 1971). Rather than viewing symptoms such as depression, anxiety, or passivity as problems to be eliminated, the feminist therapist views these patterns as indirect forms of expression that can be refocused in more direct and productive forms of communication as a client gains a stronger sense of self (Smith and Siegel, 1985; Rawlings and Carter, 1977).

The following section illustrates the complex communication of a symptom such as "dependency." If a woman seeks counseling in order to change a dependent behavior pattern, it is important to discover how she learned to behave in passive or dependent ways. What injunctions encouraged her to equate passivity with being a "good woman" and/or how was she rewarded for deferring to other people should be determined. Dependency is viewed by the feminist therapist as a reaction to inequality: a person with less power attempts to vicariously experience some semblance of power by attaching herself or himself to people who hold greater power (Hare-Mustin and Marecek, 1986). If direct forms of power are not available to a person, she or he is likely to rely on "devious" strategies such as dependency or manipulation (Gannon, 1982).

Symptoms such as dependency may not only represent a coping mechanism for the client, but may also serve an important role for significant others. A dependent pattern may protect partners with more power by providing them with opportunities to play leadership, protector, and hero roles; these roles support and affirm their self-concepts as independent and active persons (Lerner, 1983). Alternatively, the person who is labeled dependent often fulfills essential roles in caring for and nurturing others. The negative aspects of dependency are most likely to emerge when a client experiences unmet personal needs that result from dealing with children or other needy individuals, and resorts to behaviors such as manipulation, indecisiveness, or hypersensitivity (Kaplan, 1983). If the dependent person begins to initiate more independent actions, significant others may resist these changes because they upset the homeostatic balance in a relationship and call for new responses on the part of others in the social system (Lerner, 1983). The new responses of the dependent person may require others to accept more responsibility for fulfilling socially undervalued roles such as parenting, listening, and other forms of nurturing.

Although a pattern of dependency makes sense in the context in which it arises, it also creates problems for individuals because it involves overconformity to traditional feminine roles (Fodor and Rothblum, 1984). Esther Rothblum (1983) noted that many of women's psychological symptoms are related to stereotypes of femininity that contribute to feelings of powerlessness. If the dependencies of nurturing others and defining one's self in relation to others were highly valued attributes in this culture, exaggerations of these patterns would be less likely to contribute to psychological distress.

Although much of women's orientation to others is referred to as dependency, immaturity, or neurotic behavior, women's appropriate assertive behavior is sometimes inappropriately labeled as aggressive, selfish, angry, or "bitchy" (Fodor and Rothblum, 1984; Solomon and Rothblum, 1985). Thus, women who desire to make changes often experience double binds. On the one hand, traditional expectations encourage women to define themselves through relationships, but on the other hand, the larger society undervalues these roles (Jack, 1987). When women adopt more direct forms of influence, however, their behavior may be distorted by others and mislabeled in negative ways. As a result, it is essential for feminist counselors and their clients to discuss both the costs and benefits of change (Fodor and Rothblum, 1984; Rawlings and Carter, 1977). Feminist counselors must both critique a society that does not value traditional feminine behaviors as much as traditional masculine behaviors and help clients acquire behaviors that help them cope effectively with the realities they face.

THE COUNSELING RELATIONSHIP

The Feminist Therapist's Values

_____ 1. It is impossible for the therapist to practice value-free or value-neutral counseling.

_____ 2. It is the feminist counselor's obligation to disclose personal values about issues that are discussed in counseling.

_____ 3. Feminist therapists engage in continuous examination of their own values and attitudes to assure that they do not covertly or negatively influence their clients.

Each of the self-assessment items reflects important attitudes and values of feminist therapy and high endorsement reflects agreement with important feminist goals. However, it should also be noted that self-disclosure (item 2) must be based on the readiness of the client to hear the information and use it effectively.

All psychotherapy is influenced by the values of the therapist. Feminist therapists believe that it is impossible to practice value-free counseling, and as a result, they consider it essential for counselors to clarify their values and understand the potential impact of their values on clients (Brodsky, 1976; Butler, 1985; Gilbert, 1980). At a minimum, feminist therapists monitor their personal behavior in order to assure that their values do not influence clients in a covert fashion. Feminist therapists do not limit their awareness training to the clarification of their personal values, but attempt to expand their own worldviews by becoming informed about the life experiences of women in diverse life roles, such as women in poverty, minority women, and older women. In order to expand their frames of reference, feminist counselors should read widely about the vast array of political, ideological, sociological, and psychological issues that impinge on women's and men's lives.

Many feminist therapists directly communicate their feminist values to their clients. Others remain hesitant about using the label "feminist" during the counseling hour because of the popular stereotypes associated with feminism. Several studies suggest that even when one's values remain unstated, the therapist's techniques, roles, nonverbal behavior, and attitudes are still likely to reveal important aspects of the counselor's views. In two studies of feminist and nonsexist counseling (Enns and Hackett, 1990, 1993), college women and men were exposed to (1) videotaped counseling sessions in which the counselors enacted a feminist or nonsexist orientation but did not label their orientation, or (2) the same videotaped sessions with two-minute leaders in which counselors labeled their orientations as feminist or humanistic and described their values about counseling. Respondents rated "explicit" counselors, who shared their values, and "implicit" counselors, who did not share their values, in similar ways within each feminist or nonfeminist approach (Enns and Hackett, 1990, 1993).

Regardless of the implicit or explicit nature of each counselor's statements, participants also accurately identified the feminist or traditional goals of the therapists, suggesting that one cannot *not* communicate one's values (Enns and Hackett, 1993). Although several earlier studies of feminist and traditional written announcements of services suggested that potential clients respond less positively to feminist than traditional descriptions of counseling (Lewis, Davis, and Lesmeister, 1983; Schneider, 1985), no such findings emerged in studies in which respondents were exposed to counselor value statements that were communicated within the counseling hour. These results suggest that therapists should not hesitate to openly discuss their values when they are conveyed in a respectful manner and within a reciprocal exchange between counselor and client (Enns and Hackett, 1993).

Clients As Competent

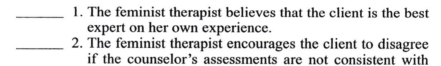

_____ 1. The feminist therapist believes that the client is the best expert on her own experience.

_____ 2. The feminist therapist encourages the client to disagree if the counselor's assessments are not consistent with the client's thinking about the issues.

_____ 3. The feminist therapist helps the client develop self-help skills and tools that allow her or him to play many of the roles of counselor for her- or himself.

Feminist therapists view clients as their own best experts (Kaschak, 1981; Laidlaw and Malmo, 1990; Rawlings and Carter, 1977). The self-assessment items measure various aspects of the view that clients know more about their own experiences than any other person. Even when their lives are in turmoil, clients have developed a great deal of expertise on coping and surviving. It is important to engage with clients as collaborators in discovering how problems should be defined, what alternative perspectives are useful, and what strategies for change will be effective (Rawlings and Carter, 1977). As a result, the therapist shares her thinking regarding how the client demonstrates competence, describes ways in which the client has learned to question her competence or believe that she is "crazy," and renames aspects of a person's behavior, such as helplessness or dependency, as *underground power* (Smith and Siegel, 1985), or indirect forms of influence that can be redirected. Because the client is her own best expert, the client's opinions and perspectives should be sought at each stage of therapy as the therapist and client brainstorm about alternatives for working through issues and problems.

Egalitarian Relationships

_____ 1. The feminist therapist recognizes that the help-seeking situation makes it impossible for the client to experience full equality with the counselor. Given this knowledge, the feminist counselor attempts to share power, but does not deny power differences that are impossible or inappropriate to erase.

_____ 2. The therapist acts on his or her beliefs about equality by describing the counselor's assessments in clear and jargon-free language.

_____ 3. The open discussion of power differences between the therapist and client demonstrates the use of negotiation. The same principles can be used in relationships outside of counseling.

_____ 4. Well-timed and brief self-disclosures about the therapist's struggles with issues model helpful responses to difficult issues and can help equalize the counselor-client relationship.

Egalitarian relationships are important as both an outcome of therapy and as a condition of the psychotherapy relationship. The four items reflect ways in which egalitarianism is often developed within counseling relationships. Counselors attempt to demystify the psychotherapy experience, promote mutuality, and establish egalitarian relationships with their clients (Ballou and Gabalac, 1985; Butler, 1985; Gannon, 1982; Kaschak, 1981).

The therapist models communication skills such as genuineness, confrontation, self-disclosure, empathy, and congruence as methods for establishing equal relationships. When clients enter counseling, they often feel alone, isolated, and crazy and may believe that the counselor is an all-powerful expert. The therapist can use brief self-disclosures in order to communicate that she is also an individual who experiences negative events such as sexism or as someone who must work consistently at resolving personal difficulties (Gannon, 1982; Greenspan, 1986). When the client has an opportunity to see the therapist as a coping role model and/or as a similar role model instead of only as an expert role model, a more egalitarian climate is established and the process of change is demystified. The identification of commonalities through self-disclosure may also decrease the client's sense of isolation and empower her to act on her own behalf. Self-disclosure must be used in the best interest of the client, and as a result, the timing, nature, and length of self-disclosure must be carefully considered for its relevance to the needs of the client (Brown and Walker, 1990; Feminist Therapy Institute, 1990).

Edna Rawlings and Diane Carter (1977) recommended that feminist therapists adopt a reciprocal model of influence in which counselors share power, avoid making decisions for the client, and communicate confidence in the client's decision-making skills. Both therapist and client should also be able to share honest feedback with each other about the goals and direction of counseling. The counselor participates as a co-worker with the client in order to assure that the client develops problem-solving skills that will help her become her own therapist in the future (Butler, 1985). Hogie Wyckoff (1977b) referred to this as a "transfer of power and expertise in the process of self-transformation" (p. 394).

Although the counselor and client work toward establishing a relationship of equality, the counselor must never assume that the counseling relationship is one of "undifferentiated egalitarianism." Laura Brown and Lenore Walker (1990) indicated that during the early years of feminist therapy, some practitioners tended to minimize or deny the existence of power differentials between feminist counselors and their clients. However, feminist therapists have become increasingly aware that they hold greater power in therapeutic relationships because of their knowledge and expertise. Lack of awareness or the denial of power differences can result in the blurring of boundaries between counselor and client and, on occasion, inappropriate role reversals (Brown, 1991a).

Instead of trying to eliminate all power differences, the feminist therapist works toward eliminating artificial boundaries, acknowledges the client's expertise regarding her or his life, and models egalitarian behaviors that will help the client negotiate effective relationships both within and outside of counseling. However, the feminist therapist must also recognize that she brings skills and professional preparation to the relationship, and that the power of position and expertise will be ascribed to her. To assume that the relationship can become fully equal is to ignore the power relationships that occur throughout life and may permit individuals to rationalize behavior that can lead to unethical practice. The open discussion of power and role differences in the counseling relationship assists the client in becoming aware of how power dynamics influence psychotherapy and other relationships, provides an opening for the counselor and client to explore ways to reduce power differentials when it is appropriate, and helps clients understand how roles can be negotiated effectively in contexts other than therapy (Smith and Douglas, 1990).

The Psychotherapy Contract and Informed Consent

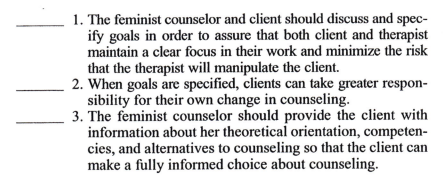

        1. The feminist counselor and client should discuss and specify goals in order to assure that both client and therapist maintain a clear focus in their work and minimize the risk that the therapist will manipulate the client.

        2. When goals are specified, clients can take greater responsibility for their own change in counseling.

        3. The feminist counselor should provide the client with information about her theoretical orientation, competencies, and alternatives to counseling so that the client can make a fully informed choice about counseling.

Feminist therapists are aware of and promote their clients' rights as consumers (Kaschak, 1981). As a result, they may offer low-cost initial decision-making sessions that allow clients to explore the compatibility of the counselor's and client's value systems, and/or inform potential clients of other resources or counseling services available to them. These procedures help clients arrive at well-informed decisions about whether to enter counseling with the feminist counselor (Brown and Liss-Levinson, 1981; Gannon, 1982).

Feminist therapists tell their clients about the nature of their skills, how they view change, their theoretical orientation, the typical length of counseling, and other relevant information about their approaches. Therapists also provide information about the costs and benefits of counseling, the responsibilities of the counselor to the client, and what the client should expect from the therapist (Hare-Mustin et al., 1979). As a client gains information about how a counselor approaches situations and why the therapist makes specific choices during counseling, she or he is able to take on an active and collaborative role in decision making and is able to take higher levels of responsibility for her or his own direction in counseling.

Whenever possible, the therapist and client specify the issues they will address and the goals they will work toward. The goals and respective responsibilities of counselor and client can be specified in a written agreement (Rawlings and Carter, 1977). When clear roles and goals are established, both the counselor and client are able to evaluate progress regularly. Verbal and/or written contracts also minimize the risk that the counselor or the client will attempt to influence each other in a covert fashion.

Informed consent should not be seen as an "all or nothing" event but as an ongoing process of negotiation and discussion (Enns 1988; Rawlings and Carter, 1977). When a client is in crisis, she may not be able to concentrate on a counselor's lengthy description about her approach. Alternatively, when the client is a child, he or she may be developmentally unprepared to assume an active planning role. Providing the client with relevant information should be based upon the client's level of interest and readiness to participate actively in collaborative discussion. Another important element in informed consent involves creating an environment in which the client can regularly ask questions about the direction and focus of counseling.

Many feminist therapists provide their clients with written descriptions of their orientation to counseling, areas of strength and specialization, and views about how feminism influences their counseling practice. Feminist therapists who use written descriptions of their approach should consider providing time during a session to discuss these documents, thus allowing the client to ask questions and the counselor to clarify statements that are difficult to convey through writing alone.

THE GOALS AND OUTCOMES
OF FEMINIST COUNSELING

Counseling for Change, not Adjustment

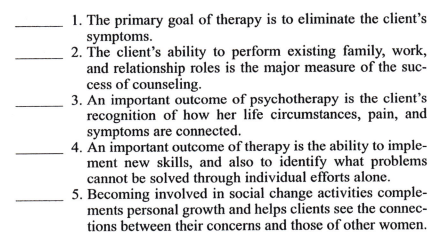

_____ 1. The primary goal of therapy is to eliminate the client's symptoms.

_____ 2. The client's ability to perform existing family, work, and relationship roles is the major measure of the success of counseling.

_____ 3. An important outcome of psychotherapy is the client's recognition of how her life circumstances, pain, and symptoms are connected.

_____ 4. An important outcome of therapy is the ability to implement new skills, and also to identify what problems cannot be solved through individual efforts alone.

_____ 5. Becoming involved in social change activities complements personal growth and helps clients see the connections between their concerns and those of other women.

These five statements are adapted from Marjorie Klein's (1976) discussion of feminist and traditional goals of therapy. Klein indicated that a strong endorsement of values associated with items 1 and 2 indicates an adjustment versus change orientation to therapy. Although some attention to these issues may be important, overemphasis encourages individuals to ignore the context and the full range of change implications for counseling. Strong agreement with items 3 to 5 is associated with a change orientation to psychotherapy.

Traditional models of psychotherapy have historically focused on removing pain and helping clients adjust to their lives as they exist (Klein, 1976). It is important for the feminist therapist to help clients explore the full range of options available to them, especially if their presenting problems are shaped by a narrow view of "what it is proper for women to complain about" (Klein, 1976, p. 90). Change goals may involve attending to personal development instead of using all of one's energy to adjust to existing relationships, choosing novel responses to difficult circumstances, or developing new attitudes toward circumstances and the realities of women's and men's lives.

One potential "change" outcome of feminist therapy is involvement in social activism. Change in the lives of individual women should be linked whenever possible to larger social issues because some problems that are experienced individually will only be altered through social change (Greenspan, 1983). Through involvement with consciousness-raising groups and community action programs, women gain experience and confidence for initiating future change activities (Brodsky, 1976).

Equality

_____ 1. The therapist should help the client gain freedom from assigned gender roles.

_____ 2. The therapist should provide information regarding the unequal status and power of women and men in this society.

_____ 3. Counselors should help clients recognize roles that are confining, restrictive, and/or oppressive for both men and women.

_____ 4. Counselors should devote time to brainstorming with clients about how to implement more flexible and less gender-bound behavior in relationships with friends, intimate others, and work colleagues.

_____ 5. Therapists should encourage clients to negotiate greater equality in the distribution of household tasks and child-rearing tasks.

_____ 6. Financial self-sufficiency is important for establishing equal personal relationships.

_____ 7. Counselors should help clients understand how factors such as race, class, and sexual orientation influence gender and power relationships.

A high level of endorsement of these seven self-assessment statements suggests that your values are consistent with the feminist principle of equality. Feminist therapists encourage their clients to work toward establishing relationships that approach equality of personal power (Butler, 1985; Kaschak, 1981; Rawlings and Carter, 1977; Sturdivant, 1980). It is also important for feminist therapists to convey to their clients why it is difficult to achieve egalitarian relationships as an individual male or female in this society. As a result, this section will outline many of the issues that limit the achievement of equality, as well as its role as a principle in feminist counseling.

One of the reasons that feminists have often emphasized the importance of financial self-sufficiency is that economic power is one of the most powerful ways of establishing equality in relationships (Rawlings and Carter, 1977). However, statistics indicate that equality is still elusive in the arena of women's and men's work. Even with gains in wage equities over the past several decades, women earn approximately 72 percent of men's pay, and the gap for women of many racial groups is wider (England and McCreary, 1987; Ries and Stone, 1992). In 1990, black women earned 62 percent of white men's pay (Ries and Stone, 1992). Although women are more frequently seen in professions and high-status jobs than in the past, most women remain clustered in low-status jobs that bring few financial benefits. The top ten jobs for women remain in traditional clerical and service occupations: secretary, typist, sales worker, sale supervisor, cashier, bookkeeper, registered nurse, nurses aide, waitress, and elementary school teacher (Needleman and Nelson, 1988). Although women's earnings often approach the income levels of men at early stages of their careers, institutional power structures, values, and promotion policies still limit the likelihood that women will achieve equal power with men over the course of a long-term career (Unger and Crawford, 1996). Within nontraditional work contexts, women often experience token status that is associated with high visibility and performance pressure, isolation, and the tendency for co-workers to view them as representative of all women (Kanter, 1977; Yoder, 1985). Women are more similar to than different from men with respect to internal qualities such as achievement motivation, but they often work within environments that treat women and men differently. In comparison to men; women generally hold less earning power, experience more devaluation of their performance and different attributions for their success, and encounter work-related hazards such as sexual harassment or discrimination (Unger and Crawford, 1996).

Despite these realities and problems, employed women generally show higher levels of mental and physical health than women who are not employed (Baruch, Biener, and Barnett, 1987). In addition to providing financial power, employment is associated with positive experiences of feedback, self-esteem, social connections, control, and challenge. Although disparities between men's and women's power still exist, egalitarian roles in heterosexual relationships are more likely to occur when the financial power of partners is similar. However, Rhoda Unger and Mary Crawford (1996) concluded that "even when wives earn more money than their husband, beliefs about the appropriate roles of women and men still influence the balance of power in favor of men" (pp. 356–357). Although employment and financial power generally contribute to equality, it is important to avoid trivializing the work of women who choose to pursue nonpaid work in their homes, or as volunteers and caregivers.

As our society has moved toward a recognition of gender inequity, gender-neutral policies have often treated women and men as though their life situations were identical. Carol Tavris (1992) indicated that equality should not be confused with identical treatment. A substantial body of research demonstrates that differences between men and women on measures of personality and ability are minimal; differences within each gender group overshadow differences between men and women. However, women and men face dramatically different reproductive events, life experiences, employment opportunities, and work responsibilities at home and at work. When men and women are treated identically, social inequities and power imbalances are often further perpetuated. Although work is considered a gender-neutral environment in which sex discrimination is illegal, it limits the potential for men's and women's achievement of real equality because the success of workers is "so thoroughly organized around a male worker with a wife at home to take care of the needs of the household—including childcare—that it transforms what is intrinsically just a male-female difference into a massive female disadvantage" (Bem, 1993b, p. 184). For example, "no fault," gender-neutral divorce laws are associated with occasions when "same" treatment results in inequality and women's loss of status. Following divorce, women experience an average 73 percent decline in their economic standard of living, and men experience a substantial average increase of 42 percent (Weitzman, 1985).

The differential earning capacities and child-care responsibilities of partners are closely related to these statistics.

When women enter feminist therapy, they may be overwhelmed by myriad life tasks and may have difficulty conceptualizing the complexities of gender equality. Women sometimes minimize their experiences of inequality in order to cope with realities that are difficult to face (Crosby et al., 1989; Unger and Crawford, 1996). Within feminist therapy, the counselor helps the client to carefully explore relationships in public and employment contexts, as well as in more private and relational spheres. Many clients may engage in self-blame for their lack of progress in achieving goals because they do not understand how institutions with gender neutral policies often perpetuate traditional power relations and status quo arrangements. When clients explore their personal experiences in light of social structures, they are able to release themselves from self-criticism, self-blame, and discouragement.

Women often feel less entitled to the same rewards as men (Major, 1993; Unger and Crawford, 1996). As they understand the full range of gender relations, they may become more confident about their rights and determined to ask for the rewards they have earned. Finally, individuals in feminist counseling often recognize that isolated personal efforts will have limited results. Support groups may help women maintain motivation and energy for negotiating the ongoing issues of establishing egalitarian intimate relationships. Seeking the assistance of advocacy groups may help women negotiate complex institutional and legal issues. In light of the reality that social change must occur for egalitarianism to permeate social and personal relationships, some clients will experience renewed energy by staying informed about political and legal issues, and by becoming involved in grassroots or community organizations that focus on achieving social change.

Balancing Agency and Communion

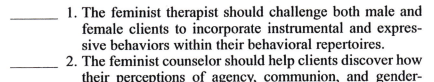

       1. The feminist therapist should challenge both male and female clients to incorporate instrumental and expressive behaviors within their behavioral repertoires.

       2. The feminist counselor should help clients discover how their perceptions of agency, communion, and gender-

appropriate behavior are influenced by gender role expectations.

_____ 3. Traits related to agency/independence and communion/ connection should be separated from traditional notions about masculinity and femininity.

_____ 4. The feminist therapist should help clients explore how their schemas of gender influence their perceptions of the behavior of others.

_____ 5. The counselor must be concerned not only with the client's ability to enact new behaviors, but she or he must also educate clients about how contexts elicit certain behaviors and how other people may misperceive or distort behaviors.

_____ 6. The development of androgyny, or the incorporation of both "masculine" and "feminine" characteristics within the person, should be a primary goal of therapy.

_____ 7. One of the most important goals of therapy is to help women identify and value the relational self.

In feminist therapy, clients explore a wide variety of personal attributes and relational options, and make choices about balancing these characteristics in a personally meaningful manner. During the past twenty years, feminist psychologists have proposed a variety of models for balancing instrumental and expressive skills. Many of the early statements on feminist therapy promoted the goal of androgyny, or the systematic integration of both traditional masculine and feminine characteristics, as an ideal model of mental health (e.g., Kaplan, 1976, 1979b; Rawlings and Carter, 1977). During the 1980s, new models of women's identity focused on the importance of revaluing the underappreciated relational skills of women rather than viewing psychological health as synonymous with independence, autonomy, and agency (e.g., Gilligan, 1982; Jordan et al., 1991). Both of these approaches to integrating agency and communion have provided useful tools for helping individuals explore personal options; both approaches have also been criticized by some feminists as popular "bandwagons" (e.g., Mednick, 1989).

Items 6 and 7 ask for your reactions to the androgyny and relational approaches for balancing interdependence and independence.

Consistent with controversies within the psychology of women, feminist counselors may disagree about the relative importance of androgyny, autonomy, and/or relational skills. The higher your endorsement of the first five items, the more likely you are to believe that the qualities of connectedness and autonomy should be balanced in flexible ways and should not be shaped by traditional notions of gender. The feminist therapist's emphasis on the relative merits of agency and communion will depend on the specific feminist philosophy she endorses. These themes are discussed at greater length in chapters on liberal and cultural feminist themes in feminist therapy.

Empowerment

_____ 1. The feminist counselor should help clients discover assertive and functional ways of expressing power and strong emotions such as anger.

_____ 2. The feminist therapist should support competence in women and men as they fulfill traditional and nontraditional roles.

_____ 3. The feminist therapist should help women experience increased self-esteem by pointing out their unique contributions, strengths, and achievements.

_____ 4. The counselor should encourage the client to evaluate her or his own change and growth.

_____ 5. The feminist therapist should be willing to act as an advocate on behalf of clients and should contribute time and support to projects that initiate social change.

_____ 6. The feminist counselor should help the client find productive ways of contributing to social change and the empowerment of other women.

_____ 7. The feminist therapist should help clients become aware of external forces that limit their freedom so that clients can release self-blame and focus their energy on circumstances that they can influence.

High levels of endorsement of these seven items indicate that you strongly agree with the feminist principle of empowerment. A major goal of feminist therapy is helping individuals see themselves as active agents on their own behalf and on behalf of other people. McWhirter (1991) defined empowerment as "the process by which people, organizations, or groups who are powerless (a) become aware of the power dynamics at work in their life context, (b) develop the skills and capacity for gaining some reasonable control over their lives, (c) exercise this control without infringing upon the rights of others, and (d) support the empowerment of others in their community" (p. 224). Within feminist therapy, empowerment involves the following: (1) an analysis of power structures in society; (2) discussion and awareness of how women are socialized to feel powerless; (3) discovery of how women can achieve power in personal, interpersonal, and institutional domains; (4) and the use of advocacy skills on behalf of women (Hawxhurst and Morrow, 1984).

Women often feel overwhelmed and incapacitated as they enter counseling, and they frequently blame themselves as the sole source of their problems. These feelings of powerlessness are often based on a long legacy of experiences that may have first emerged in childhood. Power imbalances across gender lines are already evident in interactions between boys and girls at a young age. Few differences between young boys and girls are apparent when they are observed as individuals or in same-sex pairs, but Eleanor Maccoby (1990) noted that boys as young as three years old were relatively unresponsive to girls' efforts to influence them. In general, girls learn to value enabling patterns of interaction and boys tend to value constricting styles in which conflict is exhibited directly and hierarchies are established. Although girls' typical strategies are highly effective in same-gender groups, these positive interactional styles tend to be less influential with boys. These experiences, then, set the stage for women's difficulties interacting and negotiating power across gender lines (Maccoby, 1990).

Many of women's presenting problems emerge directly from the limited power of women in society. Such problems include rape (Koss, 1993; Koss and Harvey, 1991), incest and other forms of sexual abuse (Courtois, 1988; Herman, 1992), battering (Dutton, 1992; Walker, 1979, 1989, 1994), and sexual harassment (Fitzgerald, 1993; Hotelling, 1991; Paludi, 1990a). Disorders such as eating disorders, agoraphobia, post-traumatic stress disorder, and depression often emerge from women's efforts to deal with the aftermath of traumatic events, and thus, often represent the internalization of violation and abusive power relationships. Alternatively, these problems may depict women's efforts to conform unsuccessfully with stereotyped expectations of women (Fodor and Rothblum, 1984). It is not surprising that women seek counseling more frequently than men and that they experience these problems in disproportionate numbers to men (Collier, 1982; Fodor and Rothblum, 1984; Kaplan, 1983). Furthermore, some women not only experience powerlessness because of gender, but because of the combined impact of racism, homophobia, classism, or ableism. A social analysis of power is a crucial aspect of educating a client about the contextual framework that supports and reinforces her or his problems.

After clients become aware how gender role socialization, violence, or other forms of oppression have limited their options, it is important for them to develop "response-ability" (Cline-Naffziger, 1974) in order to counteract dynamics that have constricted their life sphere or focus. As a method of reaching this goal, clients may need to have gain awareness of denied, buried, or distorted emotions. Anger is a frequent outcome of this exploration. As a part of counseling, clients learn to channel their anger effectively so that it is not expressed haphazardly or indiscriminately, but is stated in direct, constructive, assertive expressions. However, as clients gain confidence in describing their feelings directly, they will also need to identify methods of coping with individuals who respond negatively to the changes they have made (Fodor and Rothblum, 1984). Empowerment is most likely to occur when clients are fully aware of both the benefits and the costs of personal change, and base their responses on knowledge of both positive outcomes and potential risks.

Within a system in which women's overt power is often denied, women often learn to "exercise power while denying it; to reach toward a goal while pretending, to oneself and others, not to want it; to act upon others without knowledge that one's actions have any effect; and, in general, to be manipulative, sneaky, underhanded, and devious" (Smith and Siegel, 1985, p. 17). Women often express discomfort with the term *power* because of their limited experience with it or their exposure to only aggressive or forceful aspects of power. A central role of the therapist is to help the client understand the differences between *power over*, which implies dominance, coercion, and oppression; *power within,* which involves feeling that one has inner strength that will enable one to make sound decisions; and *power to,* which signifies the enactment of goal-directed behaviors that respect the rights of all parties in an interaction (Gannon, 1982; Smith and Douglas, 1990). Differentiating between coercive power and the power of information, expertise, reciprocal influence, encouragement, and reward is also a useful task for helping the client discover positive manifestations of power (Douglas, 1985).

As a part of recognizing the client's competence and coping skills, the feminist therapist helps a client explore how she currently uses power and how she can redirect efforts in line with new goals. Adrienne Smith and Mary Ann Douglas (1990) indicated that this aspect of empowerment contains four elements: (1) redefining power and reducing guilt, (2) helping clients make their own judgments and conclusions about what is right for them, (3) examining both external and internal costs and benefits of maintaining old behaviors or implementing new behaviors, and (4) helping clients assume responsibility for the choices they make. Finally, feminist counselors must "honor the client's own life agenda" (p. 48) and choices—even when they conflict with the belief system of the therapist. Empowerment often involves a complex resocialization process in which women gain permission to see themselves in new ways and skills to enact new knowledge of themselves. It is difficult to relearn behaviors that have been practiced and reinforced for many years or decades. Relearning, then, must include opportunities for practice, confidence building, and systematic, gradual change.

Empowerment does not merely involve facilitating individual change, but also engaging in advocacy roles and active support when the client needs external intervention to help her reach goals or counteract the negative impact of community systems. For example, the feminist therapist may serve as an expert witness on post-traumatic stress disorder or battered woman syndrome, help a client negotiate the complexities of a local social service network or mental health system, or advocate for the client when institutional policies block her movement (Laidlaw and Malmo, 1990; Rosewater, 1990). As clients gain confidence, they may also take on advocacy roles by becoming involved in grassroots community organizations, local sexual assault coalitions, and volunteer opportunities that benefit other people with limited power. Involvement in community action groups can expand a client's outlook, build the client's confidence in her skills, increase her awareness of both the commonalities and differences between women, and help the client transcend personal pain.

Finally, feminist therapists should consider devoting a portion of their time to social change issues (Rawlings and Carter, 1977; Rosewater, 1990; Sturdivant, 1980). These activities may focus on public policy or political issues at the national, state, or local level, but may also involve volunteering for a local women's organization, speaking to community groups, or providing low fees for potential clients who are unable to gain services through other means (Enns, 1993).

Self-Nurturance

_____ 1. The feminist therapist should help clients negotiate for their own personal area and/or time in relationships with significant others.

_____ 2. The feminist counselor should help clients assess and meet their own needs.

_____ 3. An overemphasis on self-nurturance may encourage women to neglect important people in their lives.

_____ 4. The feminist therapist encourages the client to develop an effective support network for fostering self-nurturance.

_____ 5. The feminist therapist helps the client to become less automatically "tuned in" to the needs of significant others (thus also allowing others to develop self-nurturing practices).

Helen Collier (1982) indicated that women often bring the following issues or characteristics to psychotherapy: (1) limited emotional and behavioral options, (2) difficulties expressing their needs and wants, (3) lack of trust in their own abilities and self-direction, (4) blurred boundaries between the self and others, (5) a diffused sense of self and "Who am I?" questions, (6) difficulties making choices, and (7) concerns about fulfilling obligations, rules and "shoulds." Each of these characteristics is related to the consequences of caregiving and lack of attention to self-care.

The socialization of women encourages them to nurture others effectively, but to view self-nurturing activities as "selfish" (Eichenbaum and Orbach, 1983). As a result, many women lose touch with their own emotions, desires, identity, and goals. Gilligan (1982) suggested that the outlook of may women is based on a morality of self-sacrifice that leads them to define the "good woman" as one who pleases others, denies her own needs, and gives of herself to others with no limits. Many women also learn that anger or strong emotions will jeopardize closeness, which leads them to negate their emotions or to view interpersonal conflict as their fault. The "good woman" gains the love and acceptance of others in her environment, but may lose her authentic self (Jack, 1991).

Self-nurturance involves gaining awareness of personal goals and desires, considering new options, and transcending old roles. It involves balancing concerns for oneself with concern for others. Caring for oneself involves recognizing oneself as a valuable person and setting priorities that will contribute to personal well-being (Gilbert, 1980). Self-nurturing activities should help the person experience a sense of pleasure and/or mastery. These experiences may include fantasy and goal-setting exercises, physical exercise, personal care, stress management techniques, or enrollment in classes that increase career options or allow a person to experience the joy of learning. Any activities that contribute to an increased knowledge of values and goals, a wider perspective or frame of reference, or an expanded sense of personal options are useful self-care tasks.

Self-nurturing is not only useful for helping clients discover themselves, but also for providing a buffer against future stressful events. This principle is embedded in the assumption that the skills clients learn in counseling should be applicable to multiple aspects of their lives. The client uses the tools learned in counseling for the enhancement of current functioning and the prevention of future difficulty (Butler, 1985).

Valuing Diversity

_____ 1. More attention should be paid to the special issues and needs of women of color within feminist therapy.

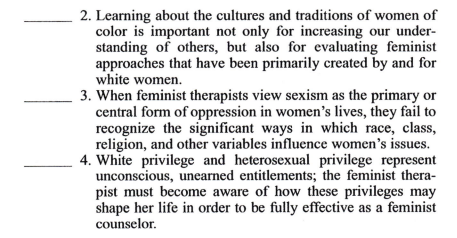

_____ 2. Learning about the cultures and traditions of women of color is important not only for increasing our understanding of others, but also for evaluating feminist approaches that have been primarily created by and for white women.

_____ 3. When feminist therapists view sexism as the primary or central form of oppression in women's lives, they fail to recognize the significant ways in which race, class, religion, and other variables influence women's issues.

_____ 4. White privilege and heterosexual privilege represent unconscious, unearned entitlements; the feminist therapist must become aware of how these privileges may shape her life in order to be fully effective as a feminist counselor.

A high level of agreement with these four items suggests that your views are consistent with recent efforts to create a more inclusive feminist approach to counseling. Feminist therapists are aware that although women share many common issues, goals, and problems, their lives are also shaped by many different experiences, roles, and life statuses. In a pluralistic and multicultural society, feminist therapists must recognize the myriad ways in which gender intersects with other factors.

Feminism has historically responded more completely to the concerns of white women than other groups, and the task of creating more inclusive forms of feminism is a critical challenge for the 1990s and the twenty-first century. Bell hooks (1984) noted that Betty Friedan's (1963) early analysis of the oppressiveness of "the problem with no name" galvanized many women to action and led to positive changes on the behalf of many women. However, this description exemplifies the inadequacy of analyses that refer primarily to the problems of a select group of women, in this case, white middle-class housewives who were dissatisfied with their stereotyped roles and lack of achievement opportunities. This assessment of women's problems inaccurately assumed that the problems of white women were synonymous with all women's concerns, and ignored the experience of the many women who had always worked outside of their homes, struggled to survive economically, and did not have the luxury to claim "the problem with no name." To assume that the dissatisfaction of one group of women reflects all women's experience or to claim that all forms of oppression are equally restrictive represents flawed thinking, minimizes the suffering of women who experience multiple forms of disadvantage, and allows more privileged women to ignore the ways in which their analyses are incomplete, racist, classist, or heterosexist. Oppression involves an absence of choices, choices which are less available to some women than others (hooks, 1984; Hurtado, 1989; Spelman, 1988). Further discussion of these issues occurs in Chapter 3.

Peggy McIntosh (1989) suggested that just as men have difficulty recognizing male privilege and power, white feminists have difficulty recognizing the unearned privileges they hold. The feminist therapist must educate herself about the unearned entitlements or status that she may hold on the basis of her class, race, sexual orientation, or ability. Involvement in antiracism (or antiheterosexism or anticlassism) consciousness-raising groups (Cross et al., 1982) provides excellent methods for increasing awareness.

Feminist therapists must also assume personal responsibility for educating themselves about the plurality of human experience, and should not assume that clients should provide this education for therapists. Members of minority cultures generally learn a wealth of information about the majority culture in order to survive and cope, but members of the majority culture often remain ignorant about important aspects of minority cultures. White feminist therapists must learn about the traditions and values of their diverse clients, read materials that inform them about relevant issues, and seek out experiences that sensitize them to important themes and concerns in their clients' lives. The competent feminist therapist must also be aware of how individual differences modify the impact of culture, race, class, religion, and sexual orientation. As a result, the feminist therapist is prepared to sensitively and carefully listen to the client and ask cogent questions that further clarify the individual client's perspective on specific issues.

Learning about women from diverse backgrounds is important not only for providing nonbiased treatment, but also for enriching our knowledge of women's lives in general. For example, Patricia

Romney (1991) proposed that gaining knowledge about women of color can "serve as a springboard to critique and advance our understanding of 'traditional feminism'" (p. 1). Similarly, becoming educated about lesbian concerns "permits us to view woman in her 'purest' form, that is, as untainted by the patriarchy as possible" (Boston Lesbian Psychologies Collective, 1987, p. 12).

Oliva Espín and Mary Ann Gawelek (1992) concluded that in order for feminist theory to be inclusive, the following must occur:

1. All women's experiences must be explored, valued, and understood.
2. Theory must be pluralistic, and differences must be appreciated for their potential to enrich our understanding of women's lives.
3. The belief in egalitarian relationships must include an understanding that women of diverse statuses can create theory and shape knowledge on their own behalf.
4. Contexts and culture must be understood as powerful influences that shape much individual behavior.

SUMMARY

Despite the reality that feminist counselors apply diverse theoretical perspectives to their work, several common themes permeate discussions of feminist therapy with women. First, some form of unequal power, victimization, or abuse often underlies the issues that women bring to counseling. Furthermore, many women experience abuse or unequal power over a long period of time, and they often enter counseling with intense feelings of guilt, isolation, and self-blame. Clients may use denial or minimization as a way of coping with the long-term, insidious effects of unequal power and abuse in relationships and often find it difficult to identify and name the problems they are experiencing. As women disclose information, the counselor and client examine how problems exist in a both a personal and social context, confront personal myths that lead to self-blame, and identify ways in which symptoms served as survival mechanisms. It is often difficult and time consuming to work through these problems that have been influenced by many years of restrictive socialization and/or relationships of unequal power.

As clients focus on these issues, it is often important for them to express feelings of anger, pain, grief, or sorrow that have been internalized or "swallowed." The discovery of personal methods for experiencing strength, capability, and power as a person is also crucial. Training in coping skills, cognitive restructuring, communication skills, imagery, self-nurturing, and decision making represent some of the tools for helping clients reach their goals. Given the reality that many individuals feel isolated as they enter counseling, the development of new support systems that reinforce the goals of counseling is important. These may include self-help or consciousness-raising groups, new family and social relationships, volunteer activities, group counseling, or groups that support social activism.

Although the basic principles of feminist therapy are well established, feminist therapists enact these principles in divergent ways. The discussion of similarities and differences between feminist therapies is the central focus of the remainder of this book. The next chapters will describe many of the prominent perspectives that have influenced feminist philosophy and how these philosophical views are incorporated within feminist therapy. An important goal for feminist therapists is to examine their personal assumptions and compare these assumptions to various feminist theories in order to create self-chosen models of feminist therapy that reflect compatibility between theory and practice. By becoming knowledgeable about the diversity of feminist theory and therapy, feminist therapists are better prepared to engage in informed decision making about the relative usefulness of various theoretical perspectives and interventions.

Chapter 2

An Overview of Liberal, Radical, and Socialist Feminisms

This chapter introduces three important political and theoretical traditions within feminism: liberal feminism, radical feminism, and socialist feminism. These feminisms have been closely associated with the emergence, ideals, and activism of the "new" feminist movement of the 1960s and the 1970s (Taylor and Whittier, 1993). Other significant themes in contemporary feminism, such as cultural feminism and the feminisms of women of color, and recent interest in feminist epistemology, including postmodern feminism, became especially influential in the late 1970s and 1980s, and will be summarized in Chapter 3. The following brief discussion of each of these strands within American feminism will not provide a comprehensive overview, but will acquaint the reader with influential themes that permeate feminist thought.

Sections summarizing each form of feminism begin with a brief set of statements that can be used to assess the degree to which your personal beliefs are consistent with specific theories. Each section also reviews historical ideas that form a foundation for each version of feminism, which is followed by an overview of current thought and emerging trends. Throughout the next two chapters, I have used a substantial number of quotes to illustrate the creative and original ways in which feminist theorists have expressed themselves over time.

LIBERAL FEMINISM

In order to use the self-assessment tools in this chapter, respond to each statement with a "yes" or "no."

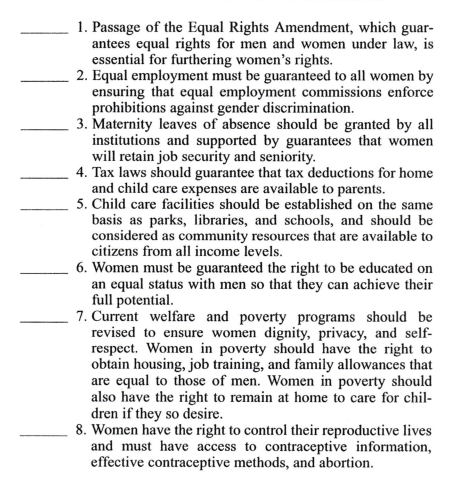

_____ 1. Passage of the Equal Rights Amendment, which guarantees equal rights for men and women under law, is essential for furthering women's rights.

_____ 2. Equal employment must be guaranteed to all women by ensuring that equal employment commissions enforce prohibitions against gender discrimination.

_____ 3. Maternity leaves of absence should be granted by all institutions and supported by guarantees that women will retain job security and seniority.

_____ 4. Tax laws should guarantee that tax deductions for home and child care expenses are available to parents.

_____ 5. Child care facilities should be established on the same basis as parks, libraries, and schools, and should be considered as community resources that are available to citizens from all income levels.

_____ 6. Women must be guaranteed the right to be educated on an equal status with men so that they can achieve their full potential.

_____ 7. Current welfare and poverty programs should be revised to ensure women dignity, privacy, and self-respect. Women in poverty should have the right to obtain housing, job training, and family allowances that are equal to those of men. Women in poverty should also have the right to remain at home to care for children if they so desire.

_____ 8. Women have the right to control their reproductive lives and must have access to contraceptive information, effective contraceptive methods, and abortion.

The preceding statements are based on the eight major points of the National Organization for Women (NOW) Bill of Rights (1970). They represent the foundational rights that contemporary liberal feminists demanded in the mid-1960s. Endorsement of the above items suggests a correspondence between your views and the philosophical underpinnings of liberal feminism. The following summary provides information about the origins and contemporary forms of liberal feminism.

Early Liberal Feminist Thought

Liberal feminism has its roots in the eighteenth and nineteenth century enlightenment and natural rights philosophies, and some of the significant contributors to this perspective include Mary Wollstonecraft (1992/1972), Elizabeth Cady Stanton, Susan B. Anthony (e.g., Stanton, Anthony, and Gage, 1881), Sarah Grimké (1838/1972), and Harriet Taylor Mill and John Stuart Mill (Rossi, 1970). These early feminist authors built their ideas on the foundation provided by liberal male theorists who proposed that men have the ability to exercise rational judgment and, thus, are entitled to exercise certain "natural" or inherent rights. According to liberal enlightenment thought, rational beings have the right to impose order on those who lack it, such as women and the nonhuman world. Enlightenment philosophers also focused on the primacy and superior nature of reason and the importance of mastering or subduing one's passions; they viewed nonrational experiences of emotion, spirituality, morality, and the aesthetic world as secondary to rational endeavors (Donovan, 1992).

Liberal feminist thinkers argued that women are also rational beings with the same capacities as men; thus, liberal feminism arose out of efforts to grant women the same rights that had been historically granted only to men. Josephine Donovan (1992) noted that although early enlightenment liberal feminists conveyed diverse views in their writings, they shared the following five major beliefs: (1) a strong faith in the power of rationality; (2) the belief that women and men share the same basic rational qualities; (3) the conviction that education, with an emphasis on critical thinking, is the most productive, efficient way to change individuals and society; (4) the assumption that individuals are independent beings who seek truth in isolation and that the rational and independent nature of persons is central to human dignity; and (5) the support of a natural rights doctrine in which each human has certain inalienable rights by virtue of their rational abilities.

Early feminists identified ways in which men oppressed women in order to preserve their superior roles, and how women's socialization hampered their ability to claim their natural rights. Mary Wollstonecraft described women's conditioning in ways that are remarkably similar to contemporary descriptions. She stated the following:

> Women are told from their infancy, and taught by the example of their mothers, that a little knowledge of human weakness, justly termed cunning, softness or temper, *outward* obedience, and a scrupulous attention to a puerile kind of propriety, will obtain for them the protection of man; and should they be beautiful, everything else is needless, for, at least, twenty years of their lives. (1792/1972, p. 6)

She also declared that women had been "stripped of the virtues that should clothe humanity" (p. 13), and deluded to follow "artificial graces" and values such as love, sentiment, gentleness, docility, and "spaniel-like affection" (p. 12). These virtues "raise emotion instead of inspiring respect" and destroy "all strength of character" (p. 13). Wollstonecraft argued that women share the same intellectual and moral core as men and should be given the opportunity to "cultivate their minds" (p. 12). She proposed that education "in common with man" (p. 12) and training in critical thinking would allow women to think clearly about their own situations, make women less naive and less easily deceived, and enable women to transcend selfishness and self-interest.

Sarah Grimké's (1938/1972) "Letters on the Equality of the Sexes and the Condition of Women" stated that "our powers of mind have been crushed" (p. 42) and that "man has exercised the most unlimited and brutal power over woman" (p. 47). Grimké wrote that it is especially through woman's union with man in marriage that her position has been lowered and she has lost her sense of individuality and independence. However, "[m]en and women were CREATED EQUAL; they are both moral and accountable beings, and whatever is *right* for man to do, is *right* for woman" (Grimké, 1838/1972, p. 40). Finally, Sarah Grimké asked "no favors for my sex" (p. 38), but requested that men "take their feet from off our necks" (p. 38), reinstate the rights that have been "wrested from us" (p. 38), and allow women to gain education and nurture their intellectual potential.

The Declaration of Sentiments and Resolutions (1848/1972), which was drafted at the Seneca Falls Convention, became an important marker for organized feminism in the United States and reflected many liberal feminist ideals. It stated the following: "We hold these truths to be self-evident; that all men and women are created equal; that they are endowed by their Creator with certain inalienable rights" (p. 77). The declaration outlined the ways in which "the history of mankind is a history of repeated injuries and usurpations of the part of man toward woman" (p. 78), usurpations that included making women morally irresponsible, monopolizing profitable employments, denying education to women, depriving married women of rights, and withholding women's right to vote. It concluded with a series of resolutions that were designed to rectify these wrongs. Elizabeth Cady Stanton and Lucretia Mott were especially influential as organizers of the Seneca Falls Convention.

Elizabeth Cady Stanton worked toward changing basic attitudes about men and women, gaining educational and coeducational opportunities for women, and securing liberalized divorce laws on behalf of women. As an extension of the principle of men's and women's basic similarity, she used liberal biblical scholarship to support the notion that God contained both masculine and feminine characteristics (Banner, 1980; Stanton, 1895/1898). Like those who preceded her, Cady Stanton emphasized feminist individualism and the importance of personal freedom, personal merit, self-reliance and self control (Banner, 1980; DuBois, 1981). She stated that "nothing strengthens the judgment and quickens the conscience like individual responsibility" (Stanton, 1892/1972, p. 159). Furthermore, "as an individual, [a woman] must rely on herself" and "make the voyage of life alone" (p. 159). In light of her belief in men's and women's similarity and individual responsibility, she asked that legislators "strike out all special legislation for us; strike the words 'white male' from all your constitutions, and then, with fair sailing, let us sink or swim, live or die, survive or perish together" (Stanton, 1860/1972, p. 121). Once "all artificial trammels are removed, and women are recognized as individuals, responsible for their own environments, thoroughly educated for all positions in life they may be called to fill," they will "be fitted for those years of solitude that come to all" (Stanton, 1892/1972, p. 159).

Elizabeth Cady Stanton contended that the natural rights doctrine should pertain not only to public life but also private life, and she stressed the importance of women having sovereignty over their own bodies and sexuality (DuBois, 1981). She stated that the "aristocracy of sex" within marriage allowed men to dominate and tyrannize women; she characterized marriage as a form of licensed prostitution, and stated that all women were kept in slavery by their constant fear of rape. Although she recommended a reformist response to these issues, radical feminists of the 1970s described the oppression of women in similar ways.

Susan B. Anthony, who often worked closely with Elizabeth Cady Stanton, is known less for her theoretical work and more for her pragmatic applications and ability to organize women on behalf of suffrage issues and other legal reforms (DuBois, 1981). In her discussion of the tenacity of tradition and the difficulties of gaining equality, she noted that:

> Even when man's intellectual convictions shall be sincerely and fully of the side of freedom and equality to women, the force of long existing customs and laws will impel him to exert authority over her, which be distasteful to the self-sustained, self-respectful women. The habit of the ages cannot, at once, be changed. (Anthony, 1877/1981, p. 148)

Susan Anthony noted that laws and amendments would not necessarily transform relationships. She speculated that during the transition of inequality to equality, women might need to opt for singleness as an alternative to the subjection inherent in marriage; singleness would assure that women could maintain self-respect and equality. Of these unmarried women she stated: "They are not halves, needing complements, as are the masses of women, but evenly balanced well rounded characters" (p. 151).

One of Anthony's strategies was to build a case for the inalienable natural rights of women by arguing that the constitution had already granted women the right to vote. She noted that the constitution made "explicit assertions of the equal right of the whole people" and that the "omission of the adjective 'female' should not be construed into a denial; but instead should be considered as of no effect" (Anthony 1872/1981, p. 155). She further argued that if men persisted in withholding women's rights on constitutional grounds, women should also be exempt from taxation and from the obligation to support the government. In a series of actions that resembled the feminist sit-ins and activism one century later, Anthony organized women to cast ballots illegally. Her arrest and later trial provided an opportunity for her to further disseminate her argument that women were already entitled to vote (DuBois, 1981; Schneir, 1972). Although interested in a wide range of issues such as equal pay for equal work, labor exploitation, international peace, and temperance, Anthony concluded that the ballot would provide women with the necessary power to secure a place of equality. She asked, "Now what do women want? Simply the same ballot" (Anthony, 1871/1981, p. 143).

Many early feminists were involved in antislavery and abolition activities, which increased their awareness of their own oppressed status and led them to adopt a feminist platform. They often linked the plight of women and slaves, noting that both male slaves and women were expected to take on the name of their masters, were denied the ownership of property, had no legal rights, and could be physically punished by their husbands or owners. Anthony (1872/1981) stated the following:

> There is and can be but one safe principle of government—equal rights to all. Discrimination against any class on account of color, race, nativity, sex, property, culture, can but embitter and disaffect that class, and thereby endanger the safety of the whole people. (p. 161)

Women of color were also actively involved in the women's movement and Sojourner Truth (1867/1972) noted the following about the concerns of black women:

> There is a great stir about colored men getting their rights, but not a word about the colored women; and if colored men get their rights, and not colored women theirs, you see the colored men will be masters over the women, and it will be just as bad as it was before. (p. 129)

Unfortunately, as it became apparent that black men would gain the vote following the civil war and women would not gain this right, white feminists became embittered, conveniently forgot their concern for all women, and resorted to racist rhetoric in their fight for the vote (Banner, 1980; Donovan, 1992). This issue and its impact on feminism even today will be discussed further in the chapter on women of color and feminism.

Roughly three-quarters of a century after the Seneca Falls Convention, women in the United States eventually the won the right to vote in 1920. A second generation of leaders, such as Carrie Chapman Catt and Alice Paul, were instrumental in organizing women in their final efforts to achieve this right (Hole and Levine, 1971). Although liberal feminists of earlier eras are sometimes described as being concerned only with gaining the vote, this conclusion is erroneous. Feminists engaged in a wide array of causes including abolitionist endeavors, issues of working women, and divorce and property rights reform (Banner, 1980). However, with the exception of a few theorists, liberal feminist theorists did not connect the battle for public rights with the private world of women. They focused primarily on how men as a class oppressed women, and they believed that legal changes would lead to equality for women; they did not attend to ways in which women's domestic roles would limit their ability to seize their rights and interfere with gaining equal economic status (Donovan, 1992). Furthermore, although early liberal feminists often viewed marriage as a primary form of oppression, they did not challenge the basic structure of marriage; women were encouraged not only to take on increased economic roles but also to practice "enlightened motherhood" (Banner, 1980).

Contemporary Liberal Feminism

After winning the right to vote, liberal feminist ideas were less influential between the 1920s and the 1960s. Many feminist activists focused less on women's rights and more on social reform (see the section on cultural feminism in Chapter 3). Most of the early ideas of liberal feminism remained intact as they were revived during the feminist movement of the late 1960s and early 1970s. Betty Friedan's book *The Feminine Mystique* (1963/1983) was an important catalyst that encouraged white middle-class housewives to examine their roles and position in society. Friedan (1963) described the ways in which women of the 1950s were manipulated and cheated by various social institutions that encouraged women to organize their lives around the "feminine mystique." The feminine mystique encompassed the belief that "the highest value and the only commitment for women is the fulfillment of their own femininity" (p. 43). Friedan (1963) argued that women had been falsely deluded into believing that "the root of women's troubles in the past is that women envied men, women tried to be like men, instead of accepting their own nature, which can find fulfillment only in sexual passivity, male domination, and nurturing maternal love" (p. 43).

As women began talking about their malaise, "the problem that has no name burst like a boil through the image of the happy American housewife" (Friedan, 1963, p. 22). Friedan indicated that this problem, which she defined as any way in which women are blocked from reaching their full potential, was likely to exact a greater toll on the mental and physical health of the country than any other disease. Her proposed solutions included the creation of new social norms, educational options, and definitions of femininity that would allow women to achieve a sense of identity, completeness, and maturity. This new identity would allow women to integrate professional and mothering roles without conflict. Friedan (1963) argued that when enough individual women successfully constructed life plans based on their own abilities and gained access to supportive services such as child-care and maternity leave, "they will not have to sacrifice the right to honorable competition and contribution anymore than they will have to sacrifice marriage and motherhood" (p. 375). In summary, women would "carry more of the burden of the battle with the world, instead of being a burden themselves" (p. 377), and both men and women would achieve greater happiness.

Betty Friedan invested her energy in various women's rights causes that would allow women to reach their full individual potential. She was active in establishing and providing direction for the National Organization for Women (NOW), which identified individual rights that would make it possible for women to make responsible choices about their own lives. The NOW Bill of Rights (1970) itemized the following demands: (1) passage of the Equal Rights Amendment; (2) enforcement of laws banning sex discrimination in employment; (3) paid maternity leave as an extension of Social Security; (4) laws allowing for the deduction of working parents' child-care expenses; (5) child care facilities that would be as accessible as other public schools, parks, and libraries; (6) equal and unsegregated education; (7) opportunities for women in poverty to gain job training and housing, and the revision of legislation that limits the dignity, privacy, and self-respect of poor women; and (8) the right of women to control their own reproduction.

Affirmative action, reproductive rights legislation, educational reforms, and equal opportunity legislation represent important liberal feminist programs that help ensure that women and other minority groups are not systematically disadvantaged. During the twentieth century, liberal feminist agendas have not only focused on the removal of structural barriers to women's success, but also have used government programs to break up power structures that have limited women's actual access to many social roles (Donovan, 1992; Ferree and Hess, 1985; Jaggar, 1983).

Summary

Liberal feminists have historically viewed the subordination of women as embedded in legal, economic, and cultural constraints that have blocked women's access to many opportunities available to men. They have emphasized that women should be entitled to the same civil rights and economic opportunities as men. Liberal feminists have consistently promoted the ideals of human dignity, equality, self-fulfillment, autonomy, and rationality, and have sought to reform existing legal and political systems that limit individual freedom. According to this view, oppression is caused by rigid gender-role conditioning and irrational prejudices that lead people to believe that women are less intellectually or physically capable than men; solutions to these problems are achieved through rational argument, the transcendence of cultural conditions, and the legislation of laws that allow for equal opportunity for all individuals. Legal measures, reforms, and the guarantee of civil rights are seen as providing opportunities for personal initiative and choices that will permit individuals to advance as far as their talents permit. Within the realm of personal relationships, a wide range of nontraditional behaviors is considered appropriate for both men and women, but these choices must be based on personal preferences and should not be externally imposed (Donovan, 1992; Jaggar, 1983; Tong, 1989).

In general, liberal feminist programs have focused on redistributing persons within power structures and have not questioned the basic assumptions of major social institutions. As a result, liberal feminism is often referred to as conservative or mainstream feminism. Ellen Willis (1975) declared that this "self-improvement, individual-liberation philosophy is relevant only to an elite" (p. 170). Despite its image as conservative, liberal feminism has increasingly moved away from the belief that individual efforts alone will liberate women, and liberal feminists have often adopted more radical politics as the struggle for women's emancipation has intensified (Eisenstein, 1981; Tong, 1989). Despite the limitations of this theory, the rights and legal gains that liberal feminists have fought for provide an important foundation for the efforts of many other feminists.

RADICAL FEMINISM

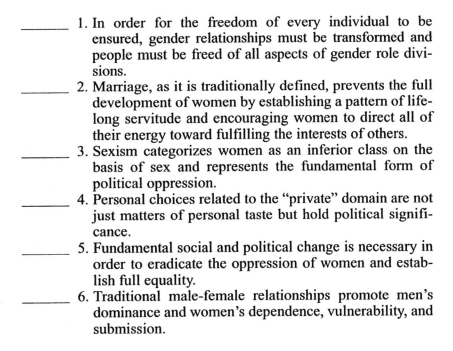

_____ 1. In order for the freedom of every individual to be ensured, gender relationships must be transformed and people must be freed of all aspects of gender role divisions.

_____ 2. Marriage, as it is traditionally defined, prevents the full development of women by establishing a pattern of life-long servitude and encouraging women to direct all of their energy toward fulfilling the interests of others.

_____ 3. Sexism categorizes women as an inferior class on the basis of sex and represents the fundamental form of political oppression.

_____ 4. Personal choices related to the "private" domain are not just matters of personal taste but hold political significance.

_____ 5. Fundamental social and political change is necessary in order to eradicate the oppression of women and establish full equality.

_____ 6. Traditional male-female relationships promote men's dominance and women's dependence, vulnerability, and submission.

_____ 7. The major causes of sexism and oppression are male domination, patriarchal values that permeate the culture, and men's control over women's bodies.

_____ 8. A high proportion of the major issues facing women are consequences of violence against women (e.g., battering, pornography, incest, and rape).

Emergence of Radical Feminism

Most contemporary feminist theories are directly related to ideas that were first expressed during the eighteenth and nineteenth centuries. In contrast, radical feminism is typically defined as having contemporary roots in the late 1960s and early 1970s. Agreement with the eight statements indicates endorsement of views consistent with radical feminism. Alice Echols (1989) indicated that in their search for fundamental change and new ideas, radical women sought inspiration from contemporary sources, such as writings by the French feminist existential author Simone de Beauvoir (1952). Three of Simone de Beauvoir's views were instrumental in shaping radical feminist directions: (1) women have always been oppressed, and despite some feminists' contention that women held significant power in ancient times (e.g., in Native American cultures), matriarchal societies in which women held equal power with men have never existed; (2) socialism and changed economic structures are not adequate for eradicating women's oppression; and (3) male domination takes on a wide variety of faces in different contexts (Sarachild, 1975a,b).

Simone de Beauvoir (1952) noted that woman has historically been understood only in comparison to men and not as an autonomous being: she has become "what man decrees" (p. xvi). Furthermore, "[s]he is defined and differentiated with reference to man and not he with reference to her; she is the incidental, the inessential as opposed to the essential. He is the Subject, he is the Absolute—she is the Other" (p. xvi). In spite of this oppressed status, de Beauvoir (1952) also described a hopeful future in which women would be viewed as independent beings. Men and women would exist for themselves as well as for each other; while "mutually recognizing each other as subject, each will yet remain for the other an *other*" (p. 731).

Many contributors to radical and socialist feminism became aware of gender oppression through involvement in "New Left" and civil rights activities (Donovan, 1992). Most of the New Left and civil rights organizations were dominated by men who gave token or no support to women's concerns. When women's concerns about sexism were introduced, they were ignored or minimized and sometimes labeled as "frivolous" or "bourgeois" in comparison to race and class oppression. At times, women were also subjected to catcalls and sarcastic remarks that were exploitive and defined women as sexual objects (Deckard, 1979; Echols, 1989; Hole and Levine, 1971). The authors of a Canadian group's manifesto (Bernstein et al., 1969) noted that a major role for women had been that of "servicing the organization's men" (p. 252) by providing the "stable, homey atmosphere which the radical man needs to survive" (p. 252) and engaging in financial and emotional support roles that allowed men to "run around being political, creative—writing, thinking, and oozing charisma" (p. 252). When women sought leadership roles in this environment, they were often named "castrating females." One manifesto stated the following:

> It is our contention that until the male chauvinists of the movement (North American and world-wide) understand the concept of Liberation in relation to us, the most exploited members of *any* society, the Women, they will be voicing political lies. (Bernstein et al., 1969, p. 253)

Some of the first radical feminists participated in NOW for a short time but reacted negatively to its hierarchical structure, use of traditional democratic methods for making decisions and organizing for change, and efforts to cooperate with existing political institutions that radical feminists hoped to eradicate. After brief participation in NOW, radical feminist activist Ti-Grace Atkinson (1974) indicated that she was resigning because "you cannot destroy oppression by filling the position of the oppressor. I don't think you can fight oppression 'from the inside'" (p. 11). Most radical feminists participated in small, loosely organized units that arose spontaneously in various parts of the country and focused on creating cultures of active resistance to mainstream society. Decision making was based on consensus and equal participation, and all members engaged in both support and leadership roles. In contrast to liberal feminist messages of the 1960s, Jo Freeman stated that "women's liberation does not mean equality with men" because "equality in an unjust society is meaningless" (quoted in Echols, 1989, p. 60). Bonnie Kreps (1973) added the following: "We, in this segment of the movement, do not believe that the oppression of women will be ended by giving them a bigger piece of the pie, as Betty Friedan would have it. We believe that the pie itself is rotten" (p. 239).

Radical Feminist Manifestos and Thought

Some of the most active radical feminist groups included the Redstockings, The Feminists, and New York Radical Feminists. During the first years of their existence, these groups demonstrated enormous energy; utilized a wide variety of tactics, speakouts, and demonstrations to raise public awareness; and created an extensive literature of pamphlets, manifestos, journals, articles, books, and creative works. From the start, women in these groups expressed diverse opinions, and conflict between groups was sometimes divisive (Echols, 1989; Willis, 1984). Most of these groups functioned actively for only a few years and acted like "a generator that got things going, cut out and left it to the larger reform engine" (Frances Chapman, quoted in Echols, 1989, p. 5). After a high level of initial activity that continued into the mid-1970s, radical feminism lost momentum as a political movement and was superseded by cultural feminist ideas in the late 1970s and 1980s (Echols, 1989).

Three fundamental beliefs are shared by radical feminists: (a) women were the first oppressed group; (b) women's oppression occurs in all cultures and is the most widespread of all oppressions; and (c) gender oppression is the most virulent and difficult form of oppression to eliminate, and cannot be abolished through other social changes, such as the erasure of class differences (Jaggar and Rothenberg, 1984). Radical feminists believe that women share roles as members of a gender-class, that these oppressive roles needed to be understood in political terms, and that these roles must be completely eradicated. Some of the most provocative works of radical feminists have critiqued the institutions of the family, love, marriage, and normative heterosexuality (Echols, 1989). The early writings on radical feminism are diverse, and were often written quickly and spontaneously in order to energize women and hasten change. As a result, these writings occasionally contain themes that are contradictory or difficult to understand (Donovan, 1992; Echols, 1989).

Radical feminist groups stressed the importance of defining a shared voice rather than encouraging individual writers to become "stars." The "manifestos" of the following groups communicated consensus values and are important sources for understanding the ideals and diversity of radical feminism.

The Redstockings

The goal of the Redstockings was to achieve "final liberation from male supremacy" for all women. The Redstockings Manifesto (1969) declared that "our oppression is total, affecting every facet of our lives" (p. 272) and that other existing ideologies, such as those that focus on class, are inadequate for eliminating male supremacy. Furthermore, the agents of oppression were defined as men:

> All other forms of exploitation and oppression (racism, capitalism, imperialism, etc.) are extensions of male supremacy: men dominate women, [and] a few men dominate the rest. All power structures throughout history have been male-dominated and male-oriented. Men have controlled all political, economic and cultural institutions and backed up this control with physical force. They have used their power to keep women in an inferior position. *All men* receive economic, sexual, and psychological benefits from male supremacy. *All men* have oppressed women. (p. 273)

The Redstockings developed the "pro-woman" stance, which viewed women's behavior and seeming submission as a consequence of unequal power, the immediate social environment, and daily pressure from men. They rejected any internal and psychological explanations that suggested that women contribute to their own oppression. They stated that women's acquiescence and apparent collaboration in their own oppression is caused by powerlessness and not passivity, as well as the reality that rebellion against "proper" roles is punished. Women's submission is based on necessity and not choice (Echols, 1989).

Carol Hanisch (1971) noted that the pro-woman stance means that:

> women are really neat people. The bad things that are said about us as women are either myths (women are stupid), tactics women use to struggle individually (women are bitches), or are actually things that we want to carry into the new society and want men to share too (women are sensitive, emotional). (p. 155)

Judith Brown (1971) added that women are not brainwashed or conditioned to behave as they do; behaviors such as "conniving, vamping, and flirting" (p. 165) are skills of survival. By using these behaviors, "we either avoid material danger (loss of a job or a man) or gain material advantage (a promotion, a man)" (p. 165). Consistent with this perspective, the Redstockings did not criticize women for maintaining intimate relationships within the flawed institution of marriage, but noted that marriage often represents the best option or bargain available to women in an oppressive world.

The literature of the Redstockings emphasized the relevance of feminism for women of all economic, racial, and educational statuses, and called on all women to unite in the struggle for liberation. They opposed the antimarriage position taken by some radical feminist groups, noting that such a recommendation reflects a class bias. Most women must remain in marriage in order to survive economically. They avoided making moralistic judgments of various women's choices and attempted to recognize how oppression varies by class and culture and how women develop a wide range of behaviors to deal with their realities. The Redstockings also recommended that white women become aware of their privileges, renounce their privileges, and identify with less privileged women (Echols, 1989; Redstockings Manifesto, 1969).

The Redstockings wrote frequently about the importance of consciousness-raising. They stated: "We regard our personal experience, and our feelings about that experience, as the basis for an analysis of our common situation" (Redstockings Manifesto, 1969, p. 274). Through consciousness-raising (CR), women were encouraged to define a program of liberation based on the daily and subjective realities of women's lives. Carol Hanisch (1971) commented:

"I've been forced to take off the rose-colored glasses and face the awful truth about how grim my life really is as a woman" (p. 154). Furthermore, "[o]ne of the first things we discover in these groups is that personal problems are political problems. There are no personal solutions at this time. There is only collective action for a collective solution" (p. 153). Ellen Willis (1984) noted that the "genius" of this strategy was its relevance and concreteness; it asked women to explore and respond to issues that created the most pain in their own lives.

The Redstockings actively raised public awareness about abortion issues, organized occasions for women to speak publicly about their personal experiences, and called these events "speakouts." Through the medium of the speakout, feminist activists successfully confronted the popular notion that abortion did not have political significance for women (Echols, 1989).

The Feminists

Another radical group, The Feminists, focused on a more psychological analysis of gender roles than the Redstockings, and believed that men oppress primarily because of their psychological needs rather than their greater access to power (Echols, 1989). They declared that the male-female role system "distorts the humanity of the Oppressor and denies the humanity of the Oppressed" (The Feminists, 1973, p. 369). Instead of engaging in creative action, men justify their existence by denying the humanity of women; women's roles represent a form of "self-defense" against the impositions of men over women. Both male and female roles must be annihilated or completely destroyed because both stabilize the male-female system as it exists. The Feminists (1973) stated the following: "If any part of these role definitions is left, the disease of oppression remains and will reassert itself again in new, or the same old, variations throughout society" (p. 370).

The Feminists agreed with the Redstockings about the centrality of male oppression, but rejected the pro-woman position. They were critical of the Redstockings' emphasis on external forces as the primary sources of women's oppression and believed that it is important for women to identify ways in which traditional gender roles are internalized and distort women's self-definitions. The Feminists also criticized women who "collaborated" in or acquiesced to their own oppression; thus, they viewed the pro-woman position as leading to self-deception or excuses for avoiding personal and social change. The Feminists believed that the "pro-woman line" condoned women's participation in sexist institutions and stifled women from making moral judgments about behavior that is inappropriate for feminists (Echols, 1989).

The Feminists also believed that consciousness-raising could retard the progress of feminism by overemphasizing feelings and personal reactions, and substituting talk for theory-building and action (Echols, 1989; Willis, 1984). Consistent with their view that women's behavior is psychologically conditioned, they believed that it is necessary for women to make changes on their own behalf. Ti-Grace Atkinson stated the following: "Only when all people, *each* of us, refuse to submit, will oppression disappear" (1974, p. 118). Furthermore, a "feminist gives up the privilege of self-deception at the moment she claims the role of social critic" (p. 119). According to The Feminists, the phrase "the personal is political" means that one's personal life must clearly reflect a commitment to feminism and radicalism. In order to help women transform themselves, The Feminists focused on setting standards or prescriptions of appropriate feminist behavior (The Feminists, 1973; Echols, 1989; Willis, 1984). Their program for change also proposed the destruction of all institutions that reinforce women's traditional roles, including institutions of love, childbearing, and heterosexual sex (The Feminists, 1973).

The Feminists' views on oppression generally reflected the statements of one of their major theorists, Ti-Grace Atkinson, who viewed marriage as inherently unequal, as debilitating for women, and as posing an easy retreat from the radical demands of feminism. Atkinson (1974) stated that "marriage and the family are as corrupt as institutions as slavery ever was. They must be abolished as slavery was" (p. 5). She also added that:

> Since our society has never known a time when sex in all its aspects was not exploitative and relations based on sex, e.g., the male-female relationship, were not extremely hostile, it is difficult to understand how sexual intercourse can even be salvaged as a *practice.* (p. 19)

Furthermore, love is "the payoff for the consent to oppression" (p. 7) and "love is the psychological pivot in the persecution of women" (p. 43).

Consistent with The Feminists' rejection of marriage in practice as well as in theory, they eventually adopted a standard that no more than one-third of the members could live with a man in a formal or informal relationship (The Feminists, 1973). Separatism was advocated as a method for altering social structures and for organizing a "counter power block to that of men" (Atkinson, 1974, p. 105). Atkinson stated the following:

> Women are still operating on a personal rather on a political basis. The proof of class consciousness will be when we separate off from men, from these one-to-one units. (For example, marriage and motherhood.) There can be no significant improvement in the situation of women until this happens. (p. 90)

The Feminists viewed ongoing association with men as undermining the liberation movement: it pointed to the inconsistency of belief and practice of members. In contrast, the Redstockings viewed separatism as impractical, unappealing and as an ineffective means for challenging male power. They believed that it is possible to work toward equality while remaining within heterosexual relationships (Willis, 1984).

The Feminists directed efforts toward eradicating sexual exploitation through rape, prostitution, and marriage. In general, they did not view sexuality as a potential source of pleasure for women (Echols, 1989), but suggested that women needed to be liberated from sex: "Sex, because it is genitally determined, is in the interests of the male and against the interests of the female" (Atkinson, 1974, p. 67). Heterosexual sex was seen as reinforcing roles of dominance and passivity (The Feminists, 1973). Thus, The Feminists encouraged women to love each other but to avoid confusing love with the distractions of sex.

In her initial statements, Ti-Grace Atkinson believed that lesbianism was primarily an alternative sexual choice, and thus, represented a distraction rather than a solution to heterosexual sex (Echols, 1989). Later, however, she defined lesbianism as a powerful political choice that could help eliminate the power of men over women (Atkinson, 1974) and stated: "Feminism is the theory; lesbianism is the practice" (cited by Koedt, 1973, p. 246).

A second highly influential member of The Feminists was Kate Millett, whose book titled *Sexual Politics* (1970) was often cited by radical feminists for its analysis of how sex is a status category with political implications. Millett (1970) argued that male supremacy is not based on biological difference but on a belief system founded on:

> needs and values of the dominant group and dictated by what its members cherish in themselves and find convenient in subordinates: aggression, intelligence, force, and efficacy in the male; passivity, ignorance, docility, "virtue," and ineffectuality in the female. (p. 26)

She identified the ways in which conditioning, family relations, class differences, economic conditions, violence and force, psychological factors, and religion support and reinforce patriarchal values across generations. Millett (1970) concluded that "patriarchy's greatest psychological weapon is simply its universality and longevity" (p. 58). Although she noted that class is also a powerful force in molding behavior, "patriarchy has a more tenacious hold through its successful habit of passing itself off as nature" (p. 58).

New York Radical Feminists

The New York Radical Feminists joined The Feminists in rejecting the social-power analysis of the Redstockings; they believed that men seek power for its own sake and find the exercise of this power to be intrinsically satisfying (Echols, 1989). Their manifesto stated: "We believe that the purpose of male supremacy is primarily to obtain psychological ego satisfaction, and that only secondarily does this manifest itself in economic relationships" (New York Radical Feminists, 1973, p. 379). In analyzing the psychological aspects of the "male ego identity," this group stated that "[i]t is not out of a desire to hurt the woman that man dominates and destroys her; it is out of a need for a sense of power that he necessarily must destroy her ego and make it subservient to him" (p. 380). Furthermore, the more powerless a man feels in relationship to other men, the more likely he is to oppress women (Echols, 1989; New York Radical Feminists, 1973). The New York Radical Feminists argued that women's behavior is enforced by external constraints, but also internalized through socialization experiences that teach women to conform to social expectations and to accept these limitations as natural. The Feminists utilized consciousness-raising, but were critical of the Redstockings' efforts to use CR to initiate personal change. They viewed CR as a method to increase women's awareness of how to change social systems.

In their analysis of sexual institutions, the New York Radical Feminists stated that positive heterosexual relationships could occur when, "the need to *control* the growth of another is replaced by love *for* the growth of another" (1973, p. 381). One of the influential members of the New York Radical Feminists was Shulamith Firestone, whose book titled *The Dialectic of Sex* (1970) proposed that patriarchy and male supremacy are rooted in inequities associated with the reproductive roles of women. She encouraged women to gain control of reproduction as a way of abolishing sexual class oppression. By renouncing biological reproduction, which leads to possessiveness and jealousy, and relying on technological reproductive advances, traditional sex roles and the biological family could be eliminated and replaced with new forms of childbearing and childrearing that could be shared by society as a whole. Women would no longer be confined to the home, but they would be free to enter the workplace unencumbered by reproductive and family roles. Finally, women would engage in sex voluntarily and as a free expression of themselves.

Lesbian Feminism

Some radical feminists, such as the Redstockings, viewed the lesbian lifestyle primarily as a sexual choice and as a substitute for working toward equality in heterosexual relationships. However, other radical feminists described lesbianism as a profoundly political choice and the logical outcome of refusing to participate in inherently unequal heterosexual relationships. Charlotte Bunch (1972/1987) noted that lesbianism is political "because relationships between men and women are essentially political: they involve power and dominance. Since the lesbian actively rejects that relationship and chooses women, she defies the established political system" (p. 162).

The Radicalesbians were among the first to challenge the heterosexism of straight feminists, to help erase the typical negative connotations associated with the term *lesbian*, and to describe feminism on their own, positive terms. In their manifesto titled "The Woman Identified Woman," The Radicalesbians stated the following:

> A lesbian is the rage of all women condensed to the point of explosion. She is the woman who, often beginning at an extremely early age, acts in accordance with her inner compulsion to be a more complete and freer human being than her society . . . cares to allow her. (p. 240)

Based on her ongoing, continuous struggle with heterosexist society, the lesbian is "forced to evolve her own life pattern" and learns earlier than her heterosexual sisters about "the essential aloneness of life (which the myth of marriage obscures)" (p. 240).

The manifesto noted that feminist women had avoided dealing with lesbianism, and that the fear of this issue demonstrated men's continued control over women. Fear of lesbianism frightens women into assuming a less militant stand, separates women from each other, and reinforces the notion that "male acceptability is primary" (p. 243). The Radicalesbians contended that "only women can give to each other a new sense of self" (p. 245) and that this identity cannot be found in relationships with men. They stated: "Our energies must flow toward our sisters, not backward toward our oppressors" (p. 245).

Although the Radicalesbians worked primarily toward creating a new way of thinking about lesbians, a second lesbian feminist group, the Furies (including, e.g., Charlotte Bunch and Rita Mae Brown) viewed lesbianism as a way to intensify the struggle for liberation (Echols, 1989; Myron and Bunch, 1975). As a part of their strategy, the Furies advocated a separatist stance. They viewed lesbian separatism as an opportunity to stop justifying themselves to the larger society to "build our own pride, strength, and unity as a people, to develop an analysis of our particular oppression, and to create a political ideology and strategy that would both force the movement's recognition of us and lead to the end of male supremacy" (Bunch, 1976/1987, p. 185).

Critical of heterosexual women, Rita Mae Brown stated: "Straight women are confused by men, don't put women first. They betray Lesbians and in its deepest form, they betray their own selves" (1975, p. 74). Charlotte Bunch noted that heterosexuality often separates women from each other and encourages women to compete for and define themselves through men. She stated the following: "Lesbianism threatens male supremacy at its core. When politically conscious and organized, it is central to destroying our sexist, racist, capitalist, imperialist system" (1972/1987, p. 161). Lesbianism dismantles beliefs about women's inferiority and erases women's need for men. The independence of the lesbian woman is a "basic threat" (p. 164) to the power of men over women. According to this view, lesbians are more likely to seek radical solutions and to fight to change society because they have no vested interest in maintaining the various institutions that support heterosexuality (e.g., the church, the state, schools, health systems). Bunch (1972/1987) concluded that "lesbianism is the key to liberation and only women who cut their ties to male privilege can be trusted to remain serious in the struggle against male dominance" (p. 166).

Charlotte Bunch (1978/1987) distinguished between a lesbian and woman-identified woman: a lesbian is a woman "whose sexual/ affectional preference is for women, and who has thereby rejected the female role on some level" (Bunch, 1978/1987, p. 198), and who may or may not adopt a lesbian feminist perspective; a woman-identified woman is a feminist who "adopts a lesbian-feminist ideology and enacts that understanding in her life" (p. 198), whether or not she defines herself as lesbian in a sexual sense. Thus, lesbian feminism could be adopted by gay and straight men and women. According to this model, lesbian feminism encompasses far more than a personal choice about lifestyle or the adoption of a dynamic women's community; it also involves a commitment to political change.

Adrienne Rich (1980/1989) indicated that compulsory heterosexuality has been imposed on all women, supports and perpetuates male dominance, and limits women's creative energy and opportunities to form positive bonds with each other. In her efforts to redefine lesbian existence, Rich used the term *lesbian continuum* to represent "a range—through each woman's life and throughout history—of woman-identified experience, not simply the fact that woman has had or consciously desired genital sexual experience with another woman" (p. 129). According to Rich, lesbian experience includes various forms of "primary intensity between and among women, including the sharing of a rich inner life, the bonding against male tyranny, and the giving and receiving of practical and political support" (p. 129). This definition emphasizes potential connections between all women, including women who participate in heterosexual or lesbian sexual relationships. In contrast, some radical lesbian feminists believe that heterosexual relationships inevitably promote the subordination of women because they require identification with institutions that are founded on male prerogatives, needs, wants, and perspectives. According to this view, the only route to full liberation is through the creation of a uniquely woman-oriented sexuality based on celibacy, autoeroticism, or lesbianism (Donovan, 1992; Rich, 1980/1989). It should be noted that although many lesbians hold views that are consistent with lesbian feminism, many other lesbians identify themselves more closely with other feminist philosophies, including liberal, cultural, and socialist feminism.

Male Dominance, Violence, and Sexuality

Throughout the past two decades, radical feminists have consistently generated theories about, and activist responses to, issues regarding violence against women. Many radical feminists believe that the origin of male dominance is connected to men's control of women's sexuality (Jaggar and Rothenberg, 1984). Catherine MacKinnon (1989) declared that "[m]ale dominance is sexual" (p. 127). Sexuality is the medium through which male supremacy defines, eroticizes, and confines men and women, their gender identities, and their sexual pleasure. Thus, male-defined sexuality is forced on women and maintains male dominance as a political system.

Barbara Mehrhof and Pamela Kearon (1971) were among the first to describe rape as a political act of oppression, a terrorist act for maintaining women's subordination. In her highly influential book titled *Against Our Will*, Susan Brownmiller (1975) defined rape as an act of violence rather than sex, as a way in which sexual violence is culturally condoned, and as a method for establishing masculinity. In contrast to Susan Brownmiller's efforts to separate sexuality and violence, Robin Morgan (1980) described rape as "the perfected act of male sexuality in a patriarchal culture—it is the ultimate metaphor for domination, violence, subjugation, and possession" (p. 134). In similar fashion, Andrea Dworkin (1981) described rape as "the defining paradigm of sexuality" (p. 136).

Catherine MacKinnon (1982/1993) contended that describing rape as an act of violence rather than sexuality allows one to reject violence while affirming heterosexual sexuality. Although Susan Brownmiller supported this view, MacKinnon asserted that violence and coercion are integrally related to sexuality in our society; thus, violence and coercion are normative aspects of heterosexual sex. Because of the difficulty separating violence and sexuality in rape, MacKinnon (1982/1993) prefers to see rape as more than the displacement of power into the realm of sexuality; she defines it as "an expression of male sexuality, the social imperatives of which define all women" (p. 208-209).

In general, radical feminists have drawn important connections between sexuality and the full range of ways in which sex, coercion, and violence are used against women. Organizations such as Women Against Violence in Pornography and Media (WAVPM) have directed efforts against the pornography industry (Russell and Lederer, 1980). Robin Morgan (1980) indicated that rape and pornography are closely intertwined: "pornography is the theory, and rape the practice" (p. 139). Catherine MacKinnon (1989) stated the following:

> Pornography is a means through which sexuality is socially constructed, a site of construction, a domain of exercise. It constructs women as things for sexual use and constructs its consumers to desperately want women to desperately want possession and cruelty and dehumanization. (p. 139)

Pornography becomes sexual reality because it defines women; men are trained to have sex with an image or object, not a real woman. Through pornography, the inequality of men and women appears natural or sexy, and men become conditioned to experience sexual arousal when themes of dominance, submission, and violence are present (Kappeler, 1986; Russell and Lederer, 1980; Russo, 1987). Women's self-determination and consent are erased.

Consistent with radical feminist views that it is impossible to overcome oppression through the application of existing policies, Catherine MacKinnon (1989) believes that the legal system renders "male dominance both invisible and legitimate by adopting the male point of view" (p. 237). The state defines the social order in the interests of men by "embodying and ensuring male control over women's sexuality at every level, occasionally cushioning, qualifying, or de jure prohibiting its excesses when necessary to its normalization" (MacKinnon, 1982/1993, p. 207). According to MacKinnon, current laws define rape as violent acts perpetrated by deviant rapists and do not address the conditions that normalize male violence against women. Some radical feminists have framed pornography as civil rights violations of women and have explored ways in which women's standpoint or point of view could be used to create a feminist theory of the state that has to this point "barely been imagined" (MacKinnon, 1989, p. 249).

Some feminists believe that radical feminists have overemphasized and oversimplified women's victimization, relied on confusing and ambiguous definitions of pornography and violence, and that they inadvertently advocated sexual repression rather than sexual liberation (Berger, Searles, and Cottle, 1991; Russo, 1987; Tong, 1989). Other opponents of radical feminist antipornography efforts point to the primacy of free speech rights of individuals. However, Andrea Dworkin (1980a) stated that in the name of freedom and the "absolute integrity" (p. 154) of the First Amendment, men have created images of women who are bound, shackled, humiliated, and mutilated. Men have used pornography to rape, torture, and terrorize women into silence. Furthermore, the First Amendment protects only the rights of those in power; it allows them to extend their power over those who are disenfranchised (Dworkin, 1980b).

In addition to antiviolence political activities, radical feminists have founded rape crisis centers and education programs, battered women's projects, and women's health clinics. These projects have built programs that countered existing cultural values, provided a safe haven for women, and emphasized the importance of self-help and women's control over their own bodies (Echols, 1989; Willis, 1984). These countercultural organizations have been an important context in which feminist therapy has occurred. Their emergence and impact will be discussed further in Chapter 5 "Radical and Socialist Feminist Themes in Feminist Therapy."

Summary

Radical feminist theorists assume that gender distinctions and restrictions encompass virtually all aspects of life. They note, however, that these distinctions are rarely questioned by most individuals because they are considered to be "natural." From a radical feminist perspective, women's oppression is the most fundamental and pervasive form of oppression. It is rooted in patriarchy, which is characterized by male dominance, competition, and heterosexism. A central objective of change efforts is to illuminate how gender divisions influence basic aspects of living, such as thinking patterns, social and sexual relationships, physical appearance, dress, and work. Radical feminists view male power and male control over women's bodies as dominating every area of life, including work, love, marriage, violence against women, housework, childbearing, and child-care. According to this view, culturally defined gender roles and concepts of masculinity and femininity distort personhood and support patriarchy, and these roles should be abolished. Furthermore, institutions such as the family and the church are seen as so completely permeated by patriarchy that they must be obliterated and replaced with new structures (Donovan, 1992; Ferree and Hess, 1985; Jaggar, 1983; Tong, 1989).

Because of the pervasive nature of male domination in society, radical feminist theorists have more frequently advocated separatism as a strategy for change than have other feminists. In order to counter the "patriarchal imperative that males *must have access* to women" (Frye, 1983, p. 103), some radical women believe that by choosing to participate in alternative institutions, they are destroying patriarchal power. Thus by participating in all-female consciousness-raising groups and all-women social events and businesses, women are refusing to endorse normative cultural values and are destroying long-standing blocks of power. Women's health centers and institutions also provide ways for women to gain control over their own bodies and destiny within nonhierarchical climates (Ferree and Hess, 1985; Jaggar, 1983). However, radical feminists believe that feminists must not only participate in supportive women's communities, but must also adopt a mandate for political change. Political change efforts include taking collective actions against rape, war, and other forms of violence, as well as supporting creative art and literary contributions of radical feminists and others who challenge the status quo.

It is sometimes difficult to differentiate clearly between cultural feminism and radical feminism; the boundaries between these two strands within feminism often blur. Alice Echols (1989) and Ellen Willis (1984) contend that cultural feminists are sometimes inappropriately labeled radical feminists because some of the early radical feminists gradually changed their views and strategy about gender and adopted views that resembled cultural feminist ideals. In general, several features are useful for differentiating between radical and cultural feminism. Radical feminism resembles cultural feminism in that women are seen by both perspectives as holding special ways of understanding and conceiving the world. Despite this commonality, Ellen Willis (1984) stated that the premises of these two feminisms are antithetical. Cultural feminists are more likely to emphasize women's innate differences from men. Rather than criticizing cultural notions of femininity, cultural feminists are more likely to embrace the assumption that women are inherently more nurturing, cooperative, and peaceful and to seek support for this perspective in literature that suggests the primacy of a matriarchal past. In contrast, radical feminists have historically viewed masculinity and femininity as socially constructed characteristics, have provided a more radical critique of traditional concepts of gender, focused on eliminating a sex-class system, and viewed an ideal world as one in which gender would be irrelevant (Echols, 1989).

Ellen Willis (1984) and Alice Echols (1989) view radical feminism as inextricably connected to the eradication of male supremacy in all areas of life; they view some women's countercultures that were offshoots of radical feminism as a retreat from social change into a nurturing community built on traditional "female values." According to Alice Echols (1989), whereas radical feminists have actively *engaged* patriarchy to change the larger society, cultural feminists have often *evaded* patriarchy in search of a haven based on "superior" female values. Thus, forms of separatism and women's communities that focus primarily on nurturing women are most consistent with cultural feminism, and separatism that focuses on utilizing a community of women to organize women's efforts and actively counteract harmful political institutions are most consistent with radical feminism.

SOCIALIST FEMINISM

_____ 1. Women must gain full economic rights and independence in order to be guaranteed the freedom and civil liberties they are entitled to.

_____ 2. Women will only gain full equality with men when institutions and social relationships undergo fundamental change.

_____ 3. Financial resources should be redistributed so that adequate education, child-care, and work are available to all.

_____ 4. Education, work, parenting practices, and sexuality (reproductive freedom) must be restructured in order to eliminate male domination and other oppressions.

_____ 5. Some of the most significant issues facing women include comparable worth issues, guaranteed maternity and paternity leave, and the feminization of poverty.

_____ 6. Oppression has multiple causes based on gender, class, and race distinctions.

_____ 7. Economic institutions are the source of some of the most virulent forms of oppression.

Agreement with these items is indicative of consistency between your beliefs and the basic tenets of socialist feminism.

Early Forms of Socialist Feminism

Unlike radical feminism, socialist feminism was built on ideas that emerged in the nineteenth century. Early socialist feminists were influenced by utopian socialists such as Robert Owen and Charles Fourier, who established small experimental, cooperative communities designed to replace systems of economic competition and exploitation. Feminist socialists hoped that within utopian communities, domestic tasks, household chores, and child-care would ideally become collective tasks shared by men and women (Banks, 1981; Bartlett, 1988). Margaret Fuller suggested that community laundries and child-care were necessary services for assuring that women would have adequate time for solitude, self-discovery, and growth (Bartlett, 1988). Charlotte Perkins Gilman viewed women's economic oppression by men as central to women's subordinate role in society. In *Women and Economics* (1898) and her utopian novel *Herland* (1915/1979), Gilman recommended the establishment of communal living patterns that would be free of male violence, based on class equality and egalitarian work roles, and committed to communal childrearing. Because domestic work and childrearing would be socialized, women would be free to pursue their full potential and attain economic independence. Unlike later feminist socialist theories that used Marxist concepts about conflict and class struggle to inform their thought, the ideas of Fuller and Gilman were based on a matriarchal and cultural feminist vision, in which the peaceful, collective action of women would replace violence (Lane, 1983).

In contrast to the relatively conservative socialism proposed by Gilman, Emma Goldman's feminism of the early twentieth century was inspired by her radical anarchistic views, which included antipathy for both capitalism and traditional socialism (Solomon, 1987). She expressed themes that were later voiced by both radical and socialist feminists in the 1960s. For example, she viewed marriage as a major form of women's oppression. She stated, "Marriage and love have nothing in common; they are as far apart as the poles; are, in fact, antagonistic to each other" (Goldman, 1917/1969a, p. 227). She believed that marriage is an economic arrangement that ensures women's dependency. "It incapacitates her for life's struggle, annihilates her social consciousness, paralyzes her imagination, and then imposes its gracious protection, which is in reality a snare, a travesty on human character" (Goldman, 1917/1969a, p. 235).

Emma Goldman was opposed to traditional suffrage efforts because she believed they would do nothing to alter women's realities, society, or a rotten capitalistic system. Suffrage could not offer true emancipation. She believed that the promise of suffrage encouraged women to accept a narrow, artificial, and superficial definition of emancipation, led women to falsely presume that the state would act in women's best interests, blinded woman to "how truly enslaved she is" (Goldman, 1917/1969b, p. 208), and did nothing to alter the lives of women who did not already enjoy class privileges.

Emma Goldman contended that in order for true emancipation to occur, the connections between marriage and subordinate status would need to be eliminated, and society would need to "do away with the absurd notion of the dualism of the sexes" (Goldman, 1917/1969c, p. 225). She viewed women's control over their own bodies as especially important to their liberation and like her contemporary, Margaret Sanger, she strongly advocated birth control for women (Douglas, 1970; Solomon, 1987). True emancipation would be associated with woman's "asserting herself as a personality, and not as a sex commodity" and "refusing the right to anyone over her body" (Goldman, 1917/1969b, p. 211).

Although contemporary socialist feminism is viewed primarily as a product of the "new" feminist movement of the 1960s, the ideas of feminist pioneers reveals that socialist feminist ideas were tested throughout the nineteenth and twentieth centuries (Banks, 1981). Furthermore, a strong connection between socialist themes and suffrage issues were especially evident in Britain, where many efforts for women's suffrage were connected to labor movements (Alexander, 1990; Banks, 1981). Terry Lovell (1990) indicated that whereas radical feminism was most significantly influenced by American feminism, contemporary socialist feminism has been strongly influenced by the writings and activities of British feminists.

Contemporary Socialist Feminism

The roots of socialist feminist activism in the 1960s were similar to those of radical feminism. Like many radical feminist activists, women who chose a socialist feminist orientation felt disenfranchised by the male-dominated New Left movements and developed manifestos that articulated their demands (Sargent, 1981). Unlike radical feminist groups, many socialist feminist groups maintained some connection with New Left organizations while also forming an autonomous feminist socialist community.

Both radical and socialist feminists share the belief that patriarchy predates capitalism and are critical of the mainstream Marxist belief that capitalism and patriarchy arose in tandem (Eisenstein, 1979). However, socialist feminists have viewed radical feminists as being overly simplistic in conceptualizing oppression, for defining patriarchy as a generalized ahistorical power structure, and for describing gender oppression as similar and universal across classes and cultures (Eisenstein, 1979; Tong, 1989). Second, socialist feminists such as Zillah Eisenstein (1979) criticized radical feminists for defining sexuality as the central form of oppression and ignoring economic and other complex factors that structure power and oppress women. For example, radical feminist Shulamith Firestone (1970) viewed women's reproductive functions as the cornerstone of oppression; thus she defined woman's body as the central component of her existence. Firestone's recommendation that women could be freed from oppression through the use of reproductive technology did not consider ways in which technology is embedded within society's economic power structure and can become another form of oppression (Eisenstein, 1979). Heidi Hartmann (1981) concluded that radical feminism provides brilliant insights regarding how sexism operates in the present; however, its overly psychological analysis can blind feminists to history and the ways in which oppression is modified by era, economics, race, sexual orientation, disability, and culture.

Radical feminists have also been critical of socialist feminists. Some radical feminists view socialist feminists as focusing too extensively on how women internalize their oppression and contribute to the maintenance of their own exploitation (e.g., Mitchell, 1974). Furthermore, many radical feminists understand Marxist theory as deeply embedded in androcentric thought and believe that it cannot be adequately modified to conceptualize women's oppression or liberation (Redstockings, 1975).

The early manifestos of socialist feminist groups articulate many of the significant ideals of socialist feminism. The Students for a Democratic Society (SDS) "National Resolution on Women" (1969) resembled the declarations of radical feminist groups and stated that "[w]omen form the oldest and largest continually oppressed group in the family of human-kind" (p. 254). However, this manifesto added that the struggle for women's freedom must be accompanied with an overthrow of the capitalistic system. The resolution elaborated the following three aspects of women's oppression: (1) women serve as "a reserve army of labor" (p. 255) and are forced to work for lower wages than men; (2) women provide free housekeeping services for working men; and (3) women are exploited and oppressed by becoming the target of men's "justified frustration, anger, and shame at their inability to control their natural and social environment" (p. 256). The Women's Liberation Collective (1969) echoed these themes by stating that the dissolution of capitalism is necessary as a precondition for women's emancipation. Although noting that socialist societies have made positive gains on women's behalf, they stated that women should organize within independent groups to ensure that their demands are not subordinated to those of men. A third group, the Charlotte Perkins Gilman Chapter of the New American Movement (1984), focused on creating a synthesis of socialism and feminism. First, they noted that "sexism has a life of its own" (p. 153) which has existed under every economic system, and second, "capitalism determines the particular forms of sexism in a capitalist society" (p. 153). They declared that the goals of feminism, such as day care, reproductive rights, and the elimination of gender roles, cannot be met in a capitalist society but can only exist in a system in which no group is exploited by other groups. The Berkeley-Oakland Women's Union Statement (1973/1979) also noted that women would need to seek liberation in cooperation with others who experience oppression. The union members stated the following:

> [O]ur struggle against sexism necessarily involves us in the struggle against capitalism, racism, imperialism, and all other forms of oppression, and must be waged simultaneously with these struggles if we are to achieve our vision of socialism. (p. 357)

As suggested by the manifestos, contemporary socialist feminists believe that Marxist analyses are useful for articulating the material or economic ways in which women are oppressed under capitalism.

The role of work and economic exploitation and its relationship to alienation and estrangement is a central area of emphasis. Nancy Hartsock (1984) explained the role of work as follows: "Work in a capitalist and patriarchal society means that in our work and in our leisure we do not affirm but deny ourselves; we are not content but unhappy; we do not develop our own capacities, but destroy our bodies and ruin our minds" (p. 270). Although Marxist concepts provide useful insights about capitalism and class discrimination, a distinctive feminist analysis is necessary because some aspects of women's oppression are not adequately explained by Marxist analysis, which assumes that women's problems will naturally be eradicated by the overthrow of capitalism or that women's condition is not as important as the oppression of workers (Eisenstein, 1979; Hartmann, 1981; Lovell, 1990; Tong, 1989). Heidi Hartmann (1981) discussed the problem of effectively combining marxism and feminism: "The 'marriage' of marxism and feminism has been like the marriage of husband and wife depicted in English common law; marxism and feminism are one, and that one is marxism" (p. 2).

Early Marxists assumed that women's participation in the paid labor force would lead to emancipation, but did not consider how the inequities of private labor also entered the public labor force in the form of the "ghettoization" of women's work and lower wages. Furthermore, although Marxism explains why the domain of work and home have been artificially separated and why home activities have been devalued in capitalist societies, it provides no adequate analysis for why women rather than men were (and still are) assigned to work tasks associated with the home (Eisenstein, 1979; Hartmann, 1981; Tong, 1989). Hartmann (1981) contended that Marxist analysis provides no insight about why women have lower status than men. Ann Oakley (1990) elaborated on this problem and indicated that the role of housewife within capitalistic society is: (1) exclusively the domain of women, (2) connected to economic dependence, (3) contrasted with primary or "real" work, and (4) seen as having priority over all other roles held by women.

Dual Systems and Unified Systems Approaches

Some of the initial views of socialist feminists have been referred to as dual systems theories because they described male supremacy and capitalism as two separate systems that intersect in the exploitation of women. In contrast to dual-systems approaches, unified systems theorists argue that capitalism, patriarchy, and other forms of oppression are often impossible to separate and must be analyzed simultaneously in order to understand the various ways in which the oppression of women operates in various contexts and cultures (Tong, 1989).

Juliet Mitchell's (1969) essay titled "Women: The Longest Revolution" concluded that four separate systems must be dramatically reconstructed in order for women to achieve liberation: (1) production, work, and earnings; (2) reproduction; (3) sexuality; and (4) the responsibility for nurturing and socializing women. She stated, "The liberation of women can only be achieved if *all four* structures in which they are integrated are transformed" (p. 166). Positive changes in one area could be offset by the maintenance or reinforcement of oppression in any other area. In her later work, Mitchell developed a dual-systems approach that combined psychoanalytic and Marxist analyses: whereas Marxist methods would be necessary for overcoming capitalism, feminist applications of psychoanalysis would be crucial for overcoming patriarchy (Mitchell, 1974). Mitchell suggested that if Freud's description of psychosexual development is viewed as a social and descriptive analysis rather than as a biologically deterministic account of childhood, the castration and oedipal complexes can be used to explain how early development and oppression operate in a patriarchal society. These complexes explain how people internalize and act out oppressive ideologies. According to Mitchell, psychoanalysis provides a more complete account of socialization than other psychological models because its analysis of the unconscious reveals the invisibility, tenacity, and extent of sexism and explains why traditional ideology is so resistant to change. Because women's oppression is internalized and buried deep within the unconscious, a revolution of the human psyche is necessary for unlocking and undoing women's oppression in private, family domains.

Gayle Rubin's (1975/1984) feminist socialist account also utilizes psychoanalysis to explain women's subordinate role and stated that "psychoanalysis provides a description of the mechanisms by which the sexes are divided and deformed, of how bisexual, androgynous infants are transformed into boys and girls" (p. 166). Rubin's model relies on a combination of psychoanalytic concepts and anthropological kinship theory to describe how gender systems are organized and perpetuated. Together, "[t]hey serve as reminders of the intractability and magnitude of what we fight, and their analyses provide preliminary charts of the social machinery we must rearrange" (p. 167). Rubin stated that pursuing political avenues for change without attending to women's internalized oppression will provide an incomplete form of liberation; a central task of women is to unite to eliminate the "oedipal residue of culture" (p. 167).

Nancy Chodorow (1978) also provided an analysis of the family structure and indicated that within capitalistic societies, men are defined first as workers and women are defined first in terms of family roles. Women become the designated and almost exclusive nurturers and caregivers of children. During the pre-oedipal stage of development, girls come to view themselves as similar to their mothers and learn to define themselves in relational and connected terms; boys become aware of their differences from their mothers and learn to define themselves as separate from others. The restructuring of capitalistic society and the participation of fathers in care-giving would eliminate this pattern and allow for greater diversity of human personality. Many cultural feminists have also incorporated Chodorow's observations about relational and separate styles of women and men, but have generally ignored her views about capitalism and the need for structural changes in society. A discussion of the limitations of Chodorow's theory from a multicultural perspective appears in Chapter 1 "Women of Color and Feminist Therapy."

The use of psychoanalytic concepts by some socialist feminists has not been received without criticism by those who believe that elaborate psychoanalytic explanations provide intricate theoretical explanations with no corresponding ideas about how to enact significant change. Ann Foreman (1977) indicated that a synthesis of Marxism and psychoanalysis is an "impossible task." Elizabeth Wilson (1990) elaborated this concept: "The last thing feminists need is a theory that teaches them only to marvel anew at the constant recreation of the subjective reality of subordination and which reasserts male domination more securely than ever within theoretical discourse" (p. 224). Wilson suggested that bringing about external and visible change in family and work structures "might do more for our psyches as well as for our pockets than an endless contemplation of how we came to be chained" (p. 224).

Although Chodorow, Mitchell, and Rubin have devised dual-systems theories that utilize psychoanalysis to understand patriarchy, other socialist feminist theorists utilize nonpsychological dual models to explain male dominance. For example, Heidi Hartmann (1981) described patriarchy as having a material or economic base that allows men to exert control over women's labor power, economic resources, sexuality, and reproduction. Through capitalism, workers are controlled and oppressed, and through patriarchy, the exploitation, underpayment, and overwork of women is established through the sexual division of labor. Like other dual-systems theorists, Hartmann believed that patriarchy and capitalism would need to be fought in different ways.

In contrast to the dual-systems approach, Iris Young argued that it is impossible to separate capitalism and patriarchy and that the marginalization of women is an *"essential and fundamental characteristic of capitalism"* (1981, p. 58). Cynthia Cockburn (1990) was also critical of traditional dual-systems approaches for trying to "mesh together two static structures, two hierarchical systems" (p. 85). According to Cockburn, the arenas of public production and family patterns have been analyzed as separate spheres, with capitalism influencing the former and patriarchy the latter. This analysis does not reveal the ways in which the patterns evident in the public work world are also present in the private work world. Analyses of how power systems of gender and class contribute simultaneously to patterns of domination and subordination are needed. Such unified theories would attend to the complex ways in which economic, physical, and social factors contribute to the perception that men's work is more valuable than women's work (Cockburn, 1990).

Toward an Integrative, Pluralistic Theory

As socialist feminist thinking has matured, authors have noted that a comprehensive analysis must move beyond traditional considerations of class and gender systems and must also focus on oppressions that are associated with racism and heterosexism (e.g.,

Joseph, 1981; Riddiough, 1981). Given its recent attention on the intersection and interaction of these multiple and complex factors, some authors view socialist feminism as a potentially unifying force for feminism. Floya Anthias and Nira Yuval-Davis (1990) stated that gender, class, and ethnicity "are intermeshed in such a way that we cannot see them as additive or prioritize abstractly any one of them" (p. 110). They added that there is no unitary category of women; each category modifies the other and may be experienced differently based on the contexts in which they come together. Theorists, researchers, and activists must be aware of the multiple ways in which gender influences women's lives and must consistently recognize the plurality of experience. Gender is experienced differently by various groups of women; furthermore, some women view gender oppression as less salient than issues such as racism and classism. Nellie Wong (1991) indicated that no woman is left out of socialist feminist analysis due to its simultaneous attention to multiple factors. She stated the following:

> Socialist feminism is a radical, disciplined, and all-encompassing solution to the problems of race, sex, sexuality, and class struggle. Socialist feminism lives in the battles of all people of color, in the lesbian and gay movement, and in the class struggle. (p. 290)

Recent socialist feminists have pointed to the importance of developing a more complex and pluralistic feminism but have yet to make significant progress responding effectively to the needs they have identified (Jaggar, 1983; Tong, 1989). If socialist feminism is to play a future unifying role with women of diversity, it will need to rethink or replace its use of models such as psychoanalysis, which propose universal truths that are based on traditional middle-class family structures, and utilize theories that are more attentive to the ways in which culture shapes both gender and class issues.

Summary

Whereas radical feminism identifies gender oppression as the fundamental source of women's oppression, socialist feminism is linked to the belief that oppression is influenced by gender but is also shaped by race, nationality, and class. Socialist feminism is based on the assumption that gender status is imposed and defined by social relationships, embedded in historical factors, and situated in systems that organize social production. Early gender learning is reinforced through a variety of social mechanisms, such as work and childrearing practices, modified by class and race (Jaggar, 1983; Tong, 1989).

Contemporary socialist feminist thought attempts to respond to the intersections of oppressions that are discussed by other feminist philosophies: (1) the structures of production, class, and capitalism stressed by strict Marxist feminists; (2) the control of reproduction and sexuality emphasized by radical feminists; and (3) the impact of socialization discussed by liberal feminists (Tong, 1989). In general, socialist feminists believe that the realization of human potential is not made possible through the legislation of individual rights alone, but must involve the restructuring of life in both personal and public spheres. The restructuring of family life and decrease in alienation and oppression will be made possible in part through universal access to adequate child-care, education, housing, birth control, and maternity/paternity leave. The gendered structure of paid and unpaid labor forces is a key issue, and socialist feminists emphasize the importance of enlarging women's options, modeling new social relationships, and valuing all forms of work, both public and private. The development of women's alternative work and social organizations is also important because both allow women to model new social relationships, overcome a sense of alienation from creative work and activity, and realize their goals in a supportive atmosphere (Hartsock, 1984). In summary, socialist feminists attempt to remove structural and psychological barriers to equality, and respond to the intersections of oppression (Ferree and Hess, 1985; Jaggar, 1983; Tong, 1989).

Chapter 3

Cultural Feminism, Feminisms of Women of Color, and Feminist Epistemologies

I have grouped the topics of cultural feminism, the feminisms of women of color, and feminist epistemologies in this chapter because they emerged as important developments within feminist theory and practice during the later 1970s and 1980s. Cultural feminism emerged as a contemporary force during the mid-1970s, gained strength during the more conservative 1980s, and spawned new varieties of feminism such as ecofeminism and feminist spirituality. The feminisms of women of color arose out of criticisms of the narrowness and ethnocentrism of feminist thought and represents an important meta-perspectives for evaluating other feminisms. I use the phrase "feminisms of color" to recognize the diversity of women of color and the multiple theoretical perspectives that they offer. Finally, the feminist epistemologies of feminist empiricism, feminist standpoint perspectives, and feminist postmodernism emerged out of the need to define strategies to support knowledge claims made by feminists. Each of these three themes within feminism has raised important questions regarding the future direction of feminist theory.

CULTURAL FEMINISM

In order to use the self-assessment tools in this chapter, respond to each statement with a "yes" or "no."

_____ 1. A major cause of sexism and oppression is the devaluation of traditional feminine qualities and the overvaluation of masculine values and patriarchy.

_____ 2. The goal of feminism should be to revalue women's traditional strengths so that women can infuse the society with values based on cooperation.

_____ 3. Solutions to sexism will come through women's discovery of internal truths, relationships with other women, and the "feminization" of the culture.

_____ 4. Key issues for women involve developing a sense of ethics based on caring and relationship values as well as organizing around issues of nonviolence.

_____ 5. Women's cooperation with other women and involvement in organized peace efforts of all kinds will give them the necessary power to influence and change society.

Agreement with these statements suggests that your views are consistent with the basic beliefs and assumptions of many cultural feminists.

Early Cultural Feminists

Although the resurgence of liberal feminism predated contemporary cultural feminism, liberal and cultural feminism share a rich nineteenth-century heritage. In the nineteenth century, cultural and liberal feminists often proposed conflicting beliefs about women's liberation: liberal enlightenment feminists tended to emphasize the importance of rationality and the similarity between men and women, and cultural feminists focused on nonrational, intuitive aspects of life and the special qualities of women that were presumed to make them different from or superior to men.

Early feminists such as Margaret Fuller (1845/1976), Jane Addams (1913/1960), and Charlotte Perkins Gilman (1915/1979, 1923) envisioned cultural transformations based on unique matriarchal visions that would act as transformative forces within society. They typically defined women's experiences as distinctly different from men's experiences and sought to revere and valorize traditional "feminine" strengths.

Margaret Fuller's (1845/1976) early cultural feminist perspective was inspired by European romantic and American transcendentalist themes, which emphasized the importance of: (1) emotional, intuitive aspects of knowledge; (2) poetic imagination and spirituality;

and (3) a holistic, organic worldview embedded in "reverence for the earth and its wisdom, beauty, and creativity" (Bartlett, 1988, p. 8). Although these values based on nonrational experiences conflicted with those of enlightenment liberalism, the traditions of transcendentalism/romanticism and liberalism shared a belief in individualism and self-responsibility (Donovan, 1992).

Margaret Fuller emphasized the special strengths of women, the way in which culture had impeded their development, and women's differences from men. She stated, "The especial genius of Woman I believe to be electrical in movement, intuitive in function, spiritual in tendency" (1845/1976, p. 263). Margaret Fuller associated female strengths with harmony, beauty, and love and male attributes with energy, power, and intellect. She noted that although "there is no wholly masculine man, no purely feminine woman . . . male and female represent the two sides of the great radical dualism" (p. 263). In an analysis that resembles contemporary feminist Jungian archetypal thought, she also noted that both men and women contain an inner potential to tap masculine and feminine strengths and suggested that "[m]an partakes of the feminine in the Apollo, Woman of the masculine as Minerva" (p. 264).

Despite the existence of women's superior intuitive powers, "the electrical, magnetic element in Woman has not been fairly brought out at any period. Everything might be expected from it; she has far more of it than Man" (p. 260). Instead, men have abused their position, trained women for servanthood, and emphasized power over values such as beauty and harmony. Margaret Fuller (1845/1976) believed that women would transform culture by exhibiting a gentle, earnest heroism and focusing on "measures which promise to bring the world more thoroughly and deeply into harmony with her nature" (p. 262). She asserted the following: "Should these faculties have free play, I believe they will open new, deeper and purer sources of joyous inspiration than have as yet refreshed the earth" (p. 264).

Fuller (1845/1976) recommended that "Woman lay aside all thought, such as she habitually cherishes, of being taught and led by men" (p. 265). Consistent with the romantic theme of individualism, she encouraged women to dedicate themselves to "the Sun of Truth" (p. 265) and "meditate in virgin loneliness" (p. 266). She also suggested that women should support each other, stating that women can be the most effective helpers of each other in their efforts to tap their "native dignity" (p. 276) and "latent powers" (p. 276).

Although Elizabeth Cady Stanton and Sarah Grimké contributed to a liberal feminist tradition by emphasizing the similarity of men's and women natures, their later writings argued that women exhibited moral superiority and power that represented the keys to enlightened motherhood and society's future progress (Banner, 1980; Bartlett, 1988). Elizabeth Cady Stanton (1891/1968) stated that the first civilizations were maternal: "The period of woman's supremacy lasted through many centuries, undisputed, accepted as natural and proper wherever it existed, and was called the matriarchate, or mother-age" (p. 143). She added that although men's early contributions were limited to inventing tools of warfare, women's roles were varied and ranged from mothering roles to the activities of protector, inventor, and breadwinner. She encouraged contemporary women to adopt a new sense of dignity and self-respect and noted that "we have every reason to believe that our turn will come again" (p. 147). Matilda Gage (1884/1968) expressed similar sentiments by indicating that in contrast to the belief that the physical world was created for man, the "feminine" principle appeared first and everywhere in science, in chemistry, geology, botany, philology, and biology. She concluded, "When biology becomes more fully understood it will also be universally acknowledged that the primal creative power, like the first manifestation of life, is feminine" (p. 140).

Jane Addams is known for her efforts in the field of social work, the founding of the settlement house named Hull House, and her involvement in international peace efforts. Like other early cultural feminists, she suggested that during earlier centuries, women demonstrated a much wider and significant role in society as they "dragged home the game and transformed the pelts into shelter and clothing" (Addams, 1913/1960, p. 109). She contended that functions which were traditionally viewed as the domain of women, such as health and education, had been wrested from women and incorporated into institutional departments that were no longer under women's control. As a part of her discussion of men's and women's differences, she noted that if the tables were turned and women held the more powerful roles granted to men, women would oppose men's suffrage and greater involvement in society for the following reasons: (1) men's fondness of fighting; (2) their carelessness about health, cleanliness, work conditions, and the well-being of both children and workers; (3) men's emphasis on profit and indifference to human life; (4) their reliance on "savage instincts of punishment and revenge" (p. 111) in their administration of the criminal justice system; and (5) and men's lack of concern for victims, such as homeless girls forced into prostitution (Addams, 1913/1960). She did not believe that women's suffrage was primarily a guarantee of individual rights or an end in and of itself, but a means to allow women to actively enter the social/public sphere and influence the society with new values. Jane Addams's commitment to social reform and pacifism emerged from her belief that women's distinctive values should permeate the family but should also humanize the world and change society. She called for "women to defend those at the bottom of society who, irrespective of the victory or defeat of any army, are ever oppressed and overburdened" and to "instinctively challenge war as the implacable enemy of the age-long undertaking" (Addams, 1916/1960, p. 257).

Although Charlotte Perkins Gilman identified herself primarily as a humanist and a socialist (Hill, 1980), many aspects of her thinking are consistent with the cultural feminist ideas of her contemporaries such as Jane Addams. Gilman was influenced by Social Darwinism and believed that although male traits, such as combat and assertion, had been necessary for the growth and evolution of some aspects of society, the original balance of society needed to be restored through the infusion of values embedded in nurturance and cooperation (Donovan, 1992; Hill, 1980). She communicated her social vision through fiction that allowed her to explore "what if" scenarios in which women held positions of power in a matriarchal, utopian society (Lane, 1980). She stated that "[t]he whole feminine attitude toward life differs essentially from the masculine, because of [woman's] superior adaptation to the service of others, her rich fund of surplus energy for such service" (Gilman, 1923, p. 270). Gilman (1923) viewed feminine traits as superior to masculine traits and noted:

The innate, underlying difference [between the sexes] is one of principle. On the one hand, the principle of struggle, conflict and competition, the results of which make our "economic problems." On the other, the principle of growth, of culture, of applying services and nourishment in order to produce improvement. (p. 271)

In 1923, women earned the right to vote and the attention of feminist activists was redirected from suffrage to social reform. The cultural feminists of the 1920s to the 1940s were often referred to as "social feminists" because they believed the maternal virtues that were typically enacted in the home could provide necessary correctives for social life in general (Black, 1989). Jane Addams's views were consistent with the views of many social feminists who became involved in the League of Women Voters, peace movements, and a variety of social reform efforts. These reformers proposed that women could help reconstruct society by using skills that men had not traditionally demonstrated in public arenas: cooperation, nurturing, and virtue. Maternal and reproductive roles had taught women how to show unselfish commitment to their own children; this unselfish commitment should also be used to benefit disenfranchised children and future children. Social feminists often assumed that because of their connection to children, they could more fully comprehend the necessity for peace than men; women who give birth and nurture life were viewed as less likely to waste time destroying life through war (Black, 1989).

Although some authors have suggested feminism virtually disappeared as a social force following the suffrage vote of 1923 (e.g., Deckard, 1979), the energies of feminists were merely redirected into social reform efforts. Legal and economic equality for women was deemed less important than the protection of women and children in a variety of vulnerable roles. Proposed equal rights legislation was often viewed with suspicion by social feminists; as feminists who viewed women and men as having different needs and strengths, they were concerned that equal rights legislation could result in the loss of protective measures that were accorded to women and children with special needs (Banks, 1981). The social/cultural feminists' emphasis on the special needs of women may have been responsible, at least in part, for the limited gains in women's rights between the mid-1920s and the 1950s and retraditionalization of women's roles (O'Neill, 1971). However, the efforts of social feminists also underline the continuity of feminist activity during the twentieth century and point out how feminist efforts are shaped by the spirit of the times.

Reemergence of Cultural Feminism

Liberal, radical, and socialist feminisms dominated the landscape during the early years of the "new" feminist movement. However, cultural feminism began to reemerge in the mid-1970s as radical feminists focused less on eradicating sex roles and more on identifying the strengths associated with traditional women's roles. The Fourth World Manifesto (Burris, 1973) reiterated the radical feminist principle that female and male cultures are artificial categories defined by male-dominated society and thus, represent caricatures of humanity. However, it also suggested that devalued female traits should not be repudiated but embraced by women. Barbara Burris (1973) stated the following:

> We are proud of the female culture of emotion, intuition, love personal relationships, etc., as the most essential human characteristics. It is our male colonizers—it is the male culture—who have defined essential humanity out of their identity and who are "culturally deprived." (p. 355)

Shortly thereafter, several authors critiqued Shulamith Firestone's (1970) position that women should be freed from reproductive roles and suggested an alternative: motherhood should be redefined in positive terms. Former "politico" feminist Jane Alpert (1973) asserted that women's biology and capacity to bear and nurture children is the basis for women's power. Her analysis relied on the premises of the book *The First Sex* (Davis, 1973), which proposed that peaceful matriarchal gynocracies had preceded patriarchal society but were crushed by barbarian male tribes, thus allowing patriarchal values to gain ascendancy. According to this perspective, motherhood was highly valued in early matriarchal societies, no sharp divisions between public and family existed, and the life of the society and industry was centered around the home. Alpert (1973) argued that women should claim the "mother right" principle, which would entail restructuring the family and society according to the characteristics of an ideal nurturing relationship between a mother and child. These qualities include the following: "empathy, intuitiveness, adaptability, awareness of growth as a process rather than as goal-ended, inventiveness, protective feelings toward others, and a capacity to respond emotionally as well as rationally" (p. 92). When a society embodies these qualities, "[m]atriarchy means nothing less than the end of oppression" (p. 92). In an elaboration of this theme, Adrienne Rich (1976) stated that women have the unique power to create life, a power of which men are both fearful and jealous. In their attempt to restrict the power of mothers, men have created rules, procedures, and medical practices that control women and alienate women from their own bodies and experiences. Women regain power by reclaiming the circumstances of childbirth and mothering on their own terms.

Some radical feminists were highly critical of efforts to revalue mothering, stating that although matriarchy provides a vision of women in power, it "mythologizes" power and bases it on some "unknown past instead of defining a real future" (p. 81). According to Brooke (1975), it promises women a nonexistent utopia and encourages women to avoid fighting patriarchy in order to establish separate women's communities that are designed to "prove to men the error of their ways by shaming them with women's superior morality" (p. 81). Visions of a matriarchal fantasy can offer a retreat from activism; "cultural feminism, then, is an attempt to transform feminism from a political movement to a lifestyle movement" (Brooke, 1975, p. 83).

In addition to receiving its initial impetus from radical and socialist feminisms, cultural feminism was also influenced by those who became disappointed with the limited gains achieved by liberal feminism. Sylvia Hewlett (1986) argued that women had traded their previous protections of traditional marriage for a "lesser life," which included limited financial gain, lower well-being, and pressures to live a superwoman existence. She noted that liberation has meant little because it has been defined under men's terms and that women remain "conditioned by and constrained by child-related responsibilities" (p. 401). In similar fashion, Suzanne Gordon (1991) stated that women had been pressured to replace the "feminine mystique" with the "masculine mystique," which was "founded on the assumption that women can find happiness, self-esteem, and self-fulfillment by emulating and ultimately internalizing the ideology of market place society; in other words, by becoming the female equivalent of economic, acquisitive man" (p. 27). In order to help women and society resolve the "crisis of caring" (p. 13), networks of collaboration and community should be integrated within the workplace. These corrective measures would allow women to revalue and balance care in both work and home settings (Gordon, 1991).

Cultural feminism owes its existence in large part to the dissatisfactions and disappointments associated with the prominent feminisms of the 1960s and 1970s. The following sections will identify some of the primary areas of study in which cultural feminist theory has become particularly influential.

Feminist Ethics

Cultural feminism has had a significant impact on feminist ethics, a field of study that emerged from the recognition that women's values and perspectives have been suppressed within traditional explorations of ethics. Contributors to feminist ethics have proposed alternative models of morality and ethics in order to correct past biases and create models that are consistent with women's experience. Winnie Tomm (1992) stated that "principles of so-called fairness have entailed discrimination against women and have tyrannized women in the name of justice" (p. 104). This reality is particularly evident in the legal treatment of rape and violence against women; skewed beliefs about morality often lead to victim blaming and decrease women's control over their own lives (Tomm, 1992).

The field of feminist ethics emphasizes the centrality of interdependence over individualism; it generally defines morality as a balance of giving and receiving rather than the enactment of specific rights. Relationships rather than the exercise of individual rights are the central priority of moral behavior. Feminist morality is connected to practical, everyday realities rather than to abstract or hypothetical values (Cole and Coultrap-McQuin, 1992).

Two theorists have significantly shaped the focus of this developing field: psychologist Carol Gilligan (1982) and educational philosopher Nel Noddings (1984). Both theorists have critiqued traditional models that equate morality with justice and rights, an approach that emphasizes the centrality of the individual in moral decision making, and stresses the importance of fairness in the application of so-called universal principles of justice (Bartlett, 1992). Carol Gilligan (1982) challenged Lawrence Kohlberg's (1981) justice model of moral development and proposed that many women resolve moral issues through an ethic of care and interdependence. She wrote the following:

> The moral imperative that emerges repeatedly in interviews with women is an injunction to care, a responsibility to discern and alleviate the "real and recognizable trouble" of this world. For men the moral imperative appears rather as an injunction to respect the rights of others and thus to protect from interference the rights to life and self-fulfillment. (p. 19)

Likewise, Nel Noddings (1984) indicated that caring, responsibility, and relationships are cornerstones of an ethic of care. Noddings declared that caring is "feminine in the deep classical sense—rooted in receptivity, relatedness, and responsiveness" (p. 2). Neither Gilligan nor Noddings described ethical decision making as a system of specific principles but as a process in which human interdependence and responsiveness are crucial to resolving concrete human dilemmas.

Closely related to feminist ethics are influential writings that have focused on women's modes of knowing and experiencing the world. Psychologists Mary Belenky, Blythe Clinchy, Nancy Goldberger, and Jill Tarule (1986) proposed that historical models of cognitive development are based on a masculine worldview in which knowledge is displayed through argument and debate that sets the knower apart from others. They noted that many women are silenced by this concept of cognition and described the development of connected knowing that values empathy with ideas, appreciation of diverse perspectives, and learning within a community of thinkers.

In *Maternal Thinking*, Sarah Ruddick (1989) outlined three "demands" of maternal thinking that contribute positively to women's ethics, activism, and a politics of peace. The activities of mothering include awareness of: (1) the need to preserve life, to enhance children's possibility of survival by minimizing their exposure to risks; (2) the complexity of fostering childrens' intellectual, emotional, and physical growth; and (3) the importance of raising children to behave in socially acceptable ways and in accordance with the values of a reference group. These demands call on women to engage in continuous "disciplined reflection" (p. 24) about their complex roles, and these practices form a foundation for thinking about and creating peace. Although Ruddick's (1989) ideas resemble nineteenth century feminists' thoughts about women's maternal roles and peace making, her assumptions diverge from those of early feminists in that she does not believe that women will automatically purify society because of their inherent peaceful qualities. She notes that both women and men can behave destructively, but that the central demands of mothering teach women to value activities that enhance the preservation of relationship and life.

Ecofeminism

Mary Daly's (1978) book titled *Gyn/Ecology* defined ecology as "the complex web of interrelationships between organisms and their environment" (p. 9), and asserted that no male efforts will be successful in counteracting the horrors committed against the earth. This concern with the interconnectedness of all things anticipated the emergence of ecofeminism, which shares with radical feminism the belief that patriarchy is the primary source of women's oppression. The patriarchal oppression of women is seen as closely connected to the domination and destruction of the earth through various forms of technology and science. "Men identify women with nature and seek to enlist both in the service of male 'projects' designed to make men safe from feared nature and mortality" (King, 1990, p. 109-110). In addition to identifying the negative connection between men and nature, ecofeminists have paid special attention to the potential for a positive connection between nature and women. Andree Collard (1989) stated that: "[n]othing links the human animal and nature so profoundly as woman's reproductive system, which enables her to share the experience of bringing forth and nourishing life with the rest of the living world" (p. 106). By virtue of their involvement in mothering, caring, and nurturing roles, women may be especially equipped to understand the interconnectedness of people and the natural world.

Three primary principles are central to ecofeminism. First, Western civilization was built in opposition to nature, which interacts with the domination of women. Because of this connection, feminists should be concerned with the struggle of all nature. The fate of human and nonhuman life is inextricably intertwined, and the struggle for social justice for women and other people cannot be achieved apart from care for the earth's resources. A second principle of ecofeminism is that all life must be considered part of an interconnected web; hierarchies associated with patriarchy must be rejected. The earth must be seen as having intrinsic value; no being is more valuable or superior to other beings. Third, a healthy and balanced ecosystem is based on diversity of human and nonhuman experience. The perspectives of non-Western and indigenous peoples, who have maintained a close connection with the earth, are especially important for showing society how to develop a new relationship to nature (Diamond and Orenstein, 1990; King, 1989, 1990).

One strand of ecofeminism has explored prepatriarchal nature-based feminist spiritualities and promoted the revival of rituals centered on goddess images of deity. Many ecofeminists believe that prior to the emergence of patriarchy and industrialization, people felt connected to the earth as a living being and believed that doing violence to her was unacceptable (Plant, 1989). Within early matriarchal societies, the earth was held in reverence, and the reproductive and life-giving powers associated with women's bodies were highly valued. According to Riane Eisler (1990),

> [i]n this highly creative and peaceful society, masculinity was *not* equated with domination and conquest. Accordingly, women and the "soft" or "feminine" values of caring, compassion, and nonviolence did not have to be devalued. (p. 30)

In addition to revaluing traditional feminine strengths, earth-based spirituality offers women the opportunity to celebrate the cycle of life, the experiences of birth, growth, decay, death, and regeneration as they appear with the seasons of the year. These rhythms appear in the moon's phases as well as in human, plant, and animal life, always with the goal of establishing balance among all the different communities that comprise the living body of earth (Starhawk, 1989). Consistent with this view, Riane Eisler stated the following in her ecofeminist manifesto:

> Let us reaffirm our ancient covenant, our sacred bond with our Mother, the Goddess of nature and spirituality. . . . Let us use our human thrust for creation rather than destruction. Let us teach our sons and daughters that men's conquest of nature, of women, and of other men is not a heroic virtue. . . . Let us learn again to live in partnership so we may fulfill our responsibility to ourselves and to our Great Mother, this wondrous planet Earth. . . . (p. 34)

Ynestra King (1990) noted that ecofeminism is closely related to cultural feminism, but suggests that it offers a more complete analysis than most forms of cultural feminism. First, ecofeminism moves beyond cultural feminism's emphasis on personal transformation and provides an important focus for activism. Second, it suggests a new basis for ethics and promotes a hopeful direction for the reconciliation of people and the earth. Third, it acknowledges the interconnectedness of all women while also recognizing diversity between women. It encourages women of all backgrounds to draw upon the earth-related imagery of their own traditions and to actively contribute to feminist theory.

Despite these strengths, Janet Biehl (1991) noted that the association of women with nature and caring/nurturing strengths can be limiting and perpetuate patriarchal stereotypes. The goddess worship of early matriarchal societies has been romanticized and idealized by ecofeminists. However, goddess worship also played a central role in patriarchal cultures and was not associated with the increased status of women. The ideal prepatriarchal world that has inspired ecofeminists and cultural feminists may be based primarily on mythology rather than historical fact.

Summary

Cultural feminists during the nineteenth and twentieth centuries have attempted to achieve broad cultural change by infusing the larger society with "female" values. They have described women's unique cultural and ethical heritage as based on altruistic, cooperative, pacifistic, life-affirming values, and they have promoted the notion that women have an obligation to better the world through social reform. Through the "feminization" of culture, violence and aggression can be overcome, and the strengths of gentleness, harmony, and peace can be realized (Donovan, 1992).

Emotional, nonrational, intuitive, and holistic elements of women's experience are considered especially important to the cultural feminist vision. Because these experiences are so rarely valued in the larger culture, women must learn to listen to themselves in new ways and affirm their inner strengths. Through identification with other women, new freedoms and visions can be fully developed. Contemporary cultural feminists have less frequently assumed that women's strengths are innate than the first cultural feminists, and they are less likely to emphasize a utopian, romantic vision of the world than were their predecessors. However, they continue to focus efforts on revaluing "female" strengths and defining a unique moral and ethical vision of women (Donovan, 1992).

THE FEMINISMS OF WOMEN OF COLOR

_____ 1. Traditional feminism has often been guilty of promoting simplistic views of feminism that overemphasize the importance of gender while ignoring significant status variables such as race, ethnicity, class, and sexual orientation.

_____ 2. Feminists have often reinforced inequality between women by defining issues according to the views of middle-class white women and assuming that these perspectives can be applied to the lives of women of color with only minor adjustments.

_____ 3. In order for a theory of feminism to be complete, it must be pluralistic and recognize the vast differences between women.

_____ 4. The lives of diverse groups of women must be understood from their own standpoints; women of color must be involved in theory development at all levels.

_____ 5. As individuals with "outsider" status, women of color often have greater awareness of the complex manifestations of oppression than middle-class white women.

Agreement with the above statements suggests that your views are consistent with the major theoretical contributions of many feminists of color. Some of the most important changes during the past decade emerged from critiques of the mainstream feminisms of the "new" feminist movement. The limitations of traditional renditions of feminism are exemplified by the critiques and proposals of women of color. This discussion will identify forms of racism and ethnocentrism that have been present within feminism and will also discuss some of the unique contributions of feminists of color. In order to provide some depth of analysis, I will pay special attention to the experience of black women and feminism.

Racism, Black Women, and Feminism

Early feminist efforts by white women in the United States were associated with the rise of the industrial era, the loss of middle-class women's central economic roles within the home, and increased leisure time for middle-class women. With increased time and leisure, white women invested time in social reform and began to reflect on their own condition (Davis, 1981). It was through involvement in antislavery efforts that many early feminists became acquainted with the nature of oppression and the ways in which it resembled their own experiences. During these early years, feminists such as Angelina and Sarah Grimké believed that women would not achieve freedom apart from black people and worked toward achieving a "common dream of liberation" (Davis, 1981, p. 45).

When placed against these hopeful beginnings, the racism and ethnocentrism of American nineteenth-century feminism is particularly disappointing. Contemporary feminists often suggest that early statements made by nineteenth-century white feminists about the solidarity between black and white women represent evidence of the antiracist views of early feminists. However, this romanticized view overlooks the reality that many antislavery activists were motivated primarily by religious sentiment. Some activists were opposed to slavery but did not recommend any alteration of the racial hierarchy evident in American life (hooks, 1981). Furthermore, as bell hooks noted, there was very little similarity between the life experiences of middle-class white women and slaves; white women were "simply appropriating the horror of the slave experience to enhance their own cause" (hooks, 1981, p. 126).

The ethnocentrism of U.S. feminism was revealed as early as the 1848 Seneca Falls convention, when delegates articulated the frustrations of middle-class women and ignored both the condition of black women in slavery and the oppression of white working-class women who were contending with long hours and inhumane working conditions. Sojourner Truth played a significant role in exposing the classism and racism present within feminism during these early years, and along with many other black women, she invested energy in feminist and antislavery efforts on behalf of both men and women (hooks, 1981). However, these efforts did not eradicate the white supremacist ideals underlying the feminist movement.

With the outbreak of the Civil War in the United States, many women's rights leaders directed their energies in support of the Union cause, and Elizabeth Cady Stanton and Susan B. Anthony were instrumental in organizing the Women's Loyal League, which called for the "civil and political rights of all citizens of African descent and all women" (Gurko, 1976, p. 211). Angelica Grimké was especially vocal about the importance of connecting the struggle for women's equality with black liberation and stated: "I want to be identified with the Negro. Until he gets his rights, we shall never have ours" (Lerner, 1971, p. 354). During postwar years, however, it became apparent that legislators in Washington were not inclined to grant suffrage to both black men and women. Notable feminists, including Susan B. Anthony and Elizabeth Cady Stanton, backed away from their earlier commitments, and revealed their unwillingness to promote black liberation if white women would not also gain immediate benefits. They argued that it was more important for white women to earn the vote than for black men to earn the vote. In a letter to the editor of *The New York Standard*, Elizabeth Cady Stanton (1865/1881) stated:

The representative women of the nation have done their uttermost for the last thirty years to secure freedom for the negro;

and as long as he was lowest in the scale of being, we were willing to press his claims; but now, as the celestial gate to civil rights is slowly moving on its hinges, it becomes a serious question whether we had better stand aside and see "Sambo" walk into the Kingdom first. (pp. 94-95)

She later added the following: "I would not trust him with my rights; degraded, oppressed, himself, he would be more despotic . . . than ever our Saxon rulers are . . ." (Stanton, Anthony, and Gage, 1881, p. 214). In spite of these racist statements, The Equal Rights Convention of 1867 declared its intent to work simultaneously for black people's and women's suffrage. However, conflict quickly emerged within the Equal Rights Association, and racist rhetoric persisted. The Fourteenth and Fifteenth Amendments, which entitled all male citizens to the ballot and prohibited disfranchisement on the grounds of race, color, or other forms of servitude, were passed without the inclusion of women's rights (Davis, 1981).

As the struggle for women's rights continued at the turn of the century, suffrage organizations adopted white supremacist and racist arguments that were fueled by the eugenics movement. Women's suffrage was viewed by white organizations as central to purifying and redeeming "the Race" (hooks, 1981, p. 127). When called upon to lend their support to fight against segregation and racism, members of the National American Woman Suffrage Association showed indifference. Many white suffragists supported racial segregation, harbored racist stereotypes of black women as morally impure, and rejected efforts of black women activists to build bridges and foster cooperation (hooks, 1981). Despite their efforts to create a multiracial movement for women's rights, women of color "were betrayed, spurned and rejected by the leaders of the lily-white suffrage movement" (Davis, 1981, p. 148).

Although they were excluded from white suffrage organizations and subjected to racist ideology, black women remained actively involved in the fight for women's rights. Women such as Mary Church Terrell, Josephine St. Pierre Ruffin, Fannie Barrier Williams, Anna Julia Cooper, Ida B. Wells, and Frances Ellen Watkins Harper worked tirelessly for women's suffrage and defined and addressed issues on black women's terms. They organized to counter stereotypes of black women and to focus on many immediate issues such as poverty, care of the elderly, prostitution, and suffrage. In her call to address the needs of all women, Josephine St. Pierre Ruffin stated:

> Our woman's movement is a woman's movement that is led and directed by women for the good of women and men, for the benefit of all humanity, which is more than any one branch or section of it. . . . [W]e are not alienating or withdrawing, we are only coming to the front, willing to join any others in the same work and cordially inviting and welcoming any others to join us. (1895, cited in hooks, 1981, p. 164)

The words of Anna Cooper also demonstrated black women's commitment:

> Not till the universal title of humanity of life, liberty and the pursuit of happiness is conceded to be inalienable to all; not till then is woman's lesson taught and women's cause won—not the white woman's not the black woman's, not the red woman's, but the cause of every man and of every woman who has writhes silently under a mighty wrong. (Hutchinson, 1982, pp. 87-88)

The 1923 passage of the nineteenth amendment, which granted women the vote, resulted in little or no change for black women. In the South, election managers and the Ku Klux Klan worked actively to prevent black people from voting. Segregation and oppression deepened as white supremacy denied black people full citizenship. Many black activist women became disillusioned with the promise of women's rights per se and shifted their attention to other important issues such as campaigns to eradicate lynching (hooks, 1981).

Racism and Ethnocentrism
Within the "New" Feminist Movement

Given the racism associated with feminism throughout its early history, it is not surprising that women of color were skeptical when white women activists during the 1970s repeated a claim that had been made over a century before: that the oppression of women resembled the oppression of minority groups in the United States (hooks, 1981). According to bell hooks, this comparison represented a form of racism based in narcissism and egocentrism. Toni Morrison (1971) indicated that white women's description of "woman as nigger" was "an effort to become Black without the responsibilities of being Black" (1971, p. 64). Linda LaRue (1970) added that although white women are "suppressed, Blacks are oppressed . . . and there is a difference" (p. 61). The assumption that white women and black women experience a similar oppression did not acknowledge the basic reality that the social experiences and status of white women and black women have been vastly different. When comparisons between women and minority groups are drawn for the sake of expediency, attention is deflected away from the ways in which women of color are simultaneously exposed to racism, classism, and sexism.

In addition to resenting comparisons to women of color, some black women expressed frustration and anger that the primarily white women's movement would "reap the benefits that the Black movement had sown" (Giddings, 1984, p. 308). As a result, some black activist women believed that white women would use the climate provided by the civil rights movement to gain prominence and power that they would reserve for white women. This possibility was especially painful in light of the fact that black women harbored a great deal of anger against white women, "a rage rooted in the historical servant-served relationships where white women have used power to dominate, exploit, and oppress" (hooks, 1989, p. 179). Linda La Rue (1970) stated: "One can argue that Women's liberation has not only attached itself to the Black movement but has done so with only marginal concern for Black women and Black liberation and functional concern for the rights of White women" (p. 60).

The writings of the "new" feminist movement did not include statements of hatred or overt racism against specific individuals or a group, but often ignored the presence of women of color by presuming that the experiences and interests of women of color and poor women were highly similar to those of white women. Early writings often assumed that "the word woman is synonymous with white woman" (hooks, 1981, p. 138), which resulted in the categorization of women of color as "others." Due to their more privileged status in American society, white women were able to "interpret feminism in such a way that it was no longer relevant to all women" (hooks, 1981, p. 149). For example, Betty Friedan's (1963/1983) analysis of "the problem with no name" identified the problems of white middle-class housewives who had become dissatisfied with their stereotyped roles and lack of opportunities for self-fulfillment and achievement. This assessment ignored the realities of many women who have always worked outside of their homes, struggled to survive economically, and have not had the luxury to claim "the problem with no name." Beginning with slavery and persisting until today, compulsory labor has permeated all aspects of many black women's identities (Davis, 1981). Whereas work was a choice for middle-class women, it was a necessity for working-class women and many women of color. As noted by bell hooks (1984), oppression involves an absence of choices. The ability to choose whether one will or will not work is a form of liberation that many women have never experienced (hooks, 1984; Hurtado, 1989; Spelman, 1988). Gerda Lerner (1979) stated the following:

> White society has long decreed that while "woman's place is in the home," Black woman's place is in the white woman's kitchen. No wonder that many Black women define their own "liberation" as being free to take care of their own homes and their own children, supported by a man with a job. (p. 82)

The prominent slogan of the feminist movement, "the personal is political," encouraged all women to define their own reality and organize around their own oppression. However, the perspectives of women of color were largely ignored. The "personal is political" became "the politics of imposing and privileging a few women's personal lives over all women's lives by assuming that these few could be prototypical" (King, 1988, p. 58).

When individuals invoke the phrase "the personal is political," they tend to presume that all women experience a universal distinction between private and public worlds (Hurtado, 1989). However, although private and public realms have often been sharply divided for white middle-class women, the economic realities of many women of color have not allowed this division to exist. Because external forces and the government have altered the private lives of many people of color and poor people, they often have had difficulty creating a private life on their own terms. Aida Hurtado indicated that for people of color, it would be more accurate to state that the "public is *personally* political" (p. 849). The concerns of women of color and white women are likely to differ because of this reality.

White women have been particularly concerned about issues that appear in the private arena but are also relevant for the public domain, such as unequal division of labor in the household, personal identity issues, equality in personal interactions with men, and the tenacity of socialized gender differences. In contrast, many women of color tend to direct their activism toward public issues such as desegregation, affirmative action, poor housing, poverty, welfare, and prison reform, issues that illustrate how public policy has limited personal choice. These issues are related to basic survival needs, while middle-class white women often focus on personal fulfillment (King, 1988).

Early feminist analyses of violence against women also revealed a narrow focus; bell hooks (1981) and Angela Davis (1981) stated that feminists have devoted inadequate attention to the ways in which the rape of black women during slavery and later generations has influenced contemporary attitudes about violence against black women. Although Susan Brownmiller (1975) noted the negative impact of institutionalized rape in women's lives during slavery, she failed to acknowledge that "it led to a devaluation of black womanhood that permeated the psyches of all Americans and shaped the social status of all black women once slavery ended" (hooks, 1981, p. 52). A primary image that remains today is that of the black woman as "fallen" woman, whore, or slut. Continued exploitation of black women has undermined the morale of black women who must still contend with an image that is imposed on them and limits their capacity to develop positive self-concepts. Furthermore, contemporary feminism has attended primarily to violence that occurs within love relationships and interpersonal relationships; discussions of cycles of violence elaborate the stages of escalation and contrition that occur between two people (e.g., Walker, 1979). A more comprehensive analysis of violence must also consider the systemic cycle of violence as it begins at work and other social institutions, where it is also influenced by racism and classism. Systemic violence has an impact on how violence exhibits itself in interpersonal relationships and negatively influences the lives of both men and women (Davis, 1981; hooks, 1981).

The reproductive rights campaigns that emerged in the 1970s tended to frame women's rights to control their own bodies in white women's terms and early analyses conveyed a lack of understanding of the legacy of sterilization abuses, the eugenics movement of the early twentieth century, and the role of abortion during slavery. Davis (1981) noted that abortion during slavery did not result in increased freedom but represented "acts of desperation" (p. 205) that were intended to avoid bringing children into the world who would know only forced labor and slavery. During the eugenics movement at the turn of the century, birth control advocates argued for compulsory birth control and the sterilization of lower classes to ensure that their growth would be restricted (Ross, 1993). Recommendations that the birth rates of minority and lower class groups should be restricted were motivated by efforts of white U.S. residents to maintain superiority of numbers and power. When understood in terms of these realities, the notion of "abortion rights" does not bring up images of freedom but may elicit images of genocide or remind women of color of the demand to limit family size to avoid greater oppression or poverty. Furthermore, suggestions about limiting family size are often imposed by outside groups looking in on the communities of people of color, thus representing another form of external pressure rather than liberation (Davis, 1981; Ross, 1993).

When white feminists focused energy on reproductive rights, they viewed voluntary motherhood as an important way to ensure that women could pursue their career and self-development dreams. However, these dreams did not seem relevant to working-class women and women of color who were struggling to maintain economic survival and who were compelled to resort to abortion in order to increase the likelihood of basic survival. If white feminists had worked with women of color from the outset and had arrived at mutually useful definitions of issues, a more comprehensive program of social activism could have been devised (Davis, 1981).

Some of the ethnocentrism of contemporary feminism emerged out the failure of white women activists to address the conflicts between black women and white women and the racism of early feminism (hooks, 1981). White feminists often failed to understand how their privileged standpoint contributed to the perpetuation of the very abuses that they attempted to eradicate. They did not acknowledge differences between women, and thus, excluded many women from the ranks of feminism. Hooks asserted that an emphasis on the common oppression of all women provided white women with a "vehicle to enhance their own individual, opportunistic ends" (1981, p. 150) and allowed white women to develop a patronizing attitude toward women of color. However, when women of color were invited to cooperate with white women, they were often invited to do so within the parameters established by white women, thus limiting opportunities for productive and mutual exchange (Hurtado, 1989). When black women have declined to participate in narrowly defined causes, their choices have been misread as lack of interest in women's liberation rather than lack of interest in a movement that is defined by and for white women.

Bell hooks (1984) also faulted white feminists for providing an overly narrow analysis of the family. Early radical feminist recommended that the family in its current forms should be eradicated without considering the differential impact of this statement on various groups of women. According to hooks (1984), middle-class women often have the financial resources that allow them to reject traditional family life without giving up options for receiving care and nurture. Furthermore, although white middle-class feminists often experienced the family as the primary source of oppression, the family provided many women of color with a haven from external oppression. Although sexism exists within families of color, many women of color experience greater self-worth and dignity within their families than in the outside world where they must face multiple oppressions. The family provides a context in which men and women of color share a common past, culture, religion, and tradition and gain mutual support for dealing with racism and classism in public interactions (hooks, 1984; Hurtado, 1989).

Finally, white women have tended to identify men as enemies rather than as potential allies, thus fueling antagonism between white women and women of color and limiting the attractiveness of their analysis to diverse groups of women. The legacy of many women of color includes shared resistance with men against racism and/or slavery. Angela Davis (1981) noted that all members of slave families were oppressed and all members worked as economic providers. As a result, male supremacy was not promoted in the black family as systematically as in middle-class America. Although sexism is also a factor in the lives of women of color, they are also aware of the hardships that men of color face and feel compassion for them. Radical feminist separatist views are especially likely to alienate women of color. According to this view, patriarchal values are so strong and overpowering that it is impossible to successfully resist male supremacy while maintaining personal connections with men. The mandate for separatism does not acknowledge the shared oppression of men and women of color, but instead, it suggests that black women should form an alliance with white women—women who have been instruments of oppression in the lives of many women of color.

Many black women have worked simultaneously for black rights and women's rights and understood the need for a connection between civil rights and feminism. Paula Giddings (1984) stated that "[in] times of racial militancy, Black women threw their considerable energies into that struggle—even at the expense of their feminist yearnings" (p. 7). In less militant times, black women also demanded rights in their relationships with black men. These demands were not "seen in the context of race *versus* sex, but as one where their rights had to be secured in order to assure Black progress" (p. 7).

The preceding section on ethnocentrism within feminist activism has focused most extensively on the relationship of black women to feminism and has not provided information about the activism and specific concerns of women from other racial/ethnic traditions. The realities of various groups of women of color are diverse. I encourage readers to view this section as an example of the difficult relationship between white feminists and women of color, and to use this material to inform their thinking about how to transcend the problems of the past within current relationships. It is also important for readers to explore the rich traditions of other diverse racial/ ethnic groups of women.

Ethnocentrism in Feminist Theory

The previous section identified ways in which the activities of mainstream feminism excluded women of color; this section will identify how academic theory has also excluded the perspectives of women of color. Radical feminists of the 1970s proposed that gender oppression is the fundamental form of oppression (e.g., Firestone, 1970; Millett, 1970). This tenet can be interpreted in various ways: gender oppression is the most virulent and most difficult oppression to eradicate; sexism is the first type of oppression learned by children; sexism predates other forms of oppression; sexism causes racism; gender oppression is the model of other forms of oppression; or sexism is used to justify other forms of oppression such as racism (Spelman, 1988). These potential conclusions imply that the most important form of oppression is discrimination on the basis of sex. However, by seeing sexism as more "fundamental" than other "isms," privileged women can ignore the role they may play in perpetuating racism. Conceptualizing sexism in this way can lead to "white solipsism," which entails the tendency "to think, imagine, and speak as if whiteness described the world" (Rich, 1979, p. 299). If gender oppression is viewed as central to understanding all other oppression, women of color may feel forced to identify primarily as women and to ignore their race and minority status as a source of pride. Furthermore, sexism and racism are often inseparable. "Sexism and racism do not have different 'objects' in the case of Black women" (Spelman, 1988, p. 122) and other women of color.

For many women of color, racism is a far more visible, virulent, and everyday experience than sexism. Bell hooks (1981) contends that although American society was built on a patriarchal values, "America was colonized on a racially imperialist base and not on a sexually imperialist base" (p. 122). As a result, racism overshadowed sexism as colonists constructed a society, and this reality still influences the lives of people of color.

In noting the different experiences of white women and women of color, Aída Hurtado (1989) stated that whereas women of color were the objects of rejection, white women were the objects of seduction. White women are "seduced into joining the oppressor under the pretense of sharing power" (Lorde, 1984, pp. 118-119). The possibility of sharing power or privilege was never an option for women of colonized peoples and slaves. Evelyn Higgenbotham (1992) concluded that the gender identity of black and white women is constructed in radically different contexts. Because of the salience of race in American culture's constructions of class, gender, and sexuality, race is inextricably linked to one's sense of self as a woman.

Some of the early statements that recognized the unique concerns of women of color spoke of the double and triple jeopardy experienced by women of color (e.g., Beale, 1970). The notion of double and triple jeopardy implied that various discriminations can be interpreted "as equivalent to the mathematical equation, racism plus sexism plus classism equals triple jeopardy" (King, 1988, p. 47). If this were the case, each type of oppression would have an independent and direct impact on one's status, and the contributions of each would be readily apparent. However, by attempting to separate sexism from other forms of oppression, our understanding of the interlocking, interactive aspects of various oppressions is limited (hooks, 1984; Spelman, 1988). When racism and sexism are seen as additive, the most likely conclusion is that all women are victimized by sexism and some women are also oppressed by racism. This thinking fails to acknowledge the differing contexts in which white women and women of color experience gender oppression. It also implies that a woman's ethnic or racial identity can be subtracted from her larger identity, when in fact, these aspects of experience may be inseparable. Bell hooks (1984) concluded: "Suggesting a hierarchy of oppression exists, with sexism in first place, evokes a sense of competing concerns that is unnecessary" (p. 35).

Elizabeth Spelman (1988) noted that even when theorists have acknowledged the diversity of women, they tend to view gender oppression as the most important oppression or to speak of women as though they were one group. For example, French existential feminist Simone de Beauvoir (1952) acknowledged differences between women, noted their lack of shared concerns across race and class lines, and recognized the unwillingness of women with sex and class privileges to share power with other women. How-ever, her analyses described the characteristics and natures of men and women as through race and class did not matter. She compared the oppression of women to slaves and other oppressed groups but did not acknowledge the experience of individuals who were both women and slaves. De Beauvoir (1952) also noted the importance of social institutions in shaping concepts of the self, but ignored the impact of racism in modifying meanings associated with skin color. In general, de Beauvoir gave lip service to diversity and oversimpli-fied issues by holding up the lives of white middle-class heterosex-ual Western women as normative (Spelman, 1988). A flawed con-clusion is that the experiences of women of color are synonymous either with those of men of color or white women, "and since the experiences of both are equivalent, a discussion of black women in particular is superfluous" (King, 1988, p. 45). Thus, the unique identities and perspectives of women of color can be "socialized out of existence" (hooks, 1981, p. 7).

The Feminisms of Women of Color: The Example of Black Feminist Thought

Despite the exclusion of women of color from major theories of feminism and positions of leadership within feminism, women of color have made important contributions to feminism. One of the earliest and most influential works about radical black feminism was contained in the statement of the Combahee River Collective (1982). The collective was formed in 1973 in response to the racism and elitism that limited the involvement of black women in femi-nism. The collective's manifesto noted that the pervasive nature of racism had not allowed many black women to examine the ways in which sexual oppression is a "constant factor in our day-to-day existence" (Combahee River Collective, 1982, p. 14). Members committed themselves to address sexism, racism, heterosexism, and economic oppression within capitalism. They also noted that con-temporary black feminism is built on a legacy of black women's resistance, sacrifice, and activism directed by generations of both prominent and unheralded black women. Furthermore, black women have never passively succumbed to oppression but have demon-strated "an adversary stance to white male communities in both dramatic and subtle ways" (p. 14). In a statement of belief, they noted that "Black women are inherently valuable" (p. 15) and that this principle is especially significant in light of the fact that all previous political movements have acted as though "anyone is more worthy of liberation than ourselves" (p. 16). They also articulated the centrality of the following four issues: (1) the impossibility of separating race, class, and sex oppression; (2) solidarity with progressive black men and a rejection of separatism; (3) a commitment to eradicating capitalist structures by raising consciousness about "the real class situation of persons who are not merely raceless, sexless workers, but for whom racial and sexual oppression are significant determinants in their working economic lives" (p. 17); and (4) the importance of expanding the definition of the "personal is political" to include issues of race and class. The Combahee River Collective identified several key issues as the focus of their activism: (1) commitment to issues for which race, sex, and class oppression operate simultaneously; (2) identification of racism within white feminism; and (3) a commitment to collective discussion and continual examination of their personal politics (The Combahee River Collective, 1982).

During the 1980s, feminist theory by and about women of color became increasingly more visible, especially the writings of black feminists (e.g., Collins, 1986, 1989, 1990; hooks, 1981, 1984). Patricia Hill Collins (1986) noted that African-American women play a particularly important role in the development of feminist theory because they have been exposed to "insider" information and the "intimate secrets of white society" (p. S14), while also maintaining outsider (and often marginalized) status that allows them to develop a unique standpoint and insight about behaviors that remain invisible to dominant members of society. This outsider viewpoint is valuable not only to black women but is central to the development of more inclusive ways of seeing the world. Black feminists utilize their relationship to dominant society to develop a standpoint "of and for Black women" (p. S16). This standpoint assumes that black women share some common perceptions and experiences as a group and thus, can articulate a unique perspective about black women. However, although black women share some common attitudes, their different experiences due to age, region, sexual orientation, and class mean that these commonalities will be expressed in different ways. Black feminist thought "articulates the taken-for-granted knowledge of African women" (1989, p. 750) and encourages African-American women to create new forms of knowledge and self-definition (Collins, 1989).

Three themes are especially central to black feminist thought: (1) the importance of self-definition and self-valuation, (2) an analysis of the interlocking factors of oppression, and (3) the significance of black women's culture. Self-definition is particularly important in light of historical distortions and stereotypes of African-American women. Black feminists seek to identify the power dynamics that have led to these distortions and redefine and "value those aspects of Afro-American womanhood that are stereotyped, ridiculed, and maligned in academic scholarship and the popular media" (p. S17). Second, black feminists are committed to focusing on the "simultaneity of oppression" (Smith, 1983, p. xxxii) and linkages between systems of oppression. Although Marxist and socialist feminists have attempted to include considerations of race and gender within existing theories, black feminists focus on developing new interpretations of these factors and treating "the interaction among multiple systems as the object of study" (Collins, 1986, p. S20). Finally, black feminists focus on explaining and redefining the significance of black women's culture, as well as revealing previously unexplored aspects of African-American women's experience. This scholarship reveals concrete ways in which women have expressed themselves through the church, family, and political and economic activity. Important areas of scholarship include previously unexplored aspects of black women's interpersonal relationships as expressed through sisterhood and mothering, as well as the role of creative expression and creative arts in "shaping and sustaining Black women's self-definitions and self-valuations" (p. S23). The exploration of black women's culture is important for several reasons: it reveals the unique and complex ways in which black women have resisted oppression over time, and it points to limitations in traditional notions of activism and redefines women's everyday activities as forms of activism (Collins, 1986).

In addition to defining important content areas, black feminists have identified a unique set of values for developing and evaluating knowledge claims. Black feminist thought incorporates both Afro-centric values that influence family, religion, culture, and community life in various parts of South and North America, the Caribbean, and Africa, as well as feminist standpoints that seek to explicate patriarchal oppression. Second, it also places special emphasis on the concrete, everyday experiences of black women, an approach to understanding womanhood that has been valued historically in black communities. Third, it is based in the belief that knowledge claims must be embedded within dialogue, a tradition that is based in both African and African-American oral traditions. Fourth, it is supported by an ethic of care that is connected to African humanism that focuses on the importance of seeing each person as a "unique expression of a common spirit, power, or energy expressed by all life" (p. 766). The ethic of care also acknowledges the appropriateness of emotion in verbal exchange, the understanding that "emotion indicates that a speaker believes in the validity of an argument" (p. 766), and the centrality of empathy for others. The connection between feminist and Afrocentric values appears particularly clear with regard to the ethic of care. Fifth, this perspective states that the person who proposes knowledge claims must endorse an ethic of accountability that includes an evaluation of the character, values, and ethics of the person who proposes knowledge claims. Reason, emotion, and ethics are combined in evaluating the degree to which a person has shown personal accountability. Patricia Collins (1989) noted that it is not the goal of black feminists to translate their ideas, which are embedded within Afrocentric feminist epistemology, into Eurocentric masculinist epistemology: "The goal here is not one of integrating Black female 'folk culture' into the substantiated body of academic knowledge, for that substantiated knowledge is, in may ways, antithetical to the best interests of Black women" (p. 772). It seeks instead to describe the preexisting standpoints of black women and to rethink and recenter the language of academic disciplines so that Black feminist standpoints are valued.

Many black women and other women of color have preferred to use the term *womanist* rather than *feminist* to highlight the uniqueness of their commitment to women of color as well as to demonstrate their rejection of approaches that propose gender-based dichotomies or a "false homogenizing" (Higginbotham, 1992, p. 273).

Alice Walker (1983) defined womanist as "a black feminist or feminist of color" (p. xi). Womanist also refers to women who love other women, appreciate women's culture, women's strength, and women's emotional flexibility. A womanist is committed to the "survival and wholeness of entire people, male *and* female." Finally, a "womanist is to feminist as purple is to lavender" (Walker, 1983, p. xii). These definitions underscore the strength, resiliency, and capacity of women of color.

The Future: New Images of Sisterhood

The skepticism that women of color hold toward white women persists. Evelyn Higginbotham (1992) suggested that although white feminists have largely rejected the notion of a homogenous woman, they "pay hardly more than lip service to race as they continue to analyze their own experience in ever more sophisticated ways" (pp. 251-252). The task of building bridges between white women and women of color is complicated. Bell hooks (1984) suggested that we must start by forging new definitions of feminism that focus less on equality of the sexes and more on the diversity of women's experience. Feminism should be defined as "the struggle to end sexist oppression" (hooks, 1984, p. 26). The aim of feminism is not to benefit one group of women over others; it should not define feminism as gaining equality with men nor should it "privilege women over men" (p. 26). New forms of feminism must focus on challenging the philosophical structures that support white supremacist institutions. Finally, feminism must not be a force that is centered only within academic circles, but should become a mass-based movement whose goals are not only communicated through writing but also through word of mouth and action (hooks et al., 1993). If women from diverse backgrounds are to feel a sense of solidarity, feminism will need to be based on shared resources and strengths, as well as the willingness to tolerate discussion, confrontation, and criticism. White women must continue to confront racism directly and move beyond feelings of guilt to a commitment to action. Conversely, women of color will need to confront the ways in which they have absorbed beliefs based in white supremacy (or internalized racism) in order to free themselves from racist stereotypes and contribute fully to feminist theory and social action.

Women of color have helped to demonstrate that although "all women are women, there is no being who is only a woman" (Spelman, 1988, p. 102). Furthermore, "[t]here is no *women's* voice, no *woman's* story, but rather a multitude of voices that sometimes speak together but often must speak separately" (Baber and Allen, 1992, p. 19). Gender cannot be isolated from other complex aspects of experience and viewed as the sole or primary source of women's problems, but must be understood in its multiple manifestations and as it is modified by individual difference, cultural/ethnic values, class, race, and sexual orientation.

FEMINIST EPISTEMOLOGIES AND THE EMERGENCE OF POSTMODERN FEMINISM

As feminist theory gained increasing acceptance as an academic area of study, it has become increasingly important to attend to issues of epistemology, or the strategies designed to support the various feminist philosophical systems that have been proposed. These emerging epistemologies have examined questions such as the following: How do we justify beliefs and philosophical positions that we hold? What types of research efforts will support our knowledge claims? How has androcentric epistemology been used in the service of sexist, classist, homophobic, and racist aims, and what strategies of justifying knowledge will replace these biased forms of knowledge? To what degree should feminists use the tools of traditional inquiry to support their claims?

Sandra Harding (1990) identified two major reasons why feminist epistemologies or justificatory strategies are necessary. First, they represent a defense against "objectivism," which states that "scientific claims can be produced only through dispassionate, disinterested, value-free, point-of-viewless, objective inquiry procedures, and that research generated or guided by feminist concerns obviously cannot meet such standards" (p. 87). Traditional objectivism places feminism strictly outside the domain of that which can be objectively studied via the scientific method. Second, feminists must use justificatory strategies to deal with interpretationism, or the discounting of feminist research in the form of grudging acknowledgment that feminists have a right to their own opinions and interpretations, but that such interpretations show no "objective" superiority over other alternatives. Thus, the claims of feminism are not convincing. Third, feminist epistemologies provide researchers with procedures for making choices with regard to theoretical, research, and political activities. Finally, these strategies provide a rationale and resources for organizing individuals to end male domination.

Three major approaches to feminist epistemology have been proposed: feminist empiricism, feminist standpoint theories, and postmodern feminism. Feminist empiricism has been used primarily by feminists in the social and natural sciences and is often associated with liberal feminism; feminist standpoint theories are typically associated with cultural and socialist feminism and the feminism of women of color and are adopted by feminists in the humanities, arts, social sciences, and natural sciences; and feminist postmodernism focuses on the limitations of any theory or knowledge base and represents a metaperspective that encourages individuals to maintain a skeptical, questioning attitude about knowledge claims and to examine the legitimacy of the notion that "a" truth exists.

Feminist Empiricism

Feminist empiricism has explored ways in which unspoken biases or gender privilege lead to "badly done science" (Harding, 1990, p. 90). According to this perspective, androcentrism appears through biases in the identification of issues to be studied, the definition of concepts, formulation of hypotheses, and collection and interpretation of data. Feminist empiricism challenges the incomplete way in which scientific inquiry is conducted and has sought to eliminate sexism by adhering more strictly to rules of good research design and the scientific method. It does not question the basic norms or tenets of science, and it utilizes respected/accepted methods of the natural and social sciences. By asking unbiased questions, using representative samples and appropriate explanatory models, interpreting data objectively, and attending to complex interactions that are influenced by culture, feminist empirical researchers seek to produce evidence that meets respected standards within science. Feminist empiricists assume that when research is free of bias, more accurate observations can be made and equitable policies for men and women can be implemented. Thus, feminist empiricists have relied on gathering various "facts" for refuting biased claims.

Feminist empiricism subverts traditional scientific inquiry or traditional "objectivism" by suggesting that feminists (men and women) are more likely than nonfeminists to bring a critical consciousness about sexism and other "isms" to the research process, and as a result, are more likely to identify and eliminate problems that lead to biased outcomes. Thus, feminist empiricism challenges the notion that the social identity of the observer is irrelevant to producing unbiased results. The observer plays an important role in selecting topics for investigation, forming hypotheses, identifying appropriate categories for grouping data, and interpreting information. Feminist researchers who rely on empirical methods expand on the range of topics studied, pay careful attention to context in which findings emerge, and utilize interpretive frameworks embedded within feminist beliefs. Feminist empiricism also challenges the traditional assumption that politics and science must remain separate from each other. Feminist empiricism asserts that political forces that call for emancipation and social change can increase the objectivity of science (Harding, 1986, 1990).

Feminist empiricism has been criticized for its reliance on scientific techniques, which are designed to control subjective biases but do not challenge the basic structure of knowledge. It has also been criticized for seeming to reject nonrational experiences and subjectivity as unimportant, and for devoting inadequate attention to the role of perceptions, personal feelings, and self-concept in research and human experience. Feminist empiricism presumes the "primacy of the senses" (Hawkesworth, 1989, p. 535) and that there is a "truth" to be known. It assumes that through the elimination of the distorting lenses of biased observers, feminist researchers can arrive at objective knowledge and "unmediated truth about the world" (Hawkesworth, 1989, p. 535). Despite criticisms, feminist empiricism remains a very important strategy for feminist exploration in the social sciences, and the results of feminist empirical studies are especially useful for conveying new information and evidence in the search for answers to gender issues. Feminist empiricism has been central to research efforts that have investigated gender biases, and has been useful for challenging many myths about gender differences. Research practices associated with this epistemology are especially consistent with and useful as supports for liberal feminist claims.

Feminist Standpoint Theories

Feminist standpoint theories are based on the assumption that "men's dominating position in social life results in partial and perverse understandings whereas women's subjugated position provides the possibility of more complete and less perverse understandings" (Harding, 1986, p. 26). According to this view, traditional academic methods are based on an androcentric view of the world that tends to categorize much of human experience according to a set of polarities: subject-object, mind-body, inner-outer, reason-sense, and public-private domains. These abstract categories are not only inadequate for explaining the experiences of women, but have been used by those in power to define women in comparison to and as less complete than men. For example, women have traditionally engaged in work, such as housework and mothering, which has not been valued in and of itself, but only because it has freed men to engage in activities valued within the culture. "Women are thus excluded from men's conceptions of culture" and women's experience is "incomprehensible and inexpressible within the distorted abstractions of men's conceptual schemes" (Harding, 1990, p. 95). In order to correct these biases, the role of feminists is to create a "successor science" that can replace the narrow views of traditional analysis with more complete and inclusive analyses. Feminist standpoint theorists argue that "while certain social positions (the oppressor's) produce distorted ideological views of reality, other social positions (the oppressed's) can pierce ideological obfuscations and attain a correct and comprehensive understanding of the world" (Hawkesworth, 1989, p. 536).

Feminist standpoint theories reject dualisms, reductionism, and linear models associated with traditional inquiry and attempt to replace these with more holistic and complex models of experience that are embedded in women's frames of reference (Hartsock, 1983; Rose, 1983). These approaches question the very methods and nature of intellectual inquiry, such as the assumptions that truth is objective, rational, and ahistorical, and that the inquirer must maintain distance from the subject matter being studied. Thus, standpoint theorists have proposed alternative visions of truth and emphasized the special knowledge and skills that women hold, such as relational thinking and an appreciation for connectedness with others (Harding, 1986; Morawski, 1990). According to this viewpoint, knowledge and truth are also influenced by factors that modify or inform women's special skills, factors such as race, class, and other aspects of diversity that shape a person's view of reality and inform knowledge claims. Feminist standpoint inquiry is also grounded in many of the social practices of feminism, including collaboration and consensus as appropriate forms of interaction for devising effective research programs. It seeks to place women at the center of inquiry and erase the boundaries between researchers and the person's studied, and as a result, the qualitative, in-depth study of women's lives is viewed as particularly useful for clarifying women's strengths, perspectives, and realities.

Feminist standpoint approaches have been criticized for being "essentialist" or assuming that there is *one* way of knowing and experiencing that is uniquely female. Elizabeth Spelman (1988) stated the following:

> Positing an essential "womanness" has the effect of making women inessential in a variety of ways. First of all, if there is an essential womanness that all women have and have always had, then we needn't know anything about any woman is particular. . . . If all women have the same story "as women," we don't need a chorus of voices to tell the story. (p. 158)

If one assumes that women have a distinctive and more complete perspective, one must also assume that there is some common experience that women share that would lead to a shared vision. Critics propose that standpoint theories put forth universal theories about women and neglect the diverse voices of women of color, working-class women, or lesbians. Jane Flax (1987) contended that feminist standpoint theory "may require the suppression of the important and discomforting voices of persons with experiences unlike our own" (p. 633). A second criticism is that although feminist standpoint theories reject the use of polarized categories, they also appear to place men's and women's strengths into dichotomous categories. In their efforts to reject an overemphasis on instrumental reason, standpoint theorists may overemphasize the "unique" female knowledge that is embedded in emotion, care, and intuition (Bohan, 1993; Hawkesworth, 1989). Third, standpoint theories rely on overly optimistic beliefs that women are not substantially damaged by their oppression and are able to retain superior observational and comprehension skills and that women, unlike men, "can be free of determination from their own participation in relations of domination such as those rooted in the social relations of race, class, or homophobia" (Flax, 1987, p. 642). Hawkesworth noted that "[g]iven the diversity and fallibility of all human knowers, there is no good reason to believe that women are any less prone to error, deception, or distortion than men" (p. 544). Thus, standpoint theories can fall prey to the very errors that have permeated traditional androcentric perspectives.

Despite claims that standpoint theorists propose universal truths and essentialism, recent theorists focus on the importance of development of multiple standpoints and standpoint pluralism. The work of feminists who have articulated standpoints unique to black and lesbian feminists illustrate that no one standpoint is useful for defining the reality of all women. The standpoints of specific groups of women of color reveal the way in which complex social interactions of race, gender, class, sexual orientation, nationality, and religion influence and modify human experience (Longino, 1993). Sandra Harding (1991) indicated that standpoint theories can guard against essentialism by incorporating *strong objectivity,* which is defined as acknowledging "the historically situated character of all knowledge claims and seeking to have one's own thought permeated with each (oppositional) standpoint" (Longino, 1993, p. 211). Traditional definitions of objectivity indicate that all values are potentially contaminating and should be eliminated as one acquires knowledge. In contrast, strong objectivity involves the recognition that values inevitably influence knowledge, and that some values should be incorporated within research because they result in less distorted and less incomplete accounts of the human experience. Furthermore, strong objectivity acknowledges that knowledge is socially and historically constructed, but that some claims of truth are more credible and defendable than others.

Standpoint epistemology is especially consistent with cultural feminism and some forms of radical and socialist feminism. Standpoint theories are perhaps most compatible with contributions related to feminist ethics, ecofeminism, and relationship theories that seek to revalue traditional qualities of women.

Postmodern Feminism

Postmodern perspectives raise metatheoretical questions about the role and function of theory and research, and are "deconstructive" in the sense that "they seek to distance us from and make us skeptical about beliefs concerning truth, knowledge, power, the self, and language that are often taken for granted" (Flax, 1987, p. 624). Postmodern theorists challenge (1) the existence of a stable coherent self that is capable of reason and self-insight; (2) the belief that reason can provide a reliable and objective basis of knowledge or that knowledge based on reason is "real and unchanging" (p. 624), ahistorical and independent of the context in which it occurs; (3) the assumption that individuals can escape a predetermined existence and live an autonomous, free life by implementing laws of reason; and (4) the notion that knowledge and truth can be defined in ways that are independent of and free of power dynamics, as well as the related view that scientific exploration will lead to the creation of laws of nature that will benefit society. Postmodernism proposes that "knowledge is the result of invention, the imposition of form on the world rather than the result of discovery" (Hawkesworth, 1989, p. 536), and celebrates "the human capacity to misunderstand, to universalize the particular and the idiosyncratic, to privilege the ethnocentric, and to conflate truth with those prejudices that advantage the knower" (p. 554). The notion of "Truth" should be rejected; it promotes a "destructive illusion" (p. 554).

Building on the base of various postmodern thinkers (e.g., Foucault, Baudrillard, Lacan), feminist postmodernism rejects the search for a distinctive, universal female standpoint because personal identities are influenced by many other individual differences and standpoints, such as race, ethnicity, sexual orientation, class, and disability. A postmodern view proposes that reality is embedded with social relationships and historical contexts and is socially constructed or invented. Rather than searching for *a* truth, the inquirer focuses on how meaning is negotiated and how persons in authority maintain control over these meanings. Knowledge can never be neutral or objective. Feminist postmodernism not only critiques androcentric biases but provides a metatheoretical perspective for evaluating the claims of feminist researchers and theorists (Allen and Baber, 1992; Harding, 1986; Hare-Mustin and Marecek, 1990; Morawski, 1990; Riger, 1992). From a postmodern perspective, all methods, including qualitative and quantitative methods, feminist empirical methods, and methods associated with standpoint perspectives, can be utilized to search for how "truth" and reality are socially constructed and influenced by power relations. Each method can provide a useful but limited perspective on reality (Riger, 1992).

Some feminist critics suggest that postmodernism that can also promote a "slide into relativism" because all realities are placed into question. The notion of women's oppression could be declared obsolete. If reality and the self are merely constructions, the individual has no real power to reflect on her or his existence, and to resist or challenge ways in which his or her life is constricted (Alcoff, 1988; Allen and Baber, 1992). If this view is taken to its logical conclusion, none of the statuses of race, class, and gender can be used to validate or support one's claims for justice. If all truth is created and relative, no group can legitimately make specific claims, and "once again, underneath we are all the same" (Alcoff, 1988, p. 421). The very appreciation of diversity that postmodern thinking seeks to provide can be lost if the realities of diverse groups are presumed to have no grounding in reality other than that which is constructed. Feminist politics, which are based on the perception of shared needs of a group, becomes impossible, and feminism would exist only as a mode of inquiry (DiStephano, 1990). As a corrective to the classic postmodern view, feminist postmodernist thinkers endorse a modified position. They believe that "the world is more than a text" (Hawkesworth, 1989, p. 555); the experiences of victims of rape, domestic, and sexual harassment do not merely represent the "arbitrary imposition of a purely fictive meaning on an otherwise meaningless reality" (Hawkesworth, 1989, p. 555).

A second criticism is that because there is no "truth," feminism is limited to reaction rather than creation; the only form of effective feminism becomes "a wholly negative feminism, deconstructing everything and refusing to construct anything" (Alcoff, 1988, p. 418). Nancy Hartsock (1987) added the following: "For those of use who want to understand the world systematically in order to change it, postmodernist theories at their best give little guidance" (pp. 190-191). This type of feminism critiques traditional forms of knowledge but has no basis on which to propose alternative views of reality.

A third criticism of postmodernism is that it "expresses the claims and needs of a constituency (white privileged men of the industrialized West) that has already had an Enlightenment for itself and that is not ready and willing to subject that legacy to critical scrutiny" (DiStephano, 1990, p. 75). Although postmodern theory deconstructs and decenters traditional androcentric theory, it was created by the very men (e.g., Foucault) who have historically held power to create knowledge. These theorists have remained insensitive or blind to issues of gender in their analysis of power and its impact on the creation of knowledge. If postmodernism becomes powerful within feminism, Mary Hawkesworth (1989) predicts that "it will not be an accident that power remains in the hand of the white males who possess it. In a world of radical inequality, relativist resignation reinforces the status quo" (p. 557). Furthermore, postmodern theories, which are highly complex and couched in language that is generally inaccessible to those outside of the academic world, may recapitulate the flaws of earlier traditional Enlightenment theories: they "deny marginalized people the right to participate in defining the terms of interaction with people in the mainstream" (Hartsock, 1987, p. 191)

Postmodernism has contributed to heightened awareness of how power and knowledge, including feminist theory, are interconnected (Butler, 1992). It has encouraged an appreciation of diversity and difference, and promoted a new appreciation of pluralism (Hawkesworth, 1989). Postmodern perspectives provide feminists with tools for guarding against creating theories that ignore issues of difference and thus, assist feminists in questioning the ways in which their own paradigms "serve to subordinate and erase that which they seek to explain" (Butler, 1992, p. 5). By applying this epistemology, feminists have gained access to a framework for examining how unconscious white privilege can lead to the type of exclusions of which normative theories have been guilty (Bordo, 1990).

In response to feminist critics of postmodernism, Judith Butler asserted (1992) that to deconstruct a theory is not to negate its validity; furthermore, "to call a presupposition into question is not the same as doing away with it" (p. 17). Jane Flax (1992) added that critics of postmodern theory overstate their case and promote dichotomous thinking when they suggest that feminists must either wholeheartedly accept postmodern philosophy or completely reject it. Linda Singer (1992) suggested that feminists can use postmodern ideas in a strategic fashion in order to increase the strength and viability of feminism in a complicated world. Feminists whose work has been influenced by postmodernism indicate that its most useful purpose is to guard against making inappropriate generalizations about men and women and to aid in the creation of more complex theories in which gender is considered as one of many relevant categories that include race, class, ethnicity, age, and sexual orientation (Fraser and Nicholson, 1990).

However, Susan Bordo (1990) speculated that "attentiveness to difference" may not necessarily lead to the "adequate representation of difference" (p. 140). "Attending *too* vigilantly to difference can just as problematically construct an Other who is an exotic alien, a breed apart" (Bordo, 1990, p. 140), as do traditional methods of inquiry. Considering the difficulties integrating postmodern perspectives and feminism, Nancy Fraser and Linda Nicholson (1990) suggested that postmodernism and feminism can be used to critique each other. Postmodern perspectives inform us of the danger of "essentialism"; feminism reveals the androcentrism and political naïveté of postmodernism. When postmodernism is used in a strategic way, it is not necessary to abandon theoretical or political tools for working on behalf of women. However, all theories and prices must be seen as nonuniversalist, pragmatic, and fallible. If researchers use methods and categories that are suited to each specific task, theory and research findings will appear "more like a tapestry composed of threads of many different hues than one woven in a single color" (Fraser and Nicholson, 1990, p. 35).

Postmodernism and Social Constructionism in Feminist Psychology

Mazarin Banaji (1993) asserted that "social constructionism is psychology's code word for postmodernism" (p. 261). At present, a social constructionistic model is the dominant perspective within psychology of women as an academic and research discipline (see, for example, Hyde, 1996; Matlin, 1996; Unger and Crawford, 1996). The major feature of social constructionism is that "one does not have gender; one does gender" (Allen and Baber, 1992, p. 13). Stephanie Riger (1992) elaborates this idea: "Gender is something we enact, not an inner core or constellation of traits that we express; it is a pattern of social organization that structures the relations, especially the power relations, between women and men" (p. 737).

In keeping with this principle, gender is not merely a static subject variable that exists within the person, but is continuously shaped by multiple levels of interaction. At a social structural level, gender becomes a form of social classification that determines the availability of resources and power to women and men. At the interpersonal level, gender acts as a cue or stimulus that informs individuals how to behave toward men and women. Finally, at an individual level, a person's self-definition as a gendered individual influences the manner in which specific behaviors and traits are attributed to the self (Unger and Crawford, 1996).

Postmodern theory may also help psychologists transcend the limitations of other epistemologies. Research endeavors and findings take on new significance or meaning. Rachel Hare-Mustin and Jeanne Marecek (1990) indicated that feminist empiricism tends to fall prey to beta bias, or the minimization of differences between men and women. In contrast, feminist standpoint epistemologies tend to exaggerate gender differences, and thus exhibit alpha bias. From a postmodern/social constructionist perspective, a single truth does not exist; thus, questions about the existence of gender differences are not useful. Instead, important questions become the following: What does gender mean? How is gender created and shaped? What do gender differences mean? Aside from difference or similarity, what else is gender? (Hare-Mustin and Marecek, 1990; Riger, 1992).

A major contribution of postmodernism to feminism is its commitment to pluralism. It challenges the notion that women's perspectives can be characterized by one privileged standpoint (Allen and Baber, 1992). In order to capture the complex realities of women's lives, it is necessary to use diverse methods of research. In utilizing diverse methods, however, the researcher should be aware of the value assumptions underlying each model, as well as the strengths and limitations of each method (Riger, 1992). Letitia Peplau and Eva Conrad (1989) stated that it is unproductive and illogical to label certain methods of inquiry as more feminist than others. Instead, "all methods can be feminist methods" (p. 395) if researchers remain cognizant of several principles: (1) knowledge claims and research findings are never completely value-neutral or objective, and (2) the meaning of gender cannot be defined by a snapshot of an individual at one point in time, but is shaped by important developmental, political, social, and historical forces. An extension of this principle suggests that all psychotherapy methods can be feminist if therapists use these methods in a carefully constructed and well-articulated social constructionist philosophy.

Postmodern thinking may provide opportunities for feminist theorists and therapists to think eclectically about feminist theory. Although it will remain important for feminist therapists to carefully consider the strengths and limitations of the various feminist theories, a postmodern perspective does not require the individual to endorse one form of feminism and reject others. Postmodern feminism or social constructionism provides a framework for organizing the multiple truths of women's lives. It offers much to feminist psychologists because it "embraces complexity and contradiction" and "surpasses theories that offer single-cause deterministic explanations about patriarchy and gender relations" (Gavey, 1989, p. 472).

LOOKING AHEAD

The remaining chapters will describe how various aspects of feminist therapy have been influenced by the theoretical traditions in feminism. For the purpose of organization, I have arbitrarily identified specific types of interventions and theories as most closely associated with liberal, cultural, radical, socialist, or women-of-color feminist philosophies. However, the very rich and evolving perspectives within feminism cannot, in actual practice, be easily categorized. A postmodern, social constructionist view also suggests that these perspectives can be integrated in meaningful ways. The final chapter of this book will revisit this question and articulate specific principles for clarifying a personally relevant combination of feminist therapy and feminist therapy.

Chapter 4

Liberal Feminism and Feminist Therapy

A major assumption underlying liberal feminism is the belief that irrational prejudice and restrictive gender socialization are the primary causes of sexism. The problem of irrational prejudice should be resolved through rational debate, argument, and the application of empirical evidence to problems; issues related to socialization can be dealt with through the resocialization of men and women who have experienced rigid gender-role injunctions. The goal of liberal feminism is to preserve individual dignity and establish individual freedom, autonomy, self-fulfillment, and equality (Donovan, 1992; Jaggar, 1983). The liberal feminist tradition places significant faith in human rationality and fairness, and as a result, promotes equality through reform, education, equal opportunity, and the legislation of personal rights (Jaggar and Rothenberg, 1984). As equal opportunities are provided to men and women, historical power structures that have hampered women's progress should gradually disappear, and gender-neutral policies should allow both men and women to achieve individual aspirations.

Mary Ballou and Nancy Gabalac (1985) indicated that the early years of feminist therapy were influenced by two overlapping perspectives that they termed a *questioning* approach and a *radical* approach. These two forms of feminist therapy were associated with two major strands or divisions of the feminist movement that appeared during the 1960s. The liberal feminist branch of the women's movement consisted of women's rights organizations, such as the National Organization for Women, which worked to implement changes within existing social, legal, and political structures. Organizations such as NOW focused on the legalization of abortion, the establishment of day care alternatives, election of women to public office, sex discrimination, the Equal Rights Amendment, and equal employment opportunities. This segment of the women's movement, sometimes called the *women's rights movement* (Carden, 1974; Deckard, 1979; Hole and Levine, 1971), was typically organized around formal, hierarchical structures and utilized democratic principles in decision making. These basic practices influenced the nature and form of liberal feminist therapy.

Feminists who subscribed to a more "radical" branch of feminism, sometimes labeled the *women's liberation movement* (Carden, 1974; Hole and Levine, 1971), eschewed the formal organizational style of institutions such as NOW; attempted to create antihierarchical, experimental, loosely organized structures; and chose to work outside of established institutions in an attempt to instigate social change. Feminist themes that are linked to the women's liberation movement are discussed in Chapters 2 and 5.

Women's rights organizations operated in ways that were generally consistent with the values of traditional psychology and mental health systems. Liberal women's rights organizations did not call for radical alteration of social or institutional systems, but worked for equality of opportunity for men and women. Thus, feminists within the mental health professions tended to be more comfortable with this approach than more radical alternatives. Feminists within the helping professions raised important questions about biases in research, diagnosis, and treatment; and provided suggestions for altering the practice of psychotherapy (Ballou and Gabalac, 1985). This chapter will review many of these significant contributions as well as discuss the strengths, limitations, and issues raised by this approach.

REVEALING GENDER BIAS

A major goal of liberal feminists is to identify gender bias as it hampers the development of individual potential and to suggest methods of correcting gender bias. A first step, then, is to identify biases through careful analysis and empirical research. This section will identify some of the important critiques and studies relevant to therapist gender bias, bias in diagnosis, and bias in personality theory.

Some of the strongest critiques of psychology came from within the profession. In 1968, Naomi Weisstein presented a paper titled "Kinder, Kuche, Kirche as Scientific Law: Psychology Constructs the Female" to a group of feminist activists. This highly influential paper has been reprinted at least two dozen times (Weisstein, 1968/1993) and continues to be applauded for its far-reaching insights (Bem, 1993a; Gault, 1993; Unger, 1993). A central argument of this paper is summarized by the following statement: "Psychology has nothing to say about what women are really like, what they need and what they want, especially because psychology does not know" (Weisstein 1968/1993, p. 197). The paper criticized psychology for creating views of women based on subjective theories and clinical impressions rather than on empirical evidence, for ignoring the impact of context on women's lives, and for adhering to flawed, biologically based theories. Most of the arguments were consistent with liberal feminist thought but also contained radical themes that called for the reconstruction of how psychology examines women's lives.

Numerous articles that were critical of psychology's treatment of women appeared in academic and professional journals during the 1970s. These articles elaborated on how therapeutic practices resulted in the endorsement of hierarchical therapist-client relationships and outlined ways in which therapeutic goals, psychological theories, and diagnostic practices encouraged adherence to masculine or biased criteria of psychological health and adjustment to traditional, stereotyped roles (e.g., Barrett et al., 1974; Holroyd, 1976; Klein, 1976; Marecek and Kravetz, 1977; Rice and Rice, 1973; Tennov, 1973; Whitely and Whitely, 1978).

Empirical studies about sexism and bias in psychotherapy provided support for the claims of feminist critics. One of the earliest and widely cited studies on bias against women reported that psychotherapists rated a hypothetical healthy woman as more submissive, less adventurous, more easily influenced, less competitive, more emotional, and less objective than a hypothetical healthy man or a hypothetical healthy adult whose gender was not specified (Broverman et al., 1970). The authors concluded that women experience a significant double bind. If they discard traditional female roles, they may be seen as unhealthy for not fulfilling these roles;

however, if women carry out traditional roles, they may be seen as unhealthy for diverging from the ideal of the healthy adult. This study served as a catalyst for numerous studies that were conducted by academic researchers with many different orientations, assumptions, and political perspectives. By the mid-1980s, over 150 studies on sex/gender bias had been conducted (Richardson and Johnson, 1984), and approximately a dozen reviews of the body of research had been written (e.g., Abramowitz and Dokecki, 1977; Betz and Fitzgerald, 1987; Brodsky, 1980; Davidson and Abramowitz, 1980; Richardson and Johnson, 1984; Sherman, 1980; Smith, 1980; Whitley, 1979; Zeldow, 1978, 1984).

Reviewers interpreted the body of gender-bias research in diverse ways. Julia Sherman (1980) saw clear evidence of bias against women, but Smith (1980) concluded that "counselor sex bias has not been demonstrated despite a dozen years of attempts to do so" (p. 406). Davidson (1983) charged that much of the research reflected the "narcissistic investment of many politically motivated researchers" (p. 181), and that results were influenced by an "agenda to expose the pernicious effect of 'sex biased' attitudes" (p. 168). Others concluded that although practitioners hold stereotypes about the mental health of men and women, there is no evidence that stereotypes actually alter the course of counseling (Abramowitz and Dokecki, 1977; Whitley, 1979).

The divergent conclusions of reviewers revealed the complexity of studying gender-related effects in psychotherapy. In general, gender-related bias appears to occur in complex contexts that are difficult to study through laboratory or analogue studies which attempt to replicate the conditions of psychotherapy (Brodsky, 1980; Lopez, 1989; Zeldow, 1984). The strongest evidence of bias is more likely to emerge in anecdotal reports, naturalistic study, or archival research rather than in paper-and-pencil surveys or counseling analogues. Gender effects are also more likely to appear when studies examine interactions between clients and therapists, when clients engage in role-discrepant behaviors, or when clients present specific types of problems, such as marital or occupational issues that appear to elicit more biased responses than many other issues (Lopez, 1983; Zeldow, 1978, 1984). Although females generally risk harsher judgments than males for engaging in norm-deviant behavior, men who behave in counterstereotypical ways are also the target of evaluative prejudice (Zeldow, 1984).

The body of research regarding mental health professionals' judgments of clients served as a consciousness-raising tool for the mental health profession. Replications of the original Broverman et al. (1970) study during the mid-1980s suggested that although some double standards for men and women still existed, clinicians had moved closer to adopting a single, more androgynous standard of mental health for men and women (Phillips and Gilroy, 1985; Thomas, 1985). Although social desirability and the transparency of gender-bias studies may have had some impact on results of later studies, the data suggest that the dramatic changes that occurred during the 1970s had at least some impact on the liberalization of therapists' values.

Feminists also identified the ways in which traditional personality theories contributed to the skewed or narrowly defined worldviews of clinicians and made it impossible for men and women to be seen objectively. Freudian concepts such as penis envy, castration anxiety, and the Oedipal complex, as well as Freud's descriptions of women's character as based on passivity, masochism, and narcissism were widely discussed as features of psychoanalytic theory that are blatantly biased (Barrett et al., 1974; Caplan, 1984; Holroyd, 1976; Marecek and Kravetz, 1977; Rawlings and Carter, 1977; Rice and Rice, 1973; Voss and Gannon, 1978). Nathan Hurvitz (1973) stated the following:

> Psychodynamic psychology with concepts such as "Electra complex," "penis envy," "vaginal orgasm," etc., has fostered a view of women as appendages to men, as less developed human beings, and as "natural" or "instinctive" mothers and homemakers, fostering conditions and attitudes that create problems for many women. Psychotherapy thus presumes to help these women overcome their problems by inducing them to accept the very conditions that give rise to their complaints. (p. 235)

Although psychoanalytic concepts of personality received the earliest attention, critiques also described ways in which a variety of developmental and personality theories were based on the examination of men's lives and presumed to be relevant to both men and women (e.g., Erikson, 1968; Kohlberg, 1981; Perry, 1970). In reaction to these theories, Doherty (1973) noted that any theory of personality that treats female development as a pathway that diverges from the male norm should not be considered a theory of personality. Later in the 1970s, feminist psychologists proposed alternative models of women's identities that are based on a woman-centered experience of the world (e.g., Gilligan, 1977, 1982).

Liberal feminists are not likely to question the utility of diagnosis, but believe that diagnostic categories can reflect gender stereotypes or can be applied in gender-biased ways. The elimination of this bias is essential. The primary contributions of liberal feminism to the study of bias in diagnosis focused on the relationship of diagnostic categories to gender role stereotypes. Phyllis Chesler (1972) stated that women are diagnosed for overconforming and underconforming to gender role stereotypes, and Marcie Kaplan (1983) noted that masculine-biased assumptions about healthy behavior are codified within diagnostic nomenclature. For example, the *Diagnostic and Statistical Manual of Mental Disorders* (American Psychiatric Association (APA), DSM-III, 1980; DSM-III-R, APA, 1987; and DSM-IV, 1994) devotes attention to the ways in which many women express dependency or emotionality in the form of *dependent personality disorder* or *histrionic personality disorder*. It does not mention, however, the dependency of people, usually men, who rely on others to take care of their children and maintain their households, nor does it label the emotional restrictiveness that often characterizes men's behavior. Marcie Kaplan (1983) concluded that the description of "histrionic personality disorder" parallels adjectives that were ascribed to healthy women in the Broverman et al. (1970) study: "It appears then that via assumptions about sex roles made by clinicians, a healthy woman automatically earns the diagnosis of Histrionic Personality Disorder or, to help female clients, clinicians encourage them to get sick" (p. 789).

Hope Landrine (1989) demonstrated the relationships between stereotypes and diagnostic labels by examining students' reactions to descriptions of personality disorders. Students indicated that a person described by a paragraph based on dependent personality disorder was most likely to be a married, middle-class, white woman, and a person depicted by a paragraph based on the criteria for antisocial personality disorder was most likely to be a young lower-class man (Landrine, 1989). As indicated by these results, diagnostic labels applied to men also coincide with gender role stereotypes, with men more likely than women to be diagnosed as displaying antisocial or "acting out" behaviors, obsessive-compulsive personality disorder, paranoid personality disorder, and alcoholism (Fodor and Rothblum, 1984; Kaplan, 1983).

In addition to pointing out ways in which gender role stereotypes appear in psychological diagnoses, feminists noted that the disorders men and women experience coincide with exaggerations of their normal gender roles (Franks and Rothblum, 1983; Kaplan, 1983). Violet Franks and Esther Rothblum (1983) indicated that although some women may be inappropriately labeled for merely subscribing to traditional feminine roles, the demands of these gender roles also increase their vulnerability to disorders such as depression, agoraphobia, eating disorders, and sexual dysfunction. The following warning summarizes this reality: "Sex-role stereotypes may be hazardous to your health" (Franks and Rothblum, 1983, p. 3).

Gove and Tudor (1973) concluded, on the basis of data gathered on differential rates of men's and women's hospital admission and outpatient treatment, that women experience higher levels of mental illness than men. They surmised that women's role prescriptions are key factors in determining rates of mental illness. Myrna Weissman and Gerald Klerman (1977) also discovered that women experienced depression twice as often as men. They proposed several hypotheses for this ratio: women's low social status, legal and economic discrimination against women, and internalization of role expectations that lead to learned helplessness (Klerman and Weissman, 1980). At least partial evidence for this hypothesis was provided by the finding that depression in middle-aged women is related to the endorsement of traditional feminine role behaviors (Tinsley, Sullivan-Guest, and McGuire, 1984). The interaction of gender role and life circumstance is also significant, as revealed by a study that found that housewives with liberal views about gender roles were more susceptible to depression and felt more restricted than housewives who endorsed traditional gender roles (Kingery,

1985). The higher rates of depression in women than men continue to be of significant concern to feminist psychologists, with a comprehensive review suggesting that women's depression should be seen within a biopsychosocial context that focuses on the interaction of gender stereotypes, life roles, reproductive events, poverty, and victimization (McGrath et al., 1990).

Liberal feminism has focused on destroying stereotypes about differences between men and women and providing men and women with a more level playing field. To support these efforts, feminist psychologists have explored the various ways in which stereotyped behavior is learned and reinforced, and how many so-called gender differences are based on myths.

ALTERNATIVES TO GENDER-BIASED THEORIES

Feminist mental health practitioners have proposed a wide range of gender-fair theories and approaches designed to overcome the biases of past mental health practices. The results of these efforts and the impact of liberal feminism on feminist therapy can be seen in the following areas: (1) nonsexist therapy as defined by Edna Rawlings and Diane Carter (1977), (2) androgyny therapy, (3) gender role analysis, (4) feminist humanistic therapy, (5) feminist cognitive-behavioral interventions and assertiveness training, (6) feminist family therapy, (7) feminist career counseling, and (8) the application of liberal feminist concepts to increase awareness of men's restrictive socialization. Each of these techniques and approaches emerged from efforts to reform practices within the academic or psychotherapy community and each application carried with it the endorsement of a professional community of psychotherapists or academics. The next section will describe these practices and their relationship to liberal feminism. I will also identify criticisms of some of these applications as voiced by more radically oriented feminists.

Nonsexist Therapy

The early writings on feminist therapy differentiated between two categories of therapy: nonsexist therapy and feminist therapy

(Marecek and Kravetz, 1977; Rawlings and Carter, 1977). Although the former approach was not labeled as explicitly feminist, it is based on assumptions embedded in liberal feminist thought. Thus, it can be appropriately labeled as liberal feminist therapy because it is based on the ideals of gender fair treatment and efforts to ensure that men and women are accorded equal treatment in psychotherapy.

Edna Rawlings and Diane Carter (1977) identified six major assumptions on which nonsexist therapy is based: (1) the importance of therapist awareness of values; (2) a belief that there should be no prescribed gender role behaviors; (3) the assumption that gender role reversals are not pathological, but that it is "fortunate" (p. 52) when two people can adopt nontraditional behavioral styles that give each satisfaction in a relationship; (4) the notion that marriage is not a better outcome of counseling for a female than a male; (5) the expectation that women should be as autonomous and assertive as men and men should be as expressive and tender as females; and (6) the rejection of theories of gender based on anatomical differences. Nonsexist therapists attempt to create a bias-free environment in which both men and women are afforded equal opportunities to define and choose personally relevant goals. In contrast to more radical feminist views, none of these tenets question the legitimacy of accepted cultural norms, traditions, or institutions.

The liberal feminist therapist works primarily within existing mental health systems in order to create the conditions that allow for equality of treatment. Gender differences are minimized, and the individual man or woman is viewed as capable of autonomy and self-determination. Deviations from prescribed gender roles are seen as normal, and the therapist conveys that a wide range of behaviors are available to both men and women. Although the nonsexist or liberal feminist therapist encourages clients to develop an understanding of gender role socialization and the impact of social forces on personal problems, the chosen direction and focus of the client is always of paramount importance. The therapist wants each client to gain full awareness of her or his options, and trusts the client's ability to make personally relevant choices. The therapist does not assume that certain outcomes, such as economic autonomy, are better than others, but believes that men and women will choose a variety of lifestyle, family, and economic options, and that whatever "works" for the individual constitutes an appropriate goal. The therapist also believes that the client's individual characteristics, such as ability, background, political identification, and traditionalism/nontraditionalism, will influence the extent to which she or he pursues specific alternatives.

Androgyny Therapy

One of the major catalysts associated with the emergence of feminist therapy was the recognition that mental health practitioners held a double standard of mental health for men and women. As information about sex bias in mental health professions emerged (see the first section of this chapter for more detail), studies heralded the "promise" of androgyny, or the combination of masculine and feminine characteristics within the person, as a new model of mental health (Bem, 1976). A "plethora" (Kaplan, 1979a, p. 221) of studies focused on defining androgyny and its characteristics, identifying androgynous individuals, creating methods of measuring this construct, and demonstrating its relationship to mental health (Cook, 1985). Lucia Gilbert (1981) suggested that practitioners who adopted a personal value system based on androgyny would be less likely to view healthy men and women differently, thus counteracting the double standard of mental health that was demonstrated in a variety of studies (Sherman, 1980). Second, Alexandra Kaplan (1976) noted that the model of androgyny would help the individual woman "broaden her sense of what is appropriate and acceptable for her, enlarging the scope of her self-definition" (p. 355).
Sandra Bem (1976) also noted the following:

> [T]he major purpose of my research has always been a political one: to help free the human personality from the restricting prison of sex-role stereotyping and to develop a conception of mental health that is free from culturally imposed definitions of masculinity and femininity. (p. 59)

Each of these viewpoints is consistent with the primary goal of liberal feminism: to free the individual person from negative conditioning so that she or he can achieve important personal goals. Joy Kenworthy (1979) also noted that androgyny would provide both men and women with greater opportunities for self-actualization and self-realization, two important goals of liberal feminism. Consistent with the liberal feminist viewpoint that differences between men and women are minimal, Sandra Bem concluded her 1976 article with three prescriptions: "Let sexual preference be ignored; Let sex roles be abolished; and Let gender move from figure to ground" (p. 61).

As the concept of androgyny gained attention and acceptance in the psychological community, questions about its definition emerged. Mary Ann Sedney (1989) noted that three major conceptualizations of androgyny existed. The first approach focuses on the *copresence* of traits traditionally associated with masculinity and femininity within a single person. The stereotypes of masculinity and femininity are not altered, but the person is sometimes expressive and sometimes instrumental depending on the demands of the situation. The *integration* approach emphasizes the mixing of feminine and masculine qualities within a single behavior so that, for example, assertiveness is combined with warmth and compassion. The final approach involves *transcendence* of traditional roles; the attributes that a person incorporates within his or her personality are not defined as masculine or feminine. The achievement of gender role transcendence involves the negotiation of several developmental stages. The first stage involves seeing gender according to polarized roles; a dualistic second stage entails combining "masculine" and "feminine" characteristics in a manner that resembles the copresence approach to androgyny; and the third stage involves creating self-definitions that incorporate instrumental and expressive traits in personally relevant ways. Although early approaches to androgyny have frequently been criticized (e.g., Lott, 1981, 1990; Morawski, 1987, 1990), the goal of integrating instrumental and expressive characteristics apart from gender role stereotypes remains an important principle for most feminist therapists (see Brown and Brodsky, 1992).

Consistent with the initial optimism about and research productivity that are typical when a new construct is introduced within psychology (Mednick, 1989; Sedney, 1989), questions about and criticisms of androgyny eventually emerged. Alexandra Kaplan (1979a) noted that "androgyny has rightly earned its place in the sun, and we can now afford to give it the more careful scrutiny that this clearer vision provides" (p. 222). Susan Vogel (1979) noted that although androgyny provided the possibility for greater behavioral flexibility and less rigid gender roles, an androgynous score is not "an automatic stamp of psychological health" (p. 255), nor will it "immediately undo the social inequities of sexism" (p. 256). Later research on androgyny noted that although the masculinity component of androgyny is related to mental health in both men and women, the femininity component is not associated with mental health. This finding suggested that an androcentric model of mental health is so firmly embedded within the culture that the individual adoption of androgyny will not result in significant political or social change. Furthermore, androgyny is not consistently related to self-esteem or the behaviors of competence, flexibility, and adaptability (Morawski, 1987).

Bernice Lott (1981) suggested that androgyny has the potential for perpetuating stereotypes and polarized notions about gender by obscuring "the essential humanness of the behaviors" (p. 172) that are labeled as masculine and feminine within our culture. In other words, the operational definitions of androgyny rely on the same gender role stereotypes that its proponents were attempting to replace (Kenworthy, 1979). Thus, the concept of androgyny suggests a false dichotomy between connectedness and autonomy, two sets of traits that already coexist at some level in all humans. Furthermore, approaches that define androgyny as a high endorsement of both masculinity and femininity create a prescription that one must incorporate twice the number of characteristics within the personality than is required by traditional role expectations. This represents an unrealistic or unattainable goal for many people and does not recognize the diversity of individuals. Joy Kenworthy (1979) noted that stereotypes are firmly embedded within the society and that androgyny does not represent "a key to social recognition" (p. 237). Instead, androgynous individuals might be labeled as "revolutionary, rebellious, or simply obnoxious" (p. 236).

Liberal feminism is founded on the belief that rationality is central to personal achievement and it is privileged over more emotional, intuitive aspects of human experience. It does not provide a critique of the major values that permeate society. Morawski (1987) indicated that androgyny research represents a liberal feminist agenda that presumes that many "differences" between men and women are superficial and that the reduction of these imposed differences will lead to equal and gender-neutral treatment. Androgyny researchers did not consider to extent to which so-called gender-neutral ideals are contaminated by notions of masculinity or "the appropriate ingredients for successful action in a male-centered world" (Morawski, 1987, p. 57). Although the androgyny model proposed adding previously devalued feminine characteristics to this new model of mental health, the success of women was predicated on their adoption of traditional values associated with masculinity.

Consistent with criticisms of liberal feminist theory, early concepts and research on androgyny did not question or critically analyze the nature of masculine and feminine values, nor did they consider the context in which these values arose and are sustained (Morawski, 1987). They presumed that "androgynous individuals seem to operate (effortlessly) in a social vacuum where expectations for gender-related behavior or gender-based constraints on choice of action are noticeably absent" (Morawski, 1987, p. 55). Researchers and therapists failed to consider the differential power structures, contexts in which men and women live, as well as the differential rewards and consequences that are accorded to men and women. Jill Morawski (1987) concluded that in their efforts to increase women's options, feminist psychologists had adopted male language, symbols, and research styles, but that women had not realized any real increase in power.

In her later assessment of androgyny theory, Sandra Bem (1993b) articulated a more comprehensive perspective and concluded that the original conceptualizations of androgyny were "theorized at too private and too personal a level to be of any value politically. The elimination of gender inequality will require institutional change, not just personal change" (p. 123). In this more complex analysis of gender, Sandra Bem (1987) indicated that gender should not be considered primarily as a set of internal characteristics, but as a method by which a culture transmits stereotypes and encourages individuals to internalize gender-polarized visions of reality. Her alternative to androgyny, gender schema theory, describes how beliefs about gender become organized around the culture's stereotypes and how these cognitive structures are used by the individual to anticipate, perceive, encode, and interpret information according to the culture's polarized images of gender. These cognitive structures not only influence one's judgments about personal behavior but also one's perceptions of the behavior of others. Gender schemas are extremely powerful and forge "a cultural connection between sex and virtually every other aspect of human experience, including modes of dress, social roles, and even ways of expressing emotion and experiencing sexual desire" (Bem, 1993b, p. 192).

The concept of gender schemas moves beyond a liberal feminist perspective in several ways. First, it acknowledges the complexity and tenacity of gender stereotypes and notes how power structures perpetuate stereotypes. The biased lenses of individuals and institutions encourage selective attention, recall, and interpretation of men's and women's behaviors; these biases have a significant impact on women's ability to realize their full potential (Deaux and Major, 1987). Gender schema theory assumes that gender operates on multiple levels: as a set of personal attributes at the individual level, as a set of relational cues at the interpersonal level, and as a system of power relations at the social level (Unger and Crawford, 1996). Second, gender schema theory does not prescribe any particular combination of agency and communion as an ideal of mental health. It acknowledges the diversity of healthy human behavior and eschews the identification of expressive traits as "feminine" and instrumental traits as "masculine." Ideal mental health is associated with the organization of the personality around some combination of personally relevant characteristics other than masculinity or femininity. Cultural relativism schemas, sexism schemas, and individual differences schemas represent some of the cognitive structures that can help the person combat gender stereotypes (Bem, 1983). Thus, gender schema theory presents a clearer understanding than androgyny of how context shapes and elicits behavior. It focuses less on the *content* of gender stereotypes and a prescription for mental health and more on the *process* of how gender stereotypes arise and are perpetuated despite individual change (Bem, 1987).

Assessing androgyny and counseling, Ellen Cook (1985) suggested that therapists and counselors "may find androgyny to be a useful label for what clients are moving *away* from, but describing what clients are moving *toward* requires considerably more specificity" (p. 569). With more complex understandings of gender, it is now possible to use concepts of gender role schemas for helping clients understand *how* stereotypes are transmitted, and *why* they are so tenacious. Gender role schemas, then, can be incorporated into a power or social analysis of behavior. This type of analysis can help clients understand the complexities of change and to minimize self-blame when others respond negatively to new choices they initiate.

Gender Role Analysis

Ellyn Kaschak (1981) noted that although feminist therapists utilize diverse theories to inform their work, a hallmark of all feminist therapy is gender role analysis. As a basic assessment tool, gender role analysis involves exploring and understanding the impact of gender on psychological well-being or distress and utilizing this information to make decisions about what gender role behaviors one wishes to enact. Gender role analysis is highly compatible with liberal feminist perspectives that focus on the importance of understanding gender role socialization. When utilized by radical or socialist feminist therapists, it is also likely to be used in conjunction with techniques that focus on how social power both influences and limits freedom of choice.

Gender role analysis represents a cooperative and phenomenological approach for exploring personal meanings attached to gender-related behaviors. It also involves exploring the costs and benefits of gender-related behaviors and engaging in decision making about future behaviors that the client wishes to explore. Laura Brown (1986, 1990a) indicated that gender role analysis should include: (1) the exploration of gender meanings in light of family values, the client's life stage, cultural background, and current environment; (2) discussion of the rewards and penalties for gender role conformity or noncompliance in the past and the present; (3) discussion of how the client-therapist relationship mirrors these issues or provides insight about the client's gender roles; and (4) exploration of the client's history related to victimization. Inquiries about potential victimization in the client's past, including interpersonal violence, sexual harassment, sexual assault, and sexual molestation, are likely to influence the client's current gender roles and represent an important component of gender role analysis.

If gender role analysis is conducted in a sensitive manner, the client develops an empathic rather than self-blaming attitude toward herself or himself because the therapist and client explore not only how traditional roles restrict the client in the present but also how these roles were learned and reinforced in the past. The therapist and client explore how traditional gender behaviors were transmitted, how they may have served a functional role within earlier contexts, and how they influence the difficulties the client encounters in making changes in behavior patterns. The therapist-client dyad also clarifies ways in which traditional coping methods have become less successful over time and contribute to the person's distress as she or he attempts to meet life tasks that require a wider range of skills (Greenspan, 1983).

Judith Worell and Pam Remer (1992) constructed a gender role analysis exercise with concrete suggestions for restructuring confining gender role patterns. During the restructuring stage, they suggest that individuals should do the following: (1) identify childhood messages that still influence the individual and the specific sources of those messages, (2) clarify the current ways in which these behaviors are reinforced or punished, and (3) consider the costs and benefits of gender role rules, including the costs and benefits of gender rules for society; this process should be followed by (4) deciding whether or not the client desires to make changes, and (5) creating new personal messages that are less restrictive and more empowering. The final facet of gender role analysis focuses on developing strategies for practicing new behavioral changes.

Humanistic Therapy

Person-Centered Therapy

Early feminist psychotherapists viewed humanistic psychology as consistent with their efforts because of the following specific features: (1) its emphasis on each person's uniqueness, human potential, and capacity for autonomy and self-directedness; (2) the assumption that the phenomenological world of the individual should be trusted and viewed as the most important frame of reference; (3) its emphasis on the capacity of individuals to be self-actualizing, self-determining, and capable of making productive choices for their own lives; and (4) the belief that symptoms are not signs of pathology but represent growing pains, and that painful feelings and behaviors can be redirected and refocused in positive directions. Furthermore, the core conditions of empathy, congruence, and unconditional positive regard proposed by Carl Rogers (1951, 1961) provide the foundation for an egalitarian relationship and for trusting the client as her own best expert (Lerman, 1992; Waterhouse, 1993).

Susan Sturdivant's (1980) discussion of a feminist therapy noted that in order to integrate feminism with humanism, one major question needed to be resolved: If humans have the capacity for autonomy and self-actualization, why have women been thwarted in their efforts to achieve this goal? She proposed that feminist humanism, the modification of traditional humanism, views women "as potentially competent and independent and as intellectually and morally equal to men; in other words, as autonomous and fully human" (p. 89). Feminist humanistic counselors "expose the myths about women for what they are" (p. 89) and pave the way for new and accurate images of women's potential. This conclusion is consistent with a liberal feminist viewpoint that rational argument and data will correct misinformation about women and pave the way for egalitarian relationships.

In one of the earliest descriptions of feminist therapy, Hannah Lerman (1976) indicated that feminist therapy is "an outgrowth of eclectic humanistic thought and represents a logical extension of humanistic thinking into the awareness of sex-role issues" (p. 378). Although she noted that feminist therapists come from various theoretical persuasions, she also stated: "I don't think I have met a feminist therapist, however, who has not been influenced by humanistic principles" (p. 378). In her later evaluation of this position, Hannah Lerman (1992) indicated that early feminist therapists borrowed heavily from the concepts of humanistic therapy because its limited number and relatively straightforward concepts did not contain overtly sexist features. Feminist therapists did not need to subtract or eliminate negative aspects of humanism in order to make it viable, but merely needed to add elements to the theory so that women would be included as a focal point. Thus, feminist therapists acted similarly to other humanistic psychotherapists, with the exception that they focused primarily on the needs and issues of women (Lerman, 1992).

In her early statement on feminist therapy, Hannah Lerman (1976) identified three major philosophical aspects of a feminist perspective: (1) the therapist views the client as competent and knowledgeable about her experience; (2) the therapist helps the client acknowledge personal power; and (3) the personal is political. The first two principles were highly consistent with the feminist modifications of person-entered therapy. However, in contrast to the notion that the personal is political, person-centered theory does not acknowledge the ways in which the external world influences the private self. In contrast to the nondirective approach of person-centered therapists, feminist therapists utilize self-disclosure and believe that it is important to share information with clients about environmental factors that may influence their choices.

As feminist therapists assisted clients in separating the internal from the external aspects of their problems, they increasingly recognized the limitations of a psychology that proposed that the only perspective of value is a subjective, internal, phenomenological view. Ruth Waterhouse (1993) criticized Carl Rogers for overemphasizing the American tradition of "vigorous self reliance" (p. 58) and stated that person-centered therapy lacks "a sensitivity to people's 'real suffering' and an understanding that personal troubles come not only from within the self, but also from the real world" (p. 58). Furthermore, person-centered therapy's emphasis on the uniqueness of each person devalues one's ability to identify commonalities between women and thus, limits the basis on which collective action on behalf of women can be conducted. Finally, the emphasis of person-centered therapy on self-growth and personal change may be potentially disempowering if it leads the client to blame herself for factors outside of herself such as racism, sexism, or violence. In sum, "the woman must change her 'self' for a society that basically remains the same. Furthermore, she must do this ultimately *by* and *for* herself" (Waterhouse, 1993, p. 63).

If one operates strictly from a liberal feminist worldview, humanistic liberal feminism may seem relatively complete. However, many feminist therapists note its inadequacy for connecting personal themes with the political implications of private concerns. The person-centered approach provides counselors with powerful relational tools that are necessary but not sufficient for feminist therapy. Optimism about the power of the individual to effect personal change must be matched with efforts to address the external oppression that may limit a person's efforts to reach his or her potential.

Gestalt Therapy

Gestalt therapy emphasizes the importance of self-awareness and self-responsibility and shares many of the same strengths and limitations of person-entered therapy. From the perspective of Gestalt therapy, problems in living occur when an individual is absorbed in what "might be" instead of "what is." The unhealthy person plays out a fantasy life, is hedged in by stereotypical behaviors and attitudes, and throws roadblocks in his or her own path, leaving little room for realizing personal potential (Polster, 1974). In contrast, healthy behavior is grounded in the subjective and sensory awareness of one's total experience, which leads to the ability to absorb, rather than explain or interpret, the present and always changing reality. The fully functioning person is self-supporting and autonomous. Role playing and the safety of routine are rejected, as stated by the following tenet: "Accept no should or ought other than your own" (Naranjo, 1970). The healthy person is relaxed, spontaneous, present-oriented, creative, productive, and joyful while also capable of freely experiencing hurt and pain. This person makes choices, takes risks, and assumes responsibility for the results of personal decisions.

Helen Collier (1982) indicated that women often enter psychotherapy with a sense of powerlessness, lack of trust in self-direction, and permeable "I" boundaries. They may adhere to numerous "shoulds" relevant to appropriate gender behavior, fail to nurture themselves, and have difficulty communicating suppressed emotions. Gestalt therapy provides useful tools for addressing these issues, especially as they pertain to the following: (1) expanding women's self-definitions and perceptions of personal power, (2) developing the courage to express strong emotion, and (3) expanding behavioral alternatives (Enns, 1987).

A societal injunction experienced by many women is that they should find their greatest satisfaction and happiness by living for and through others. As women learn to adapt to others, they may have difficulty distinguishing personal desires and wants as separate and distinct from those of others. As a result, they often experience symptoms of dependence, submission, and learned helplessness (Siegel, 1983). Through Gestalt techniques, women often become more aware of their unacknowledged personal power. Women can learn to take greater responsibility for their communication patterns and feelings by using the pronoun "I" rather than "we," "it," and "they." Instead of using soft language and qualifiers (e.g., "I guess" and "maybe"), they learn to use more powerful and assertive language. When women learn to change verbs, such as "need" to "want" and "should" to "choose," they become more aware of inner feelings and choices and experience greater courage to take risks.

Second, Gestalt therapy focuses on the importance of recognizing a full range of human emotions, gives women permission to recognize and express reactions that they have previously discounted or repressed, and encourages women to use those feelings to motivate action. Anger is expressed directly: "I'm angry" rather than "It makes me angry." Through techniques such as the "empty chair" that are designed to complete unfinished business, women can safely express feelings of disappointment, anger, or guilt to significant people in their past or present (Passons, 1975; Polster, 1974). People who have placed restrictions of the client's life can also be confronted through imaginary dialogue. Through the use of nonverbal exercises, women focus on areas of body tension and learn how strong feelings may be internalized in the form of physical constriction. Women learn "response-ability" and begin to experience a full range of emotions (Enns, 1987).

Gestalt techniques are also useful for helping women increase the number and quality of their choices. Through guided fantasy, the empty chair, and many verbal techniques, women learn to accept and integrate polarities. They learn that strength can be integrated with sensitivity, kindness with assertiveness, and dependence with independence. By trying new behaviors, women realize that few behaviors and emotions are unavailable to them. They discover the validity of their emotions and become more accepting of their own goals and desires (Brien and Sheldon, 1977; Collier, 1982; Polster, 1974).

Despite the usefulness of Gestalt tools for increasing one's sense of self as a powerful person, Gestalt therapy also poses problems for feminist therapists. Similar to person-centered therapy, Gestalt therapy has often been used to magnify the belief that people are masters of their own fates and to minimize or ignore the role of external realities and oppression on people's lives. There are many events over which clients have little control, no matter how aware and self-responsible they become (Mander and Rush, 1974). The Gestalt focus on taking responsibility for personal conduct may increase women's feelings of self-blame, guilt, and inadequacy, thus minimizing or discounting the toxic nature of oppressive social conditions. Furthermore, the identification of gender bias or socio-political factors that influence women's lives is likely to be perceived from a traditional Gestalt perspective as rationalizing, making excuses, projecting personal inadequacy on the external world, or evading responsibility (Mander and Rush, 1974). Gender role analysis, a hallmark of feminist therapy, may be viewed from a traditional Gestalt perspective as intellectualization or detachment from one's personal experiences or emotions. From a feminist perspective, however, the recognition of external constrictions completes women's awareness and releases them from self-deprecation. This examination of external factors does not encourage women to avoid responsibility by blaming boredom or pain on others, but frees them to engage in realistic action (Rawlings and Carter, 1977).

A second problem is that Gestalt therapy emphasizes the importance of personal autonomy and gives inadequate attention to the interrelatedness and interdependence of all persons. Many women seek goals other than autonomy, such as the ability to participate in relationships with others while also pursuing self-development. Unfortunately, women often have difficulty integrating autonomy and self-reliance with empathy and sensitivity because the larger society tends to view these strengths as mutually exclusive. Therapists who utilize Gestalt tools must also be aware that the consequences of autonomy are different for women than men. Autonomy and assertion in women may not be met with acceptance but with skepticism and rejection (Fodor and Rothblum, 1984).

The tools of Gestalt therapy are relatively compatible with liberal feminism, especially as they relate to emphasizing the importance of personal awareness and choice. Like person-centered therapy, this model does not adequately addresses environmental factors that limit the free choice of individuals. Feminist therapists who utilize Gestalt techniques must find ways to balance attention to internal choices with the realities of the sociocultural world in which the client and therapist live.

Cognitive Behavior Therapy and Assertiveness Training

During the early years of feminist therapy, assertiveness training and cognitive-behavioral interventions were widely adopted tools for helping clients experience their personal power and act on their own behalf (Blechman, 1980). Assertiveness was viewed as a potentially powerful resocialization tool for helping women become aware of their interpersonal rights, alter negative self-beliefs, transcend gender stereotypes, and use direct forms of power to influence their environments (Jakubowski, 1977; Moore, 1981). Feminist therapists recognized that women had historically been encouraged to practice "underground power" and that assertiveness training would allow them to reframe and redirect this power in productive ways. Assertiveness training was seen as a powerful method for helping women overcome "deficits in interpersonal functioning" (Moore, 1981, p. 403) and to assist women in expressing personal attitudes, reducing anxiety and fear about taking risks, creating positive beliefs about themselves and others, and developing new behavior patterns. The assumption underlying assertiveness training programs is that if women are educated about their interpersonal rights and learn to overcome internalized barriers to change, they will effectively combat negative socialization and meet their needs in direct ways.

In one of the earliest studies designed to explore the efficacy of assertiveness training, Janet Wolfe and Iris Fodor (1975) hypothesized that the combination of assertiveness training and rational emotive therapy concepts would help women combat harmful "shoulds" and irrational beliefs that are embedded in gender role stereotypes, such as the following ideas:

1. One should be loved by everyone.
2. Others' needs are more important than one's own.
3. It is easier to avoid rather than face difficulties.
4. Women need a strong person on which to rely.
5. Women have no control over their emotions.

Through "depropagandization," women learn to identify irrational beliefs and the ways in which they are reinforced, test these beliefs against objective reality, and replace them with more adaptive beliefs and behaviors (Wolfe and Fodor, 1975).

A variety of studies compared the outcomes of consciousness-raising groups with those that included both a consciousness-raising and a skills component, such as assertiveness training or communication skills training (e.g., Ballou, Reuter, and Dinero, 1979; Gulanick, Howard, and Moreland, 1979; Wolfe and Fodor, 1977). One study found that members of a communication skills group showed more progress toward reaching the four goals of enhancing communication, increasing awareness of women's issues, establishing a supportive environment, and learning behavioral skills than did a consciousness-raising group or a group that combined attention to women's issues (consciousness-raising) with communication training. Members of the combination group showed some progress in attaining communication skills and increasing behavioral goals (Follingstad, Robinson, and Pugh, 1977). Another study concluded that members of a group that integrated CR and assertiveness training developed more assertive behaviors and masculine behaviors related to androgyny than did members of a discussion-only consciousness-raising group (Wolfe and Fodor, 1977). A third study, which compared the outcomes of a modeling-rehearsal group, modeling-rehearsal-cognitive intervention group, consciousness-raising group, and control group, found that participants in both modeling groups displayed greater gains in assertiveness than did consciousness-raising and control group members. A final study indicated that members of both traditional and feminist assertiveness training groups showed increases in self-esteem, satisfaction, and assertiveness, but that feminist members of both types of groups demonstrated more commitment and greater gains in assertiveness than did nonfeminist members (Ellis and Nichols, 1979). In summary, these studies suggest that consciousness-raising groups are effective tools for changing attitudes and building personal self-esteem, but that behavioral change is more likely to occur in groups that emphasize a skills component.

Many concepts of cognitive-behavior therapy appear ideally suited to feminist therapy, including the assumptions that (1) problematic behavior is learned and can be modified; (2) the therapist plays a consulting role rather than an expert role; and (3) clients should be encouraged to establish their own goals and take charge of their own lives. Furthermore, cognitive-behavioral tools are based on an optimistic view about change (Fodor, 1988). Many cognitive-behavioral tools, such as modeling, contracting, functional analysis, self-monitoring, and reinforcement, stress inoculation, assertiveness training, and cognitive restructuring, can be integrated in a straightforward manner with a major goal of feminist psychotherapy, which is to increase women's confidence and repertoire of skills for pursuing their goals (Worell and Remer, 1992). Cognitive-behavioral techniques are consistent with liberal feminist assumptions that irrational beliefs and prejudices can be changed through nonsexist policies, the rational consideration of issues, and individual opportunities for growth. Cognitive-behavioral tools pose concrete methods to help individuals "transcend the constraints of their own prior socialization experience and to become the agents of their own change" (Fodor, 1988, p. 96).

After a period of initial optimism, feminist therapists raised questions about the efficacy of cognitive-behavioral interventions. First, appropriate assertive behavior may be misperceived because it is inconsistent with expectations of how women *should* behave. Laura Solomon and Esther Rothblum (1985) noted that "there are sometimes harsh contingencies in the natural environment for women behaving in nontraditional ways" (p. 318). Several studies supported this conclusion. Research participants who viewed videotapes of both nonassertive and assertive male and female models rated assertive models as more skilled but also less likable than nonassertive models. In addition to this general outcome, women who engaged in assertive behavior were rated in more negative ways than men who engaged in identical behavior. Assertive women were judged to be less warm, pleasant, likable, open-minded, good-natured, considerate, and friendly than nonassertive men and women and assertive men (Kelly et al., 1980). In a study that compared reactions to high-assertive, medium-assertive, and low-assertive men and women, men were rated as more likable and intelligent than women across all conditions. Although medium-assertive models were generally preferred over high and low assertive models, highly assertive women were most likely to be rated negatively with respect to their likability and intelligence (Lao et al., 1975). A third study demonstrated that women who behave assertively experience increases in self-respect, but also express concern about potential negative reactions of others, such as being discounted, rejected, and ignored (Fiedler and Beach, 1978). Although other studies have not found similar prejudices toward women (e.g., Kern, 1982; Linehan and Seifert, 1983; Solomon et al., 1983), the results of these studies suggest that women's assertiveness does result in negative consequences on some occasions. Amy Gervasio and Mary Crawford (1989) argued that much of the evidence for positive results of women's assertion has been based on research of inconsequential and impersonal situations that lacked ecological validity and ignored race, class, and status variables. The adage that "he's aggressive, she's pushy; he's firm, she's stubborn; he exercises his authority, she's tyrannical" (Muehlenhard, 1983, p. 163) appears to accurately reflect social attitudes in at least some circumstances.

The results of research findings suggest that feminist therapists need to help clients deal with the possibility of "intermittent success" of individual assertiveness efforts (Solomon and Rothblum, 1985, p. 318). Another option is to encourage women to develop "assertion plus empathy" responses, which entails stating one's rights and opinions while also acting in friendly ways and acknowledging the needs of others (Muehlenhard, 1983; Solomon and Rothblum, 1985). One study found that "assertion plus empathy" statements were viewed as kinder and more satisfying to recipients while also being as effective as assertion-only responses (Solomon et al., 1983; Woolfolk and Dever, 1979). Although these combined messages may help others in the environment accept women's authority, requests, and criticisms, it is disappointing that women may need to exert this extra effort while men are not expected to develop this additional skill. Although the less-than-consistent positive responses to women's assertion may be discouraging, Laura Solomon and Esther Rothblum (1985) argued that assertiveness helps women expect that responses to their requests will be positive and helps them deal with negative responses. This thinking is supported by a study that demonstrated that assertive individuals expect more positive responses from others such as admiration, respect, and understanding (Eisler, Frederiksen, and Peterson, 1978).

A second criticism is that cognitive-behavioral approaches do not critically examine androcentric or culturally normative assumptions about mental health that value rationality over emotion (Kantrowitz and Ballou, 1992). The potential pitfalls of traditional assertiveness training for women include its use of an overly narrow definition of "correct" assertive responses, the assumption that assertiveness will naturally lead to successful interpersonal interactions, the promotion of techniques that encourage traditional power tactics, and the definition of human "rights" as existing apart from an understanding of complex gender role injunctions (Stere, 1985). The greater value placed on instrumental, rational problem-solving skills implies that women must eschew and devalue traditional relational skills, or merely use these relational skills to increase the likelihood that their assertive responses will be successful. Prescriptions for assertive speech closely resemble positive stereotypes of masculine behavior; thus, assertiveness training promotes "masculine stereotypes as implicit norms" (Gervasio and Crawford, 1989, p. 9) and suggests that individualism is more important than interdependence. It is interesting to note that although the popular and academic literature has focused extensively on the problems of passivity and submissiveness, it has paid less attention to research on the negative mental health consequences associated with exaggerations of male stereotypes, such as emotional inexpressiveness and aggression (Gervasio and Crawford, 1989). Although assertiveness training was originally seen as a way of combating concepts of mental health that were gender-biased, the very "neutral" methods of assertiveness also reinforce a narrowly focused concept of mental health that is linked to dominant cultural values (Fodor, 1985).

When the cultural biases underlying assertiveness training are not explicitly identified, women are encouraged to engage in skill training to overcome so-called deficits of socialization rather than recognize that assertive skills should be understood primarily as important survival skills in a patriarchal world. Behavioral or skills training may encourage adherence to cultural stereotypes rather than transcendence of stereotypes. Instead of learning to value and build on strengths, individuals may feel deficient because of their lack of culturally valued skills. For example, a woman who displays traditional behaviors, who expresses her own wishes and desires with hesitancy, and defines herself on the basis of her nurturing roles may learn to devalue herself further after hearing feedback about what she lacks. Contrary to the stated goals of assertiveness training, she may seek change because of the negative evaluation of others. She may feel obligated to change to become a better and more productive mother, wife, sex partner, or superwoman. Thus, assertiveness training can potentially become "accommodation training" that encourages adjustment to a culture that defines health according to the "shoulds" of personal success and achievement (Fodor, 1988). Transcendence of cultural mandates occurs only if women learn to value current skills, consider a full range of behaviors and their consequences for them, and use skills training programs to enhance their existing strengths.

A third issue is that cognitive-behavioral interventions focus primarily on individual change. Although the concept of reciprocal determinism (Bandura, 1989), a core assumption of most cognitive-behavioral approaches, is predicated on the notion that individual behaviors are only "partly self-determined" (Bandura, 1989, p. 1175), cognitive-behavioral intervention tools do not suggest methods to address larger environmental issues that limit personal choice (Kantrowitz and Ballou, 1992). In her assessment of assertiveness training, Iris Fodor (1988) stated that narrowly defined programs place the burden of change on individuals and imply that through individual change alone, one can eliminate poor parenting, negative conditioning, sexist socialization, and unjust circumstances. The unidimensional focus on skills neglects analysis of the risks and realities present in the social environment, such as the realities that women are more frequently sexually harassed, interrupted in conversation, and addressed with inappropriate forms of familiarity than are men. Poverty and minority status further complicate many women's situations, situations that cannot be easily erased or altered through personal change alone. Individual change must be connected to institutional change and the transformation of societal reinforcement systems (Fodor, 1985). The assumptions of liberal feminism may be inadequate for dealing with some of these issues.

Feminists have proposed a variety of ways in which cognitive-behavioral techniques can be modified in order to lend themselves to the goals of feminist therapy. First, "ecologically valid" (Gervasio and Crawford, 1989, p. 11) assertion training must communicate the benefits, costs, and risks of assertive communication and acknowledge that women and men experience different social contexts with different types of personal infringements and rewards. Second, potentially pathologizing labels such as *distortion* and *irrationality*, which frequently appear in cognitive-behavioral literature, should be relabeled because they often deny a client's view of reality (Worell and Remer, 1992). For example, a supposedly irrational belief that mitigates against assertion is as follows: "If I assert myself, others will be mad at me." Some beliefs that have been presumed to be irrational are based on women's memories of occasions when their assertive responses have been punished rather than rewarded. These realities can be too easily discounted as misperceptions when words such as "irrational" are used. Third, cognitive-behavioral techniques can be combined with techniques that explore the client's affective experiences (e.g., Gestalt therapy) in order to decrease the likelihood that rationality is overvalued and emotion is undervalued (Fodor, 1987). Fourth, consciousness-raising principles can be integrated with assertiveness concepts in order to more consistently connect political with personal change issues (e.g., Enns, 1992b) and to encourage women to become involved in social activism. Fifth, assertiveness training should be balanced with self-esteem training that emphasizes self-affirmation rather than assuming that training should focus on decreasing interpersonal deficits. Linda Stere (1985) proposed that self-esteem training would include four major components or goals including the following: (1) learning to validate personal feelings as valid and based on one's responses to something real; (2) developing the capacity to please oneself and engage in self-nurturing behavior; (3) identifying and developing strengths; and (4) developing realistic expectations and accepting shortcomings, as well as acknowledging that perfection is not necessary or desirable. Self-confidence and self-esteem training must be based on an understanding of the complex relationship between women's social status and personal esteem and attitudes. Such training must also encourage women to develop self-defined strengths that incorporate but also move beyond the restrictions of cognitive-behavioral assumptions (Enns, 1992b; Fodor, 1985; Sanford and Donovan, 1984; Stere, 1985).

Family Systems Therapy

As with each of the other approaches described in this chapter, the family systems therapies were not initially criticized by feminist therapists because these approaches were known for their neutral views on gender, their valuing of short-term and problem-solving approaches, their recognition of the social and family environments that shape behavior, and their refusal to use traditional diagnostic labels that blame individuals for systemic problems (Ault-Riché, 1986). Family systems therapies, with their emphasis on viewing problems in context instead of as anchored in internal personality deficiencies present useful tools to feminist therapists, especially therapists with liberal feminist views.

The impetus for a feminist perspective on marital and family therapy was provided in part by the awareness of the negative relationships between women's mental health and marital status. After reviewing a host of research studies regarding women's mental health and marital roles, Judith Avis (1985) concluded that women in traditional relationships are more dissatisfied; have less power in family decision making; and experience less personal autonomy, worse physical health, worse marital adjustment, and more negative communication than women in egalitarian relationships. Other studies have revealed that whereas employed husbands experience the highest levels of psychological well-being, full-time homemakers experience the lowest levels of well-being, and employed married women experience intermediate levels of adjustment (Steil and Turetsky, 1987). A review of twenty-two studies concluded that of the demographic variables investigated—marital status, education, income, and employment—marital status was most strikingly related to women's mental health problems. In no study were single women shown to be more likely to experience mental illness than single men (Goldman and Ravid, 1980). Married women in unhappy marriages are especially vulnerable to depression. One study found that nearly half of women in unhappy marriages were depressed, and that women are three times more likely than men to be depressed in these contexts (Weissman, 1987). Each of these findings suggest that a feminist approach to marital and family therapy is highly important.

In their discussion of the positive connections between family systems therapy and feminist therapy, Libow, Raskin, and Caust (1982) indicated that both systems and feminist therapists are "appreciators" of symptoms as growing pains that have a communicative, coping, or adaptive purpose. Symptoms are not signs of personal flaws that must be overhauled, cured, or removed. Both feminist and family systems therapists show commitment to helping individuals and families investigate creative, original ways of incorporating change into their lives and affirm the capacity of persons to choose and act on new and rewarding behavioral alternatives. Given the apparent compatibility of these perspectives, some authors maintain that a family systems orientation is preferable to an explicitly feminist approach for helping a traditional family become unstuck from stereotypical roles. It allows therapists to suggest changes to a family "without directly introducing ideas (such as oppression and feminism) that would create alarm or resistance in all or some of the members" (Libow, Raskin, and Caust, 1982, p. 10).

Critics of family systems therapy note, however, that family systems models virtually ignore the powerful impact of gender on family relationships. The purportedly gender-neutral family systems approaches can lead to the further reinforcement of traditional roles because family members remain unaware of the impact of traditional middle-class family values on their daily lives; thus, they remain unaware of alternatives that might be more satisfying (Hare-Mustin, 1978). In this next section, I will elaborate two major limitations of family systems theory: (1) its exclusive reliance on the notion of circular causality to conceptualize problems and (2) its inattention to systemic issues that permeate the larger society.

From a systems view, relationship problems represent a "mutually regulated dance between oppressor and oppressed, a dance maintained by the cyclical interaction sequences between the participants" (Libow, Raskin, and Caust, 1982, p. 8). Interpersonal sequences that result in relationship problems are explained in terms of circular causality, which defines each action and/or individual as influencing every other aspect of a system as a part of a complex, reciprocal process of reinforcement. No specific situation or person is considered the antecedent, cause, or effect of problematic interactions. Although this perspective appears to offer an "equal opportunity" approach to the family that may be useful for understanding many daily interactions, it does not adequately address the pain associated with issues such as family violence. Hoffman (1981), for example, described battering as a relational pattern between an overadequate woman and an underadequate man that serves a functional role in the maintenance of the family system. From a feminist perspective, violence and abusiveness cannot be explained merely as responses to problematic reciprocal interactions (Taggart, 1985). Unequal social power and gender role socialization must be seen as the source and cause of many of women's problems within the family. Studies estimate that women are the victims of aggressive and violent acts such as battering, incest, and rape in 30 percent to 50 percent of families (Carmen, Russo, and Miller, 1984; Rosewater, 1984). It is difficult to deny the role of gender and power relationships in family problems when faced with the reality of such statistics. When power differences are denied, the consequences of abuse are also minimized (Bograd, 1988).

A second major problem is that although family therapy approaches define most issues in gender-neutral terms, many basic terms are based on "prototypically male attributes and sometimes define them as standards of healthy family functioning" (Bograd, 1988, p. 122). Terms such as *hierarchy, complementarity, autonomy,* and *differentiation* are used to signify the degree of health within the family and tend to encourage role definitions along traditional lines (Avis, 1988; Enns, 1988; Goodrich et al., 1988; Walters et al., 1988). In contrast, terms such as *enmeshment, fusion,* and *symbiosis* are used to label overinvestment in relationships, and these terms can be used to pathologize women's relational qualities.

The "neutral concepts" of family systems therapy can also contribute to mother blaming. Although all family members are viewed as contributing to the family climate, women are often more actively involved in their children's lives than men, and they are often allotted more than their share of blame for family problems (Caplan, 1989). When women play counterstereotypical roles, their behavior is often seen in pejorative terms, and in such cases, family therapists often attempt to "restore" power to the father (Minuchin, 1984). Michele Bograd (1988) concluded that "many formulations draw on stereotypical, culture-bound ideals of men and women that, in very subtle ways, denigrate women and perpetuate traditional assumptions about male-female interactions" (p. 123).

A third problem is that family systems approaches typically focus on the nuclear family alone and imply that gender role stereotypes and the larger social context are disconnected from what the family thinks, says, and does. Family therapy typically proceeds with the view that once the system has been fully "therapized," women's issues will disappear. To assume, however, that family therapists have managed to exempt themselves from the influence of cultural and social values is "self-righteousness bordering on delusion" (Taggart, 1985, p. 122). The resistance of some family therapists to deal with the social milieu is epitomized by Salvadore Minuchin's (1974) assertion that family therapy:

> is not a tool for humanistic revolution. It is often the opposite: one of the family's tasks is to provide continuity with a society which a family therapist, in his own value system, may consider restrictive. But the field for social change is not family therapy, but politics. (pp. 25-26)

Lois Braverman (1988) proposed that problematic aspects of family systems therapies are associated with their underlying values and not specific techniques. The following principles represent some basic considerations for integrating feminism and family systems therapies that are consistent with liberal feminist theory. First, the feminist family therapist models behavior that is not constrained by gender stereotypes. In cooperation with the family, the feminist therapist also engages in an analysis of gender patterns. The gender analysis explores how gender stereotypes influence the allocation of power, rewards, and labor. During this process, the therapist must be especially sensitive to the ways in which women have limited access to economic and social resources and should attend to how women's socialization often encourages them to assume greater responsibility for family relationships and childbearing. Third, the therapist assists the family in examining how sexist thinking limits the options of individuals and prevents the redistribution of tasks and roles. The family therapist helps family members transcend restrictive gender roles, increase their behavioral options, and create greater reciprocity and symmetry between family members. Out of respect for the diverse choices that individuals make, the therapist affirms the roles that women have traditionally played, such as nurturing and caring for others, while also supporting women's choices to experience rewarding achievement roles in various work and social institutions. The therapist helps the family become aware of the full range of options available to them, but also respects their preferences for traditional or nontraditional ways of negotiating their roles.

In contrast to the ease of combining family therapy with liberal feminism, it is more difficult to integrate traditional family systems concepts with radical or socialist feminist thinking. Family systems thinking is not based on a critical or historical analysis of the family but typically represents middle-class views of the family. This pattern of family life has existed since the beginning of the industrial revolution when women's roles were increasingly attached to the private sphere of the family and men's roles were attached to public domains and wage-earning activities. Socialist and radical feminists indicate that the family is a major system that supports and perpetuates male domination and that it will be impossible to radically alter the family while still using family systems thinking. The nuclear family as defined by family systems theory "best suits the needs of men as a class, and that requires the personal self-sacrifice of women" (Bograd, 1988, p. 127). Rather than examining the potentially oppressive structure of the typical family, family systems therapy stabilizes the typical family. According to a classic radical feminist view, even feminist family therapists may unwittingly encourage women to adjust to fundamentally oppressive systems.

Egalitarian personal relationships are difficult to achieve within current social structures. After reviewing the literature on intimate relationships, Rhoda Unger and Mary Crawford (1996) concluded that egalitarian marriage between heterosexual partners is relatively uncommon and represents an ideal rather than reality in both single-earner and dual-career families. In contrast to the hopes of feminists, a study of 1,500 dual-career couples found that husbands did not devote any more time to housework than did men in other types of relationships (Berardo, Shehen, and Leslie, 1987). In her book titled *The Second Shift*, Arlie Hochschild (1989) estimated that employed women perform 75 percent of household tasks. Employed women work roughly 15 hours more per week in paid and unpaid employment than men, which translates into an extra month of 24-hour days each year. The private-public distinction between "men's" and "women's" work, which is associated with nuclear families in capitalistic societies, persists despite individual efforts to make changes in these areas.

Arlie Hochschild's (1989) in-depth study of middle-class couples found that the negotiation of household tasks is highly complex and frustrating. In order to help themselves cope with remaining inequalities, many couples create a family myth or "modest delusional system" that allows couples to minimize the hard realities of unequal work distribution. Within this system, men and women explain men's lower level of involvement in household tasks on the basis of his personality, lack of skills, or dislike of rigid schedules for housework. The myth of equality is also maintained through beliefs that the individual man contributes more to the household than most other men, or that the woman is more organized or compulsive about housework than the man. Women's lower sense of personal entitlement regarding what they should expect to receive in intimate relationships also contributes to their acceptance of unequal relationships (Major, 1993). Although these cognitive exercises help women cope with their larger burden at home, they perpetuate inequities in relationships. Due to these cognitive gymnastics, women in heterosexual relationships may often be unaware of the full toll that the combination of these work and household roles exact.

In contrast to research on heterosexual partners, research on lesbian couples reveals that they typically reject traditional roles, achieve more egalitarianism in relationships, believe that both partners should work for pay, and share more social/leisure interests (Blumstein and Schwartz, 1983; Caldwell and Peplau, 1984; Peplau et al., 1978; Peplau and Gordon, 1983). These findings suggests that lesbians have been successful at questioning traditional family structures and creating new social structures that have the potential to transform relationships. Given the tenacity of gender stereotypes, it is unlikely that men and women in heterosexual relationships will achieve greater relational equality through interventions at the nuclear family level alone. Individual efforts and family efforts to achieve egalitarianism will need to be matched with the type of social change efforts that are more typically recommended by radical and socialist feminists.

Feminism and Career Counseling

The phrase "career feminism" can be viewed as a synonym for liberal feminism (Ferree and Hess, 1985). Career feminists are concerned primarily with helping women achieve equality in the labor force by encouraging "first women" in nontraditional careers, fighting sexual harassment on the job, and increasing the proportion of women in well-paying jobs. Myra Ferree and Beth Hess (1985) stated that career feminism emphasizes "the need for individual women to take their lives into their own hands and dare to be what they can become, to fight back if men try to stop or limit them, and to help other women" (p. 42). The major tools that advance career feminism include the achievement of personal career goals and the use of mentoring, networking, and support networks to help achieve these goals. Feminist career counseling, then, is a logical extension of liberal feminism.

Research on women's career choices has resulted in the development of many psychological theories and models that explain how personal family, and cultural factors influence the career paths of women (e.g., Astin, 1985; Eccles, 1987; Farmer, 1985; Fassinger, 1985; Hackett and Betz, 1981). Feminist psychologists and sociologists have also explored issues that influence women's careers, such as sexual harassment (e.g., Betz and Fitzerald, 1987; Paludi, 1990a); dual-career issues (e.g., Gilbert, 1987b); and the "second shift," multiple roles, and maternal employment (e.g., Baruch, Biener, and Barnett, 1987; Silverstein, 1991; Weitzman, 1994). Linda Brooks and Linda Forrest (1994) concluded that "research on women's vocational behavior is clearly one of the most popular topics" (p. 127) within the career literature. Unfortunately, a limited number of sources describe the implications of this vast information base for feminist career counseling. Thus, feminist career counseling is still in its infancy.

Linda Brooks and Linda Forrest (1994) reviewed the career counseling literature on women and concluded that although many authors noted the negative impact of stereotypes and cultural prescriptions on women's careers, "many authors still conceptualized internal barriers as the primary source of women's career development problems" (p. 116). Furthermore, references to the "personal as political" have been virtually absent in the women's career counseling literature. Despite the often-repeated statement that career counseling should help clients overcome the impact of societal prescriptions, few methods for doing so have been suggested.

In an effort to correct these problems, Brooks and Forrest (1994) suggested several applications of feminist therapy to career counseling. Gender role analysis is especially useful for helping women gain awareness of the subtle ways in which social contexts influence personal aspirations. As a part of gender role analysis in career counseling, clients can be encouraged to identify family and social messages about careers, discuss the impact of encounters with women who have adopted and defied traditional career roles, and clarify the meaning of gender as it relates to career and the meaning of career success or failure as a woman or man. Exploration of such themes leads to increased awareness and the consideration of a wider range of career options. Fantasy exercises can also be used to help individuals imagine attractive career goals and to prepare for the potential conflicts that one might encounter in pursuing goals (Brooks and Forrest, 1994; Hackett and Lonborg, 1994).

Career feminists have viewed mentors and role models as central to women's success. The lack of role models and mentors may significantly affect women by limiting their perceptions of what options are available to them. Feminist career counseling, then, can focus on helping women identify appropriate mentors and role models. For example, Michele Paludi's (1990b) role model/mentor survey can be used to help women identify skills that they would like to develop through interaction with a mentor. These skills include the following: communication skills, interpersonal skills, political skills, organizational skills, job specific skills, and adaptive cognitive strategies.

Feminist interventions are also essential for helping women combat internalized limited expectations and potential fears about success. Research reveals that enrollment in math courses is a critical filter for many high-status jobs. Math self-efficacy is central to achievement in many technical-scientific areas (Betz, 1994; Hackett and Betz, 1981). In addition to individual counseling interventions, it is essential to educate young women about this reality, expose them to role models, and encourage participation in math and science activities designed to increase their self-efficacy (Betz and Fitzgerald, 1987; Sadker and Sadker, 1994). Research also reveals that as women move from high school to college, they tend to adopt less-challenging career options and spend significant time and energy on romantic relationships (Holland and Eisenhart, 1990). Exploration of career-relationship dilemmas may be especially central to helping women define rewarding futures and develop multiple role realism, which entails the recognition of the complexity of multiple roles and the necessity of careful planning for enacting career-relationship goals (Weitzman, 1994). Finally, an egalitarian relationship is especially critical to feminist career counseling because it teaches women to develop the skills and knowledge that are necessary to choose and pursue challenging career goals (Brooks and Forrest, 1994).

Louise Fitzgerald and James Rounds (1994) noted that although contextual variables and structural factors are some of the most powerful determinants of work adjustment, "the literature lacks any systematic explanation of the role of structural and cultural factors in shaping individuals' work-related behavior" (p. 337). These structural factors are multiple. Three examples follow. The null environment "neither encourages nor discourages individual—it simply ignores them" (p. 17). The consequence of the null environ-ment is that women have little opportunity to receive feedback about themselves as competent people, and thus, have few opportu-nities to develop images of themselves that sustain them through difficult times. Women are left at the mercy of the specific environ-mental forces that are present at any point in time. Second, the devaluation of women's performance is often an issue when women are employed in nontraditional fields in which they are the "wrong" sex or when evaluation criteria are ambiguous or unclear (Unger and Crawford, 1996). Third, roughly one-half of all women will be sexually harassed during their educational or work careers (Fitzger-ald, 1993). Feminist counseling skills that help women become aware of political and social structures that have shaped or limited their aspirations are of great importance. The exploration of exter-nal factors often decreases self-blame for experiences outside a woman's control. The counselor's self-disclosure and bibliotherapy (e.g., popular and current articles about sexual harassment and/or discrimination) may also increase clients' awareness of these exter-nal forces. In the future, it will be important for feminist therapists to pay increased awareness to the integration of interventions that explore personal aspirations and strengths with interventions that increase awareness of the barriers that women may face.

Counseling Men About Restrictive Gender Roles

The application of feminist therapy to men's concerns is useful for helping men overcome the impact of gender role strain and restrictive gender role socialization (Ganley, 1988; Good, Gilbert, and Scher, 1990). Feminist interventions are highly consistent with a new psychology of men that has developed over the past fifteen years, has been informed by feminist scholarship, and views tradi-tional masculinity as a "problematic construct" (Levant, 1996, p. 259; see also Levant and Pollack, 1995).

Arnold Kahn (1984) noted that the average man has historically held higher levels of reward, coercive, referent, expert, legitimate, and informational power than women. As women seek increasing levels of equality, men must learn to share some of the power to which they have historically felt entitled. Developing and practicing methods of sharing power is not easy and "it may be a vain hope to picture men suddenly denied this power stepping back quietly and saying they don't mind at all" (Kahn, 1984, p. 241). Jean Lipman-Blumen (1984) suggested that men often hold onto traditional forms of power in order to deal with living in an uncertain and anxiety-filled world in which everything seems to be changing. Men sometimes attempt to claim greater power in intimate relationships in order to support their need to have at least a modicum of control over their environments. Feminist therapists can be instrumental in helping men deal with fears of power loss and the advantages and benefits of working toward equality in work and intimate relationships. This may be difficult within a current social-political climate that has suggested that men have become the "real" victims of the social changes of the past several decades (e.g., Farrell, 1993).

Although men exhibit more overt forms of power than women, men also feel powerless and oppressed by the pressure to maintain "masculine" roles that have been prescribed through many aspects of men's socialization (Levant, 1996; O'Neil and Egan, 1993). Joseph Pleck (1984) and Lucia Gilbert (1987a) noted that in contrast to the beliefs of many people, men as well as women have dependency needs. They also have difficulty communicating these needs, and believe that women hold power to express these needs for men. More specifically, men often view women as holding the following: (1) masculine validating power, which involves women's ability to help men feel important and affirmed by responding to them in positive and supportive ways, and (2) expressive power, or the power to detect and communicate men's emotions for them (Pleck, 1984). As a first step in enhancing men's relational confidence, it is useful for feminist therapists to help men acknowledge and describe these feelings of vulnerability and build skills that increase feelings of relational competence.

Joseph Pleck (1995) indicated that men's gender role strain manifests itself in three major ways. First, discrepancy strain is the consequence of enacting an internalized traditional masculine ideal, which results in gender role conflict and gender role stress. Dysfunction strain focuses on the ways in which traditional masculinity results in physical/psychological problems and negative side effects in men and those who relate to men. Finally, trauma strain depicts the traumatic consequences of male socialization associated with the stifling of emotional expression, separation from mothers, and absence of fathers. Trauma strains are especially apparent in professional athletes, veterans, gay and bisexual men, and survivors of child sexual abuse.

James O'Neil (1981) described a variety of patterns of conflict that emerge out of men's rigid socialization including the following: (1) restrictive emotionality, or the use of "anger as a mask for other emotions" (Ganley, 1988, p. 195); (2) socialized control, or the need to have power over others in order to feel validated as a man; (3) homophobia, or the fear of being viewed as "feminine" and emotionally close to other men; (4) restrictive sexual and emotional expressiveness, which often appears through men's inability to experience closeness outside of traditional sexual scripts; (5) the obsession with success and achievement, which involves a preoccupation with work, status, and performance; and (6) health care problems related to the lack of attention to self and health care needs.

Men often experience significant psychological costs when they adopt nontraditional roles. Gender role conflicts that result from unrealistic and/or contradictory socialization messages exhibit themselves in several forms including internal conflict or the violation of others' rights. Gender role conflict has been associated with depression in college men (Good and Mintz, 1990), lower psychological well-being (Sharpe and Heppner, 1991), and physical strain that appears as physical illness or poor self-care (Stillson, O'Neil, and Owen, 1991). Furthermore, John Robertson and Louise Fitzgerald (1990) demonstrated that men who display nontraditional role behaviors may be evaluated more negatively by therapists than traditional males. Although society has given lip service to the importance of men's role changes, self-esteem and self-acceptance in male students and professionals are still related to traditional measures of masculinity. Thus, men who choose to ad_____ _i-tional role definitions must eng___ _____ t-ing and developing _____ n contrast, when wo_____ y be more obvious b_____ roles that they may ado_

The basic principles of liberal feminist therapy with men mirrors the central principles for feminist therapy with women. As with women, men experience a wide range of life experiences and lifestyles, and some men hold significantly more power than other men—e.g., minority men, gay men—a reality that should influence the specific manner in which feminist principles should be employed with different men. Anne Ganley (1988) described a variety of gender counseling goals that can be modified to fit the individual man's experience and needs. The goals include the following: (1) learning to balance and integrate relational and achievement values; (2) taking risks in establishing healthy intimate relationships of shared power; (3) increasing listening skills, empathy for others, and the ability to disclose emotions and reactions that are often kept as "secrets"; (4) developing collaborative and noncoercive working and relationship practices; (5) increasing the capacity for self-nurturance rather than expecting women to play this role; (6) developing positive models of consensual sexuality; and (7) accepting and interpreting no responses as disappointments rather than as rejections or the removal of that which one is entitled to.

Glenn Good, Lucia Gilbert, and Murray Scher (1990) presented a similar model and labeled it *gender-aware* therapy. The concepts of gender-aware therapy resemble the principles of nonsexist therapy as defined by Edna Rawlings and Diane Carter (1977) and are designed to be equally applicable to work with men and women. The key components and goals of gender aware therapy include the following:

1. Viewing men's and women's problems within the social context.
2. Working toward changing gender injustices.
3. Implementing collaborative therapeutic relationships.

Although some feminist therapists have declared that only female therapists can practice feminist therapy, feminists who espouse a liberal feminist position are likely to believe that men who have examined their own gender behavior, have developed sensitivity to and awareness of gender role issues, and endorse egalitarian roles can work effectively as feminist or gender aware therapists. Anne Ganley (1988) recommended that male therapists who use feminist analyses to inform their work should refer to themselves as *profeminist* therapists. This title acknowledges the value of men's contributions as therapists, but also recognizes that the phenomenological experiences of women working with women and men working with men will be different. Principles of profeminist practice call for men to confront sexist behavior; redefine masculinity according to values other than power, prestige, and privilege; and actively support women's efforts to seek justice (Tolman et al., 1986). Profeminist therapists actively interrupt men's efforts to devalue women, confront their controlling behaviors, and help men and women establish egalitarian relationships (Adams, 1988).

CONCLUDING COMMENTS

This chapter has described the many ways in which mainstream psychological approaches can be combined with liberal feminist assumptions. Given the centrality of values such as personal choice, autonomy, independence, and individual freedom to both liberal feminism and many psychotherapy traditions, the integration of these models is relatively straightforward and uncomplicated.

Liberal feminist therapists work toward creating hospitable environments in which both men and women have equal opportunity to define and choose personal goals. Deviations from socially prescribed gender roles are seen as normal, and the liberal feminist therapist conveys that a wide range of behaviors should be available to both men and women. The liberal feminist therapist encourages the client to become aware of the impact of gender role socialization and the social/legal environment on personal problems. The therapist hopes that this awareness will influence the client's choices, but is careful to avoid imposing his or her perceptions of reality on the client. The liberal feminist therapist is particularly concerned with respecting and trusting his or her client's ability to make personally satisfying choices for her own life. As a result, the therapist does not assume that certain outcomes, such as economic autonomy, are better than others, but that men and women will choose a wide array of lifestyle, family, and economic options. In general, whatever "works" for the individual constitutes an appropriate goal for psychotherapy.

From a liberal feminist perspective, symptoms related to depression, eating disorders, or fear of success are seen as outcomes of socialization and overly rigid adherence to stereotypical feminine roles. Therapeutic solutions emphasize the building of skills to overcome individual deficits in functioning. From this perspective, the "personal is political means that once individuals are freed from gender role constructions, they will model flexible nonstereotypical behaviors that will lead to changes in the social environment.

Feminist therapists who endorse radical and socialist traditions in feminism argue that a liberal feminist perspective may merely reinforce status quo Western values. Therapists with radical orientations to feminism emphasize the importance of transforming psychotherapy and society through social activism as well as individual change. The major themes associated with these therapies will be the subject of the next chapter.

Chapter 5

Radical and Socialist Feminist Themes in Feminist Therapy

Radical and socialist feminisms are based on the assumption that society must be changed at its very roots in order for women to experience equality. A logical extension of this concept for feminist therapy is that the institution of psychotherapy must be radically altered in order to provide an alternative to forms of psychotherapy that have mirrored unequal relationships and/or supported the status quo. Radical and socialist themes in feminist therapy are closely related to the activities and values of consciousness-raising groups, radical and socialist feminist theory, and the radical therapy movement. Many significant contributions to radical feminist therapy emerged during the early years of the "new" feminist movement and remain highly relevant to the practice of feminist therapy today. As a result, I will spend substantial time developing these historical themes as well as contemporary issues and themes related to radical and socialist feminist influences on psychotherapy.

As noted at the beginning of Chapter 4, the early years of feminist therapy were marked by two major perspectives: (1) a questioning approach, which included efforts that are more consistent with liberal feminism and occurred primarily within established mental health professions; and (2) a radical approach, which was associated with elements of the feminist movement that sought to change the very nature and focus of mental health practices (Ballou and Gabalac, 1985). This chapter will explore contributions relevant to the second area. Given the overlapping, complex, and continuously evolving perspectives evident within these feminisms (see Chapter 2), it would be artificial to discuss socialist and radical feminist therapies in separate chapters. Thus, I use the term *radical* throughout this chapter to refer to forms of feminist psychotherapy that have been influenced by both radical and socialist feminist perspectives.

As noted in Chapter 2, radical feminist theory defined the subjugation of women as the fundamental and hardest form of oppression to eradicate. Socialist feminists have adopted this view and also place emphasis on class, cultural, political, and economic systems that victimize women. Feminist therapists with radical social-change orientations often combine these philosophies, as exemplified by Kirk's (1983) the following assertion:

> Radical feminism . . . is action-oriented and predicated on an analysis, not only of the plight of women in society, but of the generally oppressive nature of patriarchy, the corporate capitalist system, and the political and social institutions which they have created. It is also predicated on an understanding of how these systems oppress women in particular as well as other groups. (p. 179)

The first section of this chapter traces the evolution of consciousness raising into feminist therapy and describes some of the initial forms and values of radical feminist therapy. It is followed by an overview of a variety of versions of radical and/or socialist feminist therapy including the following: grassroots crisis and antiviolence counseling associated with rape crisis centers and domestic violence shelters, Hogie Wyckoff's integration of radical/socialist values with principles associated with the radical therapy movement, Miriam Greenspan's integration of radical and socialist feminist perspectives, and Bonnie Burstow's reinterpretation of radical therapy for the 1990s. These perspectives are presented in chronological order and together, represent a rich mosaic that demonstrates the similarities and diversity of radical and socialist feminist therapies. This section also includes a recent radical antitherapy perspective. The chapter concludes with a discussion of various issues that feminist therapists face as they consider new directions and the legacy of radical feminist perspectives for the late 1990s.

EMERGENCE AND ARTICULATION
OF THE FIRST RADICAL FEMINIST THERAPIES

Consciousness-Raising: Radical Alternative
to Male-Centered Ways of Seeking Knowledge

In order to understand the earliest forms of radical feminist therapy, it is necessary to understand the rationale for and role of consciousness-raising (CR) during the early years of the "new" feminist movement. Historical documents suggest that CR groups were first utilized by the radical feminist Redstockings group. Radical feminist women believed that most theories of women's experiences were steeped in androcentric assumptions and reflected the male-dominated disciplines and institutions that inspired them. Thus, written sources about women's lives could provide only incomplete or unsatisfactory answers to questions about who women are and how society can be changed. CR became the method for developing new theories and methods based on women's lives. Kathie Sarachild (1975b) said, "You might say we wanted to pull up weeds in the garden by their roots, not just pick off the leaves at the top to make things look good momentarily" (p. 144). The Redstockings and other radical groups explored the origins of women's problems by studying topics such as work, motherhood, and childhood as they were experienced personally by women. All generalizations about women were tested against the "living practice and action" (p. 145) of group members, and CR was defined as the "scientific method of research" (p. 145).

The San Francisco Redstockings (1969) declared the following: "OUR POLITICS begin with our feelings: Feelings are a direct response to the events and relationships that we experience; that's how we know what's really going on" (p. 285). Using women's feelings as a source of information was considered especially important because women's emotional life had historically been discounted or identified as the source of distorted perceptions and personal hang-ups (San Francisco Redstockings, 1969). According to the Redstockings, feelings "are saying something *political*, something reflecting fear that something bad will happen to us or our hope, desire, knowledge that something good will happen to us" (Sarachild, 1970, p. 78). Increased awareness of feelings helps women identify events or interactions that trigger their pain, which lead to opportunities to explore and understand how pain is not the result of "masochism, self-hate, or inferiority, but is a response to some behavior that was in fact designed to humiliate, hurt, and oppress us" (San Francisco Redstockings, 1969, p. 286). The small group was seen as a key "political unit" to help women deal with the "enormous pressure placed on us everywhere to deny our own perceptions or feelings" (p. 286).

In general, CR groups functioned in a spontaneous manner with a minimum amount of structure and a commitment to nonhierarchical norms that endorsed decision making by consensus and specified that each person shared equal responsibility for group content and process. Groups generally consisted of five to fifteen members who came together to share their perceptions and concerns and use their findings to develop a program of liberation (Redstockings Manifesto, 1969). One of the first descriptions of CR "programs" identified the following components: (1) ongoing consciousness expansion through personal testimony, and generalization from personal experience; (2) examination of the ways in which women are encouraged to resist consciousness of oppression (e.g., through making excuses, blaming women for their oppression, believing that one is exempt from discrimination) and the relationship of these activities to survival; (3) discussion of how women can overcome denial and delusions and "dare to see" oppression for what it is; and (4) the development of radical feminist theory that helps women conceptualize how oppression occurs in everyday life and increases women's understanding of how personal privilege, such as white skin and educational privilege may perpetuate oppression (Sarachild, 1970). Pamela Allen (1971) described the CR group process as consisting of four phases:

1. opening up, a time when women express their individual needs in a nonjudgmental atmosphere
2. sharing, the revelation of personal material for the purpose of identifying the commonalities of women's experience
3. analyzing, or going beyond personal experience to objectively consider women's predicament
4. abstracting, or building a vision for action

As an extension of this process, group members were encouraged to engage in consciousness-raising actions directed toward increasing public awareness about sexism and developing liberating views about women. These public actions, which consisted of "zap" actions, speak-outs, protests, writings, and media events "would waken more and more women to an understanding of what their problems were" (Sarachild, 1975b, p. 149). CR provided an ongoing place for gaining new information, analyzing obstacles, and setting new priorities for activism. The CR process also guarded against "mindless activism," or becoming sidetracked and narrowly focused on single-issue activism, and was designed to "keep [women] on the track, moving as fast as possible toward women's liberation" (p. 149). By carefully and collectively studying issues, women could respond to issues with the most practical and potentially influential actions.

The purpose of CR was to collectively "analyze the situation of women, not to analyze *her*. The idea was not to change women, was not to make 'internal changes' except in the sense of knowing more" (Sarachild, 1975b, p. 148). This goal was consistent with the Redstockings' prowoman stance, which identified women's behaviors as reactions to concrete acts of male supremacy and not as learned or conditioned behavior. Sarachild (1975b) noted that CR was not an end in itself or a tool for merely increasing self-esteem. Focusing on feelings was "not therapy, was not to give someone a chance to get something off her chest" (p. 148). The purpose of CR was "to get closer to the truth" (p. 148).

Carol Hanisch (1971) elaborated on these themes in her paper titled "The Personal is Political." She declared that through participation in CR, women discover that personal problems can only be understood as political problems. She insisted that CR should not be equated with therapy:

> [T]he very word "therapy" is obviously a misnomer if carried to its logical conclusion. Therapy assumes that someone is sick and that there is a cure, e.g., a personal solution. I am greatly offended that I or any other women is thought to need therapy in the first place. Women are messed over, not messed up! We need to change the objective conditions, not adjust to them. Therapy is adjusting to your bad personal alternative. (p. 153)

Although CR was instrumental in radicalizing women's views, some radical feminists were skeptical about the notion that CR would result in activism. The Feminists believed that the CR experience could overemphasize feelings, mire the movement in processing personal data, and thus, retard the growth of women's liberation. The Feminists indicated that the "prowoman line" could become an excuse for avoiding personal change and asserted that an analysis of external oppression must be matched with an examination of how oppression is internalized and perpetuated in the lives of individual women (Echols, 1989).

Changing Role of Consciousness-Raising

This section will discuss some of the factors that contributed to the reshaping of CR as a therapeutic tool. One of the factors that influenced the changing nature of CR groups was the decision-making structure of most CR groups. The norm of leaderlessness established by most radical feminist groups set them apart from the hierarchical New Left groups from which they broke away. However, the radical practice of egalitarianism meant that decision making was time-consuming and cumbersome, leaving limited time and energy for action. Furthermore, CR group members were involved in busy lifestyles and myriad tasks that made it difficult for them to devote significant time to political activism (Payne, 1973).

"The end of consciousness-raising leaves people with no place to go and the lack of structure leaves them with no way of getting there" (Joreen, 1973, p. 294). Cassell (1977) added that "group decisions became decision by exhaustion. By the time the final decisions were agreed upon, so many proposals had been discussed so many times that it was difficult to remember exactly who had decided what" (p. 140). The norm of leaderlessness also limited women with significant organizational background from exercising their skills. When specific individuals exerted direction or leadership, they were sometimes accused of seeking stardom, taking unilateral action, or recreating the very elitism that they had left behind in the New Left movement. Thus, the egalitarian climate of CR groups sometimes suppressed the abilities and expertise of capable members, and limited a group's potential to carry out action in a coherent and orderly fashion (Cassell, 1977; Deckard, 1979; Echols, 1989).

Although the primary intent of the original CR groups was to articulate social problems, the discussion of personal dilemmas was experienced as therapeutic by many members. Marilyn Zweig (1971) noted the following: "Although we are not a therapeutic group and do not try to solve personal problems of individual women, we want to study ways to make the condition of all women better so that individual women have fewer problems" (p. 163). Thus, the group often helped individual women "make a better life" (p. 163) and provided a "haven from hassles" (Payne, 1973).

By the mid-1970s, the political awareness or radicalizing function of CR groups became less salient, and women increasingly joined CR groups to achieve personal growth and gain support (Kravetz, 1978, 1980; Lieberman and Bond, 1976). The National Organization for Women, which emphasized the importance of individual choice and personal transformation, initially rejected CR as focusing on trivial matters, but shortly thereafter established a program for CR and distributed guidelines to small groups who wished to use this method to help members increase personal awareness. Diane Kravetz's (1978) study of CR group members revealed that only 21 percent identified themselves as "radical," thus documenting that CR was widely adopted by groups with diverse feminist orientations.

Although CR groups continued to serve a political and ideological function, the self-reports of group members suggested that personal change, rather than political or ideological change, was the primary benefit derived from these groups (Warren, 1976). Many CR groups could be more accurately labeled as "support groups" than groups that informed activism (Lieberman and Bond, 1976). Reports of group members revealed that personal change and support were perceived as primary benefits of CR groups (Lieberman et al., 1979). A survey of women who participated in CR groups revealed that 70 percent viewed examining women's roles and experiences was an important reason for their participation in a CR group, 13 percent cited personal change as an important reason for group membership, and 9 percent identified becoming more political as an important goal (Kravetz, Marecek, and Finn, 1983). As CR flourished, feminist researchers examined its impact on women. Diane Kravetz (1978, 1987) reviewed this extensive literature and identified the following personal benefits of CR groups:

1. increased feelings of self-esteem and decreased feelings of personal inadequacy
2. increased personal and intellectual autonomy
3. awareness of similarities between women and improved relationships with women
4. a new ability to express feelings such as anger
5. change in interpersonal roles and relationships
6. the development of a sociopolitical analysis of the female experience and women's oppression

Conflict: Can Feminists Also Be Therapists?

Women psychotherapists who had participated as members of CR groups were changed and radicalized through their interactions with other women and began to increasingly utilize their therapeutic skills to combat oppression in their professional work (Lerman, 1987). CR group members acknowledged that CR did not offer a simple solution to women's problems and that if these groups were to help women negate enduring, internalized stereotypical behaviors and beliefs, skilled, objective, and committed group leadership would be necessary (Lindsey, 1974). Women trained in mental health professions began to play these roles and to utilize CR in their therapeutic practices. The possibility of feminist therapy emerged.

The emergence of feminist therapy was not welcomed universally by radical feminists because it implied endorsement of an institution that had contributed to the oppression of women by convincing women that their problems were caused by internal rather than external factors. Several widely disseminated critiques of psychotherapy appeared in the early 1970s. Naomi Weisstein's (1968/1993) critique stated that psychology had nothing to offer women, and Phyllis Chesler (1971) described the therapist-client relationship as reinforcing and solidifying the roles of the dominant patriarch and submissive patient. Chesler (1971) noted that the majority of psychotherapists were male, that they acted as extensions and enforcers of the political institution of psychotherapy, and that they promoted the "covertly or overtly patriarchal, autocratic, and coercive values and techniques of psychotherapy" (p. 375). She also described the psychotherapy relationship as mirroring the inequality of marital relationships:

> Both psychotherapy and marriage isolate women from each other; both emphasize individual rather than collective solutions to woman's unhappiness; both are based on a woman's helplessness and dependence on a stronger male authority figure; both may, in fact, be viewed as reenactments of a little girl's relation to her father in a patriarchal society; both control and oppress women similarly. (p. 373).

Hurvitz (1973) added that psychotherapy as an institution is unlikely to contribute to social change:

> Psychotherapy serves as a means of social control because it is based on and fosters an ideology that accepts the status quo and proposes that changing individuals will improve the society. . . . This ideology . . . protects the status quo against those who would change it; it psychologizes, personalizes, and depoliticalizes social issues; it identifies success with personal worth; it fosters a concept of adjustment which often implies submission; . . . and it leads to misunderstanding the position, aspirations, and ways of changing the conditions of oppressed . . . groups in America. (p. 235)

Some radical feminists found it difficult to believe that the institutionalized sexism of psychotherapy could be overcome by merely replacing male therapists with female therapists in a new type of therapy. Furthermore, psychology's focus on examining internal factors and personal shortcomings was highly inconsistent with those who held to the prowoman stance that declared that women's behavior was not caused by internal issues but by day-to-day reactions to an oppressive environment (Redstockings, 1975). Dorothy Tennov (1973) used this argument in her rejection of feminist therapy as a viable option for women stating:

> What is feminist therapy? I find the two terms mutually contradictory. The feminist sees oppression from outside influences;

the therapist's task is to effect changes in the patient. That some psychotherapists have become activists in the women's movement, and have tried of late to "liberate" women instead of "adjusting" them, does not remove the problem. . . . Feminists do not practice therapy on their sisters. (p. 110)

From the perspective of Dorothy Tennov (1973), changing social structures should take priority over changing individuals. Thus, self-help was seen as the only legitimate alternative for women who were seeking help with personal issues (Tennov, 1973). However, other radical feminists noted that the internalization of oppression limits women's ability to become involved in action; thus, an examination of socialization and conditioning is important for helping women redefine themselves, overcome psychological paralysis, and become involved in action. Unlearning stereotypical behaviors becomes an important step for assisting individuals to fulfill their potential and gain necessary confidence to challenge external systems.

Although resistance to the notion of a feminist therapy existed, it became increasingly clear that many women entering CR groups were seeking an alternative to traditional therapy. Some radical feminists suggested that new forms of therapy for women could be constructed according to models and norms radically different from traditional therapy. This new model was described as:

a radical therapy of equals [in which] . . . the process would be democratized, the perspective would be on the "pathological" forces in the culture that uniquely damage women, and the therapeutic goals would go beyond internal psychic changes to creating new sensibilities, ambiances, and social contexts. (Walstedt, cited in Sturdivant, 1980, p. 10)

Karen Lindsey (1974) added the following:

The women's movement needs to form counter structures, therapy forms which incorporate some of the skills and knowledge of the existing structures (of therapy), but which gear them toward helping women find their own values and needs, rather than molding them into prefabricated roles. (p. 2)

Karen Chase (1977) suggested that the rejection of all aspects of the psychological profession would be tantamount to "throwing out the baby with the bathwater." To "abandon therapy out of hand is at once to refuse to satisfy an obvious personal need and to sacrifice a tool of potentially enormous importance to the movement" (p. 20). To create this new radical structure, however, would require feminists to "dismantle the professional/patient hierarchy, to discount formal accreditation, and to reconstruct the therapeutic situation on a basis of mutuality" (p.20). In addition to removing the therapists from the role of "high priest" (p. 20), it would require the redefinition of the concept of a symptom as "an appropriate response to an inappropriate situation" (p. 20).

Emergence of Group Feminist Therapy

As the therapeutic benefits of CR became increasingly apparent, CR groups were promoted as an alternative or adjunct to therapy (Barrett et al., 1974; Brodsky, 1977; Glaser, 1976; Kirsch, 1974; Kravetz, 1976, 1980; Lieberman and Bond, 1976; Rice and Rice, 1973; Warren, 1976). In addition to its personal benefits, CR offered a structure that was radically different from traditional psychotherapy. In one of the earliest statements on the mental health benefits of CR, Annette Brodsky (1976) indicated that CR groups help women become aware of how the "problem with no name" is exhibited in their personal lives, and encourage women to examine their unique potentials outside of traditional roles and fight the stagnation of role confinement. By adopting CR as a model of therapy, therapists can "confirm the reality" of women's experiences; women no longer need to deny experiences of discrimination or "pass them off as projections" (Brodsky, 1976, p. 376). The therapist serves as a "supporter and believer" (p. 375) of women's competence, helps women become aware of the range of goals and options available to them, and acts as an effective-coping role model. Barbara Kirsch (1974) added that CR can become a mechanism for the resocialization of women. CR as psychotherapy affirms women's view of reality, transforms consciousness, provides a release from conditioning, and highlights "the need to change society by showing individuals that their 'personal' problems are rooted in sociocultural phenomena" (p. 337).

Many of the norms of consciousness-raising were incorporated within early forms of radical feminist group therapy including

(1) an emphasis on egalitarianism, (2) an understanding that oppression and social conditioning are central to understanding women's distress, (3) the belief that the sharing of personal issues contributes to a more complete understanding of issues, and (4) and the belief that awareness should be matched with action. In keeping with CR principles, feminist therapy groups emphasized the importance of "collective rather than hierarchical structures, and [the] equal sharing of resources, power, and responsibility" (Marecek and Kravetz, 1977, p. 326). Therapy groups provided an effective antidote to negative gender socialization because women could gain power by practicing new skills in a safe environment. Women could alter their lives by making the following transitions in thinking and acting:

> "There is something wrong with me as a woman or as a person" to "There's something wrong in society." Anger could be rechanneled into active, open confrontation with the oppressing agent, increasing the potential for a sense of mastery and for more reciprocal human relationships. (Barrett et al., 1974, p. 14)

In contrast to traditional leaderless CR groups, feminist therapy groups were led by one or more trained leaders who helped members redefine issues of women, separate internal from external causes of problems, identify "corrective" actions, and develop productive personal responses (Brodsky, 1976; Johnson, 1976; Kaschak, 1981; Kravetz, 1978; Leidig, 1977). The group process diluted the power of the therapist and decreased power imbalances between therapist and clients because all members not only received assistance but also provided emotional support to each other (Burden and Gottlieb, 1987; Kaschak, 1981; Rawlings and Carter, 1977). Groups also provided a mechanism for reaching many women and energizing women to engage in active resistance. In contrast, individual therapy confines growth by limiting the number who receive assistance to a privileged few (Wyckoff, 1977b).

The feminist therapy collective became an important context in which radical and socialist feminist therapy occurred. Feminist therapy collectives emerged in many parts of the United States during the early 1970s and were often associated with feminist health clinics or women's centers. Some of these collectives were founded by professionally trained mental health professionals who had become radicalized through their experiences in CR groups, and as a consequence, preferred to work outside of hierarchical organizations that resembled oppressive patriarchal structures. Other collectives included both paraprofessional and professional therapists and provided ongoing training programs for members of the community who desired to lead therapy groups.

Although practices within therapy collectives have varied substantially, feminist therapy collectives have almost always been committed to nonhierarchical business practices and decision making. A typical experience of feminist therapy within one of the early collectives included attending an initial exploratory group that allowed each woman to ask questions, consider her level of interest in therapy, and identify aspects of her life that she would like to work on in therapy. If she decided to continue in group therapy, she would sign a twelve-week contract with members of her group that would identify what problems she would work on. During the twelve-week therapy contract, she would further explore her issues and practice new behaviors in the context of a group that would offer support and confrontation. At the conclusion of twelve weeks, she evaluated her progress and renewed her contract if she desired to work on additional issues.

One of the few research studies of feminist therapy compared the experiences of twenty-four women who received group therapy in a feminist therapy collective with similar clients who participated in individual therapy with male therapists. Although the mean length of therapy was four months for collective clients and ten months for the comparison sample, both groups showed similar levels of improvement and satisfaction (Johnson, 1976). The top three factors that collective clients saw as central to their improvement included experiencing a sense of belongingness and acceptance by the group, learning how to relate effectively in an interpersonal environment, and working with therapists who viewed them as competent (Johnson, 1976).

A second research study (Marecek, Kravetz, and Finn, 1979) compared the responses of approximately four hundred CR group members who had participated in either feminist therapy (not necessarily group feminist therapy) or traditional therapy. Women who experienced feminist therapy reported a greater number of positive evaluations than did women who were clients in traditional therapy. Sixty-seven percent of women in feminist therapy and 38 percent of women in traditional therapy reported that their experiences were very helpful. Both early studies of feminist therapy (Johnson, 1976) demonstrated that feminist therapy facilitates empowerment, affirmation, and validation in an environment that utilizes interactions between women as important therapeutic components.

Many of the earliest statements about feminist therapy appeared in unpublished works or papers that were informally distributed at psychological conventions. Although forty-three panels, symposis, and invited addresses were sponsored by the American Psychological Association between the years of 1971 and 1975 and drew standing-room-only attendance, most efforts to define basic feminist therapy principles did not appear until the mid-1970s (e.g., Lerman, 1976; Marecek and Kravetz, 1977; Rawlings and Carter, 1977). One of the most influential descriptions of feminist therapy, which was authored by Edna Rawlings and Diane Carter (1977) reflected many of the values of radical and socialist feminism. Their definition stated the following: (1) the goal of feminist therapy is social and political change; (2) oppression and environmental stress are major causes of "pathology," but should not be used as excuses to avoid personal responsibility; (3) diagnostic labels should be rejected because they have been used as instruments of oppression, and such labels focus on deficits rather than strengths; (4) feminist therapy can be most effectively accomplished in groups; (5) egalitarianism and efforts to equalize power in the therapy relationship are central to empowerment; (6) biologically based theories of male-female differences must be eschewed, and traditional role differences between men and women must be erased in order to break down the legacy of sex-role stereotypes; and (7) the therapist's participation in social-change activities on behalf of women is an important extension of her therapeutic role. These conditions remained cornerstones of feminist therapy in the 1990s.

VARIETIES OF RADICAL AND SOCIALIST FEMINIST THERAPIES

Violence Against Women and the Crisis Center Movement

At the same time that feminist therapy collectives were being established, grassroots rape crisis and domestic violence centers were emerging throughout the United States, Canada, and Europe. The crisis intervention and counseling provided by these centers represent important applications of radical and socialist feminist therapy.

The first rape crisis centers were founded in 1970 by grassroots, community-based feminist organizations and by 1973, the National Organization for Women also began to establish anti-rape projects. However, the antirape movement was most heavily influenced by a radical feminist perspective that identified "sexual violence against women as the embodiment of patriarchy" (Koss and Harvey, 1991, p. 123) and a threat to all women. This feminist analysis conceptualizes rape and the fear of rape as supporting and reinforcing male power and the social control of women. In response to their fear of rape, women lead more constricted lives, search for male protection, and limit their efforts toward becoming autonomous and independent. Furthermore, society often sees women as responsible for their own victimization, and traditional legal and medical procedures for survivors support victim blaming. In order to counteract the social control of women through patriarchy, "a feminist response must do just the opposite: encourage choice, affirm independence, and aid women's cultivation of personal and social power" (Koss and Harvey, 1991, p. 126). The rape crisis center is a context in which women are believed, supported, and receive direct help for working through the aftermath of sexual violence.

During the mid-1970s, feminist crisis workers described rape trauma syndrome (Burgess and Holmstrom, 1974), and noted the ways in which women's reactions to rape represent appropriate and understandable responses to extreme crisis and trauma. A variety of services were made available to survivors of rape including crisis hot lines, single-session debriefing and crisis management, peer support groups, self-defense training, individual and group counseling, medical assistance, rape exams, and legal assistance (Koss and Harvey, 1991; O'Sullivan, 1976). Services for rape survivors focused primarily on helping women work through their shattered beliefs and on restoring mastery and choice.

Rape crisis centers have been heavily influenced by the consciousness-raising sector of feminism and groups are central to fulfilling their mission in connecting personal and political change.

Rape crisis centers offer a range of group services that include self-help groups, education groups, crisis intervention groups, and formal psychotherapy groups. The basic goals of these groups are to provide confirmation that the assaulted woman has been violated, communicate that her actions and responses were based on her need to survive, reinforce her status as a survivor, decrease her isolation and self-blame, validate feelings, facilitate grief and mourning about psychological losses, and identify new forms of meaning. Consistent with feminist therapy principles, group members are encouraged to participate in both personal recovery and social change. When sufficient personal healing is accomplished, survivors often provide training about the dynamics of sexual assault, become volunteer crisis workers, or participate in community speakers' bureaus, antirape task forces, or "Take Back the Night" rallies (Koss and Harvey, 1991).

Consistent with radical feminist principles, rape crisis centers have usually considered social-change activities as an essential extension of their services to individual assault survivors. These social-change activities emphasize community education, risk awareness and self-defense training for women, and training programs designed to sensitize legal, medical, and mental health personnel to the needs of victims. Many efforts have also focused on correcting myths about rape and informing the public about date rape and acquaintance rape. Rape crisis personnel also engage in political activism and lobbying activities directed toward the passage of legislation designed to protect women's rights, define sexual assault in more accurate and less restrictive ways (e.g., not just forceful penetration), establish consequences for those who act violently toward others, and reform the legal system so that women who file charges are not revictimized (Koss and Harvey, 1991).

After reviewing the programs and efforts of rape crisis centers over the past two decades, Mary Koss and Mary Harvey (1991) concluded that crisis centers have had a "profound impact on virtually all aspects of the larger society's response to rape" (p. 120). During the 1980s, many crisis centers struggled to remain viable because of funding limitations (Matthews, 1994). Mary Koss (1993) noted that current issues include the need for greater support and funding for grassroots services for women as well as increased collaboration between grassroots organizations and formal systems of criminal justice, mental health, and medicine.

The emergence of the battered women's movement owes much to the inspiration of feminist antirape programs. The shelters and organizations associated with the battered women's movement were modeled after rape crisis centers (Schechter, 1982). In addition to offering a safe space away from violence, this movement contributed to new ways of conceptualizing violence against women. Activists rejected psychological theories that viewed battering as a consequence of stress, interpersonal conflict, impulse control, or intergenerational cycles of violence. Instead, battering is viewed as a consequence of "male domination within and outside the family" (Schechter, 1982 p. 216). Battering is seen as a tool for maintaining control over women. In contrast to the mythology of battered women as passive or helpless, the battered women's movement defined battered women's behaviors as active efforts to struggle and cope effectively with limited options. Like the rape crisis movement, the battered women's movement was founded on the belief that because violence against women is rooted in male domination, women's situations can only be changed through the pairing of services to women with political change efforts.

Battered women have often become radicalized through their experience with shelters and at some point, often become involved in political activism and volunteer work. As a first step, the shelter provides a safe space for women, and represents a first gigantic step in strengthening women and offering hope. As battered women share pain with each other, isolation is overcome, women feel released from personal blame, and responsibility for violent abuse is "placed squarely in the hands of a violent man" (Schechter, 1982, p. 315). Susan Schechter (1982) stated the following: "In literally six to eight weeks, shelters not only change women's self-perceptions but also their thoughts about male-female relationships, sex roles, and the meanings of violence" (p. 316). Through interaction with each other, women often develop a new pride in women as a group and a new political analysis of violence against women that can eventually lead to their own involvement in activism. Through the collective efforts of battered women and activists, the battered women's movement "created the first public spaces in history through which women were offered visible alternatives to violent men. It is not grandiose to suggest that . . . the battered women's movement has transformed the world for many" (Schechter, 1982, p. 321).

In keeping with the radical feminist perspective that services and institutions for women need to be defined in dramatically different ways than traditional institutions, most feminist service organizations, including women's health centers, rape crisis centers, and domestic violence programs, have attempted to design programs that revolutionize women's experience with service institutions. A major assumption is that hierarchical systems foster social inequality, dependency, and powerlessness in women and that these are the very factors that determine and reinforce many of women's problems. As a result, the institutional structure of the feminist agency must be based on equality and shared decision making that erases artificial boundaries and contributes to the empowerment of volunteers, professional staff members, and clients. Second, empowerment means that women must have control over their own bodies and their personal choices. An egalitarian structure facilitates women's ability to choose. Feminist methods such as self-help groups, consciousness-raising, collective action, and the support of clients' autonomy further highlight the competency of women who seek the services of the agency. In other words, "the process and the product must both adhere to basic feminist principles" (Kravetz and Jones, 1991, p. 237). These organizations also seek to link services with political change. The goal is that "people can become radicalized through such services, that they can begin to see the connection between one specific need and other needs, and finally to understand the deeper causes of their troubles" (Withorn, 1977).

As services for women have continued to evolve, the structure and services of rape crisis centers and domestic violence projects has become increasingly diverse. Whereas some centers emphasize victim services over social-change activities, others maintain their commitment to both personal service and social change. It has been difficult for many feminist agencies to sustain the high level of energy required to start feminist organizations, and some volunteers eventually become exhausted or burned out as a consequence of dealing with the struggles of maintaining services despite poor funding or lack of strong community support (Ahrens, 1980; Galper and Washburne, 1976; Matthews, 1994; O'Sullivan, 1976). Many of the changes in organizational and service structure resulted from funding difficulties or the need to define models that would work beyond the initial start-up phase. Many original grants to rape crisis centers, shelters, and health centers represented "seed money" that was only guaranteed for several years, and feminist organizations often concluded that they would need to seek government funding. Government funding provided increased resources and opportunities for expansion, but also led to greater complexity of organizational structure and staffing patterns, and resulted in more agency regulations (McShane and Oliver, 1978). Although many organizations begin their work with deeply committed volunteers who participated in all aspects of decision making, greater funding led to more specialization, hierarchical structures, and the hiring of professional administrators or staff to provide many services to women. As staffs expanded and became more professional, it was less likely that members of the organization shared feminist values, or held common assumptions about the necessity of pairing social and individual change. Conflicts between professional and grassroots activists have been complicated and continue into the present. Despite these issues, the services of women's crisis centers, shelters, and health centers endure as radical alternatives to traditional mental health services and point to the reality that different types of structures may be necessary to meet the needs of women during different decades (Koss and Harvey, 1991; Matthews, 1994; Schechter, 1982).

The Radical Therapy Movement and Radical Feminist Therapy

Some forms of radical feminist therapy were closely related to the goals and origins of the radical therapy movement, which was organized by men and women who sought to raise awareness of the oppressive nature of psychiatry and psychotherapy. The critiques of psychotherapy emerging from this movement resembled the commentary of many feminists who sought to establish a new form of therapy. The goals of radical therapy are captured by the inscription inside the cover of *The Radical Therapist* (Agel, 1971): "Therapy is political change, not peanut butter."

Michael Glenn (1971) stated that "[c]urrent therapy offers 'solutions' only to people who buy the system and want to maintain their place in it" (p. xii). The radical therapy manifesto (1971) declared the following: "Our notions of therapy are obsolete: elitist, male-centered, and obsessional. Our modes of practice are often racist and exploitive" (p. xv). Furthermore, the typical therapist:

> sells his skill like a vendor of fried chicken. He uses his prestige to discredit and slur social protest, youth, women's liberation, homosexuality, and any other different kind of behavior. Therapists' rewards come from helping the system creak on. (Glenn, 1971, p. xi)

Claude Steiner (1971) stated that "*[p]sychiatry as it is predominantly practiced today needs to be changed radically, that is 'at the root'*" (p. 3). According to radical therapists, new forms of therapy needed to eliminate the therapist's power that reinforces "one-up, one down" positions and to establish a new therapy that would need to link personal and social change. Glenn (1971) declared the following:

> Therapy is change, not adjustment. This *means* change— social, personal, and political. . . . A "struggle for mental health" is bullshit unless it involves changing this society which turns us into machines, alienates us from one another and our work, and binds us into racist, sexist, and imperialist practices. (p. xi)

In order to engage in a therapy that would lead to social change, therapists would need to eschew their former detachment and "clinical" attitude of neutrality, organize themselves against injustice and "*attack* precious, oppressive institutions" (p. xi) including mental health care systems, the nuclear family, treatment of children as property, professionalism, and the sacredness of the standard forty-hour work week. The radical therapist manifesto (1971) identified the following six major goals: (1) the liberation of therapists and the systems they work in, which are "unresponsive, bulky, privileged, and stiff" and that reinforce a "tangle of midwife myths, fantasy, and outright bias" (p. xvii); (2) the development of new training programs that are nonhierarchal, remove artificial boundaries between "professionals" and laypersons, and that utilize more open, responsive, and creative methods; (3) the elaboration of a new psychology of women and liberating theories of family and social life; (4) the development of therapy programs that would be monitored and controlled by clients; (5) the creation of new techniques of therapy that would be readily accessible to all people (not just the middle-class elite); and (6) the confrontation of social injustice ranging from the violation of natural resources to the "encroachment of our minds" (p. xxii) through advertising, biased education, and gender role stereotyping.

Hogie Wyckoff (1971, 1977a,b) developed a form of radical feminist therapy that combined her commitment to feminism with the principles of radical therapy as inspired by the principles of transactional analysis and the works of Claude Steiner, Eric Berne, Fritz Perls, and R. D. Laing (Steiner, 1971; Wyckoff, 1971, 1977a,b). According to her definition of feminist therapy, psychotherapy *is* a political activity; therapists are community organizers who teach problem-solving skills and political awareness (Wyckoff, 1977a).

Radical therapists used the term *psychiatry* to label their activity in order to communicate that radical therapists are "soul healers" as defined by the original Greek meaning of the word, and to state "the competency of our work and the coopting of power from the medical establishment" (Wyckoff, 1977a, p. 371). The intention of the "radical psychiatrists" of the 1960s and 1970s was not to create a form of therapy that coexisted with traditional psychiatry, but to put traditional therapy out of business by refusing to "diagnose" patients as sick, by helping people understand that they are basically good and powerful, and by placing therapy under the control of its recipients.

Radical psychiatry was founded on several basic principles. First, in the absence of oppression, people are "okay" and live productive lives in harmony with each other. However, coercion and discrimination lead to alienation, which is the result of mystification and deception. Alienation represents a central component of all psychiatric problems and involves "a sense of not being right with oneself, the world, or humankind" (Wyckoff, 1977a, p. 371-372). Deception and mystification, which cause alienation, refer to the ways in which individuals are led to believe that they are not oppressed. As a result, victims feel responsible for their own oppression and blame themselves. Wyckoff (1977a) indicated that the most typical ways in which women feel alienated include coercive or unsatisfactory experiences of sexuality, lack of recognition or minimization of their work, and self-contempt of themselves and their bodies.

In order for liberation to occur, two goals must be accomplished: *awareness* and *contact*. Awareness occurs when women explore how they were "deceived or mystified into colluding with their oppression" (Wyckoff, 1977a, p. 372), how they learned to believe that something is wrong with them rather than with a corrupt society. When consciousness is raised and mystification is removed, awareness leads to anger, which becomes a useful force for fighting the "real culprit" (p. 373) and reclaiming humanity. Anger is a first step toward contact, which involves working with and gaining support from others who are working toward liberation. Contact with other humans counteracts alienation and isolation. Through connection with a supportive group, people experience *permission* to engage oppressive agents and gain *protection* from the potential retaliation of oppressive people.

Claude Steiner (1971) stated: "The overcoming of oppression requires the banding together of the oppressed" (p. 7). Hogie Wyckoff (1971) indicated that group work reinforces the principle that "there are no individual solutions for oppressed people" (p. 182). Although individual solutions are unacceptable, Wyckoff (1971) suggested that group problem solving about individual problems is essential. She stated, "I cannot accept that women must suffer . . . while waiting for the revolution to come" (p. 187). The group experience does not detract from political action but helps women enact changes in their own lives so they can "carry on their struggle in a more vital way" (p. 187). Groups also encourage women to develop a sense of sisterhood and to test their problem-solving skills in a ready-made social situation (Wyckoff, 1971). Each group member develops a contract with the group; the contract both guides problem-solving efforts and guards against the leader/facilitator imposing personal values on the client. The contract is reinforced with homework that helps women translate awareness into action (Wyckoff, 1977b).

Hogie Wyckoff (1977a) utilized transactional analysis techniques to diagram and clarify the specific ways in which gender-role oppression, gender scripting, and mystification occur. The three internal ego states of transactional analysis focus on the following: (1) the internal parent, who "knows" without doubt what is right and wrong; (2) the adult, the self that processes information and makes decisions based on logical, rational thinking; and (3) the child, or the creative, open, intuitive, feeling aspect of the self. Although women are oppressed in each of the ego states, the "pig parent" represents a particularly virulent form of oppression because it includes all the internalized messages that help keep women subordinate. The pig parent communicates many "shoulds," tells women that they are never good enough, indicates that they must never perform better than men, and sets up a vicious cycle that is difficult to escape. Wyckoff (1977a) developed group exercises to "off" the pig parent. Women first identify the specific messages that the pig parent sends; then they learn to neutralize these messages through directly confronting this hurtful side of the self. Women also work toward developing a nurturing parent who silences the negative power of the pig parent and provides positive feedback (Wyckoff, 1977a,b).

By diagramming the overt and covert messages that underlie interpersonal dialogues, communication is demystified, women gain insight about the subtle dynamics of communication, and women become aware of why they often feel depressed or resentful in interactions. Wyckoff (1977a) also described typical, gendered, banal scripts, which promote stilted, repetitive, and inauthentic rela-tionships between men and women. Common banal scripts such as "Mother Hubbard," "plastic woman," "poor-little-me," or "nurse" reveal how "men and women are manipulated into believing that they are scripted to go together like sweet and sour sauce, hot and cold, or Yin and Yang" (p. 377). Women's experiences need not be defined according to this mythology; women can learn to identify satisfaction and fulfillment on their own terms.

Wyckoff (1977a) recommended that emotional release work should be integrated with problem-solving skills. Through bioener-getic breathing, emotional release, or other physical activities, women learn to express internalized anger and to become more aware of their bodies and the ways in which they physically hold emotional baggage inside themselves. Some of the strengths of this form of radical feminist therapy are that it (1) explains how freedom and spontaneity are repressed and can be regained; (2) describes in clear terms how gender roles are conditioned and how oppression is internalized and maintained; (3) links the identification of personal issues to concrete, straightforward problem-solving skills; (4) provides practice in helping women to act on their own behalf and try out new skills rather than being victims; and (5) suggests language and techniques for implementing self-nurturing activities.

Miriam Greenspan's Radical Socialist Perspective

Miriam Greenspan's (1983) description of feminist therapy may be the most clearly articulated effort to link socialist feminism and psychotherapy. Her description of the sources of women's problems integrates radical feminist perspectives regarding the body as a focus of oppression, liberal feminist perspectives on how women are trained to behave as victims, and a socialist feminist view of how economic factors and traditional labor divisions oppress women.

Consistent with a radical perspective, Greenspan (1983) stated that "under a system of male rule, a woman's body is the source of her power" and a "woman must develop herself as a body for men" (p. 163). Greenspan also described how women develop victim traits such as indirect communication, internalized anger, dependency, depression, and indirect expressions of power as methods of coping with an oppressive social system. Because psychiatric labels place blame on women and not on the circumstances that create their problems, these labels should be abandoned and replaced with descriptive terminology. Symptoms are a "response to an untenable psychopolitical situation" (p. 264), and within each symptom is a "seed of strength which lies dormant" (p. 265). Female "craziness" is a form of wisdom, and symptoms such as being overweight represent a "great refusal" (p. 268) to be controlled or to fulfill narrow expectations of what women's bodies should be like.

In keeping with her socialist feminist orientation, Greenspan indicated that gaining insight about the common socioeconomic subordination of women is central to understanding their situations. Patriarchy and capitalism cooperate to define women and assign women to perform the work of the private and family spheres. It is in this context that women's work is most devalued and that women develop relational skills in order to cope and survive. Women's wageless work is designed to focus on the needs of others, and through this activity, women's identity is constructed. Children and men are the beneficiaries of women's work; women's work makes it possible for them to enter and maintain a capitalist system. Thus, the reality that women's identity is oriented to her relationships is a direct consequence of being responsible for maintaining relationships. In order to stop the process by which women lose their identities in their relationships and families, radical economic and ideological notions about motherhood will need to change. In contrast to cultural feminist theories that tend to see women's relational capacity through interpersonal and intrapsychic lenses, Greenspan concluded that it is dangerous to separate women's relational strengths from the economic and material sources that support them.

Miriam Greenspan's book focused primarily on identifying the problems of traditional psychotherapy and provided a radical feminist interpretation of women's problems. In a 1995 autobiographical statement, Greenspan noted that she wrote this book in order to "consolidate the best of grassroots feminist therapy in the form of a book that women could use as both providers and consumers of therapy" (p. 235). It was not her intention to provide a textbook-like outline of techniques, and her thoughts about conducting therapy are embedded in a series of case studies designed to inform potential clients about what they can expect in feminist therapy and in traditional therapy. Thus, it fulfilled important goals of feminist therapy: It demystified therapy and empowered clients by providing information.

Bonnie Burstow: Radical Feminist Therapy in the 1990s

In her book titled *Radical Feminist Therapy*, Bonnie Burstow (1992) charged that many of the books on feminist therapy are "not very feminist" and "none take a radical feminist line" (p. xiii). She criticized much of the literature on feminist therapy for the following reasons: (1) feminist therapists have treated psychiatry as "simply like any other field that needs to be tidied up" (p. xiii); (2) feminist therapists have operated under the unspoken assumption that feminist therapy clients will be white, able-bodied, gentile women;

(3) feminist therapy has devoted only limited attention to "isms" such as racism, homophobia, and anti-Semitism; and (4) feminist therapists have avoided working with or pathologized populations such as prostitutes, ex-inmates, women who have been or are in psychiatric treatment, drug-dependent women, and women who engage in self-mutilation. Some of her most scathing criticism was directed at feminist therapists who have been active in criticizing current diagnostic practices, but have then attempted to use traditional tools, such as traditional diagnostic tools and psychological testing, for feminist purposes (e.g., Rosewater, 1985). A major goal of Burstow's book was to provide practical suggestions to feminist therapists for working with diverse groups of women and issues that are often ignored (e.g., Native American women, women with disabilities, with a special emphasis on issues and problems related to violence).

Bonnie Burstow (1992) indicated that her book was intended to "radicalize feminist therapy further" (p. xiv). Radical feminist therapy as defined by Bonnie Burstow is built on four interconnected perspectives, the first of which is a radical feminist perspective that sees gender and sex as central to the ways in which women are oppressed, especially through the physical violation of women's bodies. Violence is a crucial focus for feminist therapy because women are "violently reduced to bodies that are for-men" (p. xv). "Women's bodies are arranged, maimed, jeopardized, and tailored for the purposes of men-defined eroticism" (p. 4). Furthermore, all women are either subject to violence or must deal with the threat of violence throughout their lives; conceptualizing issues through the lens of violence against women gives meaning and perspective to other issues that women experience. A second important component is Burstow's reiteration of many of the principles and techniques of radical therapy as defined by Hogie Wyckoff (1977a,b). The existential feminist position of Simone de Beauvoir (1952) provides the third foundation because it views freedom as "severely and often brutally conditioned but not totally 'determined' by our social and human situation" (p. xvi). Women remain agents capable of choice despite facing limited options and enormous pressures. A fourth component is the belief that psychiatry is a "fundamentally oppressive institution propped up by hegemony and built on mystification, subordination, and violence" (p. xvi). Despite feminist efforts to reform psychiatry, it remains fundamentally oppressive because psychiatry (1) is used to limit individual freedom through mandated hospitalization and drug treatment, (2) is a massive-growth industry designed to serve its own interests and those of large pharmaceutical companies, (3) pathologizes different life-styles by labeling them as personality disorders, and (4) relies on drugs to manage people rather than facilitate their growth. Despite so-called changes in psychiatry, women are "psychiatrized" and "defiant women are blamed, are punished, and are threatened with perpetual sickness and perpetual 'treatment' if they do not cooper-ate with narrowly defined treatment" (p. 35). Each of these major perspectives reveals ways in which "power over" and power differ-ences are central to the problems that individuals experience.

One important principle of therapy includes solidarity, or "expressing honest outrage at what has been done to this person in particular and to her community generally and by joining with her in the face of this injury" (p. 51). The therapist's use of solidarity is critical for empowerment because it involves identifying commona-lities and bonds between women, communicates empathy, and views the analysis of sexism and oppression as inextricably con-nected to understanding women's issues. For example, oppression is exhibited in symptoms such as depression, which is frequently "the strongest protest that people can muster in a dehumanizing situation" (p. 63). The therapist communicates this view to the cli-ent in order to depathologize her symptoms and highlight the ways in which she has already resisted oppression.

The exploration of negative scripts that reinforce internalized oppression is a second important technique. Third, body work rep-resents "powerful stuff" (p. 62) for unearthing issues, engaging anger, gaining energy, exploring sexuality on women's terms, and developing a new body image. A focus on the physical self is especially healing for women who have been violated through their bodies. Fourth, although Burstow (1992) views "external systemic oppression . . . as fundamental to the problems that we find by living in the world" (p. 284), she does not necessarily stress the importance of political responses to these issues as an outcome of therapy. Political activity and advocacy, however, are important commitments for therapists who desire to effect real change in society, and Burstow (1992) provides practical suggestions for engaging in political activity within her book.

One of Burstow's more controversial positions is that feminist therapists must take a radical stand on the individual woman's right to choose—not only regarding standard feminist issues such as reproduction, but also regarding a woman's right to commit suicide. When women are involuntarily hospitalized in order to keep them from harming themselves, "we are complicit with having them dragged into a misogynous and violent psychiatric ward where they are likely to be drugged and shocked in an effort to sustain their lives against their will" (p. 268). She added the following: "The right to kill ourselves is in fact integral to freedom. It is part and parcel of owning our own bodies, of making choices about our bodies and our selves" (p. 268). Furthermore, "freedom means the right to make incorrect decisions—even lethally incorrect decisions" (p. 271). Interference in women's choice is "unethical" (p. 273). Although she stressed a woman's right to choose, Burstow (1992) recommended active crisis intervention that includes talking openly with the client about her fears and plans; helping the client call on trustworthy friends to provide support when she is actively suicidal; disputing distorted thinking about suicide; increasing the amount of contact with clients through additional sessions and/or phone calls; communicating that although the therapist respects the client's right to choose, she wants the client to live; and calling an ambulance if the client's free choice is not apparent.

A second controversial position is Burstow's strong antipsychiatry position, which includes the rejection of drug treatment and psychiatric hospitalization. In contrast to some radical feminists who view drug treatment for some mental health problems as a humane response (e.g., Kitzinger, and Perkins, 1993), Burstow clearly communicates that she will not consult with a psychiatrist, will not assist with the hospitalization of individuals for mental health reasons, and will not use medical backup because of its potential to leave a client "vulnerable to unwanted psychiatric intervention" (p. 285). She refers to individuals who have been hospitalized for mental health reasons as "psychiatric survivors" (p. 235) and believes that feminist therapists should help these clients explore how they have been oppressed by the psychiatric system, offer concrete and practical assistance, and protect them from further "psychiatrization." According to Burstow, the following important messages should be communicated to the client: (1) psychiatric treatment is "without basis"; (2) drugs and electroconvulsive therapy do enormous damage; (3) violation of women by the psychiatric profession is an extension of their violation as women by other institutions and people; (4) "going mad" is a way of "getting in touch with feelings and realities that were suppressed" (p. 245); and (5) drugs prevent women from working through their problems. In addition to exploring how women form a "sick" identity, helping women free themselves from psychiatric jargon, and identifying alternative ways of thinking and living, the feminist therapist should help women find shelters and safe havens as alternatives to hospitalization. The radical feminist therapist helps structure the client's gradual withdrawal from medication, which is "one of the most liberatory acts that survivors can perform" (p. 259); assists the client in securing advocacy and legal assistance to prevent "future psychiatric intrusion" (p. 252); and helps the client become involved in support groups and communal protest of psychiatrization. Burstow (1992) noted that some women will choose to remain on medication and this choice must also be respected.

Bonnie Burstow (1992) applied the same antimedication arguments to the treatment of the full range of disorders women experience, including schizophrenia, anxiety disorders, and depression. Her position diverges from the radical feminist views of Celia Kitzinger and Rachel Perkins (1993), who stated that although medication has often been used with female clients in abusive ways and that although side effects sometimes outweigh benefits, there are appropriate uses of medication with highly disabled clients: "Drugs are quite literally a lifesaver when distress becomes too great to tolerate" (p. 179).

Like Bonnie Burstow, Rachel Perkins (1991a) criticized feminist therapists for neglecting women with long-term mental health problems. The popularity of deinstitutionalization and normalization of mentally ill populations has led to the denial of the needs of these individuals, which leads to their invisibility, the denial of necessary services, and increased powerlessness. Perkins (1991a) contended that the needs of long-term mental health clients parallel needs of physically disabled clients. There is little benefit in labeling physically disabled individuals as "sick," but much can be gained by acknowledging disability and providing necessary support systems that "adapt the physical world to the needs of that individual" (Perkins, 1992, p. 187). According to this view, individuals with long-term mental health problems should be referred to as "socially disabled" individuals and their needs should be addressed through the provision of practical support that facilitates personal functioning and releases the individual from some responsibilities. Although the suffering of those who experience disorders such as schizophrenia and manic-depression may be exacerbated by living in a patriarchal world, social activism and the eradication of oppression will not eliminate these disorders. Furthermore, psychotherapy will not offer socially disabled women the full range of coping skills that are necessary for their survival. Instead, feminists should (1) refuse to withdraw from socially disabled women and offer genuine friendship, (2) offer practical assistance designed to help women cope with essential day-to-day tasks, (3) create asylums where socially disabled women can gain relief from the stresses of the social world in a safe and supportive environment, and (4) help socially disabled women gain access to medications that reduce the incapacitating effects of long-term mental health problems when such intervention is appropriate (Kitzinger and Perkins, 1993).

Radical Feminist Antitherapy Position

In their 1993 book titled *Changing Our Minds,* Celia Kitzinger and Rachel Perkins declared that "our aim is to draw attention to the political problems inherent in *the very idea* of 'feminist therapy' or 'feminist psychology'" (p. 3). A basic premise of their book is that despite the efforts of feminist therapists over the past two decades, feminism and psychology are incompatible. Their views represent a more recent articulation of the views of earlier radical feminists who believed that feminism and therapy cannot be integrated (e.g., Tennov, 1973). According to Kitzinger and Perkins (1993): "Feminism tells us our problems are caused by oppression; psychology tells us they're all in the mind—at least, the important ones are, the ones we can do something about in therapy" (p. 7). They added:

"Whatever it pretends, psychology is never 'apolitical.' It always serves to obscure larger social and political issues (sexism, hetero-sexism, racism, classism), converting them into individual patholo-gies by an insistent focus on the personal" (p. 6).

Kitzinger and Perkins's (1993) position is based in part on their perceptions of the failure of feminist therapy to influence society. Although feminist therapists have identified change rather than adjustment as a central focus of therapy, feminist therapy has typi-cally involved the alteration of a woman's state of mind rather than the alteration of structural conditions. Thus, the dynamics of oppression remain unchanged. "'Oppression' is reduced to the indi-vidual pathology of the oppressors, and liberation becomes a psy-chic rather than a political phemenon" (Kitzinger and Perkins, 1993, p. 72). These authors refuse to discuss the relative merits and prob-lems of specific types of psychology or feminist therapy because they believe that such a discussion would detract from the larger effort of identifying what all therapies hold in common: obfuscation of political issues. Furthermore, they reject the goal of helping feminist therapists become better qualified in connecting the politi-cal and personal and state: "We are asking for an end to therapy altogether" (p. 27). They assert that the existence of problems of living should not be denied but can be best addressed as political issues and not as therapeutic issues.

Many feminist therapists believe that the activity of therapy is political because by experiencing a "revolution from within" and gaining increased self-esteem, women are healing from the wounds of patriarchy and overcoming internalized oppression. These changes counteract the impact of patriarchy: When women heal from the inside out, they will be freed to engage in social change. Kitzinger (1993) argued, however, that this thinking is flawed; the majority of those who have actively engaged in social change have done so in spite of fear and personal difficulty. If women wait for internal change before engaging in external change, it is unlikely that tangi-ble and observable changes in women's conditions will occur. A second typical application of "the personal is political" in psycho-therapy comes through the validation of women's experiences. Feminist therapy techniques revalue women's realities that have been denied and thus, serve as political activity. However, therapists sometimes affirm only those activities that are consistent with their values. As a result, feminist therapists may abuse their power or harm clients. Third, the notion of empowerment implies that as women become aware of oppression and develop feminist perspectives, they will direct their activities toward social change. This notion, however, can separate personal empowerment from empowerment of all women and represents yet another way in which feminist therapy detracts from political activism and social change.

Efforts to pair feminism and psychology in the form of feminist therapy may be especially dangerous for lesbians (Kitzinger and Perkins, 1992; Perkins, 1991b). In an effort to empower lesbians, feminist therapists have often focused on helping lesbians deal with internalized homophobia or internalized oppression, which they have absorbed from the larger culture (Sophie, 1987; Margolies, Becker, and Jackson-Brewer, 1987). Rachel Perkins (1991b) indicated that such therapeutic activity depoliticizes oppression, defines lesbian responses to heterosexism as individual pathology, and encourages victim blaming. Change is centered on "reducing/eliminating the individual lesbian's irrational fear, self-hatred, and negative attitudes to achieve better 'psychological adjustment' and a 'positive self-identity'" (Perkins, 1991b, p. 327). Kitzinger and Perkins (1993) contend that it is largely because of this privatization of oppression that up to 70 percent of lesbians seek therapy and are encouraged to develop "therapeutic lifestyles" (p. 73) that are based on unequal therapist-client relationships and individualistic concepts. These therapeutic lifestyles detract from developing real friendships and community. Rather than devoting so much energy to healing the person within, they believe that lesbians should be encouraged to deal with problems in living by engaging in political action inspired through participation in consciousness-raising groups and a nurturing lesbian feminist community, reading about feminist history and culture, and establishing genuine friendships.

Laura Brown (1992b) responded to the criticisms of Perkins (1991b) by indicating that therapists who focus exclusively on internalized homophobia and personal change are not true feminist therapists. However, it is not antipolitical to deal with the ways in which oppressive forces are internalized in nonconscious, internal ways. These factors may paralyze the client and must be explicated in order for the person to focus energy outward toward social change. Rather than labeling all therapy as antifeminist, Laura Brown (1992b) recommended that feminist therapists and their clients should talk openly about the asymmetric nature of therapy and pay close attention to issues of ethics in order to assure that therapists do not abuse their power. Although many issues brought to therapy could be better dealt with through friendship or political activism, feminist therapy represents an important resource for helping women survive in and counteract a patriarchal society "until the day that a feminist revolution has succeeded" (Brown, 1992b, p. 240).

Radical Postmodern Perspectives

Radical feminist practice continues to evolve and mature as feminist psychologists engage in careful reflection about the strengths and limitations of the past twenty-five years of feminist practice. In contrast to Burstow (1992), who rejects most tools of traditional psychology, and Kitzinger and Perkins (1993), who assume a radical anti-therapy position, Laura Brown (1994) and Ellyn Kaschak (1992) have articulated approaches to radical feminist therapy that are more flexible. For example, Laura Brown suggests that although traditional psychological tools have often been used to oppress women, feminist therapists can also use traditional psychological tools to sabotage and transform patriarchal systems. These tools "can be a chainsaw, cutting down a person's sense of worth or value; or they can be turned on the structures of patriarchy, cutting the latter down to size or nicely remodeling them to be a better fit" (p. 192). The therapist's translation of the information derived from diagnosis, psychological tests, and other traditional tools is central to defining the feminist or nonfeminist nature of such tools.

Laura Brown (1994) also recommends the use of an integrative biopsychosocial perspective on the client's experience. While retaining her radical feminist views, she counters Bonnie Burstow's outright rejection of psychotropic medication by noting that although the "pressure to give pills to people" (p. 193) can lead to narrowly focused treatment and the silencing of women, many of the problems that individuals face have biological components, some of which are directly related to traumatic events. She argues that biological treatments can be integrated with methods that focus on interpersonal and sociopolitical factors. All options for healing, however, must be presented to clients in an open and noncoercive manner that articulates the potentially positive contributions of the option as well as its limitations.

Radical feminist therapy is about transformation. Consistent with early forms of radical feminism, therapists critique patriarchal values and structures in society. However, a more mature and integrated radical feminist therapy requires that therapists also adopt self-reflective attitudes that inform and transform feminist therapy from within and that reveal ethnocentrism and inadvertent biases associated with unexamined assumptions so more complete feminist models can be formed. According to Laura Brown (1994), a major challenge for radical feminist therapy is to create rich, inclusive, and flexible theories and practices that understand individuals in complex, multicultural contexts.

Ellyn Kaschak (1992) recommends a radical social constructionist approach to feminist therapy. A unique feature of her "new psychology of women's experience" (Kaschak, 1992) is the reinterpretation of the Oedipus complex in feminist terms. This reinterpretation depicts the typical ways in which Western culture teaches men and women to enact socially prescribed roles. As an outcome of the Oedipal drama, men reject women and identify with powerful men. As a result, men see women as extensions of themselves and their own needs. They feel entitled to women's attentions and seek power and sex in self-serving ways. In the less well-known part of the Oedipal legend, Antigone, the daughter of Oedipus, becomes her father's caretaker and guide after he blinds himself when he learns of his inadvertent incestuous relationship with his wife Jocasta, who is also his mother. Oedipus feels entitled to Antigone's devotion, and she gives up her independence to care for and please her father. Ellyn Kaschak suggests that this scenario exemplifies how women are trained to relate to men in a subservient manner. The task for men and women in feminist therapy is to resolve the Oedipal and Antigone complexes according to feminist principles. For men, resolution of the Oedipus complex requires that they develop the capacity to see women as independent beings and as whole beings rather than as possessions. For women, resolution of the Antigone complex requires the rejection of subservient roles, the ability to express their own needs, the development of assertiveness and independence, the definition of sexuality on their own terms, and the capacity to develop positive relationships with other women.

In contrast to Freud's view that anatomy is destiny, Kaschak uses the Oedipal story as an image of how gender roles are socially constructed. Furthermore, the basic themes associated with the respective complexes of men and women are experienced in myriad ways that are modified by race, class, sexual orientation, and age. The meanings associated with these complexes are highly complex and shaped by women's individual experiences. This basic assumption allows the feminist therapist to appreciate the diversity of women's experience and to integrate postmodern, social constructionist thinking and the perspectives of women of color within a radical feminist framework.

Both Laura Brown and Ellyn Kaschak have practiced and written about feminist therapy since its inception, and both have spoken increasingly about the importance of diversity, complexity, and inclusivity as central components of an integrated and radical feminist therapy. Both speak about the importance of transforming psychological practice but also appropriate some of the tools of traditional psychology if and when these tools can be reshaped to meet feminist goals. These types of efforts are likely to be especially important as feminist therapy continues to evolve and mature.

THE LEGACY OF RADICAL FEMINISM: ISSUES FOR THE 1990s AND THE NEXT CENTURY

Feminist therapy owes a significant debt to the basic tenets and ideals of radical feminism. Although many feminist therapists do not identify themselves as radical, radical and socialist feminist traditions have influenced feminist practice by challenging feminist therapists to eschew complacency and engage in an ongoing reflection about their practices. In the final section of this chapter, I will identify some of the significant issues associated with feminist therapy that are influenced by radical and socialist perspectives in feminism. They include the role of self-help, issues and changes in feminist group therapy, feminist ethics, relationships between feminist therapists trained in academic programs and those trained in alternative feminist agencies, issues regarding diagnosis and assessment, and the changing settings in which radical feminists work.

Self-Help

The strong commitment of radical feminists to connect individual solutions with political actions led to the establishment of a variety of self-help options for women, including CR groups, women's health and counseling collectives, abortion referral services, and rape crisis centers. Although some radical feminists have believed that feminism and therapy are incompatible (e.g., Tennov, 1973; Kitzinger and Perkins, 1993), they typically view self-help, sisterhood, and feminism as highly compatible. Jeanne Marecek and Diane Kravetz (1977) characterized feminist self-help systems as focusing on health, prevention, and personal growth rather than on recovery from illness. Second, power is centered within members and not in a professional leader. Members rely on mutual sharing, advice, support, and the pooling of member resources (Withorn, 1980). Self-help does not involve "unilateral do-it-yourself-ism" or "uninhibited individualism" (Tennov, 1973, p. 109), but is based on the collective study of issues and learning from each other within an organized group. Third, self-help is especially useful for helping individuals cope with crises such as rape and pregnancy in such a way that they are empowered rather than identified as the problem.

Ann Withorn (1980) noted that the nature and focus of self-help groups are widely divergent. One end of the self-help continuum is represented by politically focused feminist self-help groups. These groups are characterized by a "self-conscious, empowering democratic effort where women help each other and often provide an analysis and an example from which to criticize and make feminist demands on the system" (Withorn, 1980, p. 26). The other end of the spectrum consists of groups that focus on specific problems, such as twelve-step recovery groups, and rely on group process to enhance individual coping. These self-help groups do not attempt to provide alternative models for providing services or for restructuring society.

In contrast to the emphasis on community and political activism that permeated early feminist self-help agencies and self-help groups, the "recovery" movement and self-help literature for women have increasingly emphasized personal healing and a disease model over sociopolitical analysis. Kathleen Barry (1979) stated that:

> there has been resurrected an individualism which, flowing directly from the human potential movement, emphasizes taking one's own space, defining one's own reality, taking care of one's own needs. For many, concern over the quality of life is personal, individual, and focused on one's well-being. (p. 223)

The self-help literature and groups regarding codependency and women who "love too much" (Norwood, 1985) exemplify a shifting emphasis from radical politics to personal growth. Rather than fighting an uphill battle against sexism, patriarchy, and violence, women are viewed as fighting a battle against dysfunction, addiction, and relationship dependency (Brown, 1990c; Tallen, 1992; van Wormer, 1989). Codependency is popularly understood as the tendency to enter and remain in addictive relationships that are marked by dysfunctional patterns or an "excessive tendency to help other people" (Lamb, 1990, p. 26). The concept of codependency defines the victim of abuse or the partner of an addicted person as coculpable with the addicted person or perpetrator of abuse and thus, ignores the power differential between the perpetrator and the person who is the recipient of abuse (Tavris, 1990). The descriptions of codependency are also remarkably similar to women's prescribed cultural role. Bette Tallen (1992) stated the following: "I believe no difference exists between the definition of codependency and the definition of femininity. . . . In short, to be a codependent is to be a woman or to be treated as one" (p. 404). It should also be noted that many of the characteristics of so-called codependent behavior represent survival skills in a patriarchal culture (Tallen, 1990). The description of codependency also resembles the controversial label "self-defeating personality disorder" (DSM-III-R, 1987) and appears to support the very use of labels and victim blaming that radical feminists have fought so hard to eradicate (van Wormer, 1989).

Although many codependency self-help groups adopted the model of the CR group, the ideology and emphases of these two types of groups are markedly different. CR groups stress competency and an analysis of the social origins of problems, challenge power relations in the larger society, and focus efforts on empowering the group and individuals. In contrast, codependency, "process addiction," and twelve-step groups typically utilize a deficit or "disease" model of personality, examine personal and family roots of problems, encourage surrender to a "higher power" rather than involvement in social activism, and emphasize individual healing and empowerment over social change. Charlotte Kasl (1992) identified a variety of limitations of twelve-step programs for "dependency" issues including the following: (1) the assumption that members should emphasize their powerlessness over others, instead of stressing the need for women to unite and practice collective power; (2) the use of images of an all-powerful, male God; (3) the bonding of women on the basis of pain rather than shared power; (4) an emphasis on "detachment" from the abusive partner, which fails to acknowledge the woman's real suffering and pain; (5) a tendency to pathologize women's capacity to care for others; (6) the categorization of personal suffering and pain as individual issues and not the consequence of abusive systems; (7) the squelching of disagreement within the group for the sake of maintaining the value system promoted by the twelve steps; and (8) a limited emphasis on forming strong, healthy relationships.

Rather than connecting the personal with political issues, twelve-step programs tend to see relationship addiction as an illness from which no one ever completely recovers. They "promote a kind of narcissistic, continual self-examination, preventing people from accepting imperfections and having a sense of humor about the state of being human" (Kasl, 1992, p. 154). Thus, they do not foster a wider perspective that transcends self-interest. For some women, the allure of self-help groups and books is that they purport to embrace feminist principles; however, they often oversimplify and distort feminism and subtly blame women for the way in which social systems have influenced them (Lerner, 1990). Societal oppression may be ignored and individual solutions may become the rule (Brown, 1990c). As noted by Tavris (1992), "[c]odependency is an effort to solve the problem without changing the situation" (p. 43).

Wendy Kaminer (1992) stated that popular definitions of dysfunctional behavior have become so elastic that the meanings of injustice, abuse, and suffering have become distorted. Definitions of dysfunctional behavior and codependency render all claims of abuse as equal or comparable and gloss over social justice by "denying that there are degrees of injustice" (Kaminer, 1992, p. 155). Each person is seen as responsible for dealing with his or her own form of addiction or victimization, and the abuses of power associated with sexual assault, racism, and sexism are easily discounted or unrecognized. For example, the suffering and pain of survivors of sexual violence have been described increasingly with euphemisms or words that deny reality, such as "sexual correctness" (Crichton, 1993) or "rape hype" (Roiphe, 1993).

Harriet Lerner (1990) suggested that the positive outcome of some recovery movement groups and books is that they encourage women to validate themselves and take better care of themselves. They have also provided many women with a sense of community in which private pain could be validated, and they have helped women to redefine their self-worth in terms other than whether or not they are loved or "in love" (Brown, 1990c). However, recovery can become "a sort of compromise solution. It teaches women to move in the direction of 'more self' while it sanitizes and makes change safe, because the dominant group culture (never fond of 'those angry women') is not threatened by sick women meeting together to get well" (Lerner, 1990, p. 15). Furthermore, the recovery movement has been most responsive to the needs of those with greatest access to resources, time, and money while ignoring the realities of less privileged women. This practice supports a sense of complacency among more privileged women (Tallen, 1992), and it offers a method for helping these women find personal answers without considering the impact of their choices on the lives of less privileged women (Tallen, 1990).

The popular models of self-help that exist today represent very different versions than the models endorsed by radical feminists in the 1970s. Laura Brown (1990c) suggested that it is important for feminist therapists to respect the experience of women who have defined themselves as codependent. However, therapists must also help them reframe at least a part of what they are communicating in order to conceptualize issues in terms of unequal power and dominance. Charlotte Kasl (1992) indicated that feminists should work to redefine codependency as internalized oppression, which would acknowledge the utility of "codependency" as a survival tool, but also assure that oppression would be identified as the source and cause of "codependency." She also recommended that the principles of twelve-step groups should be reworked and reframed into "steps for discovery and empowerment" that connect the personal and political.

When the political meaning of personal issues is neglected, the powerful forces of denial within the larger culture gain an upper hand and support a backlash which declares that the very people who raise awareness about important issues are responsible for creating distress or false epidemics (Faludi, 1991; Herman, 1992). A recommitment to consciousness-raising and support of the grass-roots agencies that clearly connect the personal and political are necessary for ensuring that social change remains an important component of self-help and feminist therapy.

Group Feminist Therapy

During the early years of feminist therapy, feminist counseling groups emphasized the shared oppression of women and the external sources of their problems. Women were typically assigned to therapy groups on the basis of convenience rather than the type of presenting problem, and individual differences between women were minimized in order to heighten awareness of the similarities between women. By the mid-1980s, group feminist therapy had changed dramatically; group members were less likely to come together by virtue of their feminist views, and more likely to gather because they shared a specific problem. A survey of feminist therapists revealed that although approximately three-fourths of feminist therapists conducted groups, these groups tended to focus on specific issues rather than on the general interpersonal themes, which had received greater attention during the 1970s. A majority of therapists indicated that the demand for feminist groups had decreased, and only one-fourth of the therapists facilitated groups that resembled feminist therapy collective groups (Johnson, 1987). When groups based on CR principles were conducted, they were more frequently referred to as support groups, self-help groups, or as women's networks (Kirsch, 1987).

As feminist groups became more diverse and complex, group approaches were recommended for specific problems such as incest and sexual abuse (Cole, 1985; Courtois, 1988; McEvoy, 1990; Sprei, 1987), body image issues (Bergner, Remer, and Whetsell, 1985; Laidlaw, 1990), battering (Hartman, 1987; Lewis, 1983), eating disorders (Hotelling, 1987; Katzman, Weiss, and Wolchik, 1986), agoraphobia (Brehony, 1987), and sexual functioning (Cotten-Huston and Wheeler, 1987). Feminist therapists gained increased knowledge about the complexity of many of women's problems and were able to receive more extensive information about working with these problems in groups. Greater emphasis was placed on the successful individual resolution of issues and less emphasis was placed on understanding the similarities between diverse groups of women or the political ramifications of personal issues.

By the early 1980s, individual feminist therapy was the most typical form of feminist practice (Kaschak, 1981). Although the individual practice of feminist therapy has provided feminist therapists with opportunities to explore complicated issues in greater depth, there are potential costs associated with the increase of one-to-one work. Within individual counseling, "the unique capacities of people are made so evident that it is next to impossible not to treat those incapacities as *the* problems" (Kaschak, 1981, p. 275). Thus, women clients are more likely to view their problems as intrapsychic deficiencies, may feel isolated, and may experience less support for change. Although the individual feminist therapist may integrate a social analysis within therapy and point out social circumstances that influence women's lives, the therapist's analysis and statements are not verified or supported by the experiences of other women within a group. Furthermore, feminist therapists often worry about inappropriately imposing an unsolicited value system on clients; thus, they may avoid discussing political implications of personal issues (Fine and Gordon, 1989; Parvin and Biaggio, 1991). The possibility that the therapist's ideology will become imposed rather than considered as one among a variety of alternatives is more pronounced within individual settings in which the power differential between the counselor and client becomes more apparent. When women work together in groups, feminist therapists may experience greater freedom to share their ideas because clients have opportunities to test the therapist's ideas with each other and compare the realties of multiple women with the value system of the therapist (Longres and McLeod, 1980).

During the 1980s and 1990s, women have increasingly pursued individual strategies for working through personal difficulties. The move to greater individualism exhibited within self-help is also present within the professional practice of feminist therapy. Greater integration of group work and consciousness-raising within feminist therapy will be necessary in order to ensure that feminist therapists will utilize sociocultural explanations of distress and suggest collective solutions to problems (Enns, 1993). Sandra Butler and Claire Wintram (1991), in their book on feminist groupwork, stated the following:

> Feminist groupwork delabels, deconstructs boundaries, expands a sense of personal vision and makes the connections between these and wider socio-economic forces. The changes in women's personal lives have irreversible repercussions. Sustaining social change in the face of resistance and ridicule is nurtured by the bedrock of the group. Feminist groupwork breaks down the destructiveness of individualism. (p. 188)

Feminist Therapy Ethics

During the earliest years of feminist therapy, some feminist therapists naively assumed that because both the therapist and client were women, the type of power issues associated with hierarchical, patriarchal structures and relationships would not be evident in feminist therapy (Lerman and Rigby, 1990). However, assuming the title of "feminist therapist" does not insulate one from engaging in ethically problematic behaviors, including boundary violation and sexual victimization of clients (Brown, 1991a). The early radical feminist position of "undifferentiated egalitarianism" (Adleman and Barrett, 1990) represented a false sense of equality and a simplistic view of actual power differentials that exist between therapists and clients. As feminist therapy has matured, feminist therapists have recognized the importance of reflecting on the ethical practices of feminist therapists, and the Feminist Therapy Institute (FTI) has developed a feminist code of ethics.

Concerns about overlapping relationships are of particular importance to feminist therapists who work in small sociological communities that are defined by sexual orientation, ethnic minority status, or shared political values (e.g., radical feminist values). For example, a therapist and client who share feminist political values may find themselves working toward social change within the same community organization. Lesbian and ethnic minority feminist therapists, who may be involved in social networks linked to their minority status, may find it difficult to avoid social contact with clients who are members of the same small community. Laura Brown (1991a) recommended that ethical behavior should be viewed as a continuum of behaviors rather than as either-or rules or dualisms. As a first step in resolving dilemmas, feminist therapists should acknowledge the potential for overlapping relationships. When the potential for role overlap exists, feminist therapists should initiate discussion with clients so they can develop mutual plans for dealing with occasions when they may meet each other outside of therapy (FTI, 1990).

The Feminist Therapy Institute Code of Ethics (1990) clearly reflects the impact of radical feminist thinking in its redefinition of ethics according to feminist values. Traditional ethical codes tend to do the following: (1) define ethics in reactive rather than proactive terms, (2) describe issues in either-or terms rather than representing the complexity of ethical decisions, (3) pay limited attention to prevention and growth issues, (4) devote minimal attention to issues of diversity as they influence ethics, and (5) often frame issues in overly concrete, lengthy, and cumbersome language. Furthermore, recommended methods for resolving grievances are often paternalistic and tend to protect professionals rather than clients (Lerman and Porter, 1990).

The FTI Code is not intended as a substitute for existing professional codes, but represents a set of aspirational guidelines for conducting feminist therapy, training, and research (Rave and Larsen, 1990). First, it clearly exemplifies the thinking that the personal is political and reflects a proactive stance designed to eliminate oppression and empower women as a group. Second, it pays particular attention to the specific concerns of women as therapists and as clients. Third, it proposes guidelines for dealing with potentially risky situations associated with overlapping relationships. Fourth, it acknowledges that power differences between clients and therapists do exist and proposes ways in which the power of the therapist can be used in the client's best interest. Fifth, it attends to diversities of race, class, age, and ability and requires therapists to engage in constant monitoring of their attitudes, behaviors, and knowledge in order to ensure competent treatment of clients. It also highlights the importance self-care as a tool for ensuring the personal health of the therapist. Sixth, it articulates the responsibility of feminist therapists to address social change as well as personal issues (FTI, 1990; Rave and Larsen, 1990).

Social Activism

Edna Rawlings and Diane Carter (1977) identified social action as an "essential professional responsibility of therapists" (p. 63) and the first radical feminist therapists believed that limiting one's practice to counseling individuals was tantamount to treating the symptom and ignoring the disease created by social conditions. However, commitment to social action no longer remains an area of consensus among feminist therapists (Ballou and Gabalac, 1985).

It appears that there are multiple reasons for many feminist therapists' decreased emphasis on activism. Feminist therapists and their clients who did not personally experience the political activity associated with the women's movement of the 1970s may view activism as irrelevant to feminist therapy. Other feminist therapists are particularly aware of the unintended consequences of early activism: Increased options for women have sometimes led to role overload and new oppressive requirements for women. Some individuals question whether women are better off in the 1990s than they were during prefeminist eras (Meara and Harmon, 1989). Many obvious forms of sexism have been eliminated, and current forms of bias are often more subtle, possibly contributing to complacency among some feminist therapists. Finally, women have also been encouraged to pursue the "revolution within" by focusing on the implications of feminism for personal transformation (Steinem, 1992).

One of the first volumes on feminist therapy included several chapters dealing specifically with social activism as therapy (Adams and Durham, 1977; Gluckstern, 1977), but the more recent literature on feminist therapy has focused primarily on microinterventions. Some of the current confusion over the appropriateness and role of social action may be associated with feminist therapists' lack of training in social advocacy or a limited view of what type of social activism is useful.

Some feminist therapists have become involved in social activism at the national and legislative level. However, women have historically been more actively involved in grassroots efforts and citizen action groups rather than professional activism such as legislative lobbying (Reeser, 1988). It is important to affirm grassroots and community efforts as crucial social change efforts. Social action can take on myriad forms including the following: (1) conducting research that places women's issues in a larger social context (Dobash and Dobash, 1988); (2) linking research implications to social policy recommendations (e.g., Browne, 1993; Fitzgerald, 1993; Koss, 1993); (3) providing pro bono services to women in alternative/feminist agencies for women (Withorn, 1984); (4) engaging in primary prevention efforts and leading public education and support groups within the community (Albee, 1981; Koss and Harvey, 1991; Wedenoja, 1991); (5) assessing and altering organizational climates to serve clients more effectively (Harrison, 1987); (6) incorporating CR and antiracisist activities within classes and educational workshops; and (7) working with grassroots organizations to provide adequate day care and housing, to change community attitudes about violence, and to ensure equal access to medical treatment (Weil, 1986).

Relationships Between Grassroots Workers and Professionally Trained Therapists

In her discussion of feminist therapy at the end of its first decade, Ellyn Kaschak (1981) distinguished between radical grassroots feminist therapy and radical professional therapy. Whereas grassroots radical feminist counselors were most typically trained in alternative women's settings and often worked within feminist crisis centers and collectives, professional radical feminist therapists have received their training in academic institutions and typically worked in collectives, private practice, or social service agencies. Both groups of radical women have shared radical feminist values, but have emphasized somewhat different facets of their work with women. Whereas grassroots therapists tend to believe that both clients and therapists must be involved in social change, professional radical feminists tend to think that social change is central to the therapist's mission but an option for the client. Grassroots therapists have sought to erase all power differences within peer counseling, and radical professional therapists tend to believe that the therapist could use nonexploitive forms of power on behalf of clients. With respect to expertise, grassroots therapists have generally not defined themselves as experts and have viewed the client as the expert on her process; radical professional therapists agree that the client is her own best expert, but also note that the therapist brings specific skills and expertise to the relationship. Finally, whereas professionally trained therapists tend to view a wide range of interventions at the individual, group, and societal level as important, grassroots therapists more frequently emphasize the importance of societal issues and group interventions designed to influence social change (Kaschak, 1981). These two groups have generally worked together in compatible ways. However, most professional therapists do not hold radical feminist values and issues of mistrust between professionals and grassroots workers have persisted over the past several decades.

The mistrust of grassroots workers for professional mental health workers is not surprising in that prior to the establishment of anti-rape and battered women's movements, psychological models of victimized women were almost entirely negative. The discussion of violence was virtually absent within the psychological literature, and when it surfaced on rare occasions, women were typically blamed for their victimization. For example, an article titled "The Wife Beater's Wife" (Snell, Rosenwald, and Robey, 1964) described the typical wife of a batterer as experiencing a masochistic need to be the recipient of aggression; she periodically desired to be "punished for her castrating activity," and her husband would need to "re-establish his masculine identity" (p. 111). Women who charged their husbands with assault were viewed as "aggressive, efficient, masculine, and sexually frigid" (p. 111). Grassroots activists were also critical of professionals when they conveniently claimed violence as a mental health problem after activists increased social consciousness about violence. Along with the labeling of violence as a mental health problem, "political analysis disappeared, was changed, or was considered beyond the scope of professional concern" (Schechter, 1982, p. 107). Thus, grassroots activists often fear that "professionalization" of services will result in a loss of political and social vision (Cooper-White, 1989).

Despite historic tensions between grassroots organizers and professionals, the future growth of radical feminist therapy must rely on the contributions of both groups. Cooperation between grassroots and professionally trained radical feminist therapists may be especially productive when each group focuses its efforts on specific stages of recovery from violence. Peer and grassroots efforts are especially useful during crisis phases for (1) validating and supporting victims, (2) accompanying and advocating for women as they negotiate the social service and judicial systems, and (3) providing basic information about social and political reasons why battering, rape, and other forms of violence occur. In contrast, professional feminist therapists can help women address the long-term effects of violence that may appear in the form of depression, posttraumatic stress, or dissociation. The therapist can also work with the client on understanding issues in a sociopolitical context, channeling anger, and forming healthy relationships. Grassroots and professionally trained feminist therapists are most likely to work together effectively when both groups are personally involved in some form of community education, advocacy, and political activism that helps them focus concretely on their common goals (Cooper-White, 1989). Given the fact that professional therapists and grassroots activists/therapists typically work in different types of agencies, it is also important to establish positive referral and communication networks.

The Politics of Diagnosis in Feminist Therapy

Edna Rawlings and Diane Carter (1977) stated that feminist therapists do not use diagnostic labels because they reflect the inappropriate application of social power, ignore environmental influences on symptom formation, represent a major instrument of oppression, and reduce the therapist's respect for clients. Diagnostic labels encourage therapists to focus exclusively on intrapsychic symptoms, the removal of which may ignore the communicative function of symptoms, encourage adjustment to status quo norms, and reinforce stereotypes about women (Klein, 1976; Whitely and Whitely, 1978). If symptoms are removed without attention to context, the person is deprived of the indirect influence and symbolic communication associated with the problem, and thus, may be less powerful after therapy than before counseling. As a result, feminist efforts have focused less on diagnosing and controlling symptoms and more on exploring the role of strong emotions in women's lives. Clients are encouraged to use intense emotions to create satisfactory solutions for themselves (Gilbert, 1980; Marecek and Kravetz, 1977; Rawlings and Carter, 1977).

Although liberal feminist therapists have focused primarily on eliminating sex bias in diagnosis, radical feminists often rejected traditional systems, avoided diagnostic labels, and utilized descriptive narratives and gender role analysis (Brown, 1986, 1990) to assess the meaning of the client's problems. The advantage of gender role analysis over other alternatives is that it is based on a cooperative and phenomenological approach to assessment in which the client's meaning and attitudes are considered equally important as the assessor's interpretations. The client is viewed as her own best expert (Rawlings and Carter, 1977) and the interpretations of the therapist are considered as hypotheses to be tested with the client's perceptions.

During the 1970s, feminists identified rape trauma syndrome (Burgess and Holmstrom, 1974) and battered woman syndrome (Walker, 1979) as women's typical responses to traumatic external events. These syndromes connected the personal and political by indicating how violence against women influences the psychological self and avoids the victim blaming associated with formal diagnostic categories. The addition of the diagnostic category of post-traumatic stress disorder (PTSD) to the DSM-III (American Psychiatric Association) in 1980 provided the first label approved by the psychiatric community that acknowledged the impact of external events on psychological well-being. Feminist therapists, who previously eschewed all labeling, reconsidered PTSD as a potentially nonstigmatizing method of conceptualizing women's distress. Critics note that this label does not account for all of the symptoms or the complexity of responses associated with violence, nor does it adequately conceptualize the sequelae of multiple traumatic events or long-term abuse (Brown, 1994). However, it views psychological responses to trauma as normal responses to abnormal events, integrates multiple symptoms under a straightforward framework, thus supporting the development of more comprehensive models for understanding women's reactions to trauma (Goodman, Koss, and Russo, 1993). For example, many women diagnosed with borderline personality disorder, somatization disorder, or multiple personality disorder are victims of traumatic events, and their problems can be more adequately addressed when they are viewed as long-term chronic effects of PTSD (Dutton-Douglas, 1989; Herman, 1992). Although the original framework of PTSD is not based on feminist principles, it can be used in ways that are compatible with feminist principles. Other diagnostic labels, such as borderline personality disorder and other personality disorders, are virtually impossible to use without blaming victims. As noted by Laura Brown (1994), "If you call it a skunk, you will assume that it smells" (p. 131). A label such as "borderline personality disorder" presupposes the existence of internal pathology and is likely to increase the therapist's tendency to blame the client for the complex array of survival mechanisms that she has developed for coping with a difficult and often violent past.

Judith Herman (1981, 1992) has contributed substantially to the feminist therapy literature on trauma survivors and proposed a new diagnostic category termed "complex post-traumatic stress disorder." In contrast to simple post-traumatic stress disorder, which accurately describes the typical reactions to single traumatic events, complex post-traumatic stress disorder describes a complicated set of reactions to "a history of subjection to totalitarian control over a prolonged period (months to years)" (p. 121). Concentration camp survivors and survivors of sexual trauma or battering are examples of individuals who may experience this disorder, which typically involves alterations in affect regulation, consciousness, self-perception, and meaning systems. It also entails alterations in the victims' perceptions of the perpetrator and disruptions in relationships with others (Herman, 1992). By proposing new ways of conceptualizing reactions to violence and abuse, feminists may be able to change the way in which the larger mental health profession deals with disorders that affect the lives of a high percentage of women.

In another effort to create a category of disorders that could be integrated with radical feminist principles, Laura Brown (1992a) proposed the creation of "abuse and oppression artifact disorders" that would focus on "the psychological sequelae of exposure to stressors that may be unusual, but often are embedded in the framework of the culture in which an individual develops" (p. 223). Assessment for these disorders would explore how various stressors including abuse, racism, sexism, and heterosexism are connected to (1) persistent and painful behavior patterns, such as learned helplessness, avoidant behavior, or rescuing behavior; (2) the distortion of or constriction of affective capacities that is exhibited through fear, emotional numbness, or gender-stereotypical behavior; and (3) disruption/distortion of cognition that emerges in the form of self-blame, shame, denial, confusion, or pessimism. The behavior patterns associated with these disorders are typically defined as personality disorders in current psychiatric terminology.

Issues related to assessment are likely to be controversial among feminist therapists for some time to come. Some radical feminists continue to reject all diagnostic labels, including schizophrenia (e.g., Burstow, 1992). Other radical feminists believe that the categorical rejection of *all* diagnostic labels is tantamount to "throwing out the baby with the bathwater." Given our increasing knowledge of the biological/physiological contributions to some disorders such as depression, bipolar disorder, or schizophrenia, the denial of disability may result in romantization or denial of important medical services to individuals whose quality of life may be increased through access to these services (Perkins, 1991a, 1992).

Laura Brown's (1994) recent discussion of a radical feminist approach noted that the feminist maxim that the master's tools cannot be used to dismantle the master's house (Lorde, 1984) provides therapists with an inadequate basis for countering patriarchy. In order to provide alternative models of conceptualization, feminist therapists must understand the social meanings of traditional diagnosis, comprehend how they can be used to oppress individuals, and reshape these tools for feminist change. Although the master's tools cannot be the only tools for transforming psychotherapy, they can be used to "reforge, reshape, and transform each possibility for oppression into one of liberation and social change" (Brown, 1994, p. 199).

Brown (1994) noted that although some early feminist therapists concluded that diagnosis was "irrelevant" or "no more than negative labeling" (p. 125), this position is naive. If all of the complex problems that clients bring to therapy are reduced to "feeling bad," the therapist has an inadequate framework for guiding the client toward wholeness. It is essential for feminist therapists and their clients to "work jointly to develop organized hypotheses about the nature, origins, and meanings of the client's distress" (p. 128) Such a process helps the client and therapist name the distress accurately; identify the complex individual, interpersonal, and social/contextual factors that contribute to the client's issues; and clarify the course and goals of therapy.

Although radical feminist therapists may disagree about the utility of diagnostic labels, they agree that assessment of a client's problems must be based on a shared dialogue between the therapist and client. Through such discussion, clients achieve greater understanding of the personal, cultural, and social aspects of their problems. Feminist therapists should inform clients about their hypotheses, how these were developed, and what theories and beliefs influenced the therapist's thinking (Brown and Walker, 1990). Assessments should be tested with the client, who should be encouraged to ask questions or propose alternatives. The therapist should also be willing to explain why she does or does not reject the use of traditional diagnoses.

Radical feminist therapists who prefer to avoid diagnostic labels may feel forced to consider using such labels when insurance reimbursement for services depends upon the provision of a diagnostic code. In such situations, the client and therapist can choose to work within the limits imposed by insurance reimbursers or develop some other type of fee arrangement independent of insurance guidelines. Given the financial ramifications of such choices, the client's wishes should be respected. If the therapist and client opt to work with insurance providers, the choice of a diagnostic label should be based on honest assessment and the mutual discussion of the strengths and limitations of each potential diagnostic label.

Although assessment and diagnosis remain controversial issues, it is important to acknowledge the activism of feminist therapists who have worked against the inclusion of new diagnostic categories in DSM-III-R (APA, 1987) and DSM-IV (APA, 1994) that include elements of victim blaming. For example, feminists revealed the biased nature of masochistic personality disorder (later renamed self-defeating personality disorder) and late luteal phase dysphoric disorder, which appeared in a section on diagnostic categories for further study in the DSM-III-R (Caplan, 1995; Gallant and Hamilton, 1988; Walker, 1989). Feminist therapists suggested that up to 85 percent of normally socialized women exhibit many of the criteria of self-defeating personality disorder (SDPD), which describes the behaviors of persons who remain passive and immobilized in exploitive relationships (Walker and Dutton-Douglas, 1988). They noted that such a label is likely to blame women for being the target of male violence rather than placing responsibility on society and abusive partners. Furthermore, SDPD did not acknowledge the survival value of learned sacrificial or pacifying behaviors in reducing the emotional or physical violence that accompanies abusive relationships. To point out the oppressiveness of this label, Paula Caplan (1991) proposed a new diagnostic category titled "Delusional Dominating Personality Disorder," which is characterized by fourteen criteria associated with overconformity to a traditional "real man" image. SDPD also overlapped substantially with other personality disorders, lacked diagnostic usefulness, and was supported by limited empirical data. The activism of feminist psychologists was crucial in eliminating further consideration of this disorder; no mention of this proposed category appears in DSM-IV (APA, 1994).

Late luteal dysphoric disorder (LLDD) contains similar flaws as SDPD, including the fact that it highlights the biological elements of women's lives over social factors, pays limited attention to situational and environmental factors associated with women's menstrual cycles, and ignores the fact that the psychological symptoms of "premenstrual syndrome (PMS)" can be adequately conceptualized, through existing options (Gallant and Hamilton, 1988). Carol Tavris (1992) noted that to a large degree, PMS has been manufactured by the media, which has labeled it with terms such as the "monthly menace" and the "internal earthquake." Extensive credence is given to this "syndrome" during historical cycles when women's participation in the workforce is questioned. Furthermore, research on women's menstrual cycles has been riddled with methodological biases, including inadequate sample sizes, the reliance on retrospective reports, the failure of researchers to use adequate control groups, an emphasis on negative premenstrual symptoms and lack of attention to positive menstrual experiences, and the tendency to overgeneralize from psychiatric populations to all other populations of women (Gallant and Hamilton, 1988; Matlin, 1996; Tavris, 1992). Although feminists were successful in eliminating SDPD from further consideration as a diagnostic category, LLDD has been renamed premenstrual dysphoric disorder and appears in the DSM-IV in the list of proposed disorders that will receive further consideration.

Feminist Organizations

Radical and socialist feminists have sought to create organizations that are radically different from traditional structures. As noted earlier in this chapter, rape crisis centers, battered women's shelter's, and feminist therapy collectives of the early 1970s were committed to antihierarchical, egalitarian structures. Employees and volunteers often refused to become aligned with formal organizations for fear of being subtly coopted by such organizations. In order to gain the resources necessary to serve their clientele and sustain long-term services, most feminist organizations gradually adopted more formal policies or a modified collective structure. Claire Reinelt (1995) noted that although early radical feminist organizations successfully minimized differences between personnel based on status or specialized knowledge, radical collectives often had no adequate structures for ensuring the accountability of workers, for dealing with informal power coalitions (that were sometimes more difficult to contend with than formal structures), or for working through personal conflicts without disrupting relationships or influencing services in a negative manner.

Over time, the differences between formal and collective feminist organizations have blurred. Feminists have increasingly adopted more formal structures, explored how feminists can use radical beliefs to transform mainstream mental health institutions, and have learned how to use tactical maneuvers or "insider techniques" to achieve the goals of "outsiders" (Spalter-Roth and Schreiber, 1995). Reinelt (1995) stated that the modified structures of feminist organizations should not be viewed as "quiet slippage toward ever greater bureaucratization" (p. 101), but as a commitment to creating innovative strategies to deal with new challenges of new eras. Jo Freeman (1995) also noted that "movements are not institutions, but to survive beyond the initial burst of spontaneity they must take on many of the characteristics of institutions" (p. 404). In contrast to the fears of some early feminists, encapsulation and stagnation are not automatic consequences of greater formalization of organizations, provided its members create mechanisms that attend to the maintenance of important existing services as well as social activism.

During the early years of feminist therapy, radical feminist therapists were most frequently found within collectives or in independent practice. Laura Brown (1994) noted, however, that as more individuals are trained as feminist therapists, the diversity of settings in which they practice has broadened. Although participation in mainstream institutions can coopt the efforts of feminists, it is also possible for feminist therapists to coopt the efforts of mainstream organizations. Feminist therapists can successfully challenge mainstream institutions to adopt practices consistent with feminist values if they resist complacency, are knowledgeable about and attentive to the subtle biases present in mainstream mental health practices, and are aware of the ways in which their feminist values can be subverted within these settings. Laura Brown (1994) commented, "The notion that we might get patriarchy to pay for its own dismantling is an attractive one" (p. 198). The challenge for radical feminist therapists in the late 1990s is to resist making dogmatic statements about contexts in which radical feminist aims can be achieved and to maintain vigilant attention to new structures in which they can implement social change.

CONCLUDING COMMENTS

Feminists who are influenced by radical and socialist feminist perspectives assume a wide range of positions regarding the degree to which mainstream psychotherapy can be integrated with psychotherapy principles. Kitzinger and Perkins (1993) reject psychotherapy altogether as a viable method for solving women's problems, and Burstow (1992) rejects many of the tools and ethical stances of mainstream psychology. Laura Brown (1994), however, views radical feminist psychotherapy as a crucial tool for empowering individuals to become involved in social change. While highly critical of the sexism, racism, and heterosexism that permeates much traditional psychological thinking, she believes that feminist therapists can use many psychological tools to achieve radical feminist goals. A well-developed feminist consciousness is an essential catalyst for helping radical feminist therapists both critique and transform the discipline of psychology.

Despite differences regarding how radical feminist goals are interpreted, "the personal is political" remains a central theme. Issues of power and politics are central to psychotherapy. "A client comes to perceive her problem as just one knot in a power network that ties up many peers with seemingly equal tightness" (Elias, 1975, p. 58). A salient theme of radical forms of feminist therapy is that women's problems are not only the result of unequal opportunity (a liberal feminist position), but are also the consequence of the devaluation of women that permeates the very structure of institutions such as the Church, legislative bodies, the justice system, educational systems, and the family. The transformation of these systems is a salient goal of feminist psychotherapy. As a result, feminist therapy is a "disruptive force" (Brown, 1994, p. 29)," or a "subversive dialogue" designed to resist and "subvert patriarchal dominance at the most subtle and powerful levels, as it is internalized and personified in the lives of therapists and their clients, colleagues, and communities" (Brown, 1994, p. 17).

Chapter 6

Cultural Feminist Themes in Feminist Therapy

Cultural feminists have sought to revalue women's experiences that have historically been devalued. Much of the material written by feminist therapists that is most consistent with cultural feminism focuses on maternal values, mother-daughter relationships, and the relational capacities of women. This chapter begins with a summary of the early contributions of the cultural psychoanalytic feminists Karen Horney and Clara Thompson. It then describes feminist relational personality theories, provides an overview of recent psychodynamic feminist approaches to feminist therapy, and concludes with a discussion of Jungian archetypal, or goddess, psychology. The description of each orientation is followed by a critique.

EARLY CULTURAL FEMINISTS: KAREN HORNEY AND CLARA THOMPSON

From the 1920s to the 1940s, Karen Horney and Clara Thompson contributed a series of articles on the psychology of women that anticipated current versions of cultural feminism. The works of both women were collected posthumously (Horney, 1967; Thompson, 1971) and have only recently been fully appreciated (Westkott, 1986). Both theorists rejected Freud's biologically deterministic views and emphasized the way in which culture influences women's sense of self. Karen Horney (1926/1967) wrote the following:

> Like all sciences and all valuations, the psychology of women has hitherto been considered only from the point of view of

men. It is inevitable that the man's position of advantage should cause objective validity to be attributed to his subjective, affective relations to the woman, and . . . the psychology of women hitherto actually represents a deposit of the desires and disappointments of men. (p. 56)

She noted that power differences between men and women significantly influence their development and commented, "Historically the relation of the sexes may be crudely described as that of master and slave. . . . In actual fact a girl is exposed from birth onward to the suggestion . . . of her inferiority" (Horney, 1926/1967, p. 69).

According to Karen Horney (1939), masculine presuppositions of true womanhood and the devaluation of women include "the greater dependency of woman; the emphasis on woman's weakness and frailty; the ideology that it is in woman's nature to lean on someone and that her life is given content and meaning only through others: family, husband, children" (p. 113). She also noted that women had unconsciously learned to adapt to men's perceptions and had learned to see themselves "in the way that their men's wishes demanded of them" (1926/1967, p. 57). As a result of men's unconscious depreciation of womanhood, women learn to define motherhood and femininity as a burden and struggle rather than a source of strength and power.

Horney was especially critical of Freud's use of concepts such as penis envy to reinforce the inferior status of women in society and declared that "[i]n fact, there is scarcely any character trait in woman which is not assumed to have an essential root in penis envy" (1939, p. 104). Within Freud's model, traits attributed to penis envy included women's presumed sense of vanity, physical modesty, limited sense of justice, and jealousy. In keeping with her cultural analysis of men's and women's roles, Horney rejected the notion that penis envy is based on women's perceived biological inferiority to men but is based on women's awareness of their limited social power in a masculine world. She suggested that Freud's use of penis envy to explain women's feelings of inferiority represented a "simple" (1939, p. 107) solution that ignored complex social factors. Instead, women's envy of men "may be the expression of a wish for all those qualities or privileges which in our culture are regarded as masculine, such as strength, courage, independence, success, sexual freedom, [and the] right to choose a partner" (1939, p. 108).

In addition to identifying roles and privileges denied to women, Karen Horney noted ways in which women were encouraged to engage in a "flight from womanhood" (1926/1967, p. 54) because of the presumed inferiority of traditional female strengths. She noted that women had been trained to overvalue that which is male and to compete with each other for relationships with powerful men, thus leading them to ignore positive skills and qualities within themselves. Socially prescribed roles lead women to emphasize pleasing men through the pursuit of a "cult of beauty and charm" and to depend on men for care, protection, love, and prestige (Horney, 1934/1967; O'Connell, 1980).

As a part of her efforts to revalue women's experience, Karen Horney posited the existence of unique female and mothering instincts. She suggested that womb envy in men is as significant a factor in men's lives as penis envy is in women's lives (Horney, 1933/1967; O'Connell, 1980). In contrast to men's need to prove their masculinity through erections, women do not need to prove themselves in a similar way, a reality that fills men with both admiration and resentment as well as anxiety about their physical inferiority (Horney, 1932/1967). This position, which suggested women's biological superiority, represented a departure from her sociological perspective and a reliance on biological determinism reminiscent of Freud's work. This version of women's "special nature" or "differentness" has been criticized by some feminists for "essentializing" women's characteristics that are the product of culture and socialization, maximizing differences between women and men, and supporting stereotypes that legitimize differential treatment of men and women (Chodorow, 1978; Garrison, 1981).

During the second stage of her career, Karen Horney developed an inclusive theory of development and neurosis and postulated three major modes of dealing with the world: moving toward others, moving against others, and moving away from others (Horney, 1945). Her descriptions of these styles and the family factors that influence their development provided a foundation for recent feminist theories that focus on how early experiences reinforce relationship-oriented identities in women and more separate, disconnected identities in men (Chodorow, 1978; Gilligan, 1982; Jordan and Surrey, 1986).

Clara Thompson was influenced by the interpersonal school of psychoanalysis, which emphasized the centrality of relationships in development. She did not propose new theories about the causes of women's difficulties but sought to clarify how women had coped with awareness of their cultural inferiority. Like Karen Horney, she rejected the notion that "penis envy" is biologically based and proposed that it represents "a picturesque way of referring to the type of warfare which so often goes on between men and women" (Thompson, 1971, p. 74). She noted that physiological/sexual differences between men and women are easily distinguishable and thus, become the focus of "derogation in any competitive situation in which one group aims to get power over the other." (p. 75). In a patriarchal culture, the penis becomes the symbol of power, and "the restricted opportunities afforded woman, the limitations placed on her development and independence give a real basis for envy of the male quite apart from any neurotic trends" (p. 77). If hours were a matriarchal culture, the breast would become the symbol of power. In contrast to the way in which male power is associated with aggression, power associated with the breast stands for "life-giving capacity rather than force and energy" (p. 74).

Clara Thompson (1971) encouraged women to avoid accepting the dominant male model of mental health, which she termed the "masculinity complex" (p. 91) and challenged women to define themselves on the basis of their own strengths. She believed that women would lose connection with their own interests if they tried to mold their lives after men. Both Clara Thompson and Karen Horney anticipated many contemporary cultural feminists who would object to the creation of a psychology of women that is based on a psychology of men and who would encourage women to develop a psychology that is based on women's ways of being and knowing.

FEMINIST PERSONALITY THEORIES: WOMEN IN RELATIONSHIPS

Although feminist critiques of personality theory emerged during the early 1970s (e.g., Carlson, 1972; Doherty, 1973), it was not until the late 1970s and early 1980s that alternative theories informed by feminist thought began to appear. Jean Baker Miller (1976) and Carol Gilligan (1977) noted that a substantial number of mainstream personality theories are based on androcentric models of maturity, and embedded in empirical research on white middle-class men that has been generalized to the lives of women (e.g., Kohlberg, 1981; Levinson, 1978; Perry, 1970). Gilligan (1977, 1982) also criticized mainstream theorists for equating separation, autonomy, and individualism with mental health. She noted that when traditional theories pay attention to women's experience, relationship themes are often portrayed in negative ways, as exemplified by the following examples.

Erik Erikson (1968) proposed that for men, identity precedes intimacy, while for women, identity and intimacy tasks are fused. He also asserted that the interpersonal nature of female development glosses over the most vital issues of identity: the selection of an ideology to follow and the choice of an occupation. The young adult woman does not clearly resolve issues associated with career choice and the selection of a life philosophy, but defines her identity through "the selective nature of her search for a man" (p. 283). The central focus of the woman's identity is her potential for motherhood. Her capacities to hold on, hold in, include, and accept, as reflected by her anatomical design, make the woman gifted in intimacy and the "protected inner circle of maternal care" (Erikson, 1968). Although Erikson viewed women's capacity to maintain relationships as positive attributes, he also saw women's relational skills as impeding clear identity formation.

Although personality theorists often devote attention to relationships as central to the testing and developing of one's identity, the mature adult self has typically been seen as self-sufficient, self-supporting, and distinct from others. For Levinson (1978), the novice adult male is portrayed as chasing "the dream" that consists of active striving, the pursuit of competence, and rational consideration of options available to the man. Significant relationships are depicted as the means to the goal of individual achievement, or viewed as important for their potential to facilitate or detract from a person's search for personal identity.

The emphasis on the singular self is also present in humanistic psychology. Although Abraham Maslow (1956) depicted the self-actualizing person as capable of more profound interpersonal relationships than others, he also described this individual as a "self-contained" person who is "independent of the good opinion of other people" (Maslow, 1956, p. 176). For Carl Rogers (1956), genuine, congruent, empathic relationships provide the medium for self-affirmation and the prizing of the self. One's mental health, however, is ultimately expressed through an internal locus of evaluation. Individual experience is construed as the highest authority, and evaluation by others is not considered an appropriate guide for behavior.

Most mainstream personality theories are based on formative empirical research with homogenous groups of relatively privileged men. For example, Murray's (1938) psychology of needs and Perry's (1970) theory about cognitive and intellectual development in college students were based primarily on studies of male students at Harvard. Levinson (1978) explored the developmental paths of forty men, and Kohlberg (1981) studied the evolution of morality and principled behavior in eighty-four boys, whose lives he followed for approximately twenty years. Each of these theories have provided valuable insights about human behavior, but can support narrow thinking about healthy behavior. Women are evaluated according to their pursuit of the dominant goals of privileged men: achievement, individualism, self-determination, mastery, and personal success.

Many feminist psychologists have been critical of traditional theories of psychology. The unique contribution of feminist relational theorists is that they have not only criticized androcentric biases, but have also proposed theories that revalue the relational qualities of women that have been previously ignored by psychologists. I will briefly describe three major feminist personality theories in the next section. Each model builds on existing theories within psychology and reshapes theory to account for relational themes in women's lives.

Carol Gilligan: In a Different Voice

Carol Gilligan's (1982) ground-breaking study of moral development was among the first efforts to correct the biases of androcentric theory and provide an alternative model that is more consistent with women's experience. Her work has been widely recognized across disciplines and has had a significant impact on the development of feminist ethics and cultural feminist theory (e.g., Cole and Coultrap-McQuin, 1992). It has also been a catalyst for the development of other relational theories of women's identity.

Gilligan's (1982) findings about women's capacity to maintain significant attachments were formalized in her model of connected moral development, which she proposed as an alternative to Kohlberg's (1981) morality of justice and fairness. The primary source for this relational theory of moral development came from Gilligan's abortion decision-making study, which examined the choices of a group of twenty-nine women from diverse social, ethnic, and marital backgrounds. Additional data came from the study of college students' moral development as well as a rights and responsibilities study, which examined the moral decision making of thirty-six men and women from different stages of life (Gilligan, 1982).

A morality of care develops through three major phases that represent a modification of the three stages of preconventional, conventional, and postconventional morality proposed by Kohlberg (1981). At stage one, morality is based on individual survival and self-interest that is often formed as a response to feelings of powerlessness; at stage two, individuals define morality as responsibility toward others, meeting others' needs, and self-sacrifice; and at stage three, ethical behavior is defined as a morality of nonviolence that allows women to balance self-nurture with care and concern for others. In contrast to Gilligan's model, Kohlberg's (1981) theory identified relational themes as significant only during a substage of "conventional" morality. According to Kohlberg, the individual decision maker transcends this conventional form of morality as he or she moves into a postconventional stage of reasoning, which is associated with abstract considerations about issues of justice. Relational themes are limited to personal choices that are based on gaining the approval of others. Kohlberg's model did not account for the complicated and rich ways in which relationships may influence decisions as one's sense of connectedness becomes increasingly mature. It ignored the potential role of relationships for facilitating positive growth throughout the developmental process. Gilligan's model corrected many of these oversights.

The implications of Gilligan's (1982) work extend beyond the domain of moral development; they hold significance for the ways in which men and women define themselves. Nona Lyons (1983) noted that relationships play a role in all people's lives but take on different meanings for persons who define themselves in more separate or in more connected ways. For persons with a more separate sense of self, reciprocity, rules, and roles take precedence. Issues are negotiated through the application of impartial and objective rules, which are embedded in one's obligations to fulfill specific roles. For persons with a more connected sense of self, strict application of rules is less important than considering issues within their context. This orientation involves "seeing others in their own terms, entering into the situations of others in order to know them as the others do, that is, to try to understand how they see their situations" (p. 135). In contrast to the heightened role of reciprocity, rules, and roles, the relational self focuses more extensively on responses to others, care, and interdependence.

Gilligan's (1982) model has encouraged therapists to consider women's relationships as a source of empowerment. Investigations about the unique features of justice and care orientations help us conceptualize ethical decision making in a more complete fashion. It is important to note, however, that although recent studies support the existence of distinct moralities of justice and care, men and women use both orientations (Donenberg and Hoffman, 1988) and consider them fairly equally (Ford and Lowery, 1986). One study found that a morality of care is more closely related to one's gender role orientation than to one's gender. Women who demonstrated a care or other-oriented approach to moral reasoning were more likely to endorse a feminine gender role orientation (Sochting, Skoe, and Marcia, 1994). Another study found that men's and women's responses to both hypothesized and real-life parenting issues were remarkably similar, suggesting that situational demands are likely to influence the moral reasoning of both men and women (Clopton and Sorell, 1993). In summary, the different voices of justice and care seem less associated with gender than Gilligan originally asserted.

Early criticisms of Gilligan's work noted that her original research repeated the same flaws that permeated its androcentric precursors by focusing only on one gender. However, it should be noted that studying women on their own terms—especially at initial stages of inquiry—may be important to avoid viewing a male comparison group as the normative group from which women's experiences diverge. In more recent efforts to elaborate on the "different voice" of women, Gilligan and her colleagues have directly compared the moral reasoning of men and women and have explored the decision-making patterns of individuals in low-income and urban settings. Theoretical refinements have focused on how the self develops and changes during childhood and adolescence, and researchers have examined how and when care and justice orientations are typically chosen by women and men (Gilligan, Lyons, and Hanmer, 1990; Gilligan, Ward, and Taylor, 1988).

A Modification of Erikson's Formulation of Identity

Erik Erikson's model of personality development has been criticized for viewing identity formation in adolescence as an important prerequisite for the task of early adulthood, forming intimate relationships. Erikson defined the key tasks of identity formation as defining oneself as an autonomous person and developing an inner organization of one's needs, abilities, and self-perceptions. Identity formation involves gaining a sense of one's own uniqueness and developing a self-structure based on one's personal abilities, beliefs, and history. As noted earlier, Erikson (1968) indicated that women appear to have greater difficulty establishing a firm sense of self apart from their relationships, and also seem to fuse tasks of identity and intimacy. He concluded that whereas women's activities are oriented toward valuing harmonious activities associated with their "vital inner potential" (p. 275) and the "inner space" (p. 270) of women's reproductive organs, men pursue activities associated with independence, assertiveness, and "outer space" (p. 270). Although Erikson (1968) noted that women were often "gifted with a certain intimacy" (p. 284), the fact that many women did not establish a strong independent self troubled him. As with Kohlberg's model, Erikson's view of the role and nature of relational themes was narrow and androcentric, and it led to restrictive perceptions about women's identity.

Marcia (1966) elaborated Erikson's theory by identifying four potential outcomes of the identity phase of development: *moratorium, foreclosure, diffusion,* and *achievement.* Ruthellen Josselson (1987) utilized the identity status interview developed by Marcia (1966) and other survey questions as stimulus materials for her longitudinal study of women who were interviewed at two points in time: during the early 1970s at the time of college graduation and during 1983. Sixty women were interviewed in the first phase and thirty-eight women participated in the follow-up study. Josselson concluded that women hold a range of different orientations to relationships, with foreclosure women showing the most attachment to relationships and moratorium and diffusion women showing the least. Similar to women who balanced self-nurture with care for others in Gilligan's third phase of moral development, achievement women demonstrated an optimal balance of separateness and relatedness.

Only one-quarter of the women, foreclosure women, defined themselves according to the pattern that Erikson defined as normative for women. These women defined their identities in terms of a successful search for a mate, and acted as "purveyors of heritage" (p. 2). In general, they lived out unquestioned childhood dreams and organized their adult lives to be predictable, conventional, and unchanging. They typically had high scores on measures of mental health but showed little evidence of a separate self-definition.

Women with achievement identities consciously tested their identities, built self-defined paths, and demonstrated flexibility in integrating needs for self-assertion and connection. These women tended to "separate themselves from their childhood selves gradually and incrementally, preserving relatedness at each step" (Josselson, 1987, p. 187). Moratorium women gave up traditional, safe, relational anchors to try out exploratory identities and atypical roles, but also experienced greater difficulty resolving identity issues. In their thirties, moratorium woman sometimes adopted a self-chosen achievement status, but often experienced identity diffusion or opted for a foreclosure-like status. Previous research revealed that men who chose moratorium or achievement statuses during college showed more adaptive personality characteristics and higher levels of mental health than men in foreclosure and diffusion statuses. In contrast, women who displayed characteristics associated with foreclosure or achievement showed higher levels of mental health than women in moratorium or diffusion statuses (Marcia, 1980). Josselson (1987) found similar patterns in her sample of women and proposed that, unlike men, women are discouraged by social and family pressures to adopt extended exploratory identities: if identity is not achieved by the end of the college years, pressures to return to the safety of childhood experiences are strong. For women, the social expectations, choices, self-reflection, ambivalence, and isolation associated with choosing nontraditional roles are costly.

In summary, Suellen Josselson (1987) found that significant relationships provide the primary anchor for women's identity, but that these anchors do not operate according to the model defined by Erikson. Like Carol Gilligan, she concluded that relationships must be viewed positively and centrally. Furthermore, a relational orientation does not exhibit itself in uniform ways for all women, but is enacted in diverse and creative ways in women's lives.

Women's Ways of Knowing

The authors of *Women's Ways of Knowing* (1986)—Belenky, Clinchy, Goldberger, and Tarule—sought to develop a more adequate theory of women's intellectual development during the college years than the one provided by William Perry (1970), whose model was based on research with male Harvard University students. Perry proposed that students start academic careers with dualistic, either-or views of the world. At a second major stage; they gradually recognize uncertainty, ambiguity, and multiple ways of thinking, often concluding that no opinion or approach to pursuing knowledge is better than any other. Eventually, students who effectively negotiate developmental phases demonstrate the ability to deal with uncertainty and to weigh the merits and problems of various views by applying objective principles for evaluating knowledge claims. Whereas male students showed fairly distinct shifts in their approaches to knowledge, Belenky et al. (1986) noted that women appeared less dualistic than men during the initial stage, approached the middle phases of multiplicity with more caution, and defined the final stage of commitment as less of a singular, self-defining act and more of a commitment to a community and relationships. They concluded that Perry had articulated the development of separate knowing, which focuses on the development of traditional methods of objective, impersonal evaluation and analysis.

In contrast to the exclusive reliance on separate knowing, women often utilize connected knowing, which is more contextual in orientation and focuses on the importance of understanding another person's view, learning through experience, and connecting ideas and theories to personal events and relationships. Connected learning occurs primarily through participant observation, personal immersion in situations and stimulus materials, and understanding various perspectives from another person's point of view. Connected knowers rely on support and confirmation throughout the educational experience and feel isolated when they receive feedback only at the conclusion of their work. In order to correct the biases of Perry's views, Belenky et al. (1986) described a series of developmental phases that women are more likely to experience as they approach learning. During the earliest stages of development, women often feel silenced and learn to overvalue the voice of authorities and separate knowing. As women become aware of the limitations of external knowledge, they emphasize the importance of subjective, personal knowledge and connected knowing. At a final phase of development, women learn to be constructed knowers and integrate separate and connected knowing. Throughout the process of intellectual development, women's relationships remain important.

Support for the notion that women often experience learning tasks differently than men is provided by Benack (1982), who found that women's thinking is more variable, more flexible, and less sequential or linear than Perry (1970) had proposed. Magolda's (1989) quantitative study and analysis revealed similarities in the cognitive structures of men and women, but her qualitative analysis revealed gender differences in how men and women view the acquisition of knowledge. Women expressed preference for collecting others' ideas instead of debating opinions, and they relied more on personal interpretation than did men.

Relational Identity Models: An Integration

Although the language and emphasis of the relational models varies, each model proposes similar sequences, developmental issues, and goals of women's development. In general, the initial response of women to relationships is an ethic of self-preservation and "selfishness" (Gilligan, 1982), which is a normal and predictable aspect of early development. During middle phases, women become aware of the needs of others and often interpret ethical behavior as a form of self-sacrifice and responsibility to others. As women develop emotional and relational skills, they value positive growth in relationships as a primary goal and experience frustration when their relational needs are not anticipated or responded to by others. The ethic of self-sacrifice is often accompanied by an acceptance of conventional femininity and an emphasis on following social dictates for being a good woman, which leaves the woman voiceless as she relies on following the conventional wisdom of external authorities (Belenky et al., 1986). Women who conclude their identity search at this point are likely to adopt a foreclosure status and live out a traditional model of femininity (Josselson, 1987).

During the next phase, women who become aware of the limits of conventional femininity and self-sacrificial giving discover the importance of subjective, connected knowing, which helps them value how they personally feel about issues and role demands (Belenky et al., 1986). When their own needs are unmet, they search for ways to reconcile their own needs with those of others. This questioning is accompanied by a moratorium status that involves the energetic exploration and pursuit of new roles (Josselson, 1987). Women who reach this stage begin to affirm themselves more fully and learn to differentiate themselves from others while still maintaining important relationships. As women recognize the importance of integrating connectedness and self-nurturing, they begin to establish a mature morality of care, which allows women to redefine and balance personal needs with those of others (Gilligan, 1982). These women learn to construct knowledge by integrating received learning and subjective learning (Belenky et al., 1986), and develop an achievement identity that involves a commitment to roles of both interdependence and autonomy (Josselson, 1987).

Each of these relationship models has significant implications for psychotherapy. These models suggest that the quality of the client-therapist relationship is central to positive psychotherapy outcomes. They also imply that the integration of the separate and connected self is not easy in a culture that continues to encourage women to gain reinforcements by caring for others and neglecting the self. Each of the theories suggests that before learning to integrate one's personal voice with other voices, women often experience a stage in which they must work through the demands associated with traditional femininity, the giving of nurture and care to others. Rather than labeling this behavior as negative, feminist therapists can help empower clients by noting the transitional nature of these attitudes and raising questions that can provide catalysts for continued development (Enns, 1991).

Issues and Critique

Although the authors of the relational personality theories provide important advances over traditional theory, some feminist psychologists believe that they create artificial dichotomies between the identities of men and women (e.g., Lerner, 1988; Mednick, 1989). Generalizations such as "women's basic orientation is toward caretaking" (Jordan and Surrey, 1986, p. 100) and "women define their identity through relationships of intimacy and care" (Gilligan, 1982, p. 164) encourage individuals to think of autonomy and relatedness as caricatures of maleness and femaleness (Lerner, 1988). Although the revaluing of relatedness is central to creating inclusive models of personhood, the tendency to define women's affiliative capacities and men's instrumental capacities as more natural/superior than other qualities detracts attention from the ways in which the capacities to be independent and nurturing are available to all individuals as well as the ways in which personality qualities are socially constructed (Hare-Mustin and Marecek, 1986). The more we emphasize the importance of women's nurturing and caring capabilities, the less men will identify and act on their own skills in this area, further reinforcing gender inequities (Lerner, 1988).

Luria (1986) and Kerber (1986) expressed concern that theories focusing on the "superior" nurturing qualities of women might encourage romantic oversimplification, or a return to the "modern cult of true womanhood" (Luria, 1986, p. 320) and the "world of the angel in the house" (Kerber, 1986, p. 309). Feminist therapists have sought to free us from the beliefs of early American psychologists such as G. Stanley Hall, who described women as demonstrating greater sensibility, intuition, and moral superiority. In the past, these notions strengthened the myth that mothers were superlative care-givers and maintained the subordinate status of women (Lewin, 1984).

Gaining skills of autonomy or relatedness are largely an outgrowth of one's location in the social structure (Hare-Mustin and Marecek, 1986). Women's economic dependence and their responsibility for child care continue to rule out independence for many women, and pressures to be a "good provider" and to attain individual accomplishments rule out affiliative roles for many men. Furthermore, the relationship strengths ascribed to women have historically been associated with subordinate groups (Kerber, 1986; Lerner, 1988). If articulations of the relational capacities of women are not adequately connected to an analysis of the impact of power, domination, and subordination on behavior, old stereotypes that attribute gender differences to inborn qualities rather than social categories and cultural influences may persist (Deaux, 1984).

An important critique of the relationship models has come from feminists of color who note that the authors of these models have paid inadequate attention to race, class, and situational factors that interact with gender. Oliva Espín (1990) noted that women's "universal" characteristics of connectedness, empathy, nurturance, and affiliation may merely reflect middle-class white women's methods for dealing with their own oppression. Multicultural views of the role of connectedness in identity formation have only recently appeared in the feminist therapy literature and represent an important corrective to past omissions (Bradshaw, 1990; Davenport and Yurich, 1991; Turner, 1991). Refer to the chapters on the feminisms of women of color and multicultural feminist therapy for further discussion of these issues.

CONTEMPORARY FEMINIST
PSYCHOANALYTIC THEORY

At least three major approaches to feminist psychoanalysis have been integrated with feminist approaches and include feminist object relations, feminist self-psychology, and interpersonal psychoanalytic feminism. Object relations theory, self psychology, and interpersonal psychoanalysis emphasize the centrality of interpersonal relationships, especially mother-child relationships, in the formation of the self. Pathology is considered as resulting from problems in early development, and psychotherapy is viewed as a restorative relationship in which the consequences of early developmental deficits can be reworked.

Consistent with cultural feminist perspectives, feminist psychoanalytic therapists do not focus primarily on how gender roles might be reconstructed, but on revaluing traditional roles of women and mothers. Each of the feminist applications of psychoanalysis that are consistent with cultural feminism attend to the centrality of relationships in women's lives, the means by which relational qualities are developed, and the role of relationships in women's well-being. Early development, especially pre-oedipal development, is crucial to the development of gender identity, and mother-daughter dyads represent core relationships in which women negotiate self-development. Following a brief discussion of these models, I summarize criticisms of each model.

Feminist Object Relations Theory

Object relations theories emphasize the ways in which one's relationships with early caretakers are internalized and form the basis for a self-concept and relationships with other people. During the first three years of life, the infant moves from a state of symbiosis or fusion with the mother to a point of separation and individuation, which is defined as the development of a sense of self, autonomy, and separateness as a being (Mahler, Pine, and Bergman, 1975).

Internalized images of others become the basis for mental representations of oneself and others. These mental representations of others may resemble actual people but may also be based on distorted perspectives that become the foundation for the defensive processes of the following: (1) splitting, or separating people into strict good and bad categories; (2) projection, which involves attributing denied aspects of the self to others; (3) projective identification, or projecting disowned aspects of oneself on other persons who unconsciously absorb these qualities and react in accordance with expectations; and (4) introjection, which entails incorporating an aspect of another person or the external world within oneself. Object relations theories focus on how one's mental images are played out in current issues and relationships (Okun, 1992).

Nancy Chodorow's (1978) feminist socialist version of object relations theory has formed an important foundation for understanding gender roles from a psychoanalytic perspective. She noted that in capitalist industrialized family structures in which mothers play primary parenting roles, boys are encouraged to disconnect themselves from a primary identification with their mothers, but girls are encouraged to maintain more connected, fluid relationships. Boys, who recognize themselves as biologically different from their mothers, learn to view themselves as different from and separate from their mothers while girls, who see the similarities between themselves and their mothers, learn to define themselves in more relational ways. She noted that unless significant changes in parenting patterns occur, traditional roles of men and women will continue to be reinforced. Most cultural feminists use Chodorow's analysis to describe why men and women often develop different personality and behavioral styles, but rather than suggesting changes in parenting patterns, they focus primarily on appreciating the relational roles that women have historically assumed.

Luise Eichanbaum and Susie Orbach's (1983) model provides one of the clearest examples of a feminist object relations approach to psychotherapy. Eichenbaum and Orbach describe how women's problems are related to the unconscious internalization of patriarchal norms and cultural requirements. One powerful mandate requires women to defer to others and articulate their needs only in relationships. Because they are not the main characters in their own lives, women learn to feel "unworthy, undeserving, and unentitled" (p. 7). A second requirement is that women should shape their lives in relationships to others, which results in the loss of self, feelings of neediness, and feelings of insufficiency.

According to Eichenbaum and Orbach, cultural mandates are transmitted primarily through the mother-daughter relationship. The mother unconsciously projects on her daughter the same negative culturally prescribed feelings that she has about herself, including the repressed aspects of the mother's needy self that she has learned to deny and dislike in order to survive. Because the mother experiences conflict and ambivalence about her role, she unconsciously creates frustration and gratification patterns that lead the daughter to feel insecure and rejected.

The daughter learns to identify with her mother's caretaking role, gives up her expectations of being cared for by others, and instead, develops emotional antennae that are highly sensitive to the needs of others. As the daughter absorbs information from her mother, she learns to respond to other people's needs as a way of dealing with her own unmet needs. The daughter represses the "little girl" inside, develops false ways of relating to others and the world, and develops difficulty in forming personal boundaries and articulating her own needs. The woman denies that she is needy because she believes that her psychological needs will never be met, but she also searches in vain for a nurturing relationship that will result in personal fulfillment.

Through a positive psychotherapy relationship, the woman can acknowledge her own neediness and unmet dependency needs, work through these issues, and eventually integrate needs for closeness and autonomy. Early stages of therapy focus on building trust and solving specific problems, middle phases examine transference issues and help women appreciate their capacities for both closeness and separateness in a therapeutic relationship, and the final phase involves increased awareness of personal boundaries and differentiation from the therapist. Eichenbaum and Orbach (1983) concluded that "feminist therapy is about learning to love the little girl inside that patriarchy has taught us to fear and despise; it is about allowing her to grow up and become part of an autonomous woman" (p. 107). This new woman successfully integrates self-care with other-care.

Feminist Self-Psychology

Self-psychology is inspired by the work of Heinz Kohut (1971, 1984), who viewed psychotherapy as a context in which a self that has been damaged or inadequately developed during childhood can be reworked within a positive, empathic therapeutic relationship. Similar to the concepts of object relations theory, the self is seen as the internalization of the psychological functions of the caregiver.

Empathy is central to development. By experiencing the mirroring function, which is based on the caregiver's appreciation for the child's accomplishments and development, the person develops self-esteem, enjoyment, goals, and purpose. Second, the child's experience of the caretaker's idealizing function results in feelings of security and the child's belief that the parent is a caring, giving, and powerful individual (Kohut, 1971, 1984). When caregiver-child relationships do not include these positive outcomes, psychological problems ensue. The caregivers' beliefs about gender also influence the way in which these functions are experienced. Mirroring and idealizing functions associated with psychotherapy are important tools for restoring the self so that further growth can occur.

Self-psychology has been viewed by some feminist therapists as especially consistent with feminist therapy goals because of its emphasis on the importance of relationship and empathy in the formation of a healthy self (Gardiner, 1987; Hertzberg, 1990; Knox, 1985; Mitchell, 1989). Judith Gardiner suggested that self-psychology is more consistent with feminist goals than object relations theory because it places greater emphasis on "a whole life psychology in which change is normal throughout adulthood" (p. 770). One potential consequence of object relations theory's strong emphasis on examining unconscious internalized representations is that it "endows fantasy (intrapsychic life) with more significance than reality (life as it is lived with others)" (Burack, 1992, p. 502). Self-psychology may also provide a more adult model of parenting because of its emphasis on empathy rather than on object relations theory's concept of symbiosis, which suggests that during early stages of development, an adequate parent "entirely loses herself in caring for her infant" (Gardiner, 1987, p. 771). The notion of symbiosis implies that women enter an infantile-like state when they engage in some nurturing activities. Gardiner also argues that compared to object relations approaches, self-psychology places more emphasis on interdependence as a goal of therapy and less emphasis on independence and separation. The flexibility of this model is exemplified in the following statement by Kohut (1984): "There is not one kind of healthy self—there are many kinds" (p. 44).

Self-in-Relation Model of Psychotherapy

In addition to acknowledging the contribution of object relations and self-psychology perspectives to their thinking, the authors of the self-in-relation model credit Harry Stack Sullivan (1953) with reconceptualizing psychoanalysis in an interpersonal framework. Sullivan stated the following: "A personality can never be isolated from the complex of interpersonal relations in which the person lives and has his [sic] being" (p. 10). A limitation of his thinking, however, is that although he defined the "reflected appraisals" of others as crucial to self-definition, the independent self emerging from these relationships is seen as the endpoint of healthy self-development (Jordan et al., 1991).

Contributors to the self-in-relation model use Jean Baker Miller's (1976) often-quoted work titled *Toward a New Psychology of Women* as a foundation. Miller was one of the first contemporary feminist psychologists to describe the importance of women's capacities for empathy, nurturance, and affiliation and to note how these qualities are distorted and denigrated in a culture dominated by men. She also articulated how women's anger and aggression are suppressed in male-dominated societies and find their expression in many of the psychological problems women experience. As a result, clinical work should focus on revaluing women's core relational self as well as identifying ways of expressing anger and assertion in self-affirming ways.

In contrast to Eichenbaum and Orbach's (1983) emphasis on the ways in which the mother-daughter relationship transmits negative patriarchal values and limits girls' abilities to develop an integrated sense of self, the self-in-relation model emphasizes the positive impact of the mother-daughter dyad on women's relational self. The mother-daughter relationship contributes to a more "encompassing" or complete self that can be contrasted with "the more boundaried, or limited, self that is encouraged in boys from a very young age" (Miller, 1991, p. 15). Rather than viewing the successful outcome of identity development as separation and individuation apart from others (Mahler, Pine, and Bergman, 1975), this model identifies "relationship-differentiation" (Surrey, 1991, p. 38), "mutual intersubjectivity" (Jordan, 1991, p. 82), or "agency within community"

(Miller, 1991, p. 16) as central to women's identity development. It takes issue with terms such as *merger, symbiosis,* or *fusion* that are used in traditional object relations theories to describe early infant-mother relationships, and suggests that this relationship is much more complicated, complete, and rich (Miller, 1991).

The self-in-relation model underscores four positive motivational and structural aspects of the mother-daughter relationship that mold the self: (1) an early emotional attentiveness between mother and daughter, (2) the experience of mutual empathy and affective joining between mothers and daughters, (3) the expectation that relationships are a major source of personal growth, and (4) mutual empowerment, which involves seeing relationships as an important context in which to experience further growth and maturation (Jordan and Surrey, 1986; Kaplan and Surrey, 1984). According to the self-in-relation model, women's positive connections to others validate their capacities as relational beings; provide the necessary foundation for personal beliefs about autonomy, competence, and self-esteem; and are central to helping women experience continuing growth and well-being. Problems in women's development do not occur because women experience a failure to separate from others but because they have difficulties asserting a distinct self-concept that is both differentiated from that of others and also connected to others (Kaplan, 1986). Although the relational self is positive and central to women's well-being, social values that equate ego strength with self-reliance often lead women to label their core selves as dependent or immature (Jack, 1987).

Because women spend significant time enhancing their skills in relational realms (e.g., families, friends, and significant others), they are more likely than men to assume self-blame for relationship failures, thus leaving them more vulnerable to disorders such as depression and low self-esteem (Jack, 1987, 1991). Building on Carol Gilligan's (1982) model of moral development, Dana Jack (1991) suggested that depression is often associated with the second stage of moral development, which defines the "good woman" as behaving in self-sacrificial ways. Tremendous effort is required to silence the authentic self, women's creativity, and women's anger; the consequences of this effort are self-alienation, hopelessness, and depression. Learning to see for oneself versus seeing for others is a necessary step toward creating a healthy self.

Rather than defining depression negatively, Dana Jack stated that women's depression reveals "the vulnerabilities of a relational sense of self within a culture that dangerously strains a woman's ability to meet basic needs for interpersonal relatedness, while maintaining a positive sense of self" (1987, p. 44). Women's strong grief reactions to relationship loss should not be interpreted solely as dependency or neediness, but as threats to women's positive core sense of self. Revaluing and reshaping the core sense of self-in-relation is a central role of psychotherapy.

In summary, the major goals of feminist psychotherapy entail redefining behaviors that contribute to self-blame and self-denigration, developing the capacity for self-empathy, and valuing the core relational self. For example, dependency might be described as the following: "A process of counting on other people to provide help in coping physically and emotionally with the experiences and tasks encountered in the world when one has not sufficient skill, confidence, energy, and/or time" (Stiver, 1991, p. 160). Redefining dependency in this manner identifies the healthy and normal aspects of this behavior, highlights ways in which it promotes growth rather than stagnation, and frees the individual to try out a wider range of and more flexible behaviors.

Comparisons and Critique of Feminist Psychoanalysis

Object relations feminists tend to place more emphasis than interpersonal psychoanalytic feminists (self-in-relation model) on the intricacies of the internal world, unconscious processes, and the mechanisms by which the "self" is constructed. Whereas object relations theorists examine the ways in which women's roles and capacities intersect with male development, interpersonal psychoanalytic feminists (self-in-relation model) focus almost exclusively on women's development. Interpersonal psychoanalytic feminists place less emphasis than object relations theorists on unconscious dynamics and emphasize cultural prescriptions and personal experiences that influence women's affiliative self. Whereas object relations approaches are more likely to discuss the pitfalls as well as the positive aspects of the relational self, interpersonal/self-in-relation approaches focus more exclusively on the positive aspects of the relational self (Chodorow, 1989).

Feminists have been critical of traditional object relations, interpersonal, and self-psychology theories because the mother's role is considered as all-important to the formation of a healthy self. Problems of development are largely due to qualities of the "bad mother," or the lack of availability of mothers to their infants (Frosh, 1987), which leads to a narrow view of women's roles in the world and facilitates the blaming of mothers for problems in development (Caplan, 1989; Okun, 1992). Although the models described in this section have attempted to revalue the role of mothers and rethink the way in which women's subordinate status and patriarchal culture influence development, the continued overemphasis on mothering roles and lack of discussion of fathering can perpetuate old myths.

These models provide limited insight about how fathers, family interactions, and the broader sociopolitical context influence development (Frosh, 1987; Lerner, 1988). They tend to promote individualistic solutions that focus on discovering and acting on repressed aspects of the self. Methods for altering skewed relationships or changing exclusive mothering patterns in the patriarchal family are largely unexplored (Frosh, 1987; Lerman, 1986). Although the feminist psychoanalytic approaches to women's lives have moved away from mother blaming by examining the role of culture in women's lives, the continued emphasis on mother-child relationships may limit the movement that feminist psychoanalysis can make from a deficiency model of maternal parenting. In the future, fathering must also be treated as a feminist issue (Silverstein, 1996).

ARCHETYPAL AND GODDESS PSYCHOLOGY

During the 1980s and 1990s, archetypal psychology has become the focus of popular psychology and self-help books (Nelson, 1991; Pearson, 1986, 1991; Woolger and Woolger, 1989), best-sellers (Bly, 1990; Estes, 1992; Keen, 1991), and weekly news magazines (Adler, Duignam-Cabrera, and Gordon, 1991; Adler et al., 1991; Goode, 1992). During this same period of time, Jungian archetypal psychology has been adopted as a theoretical orientation by some feminist therapists. These feminist counselors and psychotherapists have embraced archetypal psychology because it defines receptivity and "feminine" instincts as valuable assets for making meaning of one's life (Wehr, 1987). Nelson (1991) stated that contemporary women have been pressured to "do it all" and have found their deep feminine values to be questioned and devalued. Archetypal psychology has been endorsed by some feminists as a method for revaluing traditional feminine strengths and for healing misunderstandings between men and women. Archetypes can serve as role models that help women identify the goddesses within themselves and expand their emotional and behavioral repertoires (Bolen, 1984).

Jung's belief that an unconscious man exists within the woman (animus) and that an unconscious woman exists within the man (anima) implies that masculinity and femininity can be united in a balanced relationship. Although Jung's notion that mentally healthy persons have a well-developed anima or animus seems consistent with feminist goals, Jung associated masculinity with rational thought and viewed it as superior to femininity. He attributed a "magic authority" (Jung, 1954/1959, p. 82) to the "feminine." In contrast to a man's "decisiveness and singlemindedness," however, Jung associated femininity with characteristics such as "indefiniteness," "passivity," and "feelings of inferiority which make her continually play the injured innocent" (Jung, 1954/1959, p. 90). Although Jung believed that a competent woman possessed a well-developed masculine animus, he considered a woman's knowledge, rationality, and objectivity to be inferior to a man's competence because her animus is less conscious than a man's masculine self. Furthermore, Jung thought that women could become possessed by the animus, a state in which the animus is corrupted, exhibiting itself in women's hostility, obstinacy, dogmatism, power-driven behaviors, and irrationally opinionated perspectives (Bolen, 1984; Jung, 1943/1953; Young-Eisendrath, 1984). The association of the animus with animosity persists in current dictionary definitions. Although no negative meanings are attached to the term *anima*, one of the meanings of animus, as identified by *The Random House Dictionary* is "strong dislike or enmity; hostile attitude" (Flexner and Hauck, 1987, p. 82).

Some feminist counselors and psychotherapists believe that although some of Jung's notions about the animus are sexist, many of his concepts can be integrated with feminist principles. Consistent with feminist ideals, Jung emphasized that symptoms represent a healthy struggle toward wholeness and an effort of the psyche to regain balance. He viewed individuals as essentially self-regulating and believed that persons move toward maturity through a natural and continuous exchange between the conscious and unconscious. Jung also deemphasized the authority of the analyst and accentuated the centrality of the client's experience, self-understanding, and insights (Lauter and Rupprecht, 1985).

One of the major problems of traditional Jungian psychology is that the archetypes, myths, and symbols that are considered the source for inspiring clients toward positive actions are based on patriarchal myths that undervalue women's experience and reinforce traditional visions of masculinity and femininity. The typical motif in fairy tales depicts the man as engaging in a heroic task, rescuing a woman, and sweeping her off to an idyllic existence. Feminist Jungian therapists, then, have been faced with the challenge of identifying and utilizing woman-centered archetypes that can provide concrete and empowering visions of women's social, economic, political, and personal behavior. Some feminists have sought to identify prepatriarchal archetypes and goddess images to avoid contaminating images associated with more recent patriarchal mythologies. According to Riane Eisler (1988), early matriarchal societies were based on egalitarian, nonviolent, earth-centered values that revered the Great Mother and other goddess figures. Humans lived in harmony with each other during these eras, and women exercised greater social power than they did during patriarchal societies, which have been associated with widespread "spiritual bankruptcy" (Woolger and Woolger, 1989, p. 17). In general, liberating archetypes that are consistent with feminist values can be found in diverse sources such as women's poetry, writing, painting, needlework, dreams, and quilts.

The goddesses associated with patriarchal Greek mythology had less power than male gods and thus, may seem to offer limited value to women who seek egalitarian relationships. Despite their lower status, however, these goddesses demonstrated significant diversity of behavior and substantial power that included the capacity to change the course of major human events. They also used creative means for counteracting the negative aspects of male gods' power (Bolen, 1984; Woolger and Woolger, 1989). According to this version of goddess psychology, knowledge of the psychic life of Greek goddesses can help women understand themselves and their relationships, as well as what motivates, frustrates, and satisfies them. The different styles and personalities of the Greek goddesses can also help women appreciate diversity between women and their various means of achieving fulfillment (Bolen, 1984).

Woolger and Woolger (1989) suggested that each woman is influenced by a combination of six major goddess types including Athena (intellectual life, wisdom, achievement), Aphrodite (love, intimacy), Persephone (spirit world and mystical experiences), Artemis (adventure, physical world), Demeter (nurturing, motherhood), and Hera (power, leadership). Jean Bolen (1984) divided her list of seven goddesses into the categories of virgin goddesses (Artemis, Athena, Hestia), vulnerable goddesses (Hera, Demeter, Persephone), and a transformative goddess (Aphrodite). These authors encourage women to explore what goddesses they are ruled by, and how the different goddesses facilitate and influence specific developmental stages and turning points in women's lives.

The task of feminist archetypal therapy is to revalue women's strengths of all kinds and to "disentangle feminine archetypes from the masculine warp of culture" (Lauter and Rupprecht, 1985, p. 19). To accomplish this task, women must explore how confining images have been internalized by men and women and how these images have become misconstrued as objective, universal facts. By exploring these issues, women gain awareness of the specific behavior patterns that women have used for many generations to cope with their lower status (Wehr, 1987). Through this form of "unconsciousness raising" (Pratt, 1985), women can gain insight about how their past behavior patterns have allowed them to cope with their lower status, which releases them from self-blame for acting on cultural imperatives. Women also gain insights that allow them to transcend narrow roles, explore new emotional and behavioral alternatives, and implement plans for achieving equality.

Critiques of Feminist Archetypal Psychology

Feminist therapists whose work is inspired by Jungian perspectives have successfully redefined many of Jung's concepts in ways that are consistent with feminist perspectives. However, the Jungian definition of archetypes as universal and internal encourages individuals to view masculinity and femininity as qualities that are fixed and lodged within the individual psyche. Pratt (1985) suggested that the notion that an unconscious man or woman exists within each person's unconscious can lead to smugness and distortion of human qualities. For example, the person who believes that the internal anima provides information about the full range of women's experience may ignore the significance of external circumstances, such as socialization, sexism, and violence, and assume that women's difficulties are caused by internal deficiencies or women's inability to balance feminine instincts and the masculine animus. This view can lead to victim blaming and the belief that "the problems associated with being a man or a woman in the social world will handle themselves" (Pratt, 1985, p. 98).

Some of the feminist revisions of Jungian archetypal psychology consistently emphasize the importance of seeing all archetypes as socially constructed and caution against essentializing masculinity and femininity (e.g., Lauter and Rupprecht, 1985). Nevertheless, the revisions of archetypal psychology that are often referred to as goddess psychology frequently emphasize the special and unique qualities or "instincts" (Estes, 1992) of women that are presumed to be a part of their essence.

As noted earlier in this chapter, efforts to revalue traditional strengths of women can be inappropriately used to create new stereotypes of "woman's nature" (Mednick, 1989). Nancy Goldenberg (1976) cautioned that any fixed or highly defined archetypes or goddesses limit the behavioral alternatives of women by establishing new boundaries on women's experience that can be as constricting as traditional female archetypes. Women can continue to internalize oppression by attributing relational, nurturing skills to innate qualities rather than viewing them as survival mechanisms that help women find meaning in a world in which they hold lower social status (Wehr, 1987). Approaches that focus exclusively on helping women look inward to recover buried images of strength may result in women's lowered expectations for external and social change and an overemphasis on changing the self (Walters, 1993).

Recent versions of goddess psychology have sometimes become trendy and disconnected from the political implications of feminism. Rene Denfeld (1995) asserts that "this vision of women as spiritually superior—and spiritually pure—has led to devastating inertia" (p. 132). Spiritual rituals associated with goddess worship have sometimes replaced activism, which is sometimes seen as distasteful or unnecessary.

A final criticism of goddess psychology is that women from multicultural backgrounds may feel invalidated, excluded, or marginalized by a psychology that is based solely on Greek mythology and the history of white women (Lorde, 1983). Reiko True (1990) noted that it is difficult for minority women to identify with "blond, blue-eyed goddesses" (p. 483). Women from ethically and racially diverse backgrounds should be encouraged to draw on their own rich heritages of mythologies that include powerful female images. These images can be used as role models to help women contend with the oppressive aspects of sexism of this own cultures as well as the racism of dominant white culture (e.g., Allen, 1989; Kingston, 1976; Larrington, 1992; Lorde, 1983). Lillian Comas-Díaz (1991) indicated that many women of color rely on spirituality that is embedded in their own traditions as a form of renewal; culture-specific archetypes can be used to enhance the power and relevance of this spirituality.

It should be noted that Jungian archetypal psychology can be used to support feminist goals or subvert feminist goals. The popular mythopoetic men's movement has borrowed extensively from Jungian psychology to access archetypes of manhood (e.g., Bly, 1990; Keen, 1991; Moore and Gillette, 1990, 1992). Authors of popular books are critical of patriarchy, and suggest that it has victimized men through performance expectations associated with work, sex, and war (e.g., Keen, 1991). Keen (1991) also argued that men experience an unconscious bondage to women and that men are "enmeshed, incorporated, inwombed, and defined by WOMAN" (p. 15).

Although feminists agree that both men and women are confined by traditional roles, the woman-blaming tone of much of the literature associated with the mythopoetic movement, its lack of recognition of male privilege associated with social power differences between men and women, and its re-adoption of traditional masculine images is highly problematic (Enns, 1994). A major feminist criticism of the mythopoetic movement arises from its use of romantic, idealized images of the wild man, king, and warrior— images that are designed to affirm men's virility, decisiveness, and power. Archetypes that demonstrate compassion, caring, and empathy are predominantly absent. Second, although a lack of fathering is viewed as a significant cause of men's pain, the role of women in promoting men's "softness" is seen as a major cause of stifling men's independence, feminizing boys, and creating their codependency (Doubiago, 1992), a view that further perpetuates the mother blaming that permeates our culture (Caplan, 1989). Third, mythopoetic approaches focus only on the oppression of men and do not explore the impact of many centuries of male privilege on men's lives. Starhawk (1992) suggested that the first step to freedom for men will not come through the reassertion of power and privilege but through the letting go of privilege and the sharing of both highly valued and undervalued life experiences with women (Starhawk, 1992). This brief commentary on the mythopoetic archetypal psychology identifies the negative consequences of endorsing a psychology that focuses on the revaluing of traditional masculine and feminine roles. If retraditionalization, the perpetuation of old myths, and the reassertion of male power are outcomes of archetypal mythopoetic psychology, similar outcomes may be associated with an overemphasis on traditional female strengths.

SUMMARY AND CONCLUDING COMMENTS

Cultural feminism was first inspired by feminists who envisioned a transformation of culture in accordance with a uniquely matriarchal vision (see Chapter 3 for a review). They defined women's experiences as distinctly different from men's and sought to revere and valorize traditional "feminine" strengths. Contemporary cultural feminists have less frequently assumed that women's strengths are innate than did the first cultural feminists, and they are less likely to emphasize a utopian, romantic vision of the world than were their predecessors. However, they continue to focus efforts on revaluing "female" strengths and outlining a unique moral and ethical vision of women (Donovan, 1992). These themes, then are reflected in cultural feminist adaptations of feminist therapy.

Cultural feminist views of women have been especially popular during the 1980s and early 1990s. At a subjective level, this perspective offers a "ring of truth" for many women. The cultural feminist vision provides validation and comfort by conveying to women that they are not flawed and that they do not need to give up the relational skills with which they may feel most comfortable. This is perhaps the greatest strength of cultural feminism as it is applied in feminist therapy.

The most significant criticism of cultural feminism is that it is "essentialist" (Bohan, 1993). Although authors of relational models of personality and psychotherapy do not propose that women are inherently different than men, the models often imply that gender is "resident within the individual" (Bohan, 1993, p. 6). Relational skills are qualities of individuals or "fundamental attributes that are conceived as internal, persistent, and generally separate from the ongoing experience of interaction with the daily sociopolitical contexts of one's life" (p. 7). In contrast, social constructionism views gender as occurring in interactions; gender is a verb rather than a set of qualities. When relationship qualities are seen as personal qualities rather than as outcomes of social arrangements, views of gender become less flexible, the diversity of women is less frequently considered as important, and women may be less likely to explore options outside of relational domains. Social change becomes a less salient mandate; the inner, connected self becomes a more important focus of attention than the social structures that shape the relational self (Bohan, 1993).

A future challenge is the integration of relational models with social constructionistic perspectives. For example, Markus and Oyserman (1989) suggested that relational traits can be conceptualized as components of a connected or a relationship self-schema, or a set of beliefs about the self that influence self-perceptions, perceptions of others, basic cognitive processes, and one's activities in the world. Many factors, including socialization, cultural factors, patriarchy, power structures, or parent-child relationships, contribute to the development of a connected or separate self-schema. By viewing the relational and separate selves as types of self-schemas, one can describe the relational and separate selves in rich terms *and* maintain awareness that each type of self is constructed and shaped by myriad factors. Such integration can help feminist therapists view the relationship models of personality, ethics, moral development, and psychotherapy as descriptive and flexible models rather than as prescriptive models.

Chapter 7

Women of Color and Feminist Therapy

In her recent book on feminist therapy, Laura Brown (1994) opened her chapter on diversity in feminist psychology by stating the following: "Feminist therapy cannot arise from a theory that would require someone to choose which aspect of her identity is the one to be liberated while other lie silenced, unattended to, or rendered marginal" (p. 69). A multicultural analysis of behavior is especially important for establishing a framework or model of viewing diversity as a central and defining characteristic of feminist therapy. Within this framework, gender cannot be seen as an isolated variable, but must be understood within an integrated analysis of oppression (Kanuha, 1990).

In large part, feminist therapy was originally developed "by and with White women" (Brown, 1990b, p. 3), and early statements concerning feminist therapy made only brief references to issues influenced by poverty, homophobia, racism, or classism. Landmark descriptions of feminist therapy (e.g., Greenspan, 1983; Rawlings and Carter, 1977; Sturdivant, 1980) were based primarily on the realities of middle-class white women; only occasional references were made to the types of oppression and life experiences that poor women and women of color encounter (Brown, 1990b). Even during the mid-1980s, the *Handbook of Feminist Therapy* (Rosewater and Walker, 1985), which heralded the coming of age of feminist therapy, included no discussion of the needs of women of color. Julia Boyd (1990) charged that white feminist therapists have often acted as though the struggles of women of color can be equated with their own struggles. When the specific or unique issues of women of color are considered, they have often been defined in comparison or in reference to white women's experiences, and not on the basis of the values, perceptions, and strengths of diverse groups of women.

When this occurs, feminism marginalizes some women and becomes a system to which women of color are expected "*to define and justify their reality, which makes it (feminism) just as oppressive as the traditional sexist patriarchal system*" (Boyd, 1990, p. 162).

As feminist therapy has matured, feminist therapists have expressed concern about the inattention of feminist therapy and theory to the issues of women of color (e.g., Brown, 1990b; Comas-Díaz, 1991; Espín, 1990, 1993). However, efforts to be more inclusive have often fallen short of including the perspectives of women of color in a fully integrated and central manner (Espín, 1993, 1995). Beverly Greene (1995) commented that "[w]hite feminists as a group have continued the American traditions of their foremothers in presenting a slowly changing but still frequently arrogant and unexamined white, middle-class perspective on what issues are important to all women" (p. 306). Without considering diversity, feminist therapy will become stagnant. Attending to diversity is essential to the relevance, vitality, and growth of feminist therapy.

It is with some trepidation that I write this chapter. As a white, middle-class woman, I am aware that my efforts to be inclusive may be limited by my own experiences and perceptions of this world. As a result, I am relying whenever possible on discussions of feminist therapy that are written by feminist therapists of color and for women of color. The chapter begins with a discussion of the limitations of feminist research and feminist personality theories that have emerged over the past twenty years, as well as commentary about some necessary correctives. The middle section of this chapter focuses on the importance of antiracism or antidomination training for white feminist therapists. The final section of the chapter describes the work of several feminist therapists of color who have contributed substantially to theory and practice in feminist therapy. This chapter focuses primarily on general principles for working with women of color. For in-depth discussion of specific populations, I recommend Lillian Comas-Díaz and Beverly Greene's (1994) edited book titled *Women of Color: Integrating Ethnic and Gender Identities in Psychotherapy.* For in-depth discussion of guidelines for antiracist practice in feminist psychology, I recommend Jeanne Adleman and Gloria Enguídanos' (1995) edited book titled *Racism in the Lives of Women: Testimony, Theory, and Guides to Antiracist Practice.*

DEVELOPING AN INCLUSIVE PSYCHOLOGY OF WOMEN: THE RESEARCH FOUNDATION

When the psychology of women was born in the early 1970s, psychologists successfully challenged a wide range of theories and research practices that held up the lives of privileged white men as normative and that evaluated all other groups in comparison to this group. During the 1970s and 1980s, a substantial amount of research was conducted regarding the lives of women; it focused on diverse areas such as work, achievement, intimate relationships, violence against women, attitudes toward women, and the socialization of women during childhood and adolescence. However, most of this research was conducted by white feminist researchers and with traditional undergraduate students, who were primarily from white, middle-class backgrounds. The initial body of knowledge that emerged was a psychology of women based largely on the lives of white women (Vaz, 1992; Yoder and Kahn, 1993).

Janice Yoder and Arnold Kahn (1993) noted that feminist psychology's reliance on traditional empirical methods and traditional comparison groups has often contributed to ethnocentrism. For example, if the researcher is studying women's attitudes toward some issue, the researcher is most likely to compare a group such as African-American women with white women. Such comparative research is very useful when it "debunks misconceptions and undermines harmful stereotypes about group differences" (Yoder and Kahn, 1993, p. 848). However, this form of research becomes harmful when white women are seen as "women in general" (p. 848), the normative group, and the baseline from which other groups deviate. Gordon, Miller, and Rollock (1990) referred to this nonconscious bias as "the tendency to make one's own community the center of the universe and the conceptual frame that constrains all thought" (p. 15). Too frequently, the attitudes and behaviors of women of color have been interpreted on the basis of their similarity and divergence from white women's values and attitudes. Furthermore, dichotomous comparisons between women of color and white women may provide a foundation for forming new stereotypes and can erase information about differences within specific groups of women. In other words, feminist psychologists have sometimes inadvertently practiced the very ethnocentrism that they have accused male psychologists of enacting.

Karen Wyche's (1993) review revealed that applied research on African-American women has consisted primarily of comparative studies and studies of poor, single mothers. This narrow focus ignores the diversity of African-American women and results in inappropriate generalizations from one subgroup of women to African-American women in general. Wyche (1993) also noted that white researchers have often assumed that the life experiences of black women have the same meaning as they do for white women, which further contributes to biased understanding and knowledge. Finally, past research has tended to focus on African-American women's negative or dysfunctional behaviors rather than positive reactions to stress. Each of these examples reveals aspects of ethnocentrism and bias that will need to be corrected before research findings can be seen as inclusive.

Efforts to create an inclusive research foundation have increased in recent years, but they often remain inadequate. In the first approach, oppression is studied additively. In other words, the perspectives of people of diversity have been added to existing theory, which means that the assumptions underlying research are not challenged. White middle-class norms remain central. In a second model, researchers focus on race, gender, class, and other factors as they interact. The relationships between class, gender, race, and culture are studied as parts of a complex equation. Although this model offers an improvement over previous alternatives, specific groups such as middle-class, black, and heterosexual women are still likely to be seen in definitive and fixed ways. Researchers create a "homogeny of heterogeneous types" (Morawski and Bayer, 1995, p. 118). Jill Morawski and Betty Bayer (1995) contended that neither approach sufficiently challenges the centrality of a white, middle-class perspective. White, middle-class individuals remain the norm; other groups are treated as "special cases" or as "fixed social categories" (p. 121), and the status quo is maintained. In future efforts, it is important for feminist researchers to more fully consider how the experiences of individuals are socially constructed, how they shift and change over time, and how they are shaped by history and social relationships.

Hope Landrine, Elizabeth Klonoff, and Alice Brown-Collins (1992) called for a revision of methodology in feminist psychology that combines empirical and phenomenological approaches. Their study of white women and ethnically diverse women of color found no differences between groups on objective ratings of phrases such as the following: I am passive; I am independent; I am assertive; and I am independent. However, members of these groups differed in terms of how they interpreted some of these phrases. Whereas white women most frequently endorsed "laid-back or easygoing" as the definition of passive, women of color were more likely to choose "not saying what I really think." With regard to assertiveness, women of color were most likely to define this term as "saying what's on my mind openly," and white women were most likely to define this behavior as "standing up for myself and expressing myself well." These subtle differences illustrate the importance of gathering qualitative information about the meanings attached to terms that are generally presumed to be shared by all women.

In addition to expanding the range of methods that are used, feminist psychologists must expand the range of topics they explore. Pamela Trotman Reid and Elizabeth Kelly (1994) noted that white women are generally viewed as having no race. In the future, research should examine the impact of ethnicity on all women (see also Frankenberg, 1993). Second, women of color need to be studied as "enactors, not victims" (Reid and Kelly, 1994, p. 483). An examination of the survival strategies and strengths of women of color is necessary for viewing groups of diverse women as complete individuals. Third, research on women of color must focus on the issues, definitions, and perspectives that women of color identify as relevant to their lives. The contributions of women of color must be considered as central to defining feminist theory, therapy, and research as well as understanding the diversity and similarities of all women's experiences (Espin, 1995).

DEVELOPING AN INCLUSIVE PSYCHOLOGY OF WOMEN: ISSUES ASSOCIATED WITH PERSONALITY THEORY

The problems of a middle-class, white bias are also evident in feminist personality theories. The chapter on women of color and feminism (Chapter 3) articulated how subtle biases are evident in Simone de Beauvoir's (1952) feminist theory. This chapter will describe some of the issues associated with the relational models of women's identity (see also Chapter 6, which focuses on cultural feminism). It will begin with commentary about the limitations of Nancy Chodorow's theory, which has provided a foundation for more recent psychological relational theories.

Nancy Chodorow's (1978, 1989) discussion of mothering within capitalist society is highly influential among theorists who seek to describe why men often define themselves in more separate terms and women in more relational terms. The strength of Chodorow's work is that she discussed the importance of viewing mothering in a social context (Segura and Pierce, 1993). However, based on her analysis of white nuclear families, she proposed some universal principles about parent-child relationships without adequately considering how parenting might be modified by class, race, and sexual orientation. One of the principles proposed by Chodorow is that the sexual division of labor, especially as it relates to mothering, is reinforced by a split between private and public work realms in capitalistic society. Women are responsible primarily for relational work in the private domain of the family while men are responsible for work that establishes themselves as autonomous beings in the public domain. Girls learn to define themselves in connection to others because of the awareness of their similarity to mothers and the sexual division of labor; in contrast, boys define themselves as different from their mothers, and hence, as separate from others.

Although Chodorow's observations about mothering have been very useful for understanding how the psychological self may be influenced by the nuclear family and capitalist economic structures, it does not adequately allow for an analysis of how identity is shaped by factors such as race and class. Chodorow's model is predicated on the assumptions that women's mothering occurs primarily within the nuclear family, that there is a strict division of labor between adult men and women, and that girls' relational selves are based on their perceived similarities to their mothers. However, for people of color, race and ethnicity may be more powerful or salient sources of perceived similarity or difference than gender. Thus, a mother who is a woman of color may feel a strong sense of sameness to both her male and female children based on their shared ethnic and racial background. Rather than proposing that gender identity is either relational or separate, it may be more productive to speak of multiple selves that are enacted in different social contexts. Elizabeth Spelman (1988) noted the following: "Because mothering may be informed by a woman's knowledge of more than one form of dominance, the development of gender occurs in a context in which one learns to be a very particular girl or boy, and not just simply a girl or boy" (p. 97).

The dangers inherent in proposing universal mothering roles or activities are illustrated by an example of how mothering varies by culture. The notion of motherhood as woman's highest calling is embedded within white Eurocentric culture; black Afrocentric views are more flexible. Patricia Hill Collins (1991) identified several aspects of Eurocentric thought that are problematic for understanding mothering within an African-American context: (1) mothering occurs in the context of a private, nuclear household; (2) strict gender role segregation separates male and female spheres of influence; and (3) to be a "good" mother, one must stay at home and make motherhood a full-time occupation. Within many black communities, however, the boundaries that differentiate biological mothers from other women who provide care and nurture of children are less rigid and more fluid than in many white communities. Mothering is not only associated with the private realm of the home, but involves the integration of economic and caregiving roles. Providing for the economic needs of children is seen as a significant part of mothering. Because mothering is not only associated with the nuclear family but also with service to other children, black women often develop a sense of social activism based on their sense of accountability to the larger community of children. These realities suggest that Chodorow's analysis of mothering is based primarily on white, middle-class realities and is inadequate for understanding the variations of family and individual identities.

Denise Segura and Jennifer Pierce (1993) noted that the structure of Chicana/o families also shapes personality. A prominent feature of Chicana/o families is *campadrazgo*, which refers to relationships with godparents that serve to enlarge the family and create connections between families. Extended households and networks that cross generations are often central to the family and identity development. Attachments with multiple mother figures, such as godmothers and grandmothers, shape the nature of gender-related behaviors. Denise Segura and Jennifer Pierce (1993) indicated that consistent with Chodorow's theory, Chicanas often develop a strong relational self. However the relational self is not only influenced by an exclusive mother-child relationship, but by multiple mothering individuals and collective cultural values that ask children to "think and act communally—for the good of the family and the community" (p. 81). Thus, the meaning of the relational self may be somewhat different for Chicanas than for most white women.

Most of the popular relational models of women's identity are based in part on Chodorow's analysis of mothering (e.g., Eichenbaum and Orbach, 1983; Gilligan, 1982; Jordan et al., 1991). Carol Gilligan's (1982) model of women's moral development and the relational self has perhaps been the most influential relationship model of women's identity. A summary of her theory appears in the chapter on cultural feminist themes in feminist therapy. In addition to her model of moral development, Carol Gilligan and colleagues (Brown and Gilligan, 1992; Gilligan, Lyons, and Hanmer, 1990) have conducted qualitative studies that have explored the development of the relational self in girls. Based on their studies of primarily middle-class adolescent girls, they concluded that although young girls generally express their ideas and opinions with confidence, they begin to silence themselves during adolescence rather than express open disagreement or conflict. Because of the fear of endangering relationships, they begin to monitor their own responses and often avoid expressing their true feelings. This change in behavior is an outcome of girls' awareness of cultural expectations about what it means to be a "perfect" or "good" woman in the dominant society. However, a qualitative exploration of the experiences of adolescent urban girls, who were predominantly young women of color and from poor and working-class backgrounds, revealed that many of these girls maintained the ability to speak their minds and to express both disagreement and caring in relationships (Way, 1995). Niobe Way (1995) suggested that this ability to speak out may be a result of the unique socialization experiences and mother-daughter relations that are evident in many families of color. For example, black women are encouraged by adult models to be strong and independent. To survive in the world, these young women learn that they must speak out: "[I]nner-city adolescent girls, especially girls of color, may realize that they will be offered little, if anything, if they do not speak up for what they want" (pp. 124-125). These findings demonstrate the importance of exploring the views of women of color on their own terms. These findings also highlight the strengths of women of color and the ways in which white women can learn from women of color. Finally, they also point out that socialization factors are likely to have significant impact on the nature of the relational self, and they reinforce the reality that white girls' and white women's experiences are not generalizable to all women's experiences.

Relationship models of women's identity are likely to hold relevance for many women of color (Segura and Pierce, 1993). However, it is also important for feminist therapists to be aware that the notion of the *self*, including the relational self, varies across cultures. Within most individualistic cultures such as the dominant U.S. culture, the relational self is generally defined as a orientation that exists within the individual. The person who defines herself or himself in relational terms values a sense of emotional connectedness to others. The relational self becomes a medium for self-expression. In cultures based on collectivist values, however, the notion of a distinct personal self-concept may not be as relevant. The self may not exist apart from the social systems in which one participates; it is flexible and defined differently in specific social situations that call for specific responses. This self is influenced by relationships but does not operate in the same manner as a relationship-oriented person within most dominant western cultures. Within collectivist cultures, the relational self is not merely a vehicle for self-expression but is based in a sense of interdependence, unity, and harmony with others as well as the physical world (Bradshaw, 1990, Campbell et al., 1996; Comas-Díaz, 1994; Kashima et al., 1995; Markus and Kitayama, 1991; Triandis, 1989).

Most of the personality theories that form a foundation for psychotherapy are embedded in white, middle-class traditions. It is essential for feminist therapists to be aware of the limitations of major personality theories as well as current feminist relational theories of women's identity, which are generally informed by research on white women and may reflect the way in which white women are socialized to deal with the forms of oppression they are most likely to experience (Espín, 1990). It is important for feminist therapists to critically evaluate personality theories, to point out occasions in which these theories are not inclusive, and to develop theory that is informed by and applicable to the lives of women of color.

Oliva Espín and Mary Ann Gawelek (1992) summarized major characteristics of inclusive theories that feminist therapists can use to evaluate the personality theories informing their work. First, the experiences of all women must be understood and valued. The feminist therapist must regularly ask whether the diverse experiences of women are valued on the basis of the experiences of women of color or whether these experiences are understood only in comparison to the standards of dominant culture. Second, the feminist therapist must question whether the theory adequately attends to the social context in which women live. Race, class, and ethnicity all have a significant impact on women's self-definitions, and attention to these aspects must be considered central components of theory. Third, therapists should explore whether theory is pluralistic: Is theory flexible enough to conceptualize differences between women? Finally, egalitarian relationships must be central to the development of theory. The therapist must ask to what degree the women whose reality is being depicted by the theory have had an opportunity to shape this knowledge. Women of color must be involved in the formation and testing of all aspects of theories applied to their lives.

ANTIRACISM/DOMINATION TRAINING FOR WHITE FEMINIST THERAPISTS

It is essential for feminist therapists to implement therapeutic methods that correct the limitations of previous research, theory, and practice perspectives (Adleman and Enguídanos, 1995). In order to implement inclusive methods, feminist therapists must be aware of their own values. As noted in the chapter on the feminisms of women of color, contemporary racism operates in subtle ways. Feminist therapists are not likely to be aware of their subtle ethnocentric or racism beliefs unless they carefully examine their own experiences of white privilege and become educated about the lives and histories of diverse women (Brown, 1991b, 1993, 1995; McIntosh, 1989; Frankenberg, 1993). Bell hooks (1984) suggested that middle-class feminists have overemphasized the ways in which they have been victimized in order to define feminism as relevant to their lives. The basis for solidarity among white women has been shared victimhood. Ironically, white women are the very women who experience higher levels of power and privilege than most other women in society. In contrast, "women who are exploited and oppressed daily cannot afford to relinquish the belief that they exercise some control, however relative, over their lives" (hooks, 1984, p. 45). When white women view themselves primarily as victims, they are conveniently absolved of responsibility for confronting the ways in which they may help maintain and perpetuate racism, classism, and sexism.

One of the most problematic attitudes of white feminists emerges when they attempt to respond to issues of women of color while remaining ignorant about the experiences and worldviews of women of color. Feminists of color note that white feminists who are unaware of the context of the lives of diverse groups of women are often guilty of condescension. For example, Gloria Anzaldúa (1983) compared some of the activity of white feminists to "the monkey in the Sufi story, who upon seeing fish in the water rushes to rescue it from drowning by carrying it up into the branches of a tree" (p. 206). Merle Woo (1983) added the following: "I have seen how white women condescend to Third World women because they reason that because of our oppression, which they know nothing about, we are behind them and their 'progressive ideas' in the struggle" (p. 143). Both statements reveal the importance of listening to women of color on their own terms and respecting their leadership and insight about the issues relevant to them.

Patricia Collins (1991) notes that women of color have typically developed intimate knowledge of the dominant culture in order to survive in it while members of white society remain oblivious to issues of diversity. Judit Moschkovich (1983) noted the following: "As a bilingual/bicultural women, I live in an American system, abide by American rules of conduct, speak English when around

English speakers, only to be confronted with utter ignorance or concocted myths and stereotypes about my own culture" (p. 80). Feminists therapists must acquire knowledge of the cultures of their clients in order to deal effectively with clients whose cultures are different than their own. This is especially important for white women because unlike most women of color, they have not needed to become educated about other cultures in order to cope with the social roles they must enact. By becoming aware of the cultures of women of color, white feminists also acquire information that will help them explore their unexamined perceptions about life experiences, which they may have presumed to be universal.

One of white women's most common sources of information about diversity comes from their knowledge of exceptional women of color. This information is often gained through media reports, academic experiences, or biographies/autobiographies. The lives of exceptional women of color provide rich information about how individual women have overcome sexism, violence, and racism. However, accounts about exceptional women can sometimes be used to support white supremacist notions that although racism exists, it is not a particularly significant factor if women are determined to achieve and willing to "pull themselves up by their bootstraps" (Crawford and Marecek, 1989). Thus, it is important for white feminist therapists to become aware of the everyday struggles of women of color.

Another potential problem that merits attention is the danger of inadvertently romanticizing women of color. As white feminists become aware of the rich traditions of women of color (rich spiritual traditions, healing rituals) they may desire to incorporate some of these activities within their own experience. However, if these practices are borrowed merely as forms of convenience that are not matched with knowledge and appreciation of the full significance of these traditions, white feminists may engage in a form of colonization or objectification of people of color. Another form of romanticizing women of color may occur when white feminists emphasize the strength of women of color without acknowledging the very real struggles that they encounter. An overemphasis on strength does not allow women of color to be seen as humans, or as persons who experience ordinary stresses and strains of living. For example,

Carolyn West (1995) indicated that the "mammy" stereotype reinforces the notion that black women are able to "selflessly meet the needs of others" (p. 461). The stereotype does not give black women permission to acknowledge genuine vulnerability and fear when these emotions are natural outcomes of their experiences. Bell hooks (1981) elaborated on this issue by stating the following:

> When feminists acknowledge in one breath that black women are victimized and in the same breath emphasize their strength, they imply that though black women are oppressed they manage to circumvent the damaging impact of oppression by being strong—and that is simply not the case. . . . They ignore the reality that to be strong in the face of oppression is not the same as overcoming oppression, that endurance is not to be confused with transformation. (p. 6)

Subtle racism is often perpetuated by nonconscious assumptions about the world that have so permeated the lives of most white U.S. residents that they seem as natural as breathing. Laura Brown (1991b) refers to this process as internalized domination, which she defines as:

> the sense of self within dominant group members in which images of the inherent superiority of ourselves and our cultural reference group are predominant, leading us to define normalcy, reason, and wisdom in terms of our own experience, to assume that "human" is isomorphic with membership in our group. (p. 83)

Laura Brown (1991b) also noted that when white people grow up in the dominant white culture, they will be either covertly or overtly racist to some degree. In order to eradicate nonconscious racism, feminist therapists should participate in antiracism training (Adleman and Enguídanos, 1995; Cross et al., 1982) designed to increase awareness of how white privilege and internalized domination perpetuate power differentials (Boyd, 1990; Brown 1990b, 1991b, 1993, 1995; Rave, 1990).

Peggy McIntosh (1989) suggested that just as men have difficulty recognizing male privilege and power, white feminists have difficulty recognizing white privilege or the "invisible package of unearned assets which I can count on cashing in each day, but about which I was 'meant' to remain oblivious" (p. 10). These unearned privileges resemble a "weightless knapsack" of special tools and blank checks that are accorded to people who have greater social and economic power. In order to raise consciousness, Peggy McIntosh provided a sample of twenty-six privileges that white people can expect to receive. The list included items such as the following: (1) being able to count on skin color adding to rather than detracting from perceptions of personal reliability, (2) being able to accept a job with an affirmative action employee without individuals being suspicious that the job was awarded on the basis of race versus competence, (3) being able to associate with members of the white race as one desires, (4) and being assured that educational materials will give ample attention to the existence of one's race. The listing of these privileges is useful for revealing how white supremacy and white privilege are much more than individual acts of racism, but represent ways in which some people are systematically excluded from positions of influence (McIntosh, 1989).

In addition to examining privilege, it is important for feminist therapists to become aware of the typical ways in which modern racism manifests itself. Racism is apparent in the following activities: (1) dysfunctional rescuing, or assisting women of color based on the belief that they do not have the background or knowledge to help themselves; (2) blaming the victim, or ignoring the impact of systemic racism on people's lives, and blaming women of color for not acting on their own behalf; (3) avoiding contact with women of color for various reasons, including fear or unwillingness to learn about the experiences of women of color; (4) denying differences or discounting the impact of culture on personal behavior; and (5) denying that racial, social, political, and economic differences between people have political significance (Essed, 1991; McIntosh, 1989).

Philomena Essed (1991) elaborated on three behaviors that support everyday racism: marginalization, containment, and problematization. Through marginalization, the "other" status of people of color is perpetuated by denying women access to power, considering the perspectives of people of color to be irrelevant, ignoring problems of racism, or ignoring the contributions of people of color.

Through containment, the efforts of people of diversity to achieve equality, justice, and power are suppressed through denial of racism or verbal aggression. Through problematization, people of color are viewed as deficient in some way and responsible for the very problems they experience. For example, a woman of color who expresses anger may be labeled as too emotional, and the problem of oppression may be denied and defined as an individual problem.

Bell hooks (1989) suggested that the phrase *white supremacy* reflects problems in relationships between white people and people of color more adequately than the term *racism*. The phrase white supremacy defines the way in which white people and the institutions in which they are involved internalize the values of a racist society and inadvertently "support and affirm the very structure of racist domination and oppression that they profess to wish to see eradicated" (p. 113). White supremacy is also a useful phrase for depicting the complicity that people of color can demonstrate as they are socialized to assume the values of white supremacy and thus, help maintain class and racial hierarchies. Bell hooks (1989) prefers this phrase to "internalized racism," which implies that people of color have consciously adopted negative feelings toward themselves that are promoted by the dominant society.

White feminist therapists must take personal responsibility for educating themselves about the plurality of human experience, and not assuming that women of color should provide this education and information to them. Oliva Espín (1995) cautions that even when white women have good intentions, they often remain blinded by their own privilege. Self-examination must be rigorous and continuous. Despite the long-standing distrust between women of color and white women, bell hooks suggests that there is opportunity for rapprochement in the future. If the goal of feminism is for women to gain the power that white men hold, relationships between white women and women of color are likely to remain divisive because this form of power is based on gaining power at the expense of others. White feminist therapists will need to counter white supremacy, refuse to accept myths and stereotypes about women of color that separate women, listen to women of color on their own terms, and engage in honest, open discussion of similarities and differences.

FEMINIST THERAPY FOR WOMEN OF COLOR

Despite some of the ethnocentrism present in the first forms of feminist therapy and the difficulties creating truly inclusive forms of theory and practice, Lillian Comas-Díaz (1988, 1991) stated that feminist therapy is highly relevant to the lives of women of color. Feminist therapy is especially useful for helping women of color (1) acknowledge the harmful and interactive effects of racism, sexism, and classism; (2) explore feelings of anger and self-degradation related to racism and ethnic minority status; (3) recognize themselves as competent, powerful individuals with the capacity to enact solutions to problems; (4) clarify the interaction between the sociocultural environment and their internal experiences; and (5) identify and implement opportunities to change social and institutional responses. The following two sections will describe important features of feminist therapy for women of color as defined primarily by Lillian Comas-Díaz (1991, 1994), Oliva Espín (1994), and Beverly Greene (1986, 1990, 1992, 1994).

Feminist Therapy As Decolonization

People of color often have a personal and cultural history that has been influenced by colonization. People of color have been obligated to accommodate themselves to the norms of a dominant, colonizing culture that has demanded the sacrifice and eradication of their cultures of origin. Lillian Comas-Díaz (1994) indicated that *colonization* is a more useful term than oppression to conceptualize the unique experiences of people of color because the term implies that people of color have been required to accept the norms of the dominant culture in order to survive. Although groups such as the elderly, disabled, white women, and gay people have experienced oppression and discrimination, only people of color have experienced the suppression of their own cultures through colonization. Some of the personal consequences of colonization include victimization, alienation, self-denial, assimilation within the dominant culture, and/or ambivalence about oneself and the dominant culture.

Colonized peoples often become convenient scapegoats for social problems and the recipients of narrow stereotypes. Women of color are especially vulnerable to being blamed for family problems and stresses that are the products of institutional racism (Greene, 1990). Women of color have also been perceived as the colonizer's bounty as individuals who can be enslaved or sexually abused (Comas-Díaz, 1994). They experience sexual objectification, are viewed as oversexual or asexual beings, or are confined to polarized or narrow images. For example, the concept of *marianismo*, based on image of the Virgin Mary, confines many Hispanic women to images of women as virgin and Madonna who are spiritually superior to men and capable of surviving all suffering at the hands of men (Comas-Díaz, 1988). Beverly Greene (1992) indicated that black women are subjected to the following three stereotyped images: "as angry, volatile, castrating bitches, as nurturing, pious, caring mammy figures, or as morally loose and sexually promiscuous 'whores'" (p. 20). The psychological wounds of forced assimilation and imposed stereotypes are highly significant. As a result, feminist therapy for women of color may be best understood as a process of decolonization, which involves the restoration of personal dignity and the transformation of oneself and the world (Comas-Díaz, 1994). Through decolonization, women experience the recovery of themselves, develop autonomous self-identities, and engage in action that results in change of themselves and/or the conditions they experience as colonized individuals.

Conscientização, or the development of a critical consciousness (Freire, 1970), is a central component of feminist therapy for women of color. Through consciousness-raising, the woman becomes aware of the nature of colonization and internalized racist beliefs associated with it, the impact of these beliefs on the self, and methods for countering these beliefs. In the case of black women, for example, the dominant culture's standards of beauty that idealize Caucasian features and devalue African features are especially harmful (Greene, 1992). Black women are rewarded for attempting to replicate Caucasian standards, and the internalization of these standards is reflected in many black women's concerns about body type, facial characteristics, hair texture, and skin color. The narrow range of cultural images of black women (as mammy, sexually loose, or angry woman) can also be internalized and severely restrict women's self-perceptions, contribute to high levels of stress, and limit women's capacity to enact authentic roles (West, 1995).

Although black women are criticized for fitting stereotypes associated with these images, they are also often criticized by the wider society for undermining black men when they choose to adopt a wider array of roles. This type of double bind is especially painful and difficult to transcend. Awareness of these types of issues and their consequences is important as a precursor to challenging these images and developing a healthy self-concept (Greene, 1992; West, 1995).

Lillian Comas-Díaz (1994) indicates that developing an understanding of the personal consequences of colonization is important for transcending it. That which is associated with the dominant culture is often seen as good, even by colonized peoples, and that which is associated with the minority or colonized culture is seen as negative. Deconstructing polarized images and finding ways to understand oneself and the world in more meaningful ways is highly challenging. As a part of self-recovery, clients need opportunities to express anger about confining images and correct cognitive distortions that are a consequence of the narrow images of themselves which are promoted by society. Women's ability to express anger may be complicated by the fact that the expression of strong feelings outside of psychotherapy may result in becoming the target of institutional racism. The legitimate expression of anger may be labeled as misplaced expressions of an "angry minority" (Comas-Díaz and Greene, 1994). Thus, working through anger within the therapy relationship and finding productive methods for anger expression in daily life are especially important activities.

As women of color become aware of the impact of the interactive impact of racism, gender, and/or classism on their lives, they are likely to become aware of how self-hatred and/or ambivalence toward themselves and their cultures of origin are reactions to or methods of coping with colonization. This awareness forms the foundation for more flexible and positive thinking about themselves. Lillian Comas-Díaz (1994) also indicates that it is helpful for clients to differentiate between the ways in which they experience discrimination from external sources and how their internalized negative images influence behavior. This process helps women make informed decisions about what they can change as individuals and what desired outcomes will require social change and organized action.

Following this awareness stage and recovery of the self, decolonization therapy focuses on the creation of an autonomous, integrated, and healthy identity that is "independent of the colonizer's idealized White female standard" (Comas-Díaz, 1994, p. 291). An exploration of the positive aspects of womanhood associated with one's personal culture may be especially useful. For example, although the concept of *marianismo,* which is embedded in the Catholic and colonial tradition, may be confining and limiting, the concept of *hembrismo* may provide a rewarding and freeing alternative (Comas-Díaz, 1987, 1988). Hembrismo "connotes strength, perseverance, flexibility, and an ability for survival" (Comas-Díaz, 1988, p. 45). This image, based in indigenous Puerto Rican matriarchal culture, conveys an image of women who are powerful but not oppressive and whose influence is reinforced through spiritual leadership.

Yvette Flores-Ortiz (1995) noted that Chicanas often feel pressed to simultaneously fulfill the multiple roles such as mother, sister, spouse, and comrade (*compañera*) in the political struggle. While attempting to fulfill these multiple roles, Chicanas may struggle with the demands of being "La Superchicana" and/or may feel alienated from both the mother culture and the dominant white society. Sorting out these conflicts, finding ways to balance these roles, and/or choosing what roles to emphasize are important to the formation of an autonomous, integrated identity.

Comas-Díaz (1994) also suggested that asking the client to tell her personal and cultural and story, including information about her ethnocultural group's origins, migration, and identity, may be especially helpful in developing and reinforcing a healthy personal identity. Storytelling about mothers or other significant persons, which involves recollections of significant others, how they dealt with racism and sexism, and/or how they negotiated life tasks, can form the foundation for further clarification of personal hopes and dreams. Utilizing culturally relevant myths, legends, and spiritual traditions may also provide a rich source of positive images for women of color (Comas-Díaz, 1991; LaFramboise, Heyle, and Ozer, 1990; True, 1990).

The development of an integrated identity includes the building of skills to deal with discrimination and the channeling of anger into social action. A final stage of decolonization involves the planning of healthy action on behalf of oneself and others, including the social structure in which one lives. In other words, advocacy, political action, and other methods of improving the conditions and opportunities of people of color are crucial features of a fully integrated approach to feminist therapy with women of color.

Many of the personal and identity changes that emerge through involvement in decolonization therapy are also addressed by various models of ethnic minority development (e.g., Cross, 1991; Helms, 1990; Sue, 1981), which propose that people of color acquire a positive and integrated sense of themselves by negotiating a series of developmental stages. At a preencounter stage, individuals are generally unaware of oppression and accept racism and discrimination as "givens." As they become aware of racism and colonization, the experience of anger is likely to be intense and becomes an important focus of therapy. During a third phase, individuals are likely to think in polarized ways, to reject the dominant culture, and to immerse themselves in the values and traditions of their heritages. They may also prefer to associate primarily with other members of their racial-ethnic group. At the final phases of internalization and commitment, individuals create self-chosen, integrated identities. As a part of this process, they often learn how to become bicultural individuals who can effectively negotiate across the borders of the dominant culture and their personal cultures. This internalization also becomes the basis for a commitment to social change.

Ethnospecific Feminist Therapy

Many feminist therapists believe that a female-female therapeutic dyad is essential for effective feminist therapy. Oliva Espín (1994) takes this concept one step further and articulates the advantages of a feminist ethnospecific approach, which is defined as therapy in which the therapist and client are from the same ethnic-racial background.

The positive aspects of an ethnospecific approach are multiple. First, the therapist is aware of the client's language and culture through first-hand experience. Espín cautions that when the therapist is white and the client is a woman or man of color, the client is often expected to inform the therapist about her racial/cultural traditions, which detracts from the focus of therapy. Second, a therapist from the same racial background as the client serves as a more powerful role model than a white feminist therapist. Through her presence alone, the feminist therapist of color raises the client's consciousness about the possibilities available to her. Third, there is greater likelihood that power will be equalized. Because of racial and cultural similarity, it is less likely that a relationship of dominance and submission will be recreated. When the therapist is white, her greater power than the client is magnified: She holds greater power due to her expertise as well as her dominant status in society at large. The therapeutic relationship can resemble the colonizer-colonized relationship in which the woman of color's less powerful position in society is reinforced (Comas-Díaz, 1994). Fourth, "the therapist is more likely to be invested in the client's success in therapy and life" (Espín, 1994, p. 276). Although there is some danger that the therapist may overidentify with the client, it is more likely that similarity will be an advantage.

As individuals who have experienced multiple forms of oppression, such as both racism and sexism, feminist therapists of color often develop a heightened sense of awareness of their clients' needs, which Virginia Hammond (1987) refers to as "conscious subjectivity." Conscious subjectivity operates in several ways. First, through mutual identification points, the feminist therapist is able to note common or shared experiences with the client, which allows her to both validate the client's perceptions that racism exists and model the reality that it is possible to survive and transcend oppression. Second, the therapist helps the client understand that many of her internalized racist or sexist beliefs evolved as tools for coping with a racist society; this process further validates the client and her inherent strengths. Timely therapist self-disclosure facilitates both of these activities. Third, because of her own experience with racism and sexism, the feminist therapist of color may be especially aware of how to act as an advocate or power agent on behalf of the client as she negotiates institutions or systems that have often limited her options. Fourth, by teaching specific skills, the therapist helps the client develop mastery and competence. The feminist therapist's actual encounter with multiple forms of oppression helps her engage in effective teaching.

An ethnospecific approach may also be advantageous because the facets of each person's experience are complex and multiple. Beverly Greene (1986) noted that because skin color is a highly visible difference between individuals, it may evoke transference and countertransference issues in more pronounced ways than other differences. Racial-ethnic similarity between therapist and client decreases the number of differences that the therapist and client need to transcend and may help the counselor and client establish an initial relationship of trust. Even when the therapist and client share a common racial heritage and/or commonalities that may be defined by language, religion, and/or culture, many differences between women exist. Hispanic women, for example, identify themselves in many ways: as Cuban, Spanish/Hispanic, Puerto Rica, Chicano/ Chicana, Mexican, Mexican American, or Latino/Latina. The therapist working with these populations should be knowledgeable about historical influences such as colonization and unique cultural values, the client's level of acculturation and/or experience with immigration, and the client's relationship with language, such as Spanish. Variables such as class, professional status, and sexual orientation must also be considered (Espín, 1986, 1987; Comas-Díaz, 1988). Thus, even ethnospecific approaches must be informed by knowledge of diversity within racial-ethnic groups.

Despite the many advantages of an ethnospecific approach, the number of feminist therapists of color is small, and most women of color who seek out a feminist therapist will need to work with a white feminist therapist. At its best, therapy between a white therapist and a woman of color client can provide a useful context for learning to deal effectively with similarities and differences (Espín, 1994). When the therapist is white and the client is from an ethnic minority group, it is likely that the fear, angers, and tensions present in the wider society will influence therapy in some way. The white feminist therapist must be cognizant of the legacy of distrust that may exist between her racial group and the client's ethnic-racial group. The therapist must also recognize that the client may bring a healthy "cultural paranoia" to psychotherapy, and that the client's potential testing of the therapist's trustworthiness represents a healthy and productive survival skill and may reflect methods the client uses to protect herself from additional discrimination within her social world. A nondefensive exploration of issues related to difference and discrimination may lead to the client's increased ability to deal effectively with white people and people of color (Greene, 1986).

It is important for white feminist therapists to recognize occasions when they are not able to adequately empathize with a client of color. Lillian Comas-Díaz (1994) suggested that although therapists in cross-cultural dyads may understand the client's experience from a cognitive perspective, they may have difficulty empathizing at an affective level. She suggests that the experience between a white therapist and person of color can be enhanced through "empathic witnessing," in which "the therapist recognizes his or her ethnocultural ignorance of the client's reality and reaffirms, through empathic witnessing, the client's experience and reality" (pp. 294-295).

At times, therapists' need to seem "color-blind" or their fear of acknowledging difference may lead them to avoid dealing with issues of difference (Greene, 1986). The open, honest willingness of the white therapist to deal with difference through antiracism training and as a relationship issue in psychotherapy is essential. The therapist must be careful, however, to avoid interpreting "dealing with difference" as asking the client to teach the therapist about his or her reality. It is the responsibility of the therapist to become educated about the values, experiences, and worldviews of the client.

Beverly Greene (1986) argues that although color blindness is dangerous, it is equally dangerous for therapists to uncritically comply with client rhetoric associated with the belief that "one's discriminated status justifies a failure to take into account the feelings or needs of others" (p. 54). Because of anxiety, guilt feelings about racism, or fears about her own racism influencing the psychotherapy experience, the white feminist therapist may fear confronting the client about occasions when his or her behaviors have been hurtful to others. Feminist therapists must be engage in consistent self-monitoring of their behavior in order to guard against minimizing the impact of race on the client's experience as well as ignoring factors other than race and ethnicity that the client and therapist must confront.

Ethnospecific Therapy and Indigenous Therapies

An ethnospecific approach to feminist therapy can sometimes be enhanced by integrating indigenous therapies with feminist therapy. For example, Lily McNair (1992) recommended a synthesis of Afrocentric and feminist therapy. Many feminist models do not adequately attend to cultural issues, and most Afrocentric models do not deal with issues related to gender. However, the combination of these approaches may be especially suited to the needs and values of many African-American women. The following summary will briefly describe the central features of one form of Afrocentric psychotherapy that can be used to enhance feminist therapy.

NTU psychotherapy (Phillips, 1990) is based on an Afrocentric worldview and emphasizes the interrelatedness of internal psychic forces and social-environmental factors that influence human capacity to deal with daily issues and problems of living. The term *NTU* is a Bantu word that refers to the unity of mind, body, and spirit, or the harmonizing force that leads to balanced and authentic living. This form of Afrocentric therapy is based on the core principles of (1) harmony, the spiritual belief that unity of mind, body, and spirit allows individuals to align themselves effectively with the basic forces of life; (2) balance, the process by which seemingly competitive aspects of experience are combined in a holistic manner; (3) interconnectedness, the notion that all experience is linked and creates a bridge between internal and external experiences; (4) authenticity, or the valuing of spontaneous, genuine, and intentional relationships within a community; and (5) cultural awareness, or the importance of discovering one's identity as it is influenced by Afrocentric values. Underlying these principles is an affective epistemology that places significant value on emotional self-knowledge and well-being (Phillips, 1990). Whereas a Eurocentric worldview tends to emphasize individualism, control over nature, and material values, this Afrocentric approach places priority on collective responsibility and cooperation, harmony and unity with nature, and the equal valuing of spiritual and material aspects of living (Jackson and Sears, 1992).

Anita Jackson and Susan Sears (1992) suggested that the application of an Afrocentric worldview to women's concerns is especially positive for several reasons. First, an Afrocentric approach provides the client with knowledge about her history, gives relevance to black women's heritage, and fosters self-worth and a positive identity. Second, this knowledge of Afrocentric values provides a positive framework from which to counteract negative images of black women in the dominant culture. Third, the holistic and multidimensional approach associated with Afrocentric psychology forms a foundation for stress management and problem solving while helping women cope with and transcend difficult circumstances. Finally, this approach fosters a communal orientation and the development of positive support networks. These principles are highly consistent with feminist therapy's emphasis on empowerment, women's strengths, and the enhancement of women's functioning rather than a focus on deficits and pathology.

Although the integration of indigenous therapies with feminist principles is often valuable, some cultural/indigenous therapies are embedded in social values that maintain a patriarchal social structure. The feminist therapist must be careful not to romanticize culturally defined therapies that reinforce male domination and minimize the realities of women's oppression (Bradshaw, 1994; True, 1990).

Ethnospecific Therapy, Groups, and Support Systems

Many women of color come from cultures that value collectivism, community, and interdependence. For example, the Japanese value of *amae* emphasizes the centrality of reciprocity, belongingness, and indebtedness between individuals. Amae involves the "indivisibility of subject from object, self from other" (Bradshaw, 1990, p 73). Relationships within the inner circle of family and relatives are characterized by oneness between persons, unconditional love, affirmation, and indulgence. In may Hispanic cultures, the values of *respeto*, or respect and *familiarismo*, or familism, emphasize the manner in which family members share responsibility for the health and well-being of the extended family (Comas-Díaz and Duncan, 1985). Many black women value an Afrocentric worldview, which underscores the importance of collective responsibility, extended kinship systems, and harmony between humanity and nature (Greene, 1992, 1994; Jackson and Sears, 1992). Native American women often experience their identity as an extension of the extended family, the tribe, and a spiritual perspective that stresses the interconnectedness of people and their environments (LaFromboise, Berman, and Sohi, 1994).

Given the importance of interdependence to many women of color, culturally relevant consciousness-raising groups, support networks, and self-help networks that develop these values may be especially productive forms of feminist therapy. Such experiences are likely to help women of color strengthen their historical, ethnic, and cultural identities; emphasize issues that are primary concerns of their specific ethnic group; provide concrete assistance and emotional support to each other; and empower them to make changes in their lives and in the larger community (Fulani, 1988; True, 1990; Vasquez, 1994). For example, Teresa LaFromboise, Joan Saks Berman, and Balvindar Sohi (1994) recommended several types of groups for American Indian women. Culturally sensitive time-limited workshops of skills groups can be used to focus on specific issues such as sexual abuse, self-esteem, or alcoholism. Groups may also be built on traditional healing practices. The "talking circle" incorporates aspects of ritual, prayer, role-playing, and modeling, but does not require direct interaction between members. The "four circles" option involves discussion of issues associated with four levels of interaction, which include the Creator at the center; one's spouse or partner; the immediate family; and the extended family, community, and tribe. Finally, family network therapy allows for the recreation of a clan network for the purpose of mobilizing a social support system for an individual or family.

Spirituality and religious experience may represent additional support systems for women of color. Toinette Eugene (1995) indicated, for example, that the black church has been an important aspect of a therapeutic community and an impetus for social activism in the lives of black women. First, the singing of spirituals and gospel songs is a way of articulating the suffering of black women, and also becomes a way of protesting and confronting evil. Second, through prayer and singing, individuals name the oppression that faces them. This expression of suffering provides a powerful emotional release and healing. Third, spiritual expressions validate the suffering and persecution of black women, increase women's self-esteem, and decrease women's sense of isolation and self-blame. These activities are consistent with Alice Walker's (1983) definition of a womanist identity, which emphasizes the importance of black women's commitment to the wholeness and survival of other women and an entire people. In summary, feminist therapists should value women's diverse expressions of themselves in communal environments as central components of healing.

CONCLUDING COMMENTS

Although it is easy to give lip service to the importance of a multicultural perspective in feminist therapy, enactment of inclusive, antiracist practice is difficult. Oliva Espín (1995) noted the following reality:

> When statements are made about the "need to include" women of color in theories or organizations, in the very statement of the need for their inclusion the assumption is being made that some other group (meaning, of course, *white* women) "owns" and defines the movement in which the women of color are to be included. (p. 128)

In order for feminist psychotherapy to transcend this historical problem, the work of feminist therapists of color, antiracist practice, and multicultural perspectives will need to become a cornerstone of all feminist psychotherapy practice. Attention to diversity should be central to all theory building and practice. Feminist psychologists who met at the National Conference of Feminist Practice in Psychology (Chin, 1993) defined diversity as the following: (1) empowerment; (2) an openness to differences among and between people; (3) the appreciation, cultivation, and nurturing of different perspectives; (4) a recognition of the value of difference; (5) a receptivity and respect for difference; and (6) a noun and a verb in which we are all subject and object. An appreciation for diversity is *not* associated with tokenism or multiculturalism; deficit language, such as "underprivileged"; an "add-and-stir" or elective approach to psychotherapy; or psychological models that compare nondominant groups to the "normative" groups of white men and women. Each of these values are central to defining approaches to feminist therapy that are relevant to the lives of women of color.

In order to create an inclusive feminist therapy, the following foundation must be constructed. First, it is necessary for white feminist therapists to explicitly identify their unconscious assumptions that have supported ethnocentrism. Feminist therapists must also work toward destroying the myth of the "universal woman" and stereotypes about women of color by examining the complexity and diversity of women's lives. Feminist therapists must continue to increase their understanding of the multiple experiences, multiple realities, multiple truths, and multiple oppressions that individuals experience. Feminist therapists must listen to and understand all women of color on their own terms, and they must see the experiences of women of color as lived and embodied rather than as statistics and generalizations about women. An inclusive feminist therapy must be based on comprehensive knowledge about how the inner and outer lives of women are intertwined, how women's lives are socially constructed, and how political forces influence the inner experience of the self. A feminist therapy that respects diversity must also be based on an understanding of the myriad coping skills and strengths of women of color. This knowledge requires awareness of how women resist the limitations placed on their lives by race, gender, and class, and how women reinvent their lives in response to the challenges they face.

Chapter 8

Toward Integration

In this final chapter, I comment on the following three topics: (1) salient differences in how feminist therapists with various theoretical orientations are likely to practice feminist therapy, (2) recent efforts to develop an integrated theory of feminist therapy, and (3) possibilities for eclecticism in feminist therapy.

THE DIVERSITY OF FEMINIST THERAPY PRACTICE

Basic Principles of Feminist Therapy

In her 1980 review of feminist therapy, Lucia Gilbert identified two unifying principles of feminist therapy: (1) the personal is political and (2) the therapist-client relationship is egalitarian. Most of the principles that I identified in Chapter 1 can be organized under these two themes.

Liberal feminist therapists acknowledge the relationship between women's problems and their environments, facilitate women's awareness of how social conditioning influences their lives, and assist individuals in making choices based on their personal strengths and interests. Deviations from prescribed gender roles are seen as positive and beneficial, and these choices must be based on "what works" for the individual. The notion that "the personal is political" (principle 1) is realized when individuals act on the rights and opportunities provided them. Eventually, these individual choices lead to changed social structures. An egalitarian relationship (principle 2) is defined as one in which the therapist carefully monitors personal behavior to ensure that personal values do not covertly influence the client. As a result, the therapist does not assume that certain outcomes, such as economic autonomy, are better than other outcomes that reflect more traditional choices. The self-determination of the client is highly valued, and a wide rage of lifestyle, family, and economic options are considered appropriate outcomes of therapy, provided they lead to client satisfaction.

Feminist therapists influenced by cultural feminism hold some values that are similar to those of liberal feminist therapists, and as a result, emphasize the importance of self-knowledge and personal choice. However, they are more likely to actively revalue traditional female strengths such as empathy, cooperation, and other relationship skills. The "personal is political" means that traditional feminine relational values should be used to develop affirming, supportive networks among women and that these connections can empower women to influence and reform a culture that overvalues individualism, competition, and traditional concepts of success. As women's values permeate the larger culture, greater flexibility of behavior will be accorded to both men and women. An egalitarian relationship is seen as one in which the female therapist and client will form a bond built on their common, personal knowledge of women's lives, and the therapist's unconditional acceptance, trust of and emotional sensitivity to the client may take on mothering, nurturing qualities (Chaplin, 1988). As a result, women learn to reconstruct and revalue their inner selves, which they have often rejected as unattractive or unlovable in order to survive in contemporary culture. The egalitarian relationship is "about being loved by another woman and helped by her to grow and become separate." (Eichenbaum and Orbach, 1983, p. 107). Although one person is the primary beneficiary of the relationship, both client and therapist are touched emotionally and experience empathy and genuine caring (Jordan, 1991).

Radical and socialist feminist theorists call for the dramatic alteration of gender roles, institutions, and society. For both radical and socialist feminist therapists, the statement "the personal is political" is understood to mean that therapists will be involved in social action and advocacy on behalf of clients and women in general. In addition to facilitating awareness of the impact of social conditioning, they engage in sociopolitical analysis of women's problems, actively identify how sexism influences women's lives, and encourage women to rechannel their frustration into active confrontation with oppressive circumstances. An egalitarian relationship means that the client is her own best expert. Therapists engage in self-disclosure and state their values explicitly in order to demystify the relationship, empower clients, and emphasize the commonalities among women. Although there are some differences between radical and socialist feminist therapists, both groups emphasize the importance of consciousness-raising, social change, and the transformation of institutional systems.

For women of color, the personal is political must apply not only to gender but also to race and class. Feminist women of color are critical of feminists who view women's oppression as the most fundamental oppression or who assert that women have more in common with other women than men of color, regardless of their ethnic, racial, or socioeconomic status (Comas-Díaz, 1991). Many women of color have experienced more virulent oppression as a consequence of skin color than gender; thus, the intersections of race, class, and gender must be carefully integrated when considering the political implications of personal dilemmas and problems. As a part of an egalitarian relationship, the feminist therapist must become aware of how white privilege or subtle racism and classism may limit her ability to comprehensively enact the principle of egalitarianism. White feminist therapists must examine ways in which they have contributed to the oppression of women of color by benefiting from their own participation in traditional power structures. They should also consider participating in antiracism and anti-domination training.

Diagnosis and Conceptualization

The philosophical assumptions of therapists influence their assessment of problems. Liberal feminist therapists are likely to endorse the "woman as problem" framework, which Mary Crawford and Jeanne Marecek (1989) described as the dominant perspective within the psychology of women. According to this model, women's difficulties or diminished accomplishments are the consequences of learned behaviors and socialization, and are labeled by phrases such as "the imposter syndrome" (Clance and Imes, 1978), the "Cinderella complex" (Dowling, 1981), and "fear of success" (Horner, 1970). Furthermore, the symptoms of disorders such as agoraphobia, depression, and eating disorders are linked to the stereotyping of women and/or women's overly rigid adherence to traditional gender roles (Franks and Rothblum, 1983). Liberal feminist therapists are likely to use traditional diagnostic categories but make efforts to apply diagnoses fairly by applying a single standard of mental health to men and women.

Cultural feminists, radical feminists, socialist feminists, and feminists of color share a basic mistrust of traditional diagnostic criteria, but emphasize different criticisms and propose different solutions. Cultural feminists are most likely to oppose mainstream conceptualizations of distress because these concepts devalue women's traditional strengths and are based on an androcentric view of the world (Stiver, 1991). To revalue women's experiences, cultural feminist therapists attempt to provide woman-centered explanations of women's disorders. For example, the self-in-relation model of depression indicates that a woman's core self is built on relational strengths. Because society denigrates a woman's capacity to be attuned to others, she may be defined as dependent or immature, and she becomes vulnerable to depression and low self-esteem (Jack, 1987, 1991; Kaplan, 1986).

Radical feminists, socialist feminists, and feminists of color are more likely than other feminists to operate from a "transformation" framework (Crawford and Marecek, 1989), which questions the basic tenets and foundation of mental health systems. Some radical and socialist feminist therapists will avoid using diagnostic labels, except in rare circumstances, because they are seen as embedded in patriarchal, culturally circumscribed beliefs that exaggerate power differentials, label personal rather than social circumstances as the cause of problems, and lead to a overemphasis on individual change efforts (Rawlings and Carter, 1977). For radical feminists, socialist feminists, and feminists of color, the DSM-IV (APA, 1994) is understood as a political and economic document that controls who can provide and receive remuneration for services and often reinforces current hierarchical power structures within society (Kaplan, 1983; Russell, 1986).

Many radical and socialist, and feminist therapists of color prefer to use descriptive terms or culturally appropriate terms to avoid the mystification of standard diagnostic terminology, but they may use traditional categories on behalf of clients if the denial of service is at stake (e.g., health insurance reimbursement). *Transformation* feminists also focus on how diagnosis can become a shared dialogue that increases a client's understanding of the cultural and social implications of distress. As a part of this process, the therapist informs clients about how hypotheses are formed, what theories influence conceptual formulations, and why traditional categories are accepted or rejected (Brown, 1994; Brown and Walker, 1990).

Feminists of color are especially attentive to the manner in which diagnostic categories equate characteristics associated with white, middle-class American values with normalcy. They are especially cognizant of the way in which subtle racist assumptions influence the manner in which diagnostic categories are applied. Feminists of color are also attentive to how the intersections of race, sex, and class influence the type of psychological distress that clients display.

Interventions

Feminist therapists operate from diverse psychotherapeutic systems and assume that most techniques can be potentially effective if applied in a gender-fair manner (Kaschak, 1981). This practice has resulted in "a myriad of feminist therapies that share certain core precepts but vary widely in their descriptions of normative human growth and development, pathology, and appropriate intervention strategies" (Brown, 1990b, p. 2). Feminist therapists use a common pool of psychotherapeutic options, and most feminist therapists use some form of gender role analysis, which involves "bringing to the client's attention whenever relevant, unconscious sex-role expectations" that should be discussed (Rawlings and Carter, 1977, p. 64). However, some schools of therapy are more easily integrated with specific forms of feminist therapy than others.

Liberal feminist theory is built on a humanistic model of personhood and the assumption that all individuals should be free to reach their potential. The humanistic therapies, which emphasize personal growth, wholeness, and choice, can be easily combined with liberal feminism (Sturdivant, 1980). Consistent with humanistic goals, androgyny therapy can be used to help clients overcome gender socialization and increase their repertoire of behaviors (Gilbert, 1981; Kaplan, 1979b). A cognitive-behavioral framework also lends itself to integration with a liberal feminist perspective because problems in living are viewed as learned thinking and behavior patterns. As a result, cognitive-behavioral techniques are useful tools for developing corrective resocialization experiences and overcoming deficits resulting from gender role injunctions. Assertiveness training has been a particularly prominent technique derived from this tradition and focuses on helping women "who want to be assertive in going after what they want in the same way that men do" (Williams, 1976, p. 6). Liberal feminist therapists rely on a wide range of interventions to help individuals express their emotions openly and overcome social conditioning. It should be noted that for the feminist therapist who desires to be technically eclectic, the use of these techniques is not limited to a liberal feminist framework.

Cultural feminist therapists focus on reformulating mainstream therapies in a woman-centered framework. The early efforts of feminist cultural psychoanalysts Karen Horney (1967) and Clara Thompson (1971) described the cultural denigration of women and challenged women to define themselves on the basis of their own strengths. More recently, Gilligan's (1982) "different voice" and Miller's (1986) "new" psychology of women have informed the work of many feminist therapists who have sought to validate women's relational qualities. The psychodynamic feminist therapies, including feminist object-relations therapy (Eichenbaum and Orbach, 1983), the self-in-relation model (Jordan et al., 1991), and Jungian feminist therapy (Bolen, 1984; Romaniello, 1992; Young-Eisendrath and Wiedemann, 1987), are especially consistent with the goals of cultural feminism. Most of these approaches discuss how women's relational self develops, placing special emphasis on mother-daughter dynamics, the "feminine" self, and the "essential cooperative nature of human existence" (Miller, 1986, p. 41). Typical interventions focus on understanding the role of culture in defining and reinforcing women's difficulties, identifying women's relational strengths, discovering an authentic self free of cultural biases, and building mutual empowerment through association with other women.

Feminist therapists operating from radical and socialist feminist frameworks are likely to view the "marriage of humanist therapy and feminism" as unsuccessful (Greenspan, 1983, p. 134). Radical and socialist feminists believe that liberal feminist therapists do not provide the necessary social-political analysis of women's problems, thus inadvertently defeating feminist purposes in therapy. Miriam Greenspan (1983) charged that the liberal feminist goals of increasing self-awareness, making meaningful personal choices, and experiencing an integrated self do not question male-style values or contribute to a changed society. Instead, liberal feminist approaches groom women for male-style careers and lives.

Similar to cultural feminist views, radical feminist theory emphasizes the significance of the unique, personal knowledge of women that has been discounted by patriarchal society. However, they are less likely than cultural feminist to value feminist psychodynamic contributions because they build on traditional definitions of femininity and "essentialize" mothering (Fine and Gordon, 1989). An exception to this blending of cultural feminist and psychoanalytic concepts occurs in Ellyn Kaschak's (1992) approach to feminist therapy, which uses the oedipal story in a social constructionist manner.

Radical feminist therapists are more likely than most feminists to reject mainstream approaches or to radically alter traditional frameworks as foundations for feminist therapy. Some radical feminist therapists have been influenced by the radical therapy tradition (Agel, 1971; Holroyd, 1976), which criticizes established therapeutic practices and institutions, rejects hierarchical relationships, eschews established personality theory, and advocates social and political change. Other radical feminists have created approaches that integrate radical feminist and socialist principles, radical therapy, and transactional analysis (Wyckoff, 1977a,b; Burstow, 1992). The notion of feminist therapy remains controversial in some radical feminist circles. Rachel Perkins (1991b) charged that "no matter how feminist a therapy purports to be, it essentially transforms the political into personal, individual and pathological terms" (p. 331).

Radical feminist theorists have disseminated their views through many forms of creative and artistic expression. In similar fashion, radical feminist therapists often incorporate creative expression and nontraditional techniques within their therapeutic practices, including feminist spirituality and mythology (Conarton and Silverman, 1988; Hendricks, 1985), touch/body therapy (Moss, 1985; Turner, 1990), poetry (Ellis, 1990), photography (Weiser, 1990), and storytelling (Buffalo, 1990).

Socialist feminist practitioners are likely to apply a variety of approaches already discussed but will place special emphasis on economic and class distinctions that shape individuals. Psychological interventions that rely on social-systems perspectives are especially valued. Socialist feminist therapists are also likely to view psychotherapy as a useful but incomplete method for altering social, class, and political structures, and see community organization, advocacy, and coalition-building as essential methods for helping individuals meet their basic needs, changing systems of domination, and creating social structures that allow individuals to live productively (Nes and Iadicola, 1989). In recognition of the multiple influences on people's lives, socialist feminist therapists are also likely to use multiservice approaches that link psychotherapy with economic assistance, as well as educational, health, child-care, and social services.

Feminists of color note that all psychotherapy systems are culturally determined and based on Western, middle-class values (Brown, 1990b). Women of color who are feminists attempt to choose interventions that acknowledge the unique effects of race, class, sexual orientation, and other minority statuses on women's lives. They will also use culturally valued rituals, religious practices, worldviews, and indigenous therapies to help women engage in feminist psychotherapy that is as consistent as possible with their cultural values and traditions.

TOWARD CREATING INTEGRATED THEORIES
OF FEMINIST THERAPY

In recent years, several feminist psychologists have proposed models for creating a integrated theory of feminist therapy. The efforts of two psychologists, Laura Brown (1994) and Ellyn Kaschak (1992), are particularly noteworthy. Both individuals have identified principles for creating a unified approach to feminist therapy that recognizes the diversity of women and the impact of various contexts on women's lives. Both propose principles that are highly consistent with radical, social constructionist, and postmodern perspectives in psychology (Chapter 5 also comments on their approaches).

Ellyn Kaschak (1992) stated that in order to create an integrated model, feminist therapists must recognize that experiences have multiple meanings and that the essence of being human is understanding how different individuals attribute meaning to events in their lives. Feminist psychologists must ask the following questions: "What are the *various* meanings of this event or experience to or about this person? What can be understood from *all* of them rather than from choosing one correct insight?" (Kaschak, 1992, p. 35). In contrast, efforts to identify *the* right meaning of women's experience lead to narrow thinking.

According to Kaschak (1992), several assumptions are especially useful for creating an integrated model of feminist therapy. First, all experience is organized by the meaning that individuals attribute to events. Personal meanings are influenced by various agents of socialization, including the family, peer groups, institutions, and the media. However, the messages conveyed through these agents do not have uniform meanings, but are organized and elaborated in unique ways by the individual. Second, "the most centrally meaningful principle on our culture's mattering map is gender" (p. 211), which interacts with sexual orientation, race, ethnicity, culture, and class. Within each of the latter categories, society and individuals associate different meanings with maleness and femaleness. The task of feminist therapy is to help clients identify the complexity of meanings associated with gender in their lives and to engage in meaningful self-identified change. A major task of the feminist therapist is to "maintain the tension between women as a category and each individual woman, between micro details and broad strokes, similarities and differences. Neither should be used as a way to avoid dealing with the others if we are to achieve as full a picture as possible of each woman's experience." (Kaschak, 1992, p. 224).

In addition to echoing many of the themes discussed by Ellyn Kaschak (1992), Laura Brown (1994) noted that an integrated model of feminist therapy must be built on a multicultural foundation and principles of diversity and antidomination. A feminist biopsychosocial model holds promise for ensuring that feminist therapists consider the interactions of biology, psychological experience, and social interaction and pay adequate attention to the multiple causes of human distress.

The ideas of both Ellyn Kaschak and Laura Brown are reflected in a document that summarized principles of feminist theory articulated at the 1993 National Conference on Education and Training in Feminist Practice (Chin, 1993). These basic principles are summarized in the following:

1. Feminist theory is not static but evolving.
2. Diversity is an essential foundation for feminist practice. Feminist theory redefines the experiences of those who have been marginalized as central to developing new knowledge and practice. Feminist theory gives voice to oppressed individuals in their own language and from their own perspectives.
3. Gender is a central aspect of women's oppression and interacts with other status variables such as culture, class, age, race, and sexual orientation.
4. Feminist theory and practice seeks new models of human growth, development, and personality that transcend traditional models of the "self" and identity.
5. Feminist theory seeks to appreciate the multifaceted causes of distress, paying particular attention to the sociopolitical context in which individuals are located.
6. Feminist theory pays explicit attention to issues of power. Political and social transformation consistent with feminist goals and the creation of feminist consciousness are central to feminist theory and practice.

In order for feminist therapists to create strong theoretical frameworks, it is important to consider the compatibility of specific theoretical approaches with one's own worldview. Judith Worell and Pamela Remer (1992) developed a decision-making sequence designed to help feminist therapists consider the compatibility between specific psychological theories and feminist therapy principles. A similar process is useful for therapists making decisions about the consistency between specific feminisms and their assumptions and worldviews. I have adapted Worell and Remer's (1992) exercise for this purpose. This activity can be used most productively by applying these questions to each of the feminist theories that can be potentially combined with feminist therapy principles.

1. Outline the historical development of the theory, including important contributors and their perspectives.
2. Identify the main assumptions underlying the theory.
3. How does this theory explain sexism, racism, and other forms of oppression?
4. How does this approach conceptualize women's problems? How, according to this perspective, can these problems be eradicated?
5. What are the primary goals associated with this theory? What methods and strategies are recommended for achieving these goals? What is the role of the individual in effecting change? Groups and social activism?
6. What issues have received the greatest attention? Are some issues overemphasized? Are some issues ignored? What gaps between theory and practice exist?
7. To what degree does this theory consider diversity and the multiple realities of women?
8. What are the consistencies and inconsistencies between this theory and the psychological theories that inform your work with clients?
9. Write a statement that identifies how this theory is compatible and incompatible with your views of human experience.
10. What theory or theories can be used to fill in gaps or to clarify issues not addressed by this theory? Is it possible to combine the strengths of these theories and eliminate limitations?

ECLECTICISM IN FEMINIST THERAPY?

It is possible that readers will find none of the feminist theories entirely consistent with their belief systems. In those cases, an eclectic approach to feminist philosophy may be necessary. Nancy Chodorow (1989) indicated that as our knowledge of gender issues has become more complex, the "single cause" theories of the 1970s have become inadequate. A social constructionist or modified post-modern perspective may provide a useful metaperspective for inte-grating the various systems within feminist theory.

Several aspects of postmodern or social constructionist thought lend themselves to eclecticism. First, postmodern feminist thought places emphasis on pluralism and the appreciation of difference. Consistent with an appreciation for multiculturalism, it "allows for more than one answer to a problem and for more than one way to arrive at a solution" (Gonzalez, Biever, and Gardner, 1994, p. 517). This flexibility allows for the creative integration of perspectives. Second, a postmodern perspective argues that gender is created through social arrangements and interactions among people, cul-tures, and institutions. This principle allows for analysis of gender that is multifaceted. Because interactions between people and insti-tutions are variable and complicated, we must understand that gen-der has many types of influences on people. Third, postmodern/social constructionist thinking proposes that truth and reality are modified by circumstances. There is no one truth that defines all reality; truth and reality are influenced by context, history, and the perceptions of observers. Thus, each of the "truths" of the various feminist theories may have value in certain contexts. Finally, post-modern thinking encourages feminists to engage in ongoing self-reflection. It asks individuals to reflect on how theory and practice are embedded in and shaped by power dynamics. It asks individuals to consider how the power of the person who creates theory is reflected in the nature of the theory that is created. This principle encourages feminists to develop theories that can be modified when they outlive their usefulness. It also helps ensure that egalitarianism is given more than lip service in the creation of theory.

Perhaps the major drawback of postmodern thinking is its poten-tial for "depoliticized relativism where every viewpoint becomes equally valid and true" (Allen and Baber, 1992, p. 6). If all truth is relative, there is no clear basis for political action and social change. Thus, a modified postmodern perspective may be most useful to feminist thinking. For example, the reality that gender oppression exists is a central "truth" of feminism and is not erased by context or a certain perspective on reality. A second drawback is that many articles and books that articulate feminist postmodernism are written in academic jargon that is relatively inaccessible to most readers. Thus, the translation of postmodern concepts into practical language is necessary. Some of this translation is already occurring in the works of feminist psychologists who have discussed the implications of postmodernism and social constructionism for psychology (e.g., Allen and Baber, 1992; Bohan, 1993; Hare-Mustin and Marecek, 1990).

CONCLUDING COMMENTS

In order to connect feminist political theories with feminist therapy, I have drawn divisions between liberal, cultural, radical, socialist, and women-of-color feminisms more sharply than they exist in reality. Feminist philosophy is never static; it continually evolves. In the same fashion, feminist therapists cannot be easily categorized; they hold diverse views of feminism and the practice of psychotherapy. The purpose of this book has not been to pigeonhole specific forms of feminist therapy but to encourage psychologists to reflect on how their therapeutic approaches may or may not be consistent with certain forms of feminist philosophy.

Feminist therapy has grown and expanded dramatically during the past three decades. As feminist therapy becomes more diverse and complex, it is especially important for feminist therapists to examine how their philosophical perspectives influence practice. As students in clinical, counseling, and social work training programs, we learn that our assumptions about the nature of humanity have wide-ranging influences on our practices. We spend time examining the assumptions underlying systems of psychotherapy in order to develop personal theories that are well integrated and internally consistent. As a logical extension of this process, we need to clarify the nature of our personal feminist visions and how they are informed by the various forms of feminist thought.

References

Abramowitz, C. V., and Dokecki, P.R. (1977). The politics of clinical judgment: Early empirical returns. *Psychological Bulletin, 84,* 460-476.

Adams, D. (1988). Treatment models of men who batter: A profeminist analysis. In K. Yllo and M. Bograd (Eds.), *Feminist perspectives on wife abuse* (pp. 176-199). Newbury Park, CA: Sage.

Adams, H. J., and Durham, L. (1977). A dialectical base for an activist approach to counseling. In E. I. Rawlings and K. K. Carter (Eds.), *Psychotherapy for women* (pp. 411-428). Springfield, IL: Charles C Thomas.

Addams, J. (1913/1960). If men were seeking the franchise. In E. C. Johnson (Ed.), *Jane Addams: A centennial reader* (pp. 107-113). New York: Macmillan.

Addams, J. (1916/1960). Maturing concepts of peace. In E. C. Johnson (Ed.), *Jane Addams: A centennial reader* (pp. 252-257). New York: Macmillan.

Adleman, J., and Barrett, S. E. (1990). Overlapping relationships: The importance of the feminist ethical perspective. In H. Lerman and N. Porter (Eds.), *Feminist ethics in psychotherapy* (pp. 87-91). New York: Springer.

Adleman, J., and Enguídanos, G. (Eds.). (1995). *Racism in the lives of women: Testimony, theory and guides to antiracist practice.* Binghamton, NY: The Haworth Press.

Adler, J., Duignam-Cabrera, A., and Gordon, J. (1991, June 24). Heeding the call of the drums. *Newsweek, 117*(25), 52-53.

Adler, J., Springen, K., Glick, D., and Gordon, J. (1991, June 24). Drums, sweat, and tears. *Newsweek, 117*(25), 46-47, 49-51.

Agel, J. (Ed.). (1971). *The radical therapist.* New York: Ballantine Books.

Ahrens, L. (1980). Battered women's refugees: Feminist cooperatives vs. social service insititutions. *Radical America, 14*(3), 41-47.

Albee, G. W. (1981). The prevention of sexism. *Professional Psychology, 12,* 20-27.

Alcoff, L. (1988). Cultural feminism versus post-structuralism: The identity crisis in feminist theory. *Signs: Journal of Women in Culture and Society, 13,* 405-436.

Alexander, S. (1990). Women, class and sexual differences in the 1830s and 1840s: Some reflections of the writing of a feminist history. In T. Lovell (Ed.), *British feminist thought: A reader* (pp. 28-50). Cambridge, MA: Basil Blackwell Ltd.

Allen, K. R., and Baber, K. M. (1992). Ethical and epistemological tensions in applying a postmodern perspective to feminist research. *Psychology of Women Quarterly, 16,* 1-15.

Allen, P. (1971). Free space. In A. Koedt, S. Firestone, A. Rapone, and E. Levine (Eds.), *Notes from the third year* (pp. 93-98). New York: Notes from the Third Year.

Allen, P. G. (Ed.). (1989). *Spider woman's granddaughters.* New York: Fawcett Press.

Alpert, J. (1973, August). Mother right: A new feminist theory. *Ms.*, *2*(2), 52-55, 88-94.

American Psychiatric Association. (1980). *Diagnostic and statistical manual of mental disorders,* third edition. Washington, DC: Author.

American Psychiatric Association. (1987). *Diagnostic and statistical manual of mental disorders,* third edition, revised. Washington, DC: Author.

American Psychiatric Association. (1994). *Diagnostic and statistical manual of mental disorders,* fourth edition. Washington, DC: Author.

Anthias, F., and Yuval-Davis, N. (1990). Contextualizing feminism: Gender, ethnic, and class divisions. In T. Lovell (Ed.), *British feminist thought: A reader* (pp. 103-118). Cambridge, MA: Basil Blackwell Ltd.

Anthony, S. B. (1981). Suffrage and the working woman. In E. C. DuBois (Ed.), *Elizabeth Cady Stanton/Susan B. Anthony: Correspondence, writings, speeches* (pp. 139-145). New York: Schocken Books (Originally published in 1871).

Anthony, S. B. (1981). Constitutional argument. In E. C. DuBois (Ed.), *Elizabeth Cady Stanton/Susan B. Anthony: Correspondence, writings, speeches* (pp. 152-165). New York: Schocken Books (Originally published in 1872).

Anthony, S. B. (1981). Homes of single women. In E.C. DuBois (Ed.), *Elizabeth Cady Stanton/Susan B. Anthony: Correspondence, writings, speeches* (pp. 146-151). New York: Schocken Books (Originally published in 1877).

Anzaldúa, G. (1983). La Prieta. In C. Moraga and G. Anzaldua (Eds.), *This bridge called my back* (pp. 198-209). New York: Kitchen Table, Women of Color Press.

Astin, H. S. (1985). The meaning of work in women's lives: A sociopsychological model of career choice and work behavior. *The Counseling Psychologist, 12,* 117-128.

Atkinson, T. G. (1974). *Amazon Odyssey.* New York: Links.

Ault-Riché, M. (Ed.). (1986). *Women and family therapy.* Rockville, MD: Aspen.

Avis, J. M. (1985). The politics of functional family therapy: A feminist critique. *Journal of Marital and Family Therapy, 11,* 127-138.

Avis, J. M. (1988). Deepening awareness: A private study guide to feminism and family therapy. In L. Braverman (Ed.), *Women, feminism, and family therapy* (pp. 15-46). Binghamton, NY: The Haworth Press.

Baber, K. M., and Allen, K. R. (1992). *Women and families: Feminist reconstructions.* New York: Guilford Press.

Ballou, M., and Gabalac, N. W. (1985). *A feminist position on mental health.* Springfield, IL: Charles C Thomas.

Ballou, M., Reuter, J., and Divero, T. (1979). An audio-taped consciousness-raising group for women: Evaluation of the process dimension. *Psychology of Women Quarterly, 4,* 185-193.

Banaji, M. R. (1993). The psychology of gender: A perspective on perspectives. In A. E. Beall and R. J. Sternberg (Eds.), *The psychology of gender* (pp. 251-273). New York: Guilford Press.

Bandura, A. (1989). Human agency in social cognitive theory. *American Psychologist, 44,* 1175-1184.

Banks, O. (1981). *Faces of feminism.* New York: St. Martin's Press.

Banner, L. W. (1980). *Elizabether Cady Stanton: A radical for woman's rights.* Boston, MA: Little, Brown and Co.

Barrett, C. J., Berg, P. I., Eaton, E. M., and Pomeroy, E. L. (1974). Implications of women's liberation and the future of psychotherapy. *Psychotherapy: Theory, Research and Practice, 11,* 11-15.

Barry, K. (1979). *Female sexual slavery.* New York: New York University Press.

Bartlett, E. A. (Ed.) (1988). *Sarah Grimke: Letters on the equality of the sexes and other essays.* New Haven, CT: Yale University Press.

Bartlett, E. A. (1992). Beyond either/or: Justice and care in the ethics of Albert Camus. In E. B. Cole and CS. Coultrap-McQuin (Eds.), *Explorations in feminist ethics* (pp. 82-88). Bloomington: Indiana University Press.

Baruch, G. K., Biener, L., and Barnett, R. C. (1987). Women and gender in research on work and family stress. *American Psychlogist, 42,* 130-136.

Beale, F. M. (1970). Double jeopardy: To be black and female. In R. Morgan (Ed.), *Sisterhod is powerful* (pp. 340-353). New York: Random House.

Beauvior, S. de. (1952). *The second sex.* New York: Knopf.

Belenky, M. J., Clinchy, B. M., Goldberger, N. R., and Tarule, J. M. (1986). *Women's ways of knowing.* New York: Basic Books.

Bem, S. L. (1976). Probing the promise of androgyny. In A. G. Kaplan and J. P. Bean (Eds.), *Beyond sex-role stereotypes: Readings toward a psychology of androgyny* (pp. 47-62). Boston, MA: Little, Brown and Co.

Bem, S. L. (1983). Gender schema theory and its implications for child development: Raising gender-aschematic children in a gender-schematic society. *Signs: Journal of Women in Culture and Society, 8,* 598-616.

Bem, S. L. (1987). Gender schema theory and the romantic tradition. In P. Shaver and C. Hendrick (Eds.), *Sex and gender* (pp. 251-271). Newbury Park, CA: Sage.

Bem, S. L. (1993a). Is there a place in psychology for a feminist analysis of the social context? *Feminism and Psychology, 3,* 230-234.

Bem, S. L. (1993b). *The lenses of gender: Transforming the debate on sexual inequality.* New Haven, CT: Yale University Press.

Benack, S. (1982). The coding of dimensions of epistemological thought in young men and women. *Moral Education Forum, 7*(2), 3-24.

Berardo, D. H., Shehen, C. L., and Leslie, G. R. (1987). A residue of tradition: Jobs, careers, and spouses' time in housework. *Journal of Marriage and the Family, 49,* 381-390.

Berger, R. J., Searles, P., and Cottle, C. E. (1991). *Feminism and pornography.* Westport, CT: Praeger.

Bergner, M., Remer, P., and Whetsell, C. (1985). Transforming women's body image: A feminist counseling approach. *Women and Therapy, 4*(3), 25-38.

Berkeley-Oakland Women's Union Statement. (1973/1979). Principles of unity. In Z. R. Eisenstein (Ed.), *Capitalist patriarchy and the case for socialist feminism* (pp. 355-361). New York: Monthly Review Press.

Bernstein, J., Morton, P., Seese, L., and Wood, M. (1969). Sisters, brothers, lovers . . . listen . . . In B. Roszak and T. Roszak (Eds.), *Masculine/feminine: Readings in sexual mythology and the liberation of women* (pp. 251-254). New York: Harper Colophon Books.

Betz, N. E. (1994). Basic issues and concepts in career counseling for women. In W. B. Walsh and S. H. Osipow (Eds.), *Career counseling for women* (pp. 1-41). Hillsdale, NJ: Erlbaum.

Betz, N. E., and Fitzgerald, L. F. (1987). *The career psychology of women.* New York: Academic Press.

Biehl, J. (1991). *Rethinking ecofeminist politics.* Boston, MA: South End Press.

Black, N. (1989). *Social feminism.* Ithaca, NY: Cornell University Press.

Blechman, E. A. (1980). Behavior therapies. In A. M. Bordsky and R. T. Hare-Mustin (Eds.), *Women and psychotherapy: An assessment of research and practice* (pp. 217-244). New York: Guilford Press.

Blumstein, P., and Schwartz, P. (1983). *American couples.* New York: William Morrow and Co.

Bly, R. (1990). *Iron John.* Reading, MA: Addison-Wesley.

Bograd, M. (1988). Enmeshment, fusion, or relatedness: A conceptual analysis. In L. Braverman (Ed.), *Women, feminism, and family therapy* (pp. 65-80). Binghamton, NY: The Haworth Press.

Bohan, J. S. (1993). Regarding gender: Essentialism, constructionism, and feminist psychology. *Psychology of Women Quarterly, 17,* 5-21.

Bolen, J. S. (1984). *Goddesses in every woman.* San Francisco: Harper and Row.

Bordo, S. (1990). Feminism, postmodernism, and gender-scepticism. In L. J. Nicholson (Ed.), *Feminism/postmodernism* (pp. 133-156). New York: Routledge.

Boston Lesbian Psychologies Collective (Eds.). (1987). *Lesbian psychologies.* Urbana: University of Illinois Press.

Boyd, J. A. (1990). Ethnic and cultural diversity: Keys to power. *Women and Therapy, 9*(1/2), 151-167.

Bradshaw, C. K. (1990). A Japanese view of dependency: What can amae psychology contribute to feminist theory and therapy? *Women and Therapy, 9*(1/2), 67-86.

Braverman, L. (Ed.). (1988). *Women, feminism, and family therapy.* Binghamton, NY: The Haworth Press.

Brehony, K. A. (1987). Self-help groups with agoraphobic women. In C. Brody (Ed.), *Women's therapy groups: Paradigms of feminist treatment* (pp. 82- 94). New York: Springer Publishing Co.

Brien, L., and Sheldon, C. (1977). Gestalt therapy and women. In E. I. Rawlings and D. K. Carter (Eds.), *Psychotherapy for women* (pp. 120-127). Springfield, IL: Charles C Thomas.

Brodsky, A. (1976). The consciousness-raising group as a model for therapy with women. In S. Cox (Ed.), *Female psychology: The emerging self* (pp. 372- 377). Chicago: Science Research Associates.

Brodsky, A. (1977). Therapeutic aspects of consciousness-raising groups. In E. I. Rawlings and D. K. Carter (Eds.), *Psychotherapy for women* (pp. 300-309). Springfield, IL: Charles C Thomas.

Brodsky, A. (1980). A decade of feminist influence on psychotherapy. *Psychology of Women Quarterly, 4,* 331-343.

Brooke. (1975). The retreat to cultural feminism. In Redstockings (Eds.), *Feminist revolution* (pp. 79-83). New York: Redstockings, Inc.

Brooks, L., and Forrest, L. (1994). Feminism and career counseling. In W. B. Walsh and S. H. Osipow (Eds.), *Career counseling for women* (pp. 87-134). Hillsdale, NJ: Erlbaum.

Broverman, I. K., Broverman, D. M., Clarkson, F., Rosenkrantz, P., and Vogel, S. (1970). Sex-role stereotyping and clinical judgments of mental health. *Journal of Consulting and Clinical Psychology, 45,* 250-256.

Brown, J. (1971). Mothers of the millennium. In J. Agel (Ed.), *The radical therapist* (pp. 164-168). New York: Ballantine Books.

Brown, L. S. (1986). Gender-role analysis: A neglected component of psychological assessment. *Psychotherapy: Theory, Research, and Practice, 23,* 243-248.

Brown, L. S. (1990a). Taking account of gender in the clinical assessment interview. *Professional Psychology: Research and Practice, 21,* 12-17.

Brown, L. S. (1990b). The meaning of a multicultural perspective for theory-building in feminist therapy. *Women and Therapy, 9*(1/2), 1-22.

Brown, L. S. (1990c). What's addiction got to do with it: A feminist critique of codependence. *Psychology of Women Newsletter, 17*(1), 1, 3-4

Brown, L. S. (1991a). Ethical issues in feminist therapy: Selected topics. *Psychology of Women Quarterly, 15,* 323-336.

Brown, L.S. (1991b). Antiracism as an ethical imperative: An example from feminist therapy. *Ethics and Behavior, 1*(2), 113-127.

Brown, L. S. (1992a). A feminist critique of the personality disorders. In L. S. Brown and M. Ballou (Eds.), *Personality and psychopathology: Feminist reappraisals* (pp. 206-228). New York: Guilford Press.

Brown, L. S. (1992b). While waiting for the revolution: The case for a lesbian feminist psychotherapy. *Feminism and Psychology, 2*(2), 239-253.

Brown, L. S. (1993). Antidomination training as a central component of diversity in clinical psychology education. *The Clinical Psychologist, 46,* 83-87.

Brown, L. S. (1994). *Subversive dialogues: Theory in feminist therapy.* New York: Basic Books.

Brown, L. S. (1995). Anti-racism as an ethical norm in feminist therapy practice. In J. Adleman and G. Enguidanos (Eds.), *Racism in the lives of women: Testimony, theory, and guides to antiracist practice* (pp. 137-148). Binghamton, NY: The Haworth Press.

Brown, L. S., and Ballou, M. (Eds.). (1992). *Personality and psychopathology: Feminist reappraisals.* New York: Guilford.

Brown, L. S., and Brodsky, A. M. (1992). The future of feminist therapy. *Psychotherapy: Theory, Research, and Practice, 29,* 51-57.

Brown, L. M., and Gilligan, C. (1992). *Meeting at the crossroads: Women's psychology and girls' development.* Cambridge, MA: Harvard University Press.

Brown, L. S., and Liss-Levinson, N. (1981). Feminist therapy. In R. Corsini (Eds.), *Handbook of innovative psychotherapies* (pp. 299-314). New York: Wiley.

Brown, L. S., and Walker, L. E. A. (1990). Feminist therapy perspectives on self-disclosure. In G. Stricker and M. Fisher (Eds.), *Self-disclosure in the therapeutic relationship* (pp. 135-154). New York: Plenum.

Browne, A. (1993). Violence against women by male partners: Prevalence, outcomes, and policy implications. *American Psychologist, 48,* 1077-1987.

Brownmiller, S. (1975). *Against our will: Men, women, and rape.* New York: Simon and Schuster.

Buffalo, Y. R. D. (1990). Seeds of thought, arrows of change: Native storytelling as metaphor. In R. A. Laidlaw and C. Malmo (Eds.), *Healing voices* (pp. 118-142). San Francisco, CA: Jossey-Bass.

Bunch, C. (1972/1987). Lesbians in revolt. In C. Bunch (Ed.), *Passionate politics: Feminist theory in action* (pp. 161-181). New York: St Martin's Press.

Bunch, C. (1987). Learning from lesbian separatism. In C. Bunch (Ed.), *Passionate politics* (pp. 182-191). New York: St. Martin's Press (Originally published in 1976).

Bunch, C. (1987). Lesbian-feminist theory. In C. Bunch (Ed.), *Passionate politics* (pp. 196-202). New York: St. Martin's Press (Originally published in 1978).

Burack, C. (1992). A house divided: Feminism and object relations theory. *Women's Studies International Forum, 15,* 499-506.

Burden, D. S., and Gottlieb, N. (1987). Women's socialization and feminist groups. In C. Brody (Ed.), *Women's therapy groups: Paradigms of feminist treatment* (pp. 24-39). New York: Springer Publishing Co.

Burgess, A. W., and Holmstrom, L. L. (1974). Rape trauma syndrome. *American Journal of Psychiatry, 131,* 981-986.

Burris, B. (1973). The fourth world manifesto. In A. Koedt, E. Levine, and A. Rapone (Eds.), *Radical feminism* (pp. 322-357). New York: Quadrangle Books.

Burstow, B. (1992). *Radical feminist therapy: Working in the context of violence.* Newbury Park, CA: Sage.

Butler, J. (1992). Contingent foundations: Feminism and the question of "postmodernism." In J. Butler and J. Scott (Eds.), *Feminists theorize the political* (pp. 3-21). New York: Routledge.

Butler, M. (1985). Guidelines for feminist therapy. In L. B. Rosewater and L. E. A. Walter (Eds.), *Handbook of feminist therapy* (pp. 32-38). New York: Springer Publishing Co.

Butler, S., and Wintram, C. (1991). *Feminist groupwork.* Newbury Park, CA: Sage.

Caldwell, M. A., and Peplau, L. A. (1984). The balance of power in lesbian relationships. *Sex Roles, 10,* 587-599.

Cammaert, L. P., and Larsen, C. C. (1988). Feminist frameworks of psychotherapy. In M. D. Douglas and L. E. Walker (Eds.), *Feminist psychotherapies: Integration of therapeutic and feminist systems* (pp. 12-36). Norwood, NJ: Ablex.

Campbell, J. D., Trapnell, P. D., Hein, S. J., Katz, I. M., Lavallee, L. F., and Lehman, D. R. (1996). Self-concept clarity: Measurement, personality corre-·lates, and cultural boundaries. *Journal of Personality and Social Psychology, 70,* 141-156.

Caplan, P. J. (1984). The myth of women's masochism. *American Psychologist, 39,* 130-139.

Caplan, P. J. (1989). *Don't blame Mother: Mending the mother-daughter relationship.* New York: Harper and Row.

Caplan, P. J. (1991). Delusional dominating personality disorder (DDPD). *Feminism and Psychology, 1,* 171-174.

Caplan, P. J. (1995). *They say you're crazy.* Reading, MA: Addison-Wesley.

Carden, M. L. (1974). *The new feminist movement.* New York: Russell Sage Foundation.

Carlson, R. (1972). Understanding women: Implications for personality theory and research. *Journal of Social Issues, 28,* 17-31.

Carmen, E. H., Russo, N. F., and Miller, J. B. (1984). Inequality and women's mental health: An overview. In P. R. Rieker and E. H. Carmen (Eds.), *The gender gap in psychotherapy* (pp. 17-39). New York: Plenum.

Cassell, J. (1977). *A group called women: Sisterhood and symbolism in the feminist movement.* New York: McKay.

Chaplin, J. (1988). *Feminist counseling in action.* London: Sage.

Charlotte Perkins Gilman Chapter of the New American Movement. (1984). In A. M. Jaggar and P. S. Rothenberg (Eds.), *Feminist frameworks* (pp. 152-154). New York: McGraw-Hill.

Chase, K. (1977, March-April). Seeing sexism: A look at feminist therapy. *State and Mind,* 12-22.

Chesler, P. (1971). Patient and patriarch: Women in the psychotherapeutic relationship. In V. Gornick and B. Moran (Eds.), *Woman in sexist society* (pp. 362-392). New York: Mentor.

Chesler, P. (1972). *Women and madness.* New York: Doubleday.

Chin, J. L. (Ed.). (1993). *Proceedings of the National Conference on Education and Training in Feminist Practice.* Boston, MA: Boston College.

Chodorow, N. J. (1978). *The reproduction of mothering.* Berkeley, CA: University of California Press.

Chodorow, N. J. (1989). *Feminism and psychoanalytic theroy.* New Haven, CT: Yale University Press.

Clance, P. R., and Imes, S. A. (1978). The imposter phenomenon in high-achieving women: Dynamics and therapeutic intervention. *Psychotherapy: Theory, Research, and Practice, 15,* 241-247.

Cline-Naffziger, C. (1974). Women's lives and frustration, oppression, and anger. *Journal of Counseling Psychology, 21,* 51-56.

Clopton, N. A., and Sorell, G. T. (1993). Gender differences in moral reasoning: Stable or situational? *Psychology of Women Quarterly, 17,* 85-101.

Cockburn, C. (1990). The material of male power. In T. Lovell (Ed.), *British feminist thought: A reader* (pp. 84-102). Cambridge, MA: Basil Blackwell Ltd.

Cole, C. L. (1985). A group design for adult female survivors of childhood incest. *Women and Therapy, 4*(3), 71-82.

Cole, E. B., and Coultrap-McQuin, S. (1992). Toward a feminist conception of moral life. In E. B. Cole and S. Coultrap-McQuin (Eds.), *Explorations in feminist ethics* (pp. 1-11). Bloomington: Indiana University Press.

Collard, A. (1989). *Rape of the wild: Man's violence against animals and the earth.* Bloomington: Indiana University Press.

Collier, H. V. (1982). *Counseling women.* New York: Free Press.

Collins, P. H. (1986). Learning from the outsider within: The sociological significance of black feminist thought. *Social Problems, 33*(6), S14-S32.

Collins, P. H. (1989). The social construction of black feminist thought. *Signs: Journal of Women in Culture and Society, 14,* 745-772.

Collins, P. H. (1990). *Black feminist thought: Knowledge, consciousness, and the politics of empowerment.* Boston, MA: Unwin Hyman.

Collins, P. H. (1991). The meaning of motherhood in black culture and black mother-daughter relationships. In P. Bell-Scott, B. Guy-Sheftall, J. J. Royster, J. Sims-Wood, M DeCosta-Willis, and L. P. Fultz (Eds.), *Double stitch: Black women write about mothers and daughters* (pp. 42-60). New York: HarperCollins.

Comas-Díaz, L (1987). Feminist therapy with mainland Puerto Rican women. *Psychology of Women Quarterly, 11,* 461-474.

Comas-Díaz, L. (1988). Feminist therapy with Hispanic/Latina women: Myth or reality? In L. Fulani (Ed.), *The psychopathology of everyday racism and sexism* (pp. 39-61). Binghamton, NY: Harrington Park Press.

Comas-Díaz, L. (1991). Feminism and diversity in psychology: The case of women of color. *Psychology of Women Quarterly, 15,* 597-609.

Comas-Díaz, L. (1994). An integrative approach. In. L. Comas-Diaz and B. Greene (Eds.), *Women of color: Integrating ethnic and gender identities in psychotherapy* (pp. 287-318). New York: Guilford Press.

Comas-Díaz, L., and Greene, B. (1994). Women of color with professional status. In L. Comas-Díaz and B. Greene (Eds.), *Women of color: Integrating ethnic and gender identities in psychotherapy* (pp. 347-388). New York: Guilford Press.

Combahee River Collective. (1982). A black feminist statement. In G. T. Hull, P. B. Scott, and B. Smith (Eds.), *All the women are white, all the blacks are men, but some of us are brave* (pp. 13-22). Old Westbury, NY: The Feminist Press.

Conarton, S., and Silverman, L. K. (1988). Feminine development through the life cycle. In M. D. Dutton-Douglas and L. E. Walker (Eds.), *Feminist psychotherapies* (pp. 37-67). Norwook, NJ: Ablex.

Cook, E. P. (1985). Androgyny: A goal for counseling? *Journal of Counseling and Development, 63,* 567-571.

Cooper-White, P. (1989, May). "Peer and clinical counseling–Is there a place for both in the battered women's movement?" Paper presented to the Third National Nursing Conference on Violence Against Women. Concord, CA.

Cotten-Huston, A. L., and Wheeler, K. (1987). Preorgasmic group treatment: Marital adjustment and sexual function in women. In C. Brody (Ed.), *Women's therapy groups: Paradigms of feminist treatment* (pp. 227-240). New York: Springer.

Courtois, C. A. (1988). *Healing the incest wound.* New York: Norton.

Crawford, M., and Marecek, J. (1989). Psychology reconstructs the female: 1968-1988. *Psychology of Women Quarterly, 13,* 147-165.

Crichton, S. (1993). Sexual correctness: Has it gone too far? *Newsweek, 122*(17), 52-56.

Crosby, F. J., Pufall, A., Snyder, R. C., O'Connell, M., and Whalen, P. (1989). The denial of personal disadvantage among you, me, and all the other ostriches. In M. Crawford and M. Gentry (Eds.), *Gender and thought* (pp. 79- 99). New York: Springer-Verlag.

Cross, W. E. (1991). *Shades of black.* Philadelphia: Temple University Press.

Cross, T., Klein, F., Smith, B., and Smith, B. (1982). Face-to-face, day-to-day– Racism CR. In G. T. Hull, P. B. Scott, and B. Smith (Eds.), *All the women are white, all the blacks are men, but some of us are brave* (pp. 52-56). Old Westbury, NY: The Feminist Press.

Daly, M. (1978). *Gyn/Ecology: The metaethics of radical feminism.* Boston, MA: Beacon Press.

Davenport, D. S., and Yurich, J. M. (1991). Multicultural gender issues. *Journal of Counseling and Development, 70,* 64-71.

Davidson, C. V. (1983). Making the conceptual leap from sex bias to countertrans-ference: A closer look at the patient-therapist dyad. In J. Murray and P. R. Abramson (Eds.), *Bias in psychotherapy* (pp. 168-191). New York: Praeger.

Davidson, C. V., and Abramowitz, S. I. (1980). Sex bias in clinical judgment: Later empirical returns. *Psychology of Women Quarterly, 4,* 377-395.

Davis, A. Y. (1981). *Women, race, and class.* New York: Vintage Books.

Davis, E. G. (1973). *The first sex.* Baltimore, MD: Penguin Books.

Deaux, K. (1984). From individual differences to social categories. *American Psychologist, 39,* 105-116.

Deaux, K., and Major, B. (1987). Putting gender into context: An interactive model of gender-related behavior. *Psychological Review, 94,* 369-389.

Deckard, B. S. (1979). *The women's movement.* New York: Harper and Row.

Declaration of sentiments and resolutions, Seneca Falls (1848/1972). In M. Schneir (Ed.), *Feminism: The essential historical writings* (pp. 76-82). New York: Vantage Books.

Denfeld, R. (1995). *The new Victorians.* New York: Warner Books.

Diamond, I., and Orenstein, G. F. (Eds.). (1990). *Reweaving the world: The emergence of ecofeminism.* San Francisco, CA: Sierra Club Books.

DiStephano, C. (1990). Dilemmas of difference: Feminism, modernity, and post-modernism. In L. J. Nicholson (Ed.), *Feminism/Postmodernism* (pp. 63-82). New York: Routledge.

Dobash, R. E., and Dobash, R. P. (1988). Research as social action: The struggle for battered women. In K. Yllö and M.Bograd (Eds.), *Feminist perspectives on wife abuse* (pp. 51-74). Newbury Park, CA: Sage.

Doherty, M. A. (1973). Sexual bias in personality theory. *The Counseling Psychologist, 4,* 67-74.

Donenberg, G. R., and Hoffman, L. W. (1988). Gender differences in moral development. *Sex Roles, 18,* 701-717.

Donovan, J. (1992). *Feminist theory,* expanded edition. New York: Continuum Publishing Co.

Doubiago, S. (1992, March/April). Enemy of the mother: A feminist response to the men's movement. *Ms. 2*(5), 82-85.

Douglas, E. T. (1970). *Margaret Sanger: Pioneer of the future.* New York: Holt, Rinehart and Winston.

Douglas, M. A. (1985). The role of power in feminist therapy: A reformulation. In L. B. Rosewater and L. E. A. Walker (Eds.), *Handbook of feminist therapy* (pp. 241-249). New York: Springer Publishing Co.

Dowling, C. (1981). *The Cinderella complex.* New York: Pocket Books.

DuBois, E. C. (Ed.). (1981). *Elizabeth Cady Stanton/Susan B. Anthony: Correspondence, writings, speeches.* New York: Schocken Books.

Dutton, M. A. (1992). *Empowering and healing the battered woman.* New York: Springer Publishing Co.

Dutton-Douglas, M.A. (August, 1989). Post-traumatic stress disorder and battered women. In N. Porter (Chair), "Post-traumatic stress disorder in women: Normal reactions to abnormal events." Symposium conducted at the Annual Convention of the American Psychological Association. New Orleans, LA.

Dutton-Douglas, M. A., and Walker, L. E. (Eds.). (1988). *Feminist psychotherapies: Integration of therapeutic and feminist systems.* Norwood, NJ: Ablex.

Dworkin, A. (1980a). Why so-called radical men love and need pornography. In L. Lederer (Ed.), *Take back the night: Women on pornography* (pp. 148-154). New York: William Morrow and Co.

Dworkin, A. (1980b). For men, freedom of speech; for women, silence please. In L. Lederer (Ed.), *Take back the night: Women on pornography* (pp. 256-258). New York: William Morrow and Co.

Dworkin, A. (1981). *Pornography: Men possessing women.* New York: Perigee.

Eccles, J. S. (1987). Gender roles and women's achievement-related decisions. *Psychology of Women Quarterly, 11,* 135-172.

Echols, A. (1989). *Daring to be bad: Radical feminism in America.* Minneapolis: University of Minnesota Press.

Eichenbaum, L., and Orbach, S. (1983). *Understanding women: A feminist psychoanalytic approach.* New York: Basic Books.

Eisenstein, Z. (1979). Developing a theory of capitalist patriarchy and socialist feminism. In Z. Eisenstein (Ed.), *Capitalist patriarchy and the case for socialist feminism* (pp. 5-40). New York: Monthly Review Press.

Eisenstein, Z. (1981). *The radical future of liberal feminism.* Boston: Northeastern University Press.

Eisler, R. (1988). *The chalice and the blade.* San Francisco, CA: Harper.

Eisler, R. (1990). The Gaia tradition and the partnership future: An ecofeminist manifesto. In I. Diamond and G. F. Orenstein (Eds.), *Reweaving the world: The emergence of ecofeminism* (pp. 23-34). San Francisco, CA: Sierra Club Books.

Eisler, R. M., Frederiksen, L. E., and Peterson, G. L. (1978). The relationship of cognitive variables to the expression of assertiveness. *Behavior Therapy, 9,* 419-427.

Elias, M. (April, 1975). Sisterhood therapy. *Human Behavior,* 56-61.

Ellis, J. (1990). The therapeutic journey: A guide for travelers. In T. A. Laidlaw and C. Malmo (Eds.), *Healing voices* (pp. 243-271). San Francisco, CA: Jossey-Bass.

Ellis, E. M., and Nichols, M. P. (1979). A comparative study of feminist and traditional group assertiveness training with women. *Psychotherapy: Theory, Research, and Practice, 16,* 467-474.

England, P., and McCreary, L. (1987). Gender inequality in paid employment. In B. B. Hess and M. M. Ferree (Eds.), *Analyzing gender: A handbook of social science research* (pp. 286-320). Newbury Park, CA: Sage.

Enns, C. Z. (1987). Gestalt therapy and feminist therapy: A proposed integration. *Journal of Counseling and Development, 66,* 93-95.

Enns, C. Z. (1988). Dilemmas of power and quality in marital and family counseling: Proposals for a feminist perspective. *Journal of Counseling and Development, 67,* 242-248.

Enns, C. Z. (1991). The "new" relationship models of women's identity: A review and critique for counselors. *Journal of Counseling and Development, 69,* 209-217.

Enns, C. Z. (1992a). Toward integrating feminist psychotherapy and feminist philosophy. *Professional Psychology: Research and Practice, 23,* 453-466.

Enns, C. Z. (1992b). Self-esteem groups: A synthesis of consciousness-raising and assertiveness training. *Journal of Counseling and Development, 71,* 7-13.

Enns, C. Z. (1993). Twenty years of feminist counseling and therapy: From naming biases to implementing multifaceted practice. *The Counseling Psychologist, 21,* 3-87.

Enns, C. Z. (1994). Archetypes and gender: Goddesses, warriors, and psychological health. *Journal of Counseling and Development, 73,* 127-133.

Enns, C. Z., and Hackett, G. (1990). Comparisons of feminist and nonfeminist women's reactions to variants of nonsexist and feminist counseling. *Journal of Counseling Psychology, 37,* 33-40.

Enns, C. Z., and Hackett, G. (1993). A comparison of feminist and nonfeminist women's and men's reactions to nonsexist and feminist counseling: A replication and extension. *Journal of Counseling and Development, 71,* 499- 509.

Epperson, D. L., and Lewis, K. N. (1987). Issues of informed entry into counseling: Perceptions and preferences resulting from different types and amounts of pretherapy information. *Journal of Counseling Psychology, 34,* 266- 275.

Erikson, E. H. (1968). *Identity: Youth and crisis.* New York: Norton.

Espín, O. M. (1986). Cultural and historical influences on sexuality in Hispanic/Latina women. In J. Cole (Ed.), *All American women* (pp. 272-284). New York: Free Press.

Espín, O. M. (1987). Psychological impact of migration on Latinas: Implications for psychotherapeutic practice. *Psychology of Women Quarterly, 11,* 489-503.

Espín, O. M. (Fall, 1990). How inclusive is feminist psychology? *Association for Women in Psychology Newsletter,* 1-2.

Espín, O. M. (1993). Feminist therapy: Not for or by white women only. *The Counseling Psychologist, 21,* 103-108.

Espín, O. M. (1994). Feminist approaches. In L. Comas-Díaz and B. Greene (Eds.), *Women of color: Integrating ethnic and gender identities in psychotherapy* (pp. 265-286). New York: Guilford Press.

Espín, O. M. (1995). On knowing you are the unknown: Women of color constructing psychology. In J. Adleman and G. Enguidanos (Eds.), *Racism in the lives of women: Testimony, theory, and guides to antiracist practice* (pp. 127-136). Binghamton, NY: The Haworth Press.

Espín, O. M., and Gawelek, M.A. (1992). Women's diversity: Ethnicity, race, class, and gender in theories of feminist psychology. In L. S. Brown and M. Ballou (Eds.), *Personality and psychopathology: Feminist reappraisals* (pp. 88-107). New York: Norton.

Essed, P. (1991). *Understanding everyday racism: An interdisciplinary theory.* Newbury Park, CA: Sage.

Estés, C. P. (1992). *Women who run with the wolves: Myths and stories of the wild woman archetype.* New York: Ballantine Books.

Eugene, T. M. (1995). There is a balm in Gilead: Black women and the black church as agents of a therapeutic community. *Women and Therapy, 16*(2/3), 55-71.

Faludi, S. (1991). *Backlash: The undeclared war against American women.* New York: Crown.

Farmer, H. S. (1985). Model of career and achievement motivation for women and men. *Journal of Counseling Psychology, 32,* 363-390.

Farrell, W. (1993). *The myth of male power: Why men are the disposable sex.* New York: Simon and Schuster.

Fassinger, R. E. (1985). A causal model of college women's career choice. *Journal of Vocational Behavior, 27,* 123-153.

Feminist Therapy Institute. (1990). Feminist Therapy Institute code of ethics. In H. Lerman and N. Porter (Eds.), *Feminist ethics in psychotherapy* (pp. 37-40). New York: Springer Publishing Co.

The Feminists. (1973). The Feminists: A political organization to annihilate sex roles. In A. Koedt, E. Levine, and A. Rapone (Eds.), *Radical feminism* (pp. 368-378). New York: Quadrangle Books.

Ferree, M. M., and Hess, B. B. (1985). *Controversy and coalition: The new feminist movement.* Boston, MA: Twayne.

Fiedler, D., and Beach, L. R. (1978). On the decision to be assertive. *Journal of Consulting and Clinical Psychology, 46,* 537-546.

Fine, M., and Gordon, S. M. (1989). Feminist transformations of/despite psychology. In M. Crawford and M. Gentry (Eds.), *Gender and thought: Psychological perspectives* (pp. 146-175). New York: Springer-Verlag.

Firestone, S. (1970). *The dialectic of sex.* New York: Morrow.

Fitzgerald, L. F. (1993). Sexual harassment: Violence against women in the workplace. *American Psychologist, 48,* 1070-1076.

Fitzgerald, L. F., and Rounds, J. (1994). Women and work: Theory encounters reality. In W. B. Walsh and S. H. Osipow (Eds.), *Career counseling for women* (pp. 327-353). Hillsdale, NJ: Erlbaum.

Flax, J. (1987). Postmodernism and gender relations in feminist theory. *Signs: Journal of Women in Culture and Society, 12,* 621-643.

Flax, J. (1992). The end of innocence. In J. Butler and J. W. Scott (Eds.), *Feminists theorize the political* (pp. 445-463). New York: Routledge.

Flexner, S. B., and Hauck, L. C. (Eds.). (1987). *The Random House dictionary of the English language,* second edition. New York: Random House.

Flores-Ortiz, Y. G. (1995). Psychotherapy with Chicanas at midlife: Cultural/clinical considerations. In J. Adleman and G. Enguidanos (Eds.), *Racism in the lives of women: Testimony, theory, and guides to antiracist practice* (pp. 251-259). Binghamton, NY: The Haworth Press.

Fodor, I. G. (1985). Assertiveness training for the eighties: Moving beyond the personal. In L. B. Rosewater and L. E. A. Walker (Eds.), *Handbook of feminist therapy* (pp. 257-265). New York: Springer Publishing Co.

Fodor, I. G. (1987). Moving beyond cognitive-behavior therapy: Integrating gestalt therapy to facilitate personal and interpersonal awareness. In N. S. Jacobson (Ed.), *Psychotherapists in clinical practice* (pp. 190-231). New York: Guilford Press.

Fodor, I. G. (1988). Cognitive behavior therapy. Evaluation of theory and practice for addressing women's issues. In M. A. Dutton-Douglas and L. E. Walker (Eds.), *Feminist psychotherapies: Integration of therapeutic and feminist systems* (pp. 91-117). Norwood, NJ: Ablex.

Fodor, I., and Rothblum, E. D. (1984). Strategies for dealing with sex-role stereotypes. In C. Brody (Ed.), *Women therapists working with women* (pp. 86-95). New York: Springer.

Follingstad, D. R., Robinson, E. A., and Pugh, M. (1977). Effects of consciousness-raising groups on measures of feminism, self-esteem, and social desirability. *Journal of Counseling Psychology, 24,* 223-230.

Ford, M. R., and Lowery, C. R. (1986). Gender differences in moral reasoning: A comparison of the use of justice and care orientations. *Journal of Personality and Social Psychology, 50,* 777-783.

Foreman, A. (1977). *Femininity as alienation: Women and the family in Marxism and psychoanalysis.* London: Pluto Press.

Frankenberg, R. (1993). *The social construction of whiteness: White women, race matters.* Minneapolis: University of Minnesota Press.

Franks, V., and Rothblum, E. D. (Eds.). (1983). *The stereotyping of women.* New York: Springer Publishing Co.

Fraser, N., and Nicholson, L. (1990). Social criticism without philosophy: An encounter between feminism and postmodernism. In L. J. Nicholson (Ed.), *Feminism/Postmodernism* (pp. 19-38). New York: Routledge.

Freeman, J. (1995). From seed to harvest: Transformations of feminist organizations and scholarship. In M. M. Ferree, and P. Y. Martin (Eds.), *Feminist organizations: Harvest of the new women's movement* (pp. 397-408). Philadelphia, PA: Temple University Press.

Freire, P. (1970). *Pedagogy of the oppressed.* New York: Seabury Press.

Friedan, B. (1983). *The feminine mystique,* (twentieth anniversary edition). New York: Norton (Originally published in 1963).

Frosh, S. (1987). *The politics of psychoanalysis.* New Haven, CT: Yale University Press.

Frye, M. (1983). *The politics of reality: Essays in feminist theroy.* Trumansburg, NY: Crossing Press.

Fulani, L. (1988). Poor women of color do great therapy. In L. Fulani (Ed.), *The psychopathology of everyday racism and sexism* (pp. 111-120). Binghamton, NY: Harrington Park Press.

Fuller, M. (1976). Woman in the nineteenth century. In B. G. Chevigny (Ed.), *The woman and the myth: Margaret Fuller's life and writings* (pp. 239- 279). Old Westbury, NY: The Feminist Press (Originally published in 1845).

Gage, M. J. (1884/1968). Address at a convention. In A. S. Kraditor (Ed.), *Up from the pedestal* (pp. 137-140). Chicago, IL: Quadrangle Books.

Gallant, S. J., and Hamiliton, J. A. (1988). On premenstrual psychiatric diagnosis: What's in a name? *Professional Psychology, 19,* 271-278.

Galper, M., and Washburne, C. K. (1976). A women's self-help program in action. *Social Policy, 6*(5), 46-52.

Ganley, A. L. (1988). Feminist therapy with male clients. In M.A. Dutton- Douglas and L. E. Walker (Eds.), *Feminist psychotherapies: Integration of therapeutic and feminist systems* (pp. 186-205). Norwood, NJ: Ablex.

Gannon, L. (1982). The role of power in psychotherapy. *Women and Therapy, 1*(2), 3-11.

Gardiner, J. K. (1987). Self psychology as feminist theory. *Signs: Journal of Women in Culture and Society, 12,* 761-780.

Garrison, D. (1981). Karen Horney and feminism. *Signs: Journal of Women in Culture and Society, 6,* 672-691.

Gault, U. (1993). "Psychology constructs the female": A comment. *Feminism and Psychology, 3,* 225-229.

Gavey, N. (1989). Feminist poststructuralism and discourse analysis. *Psychology of Women Quarterly, 13,* 459-475.

Gervasio, A. H., and Crawford, M. (1989). Social evaluations of assertiveness. *Psychology of Women Quarterly, 13,* 459-475.

Giddings, P. (1984). *When and where I enter: The impact of black women on race and sex in America.* New York: William Morrow and Co.

Gilbert, L. A. (1980). Feminist therapy. In A. Brodsky and R. T. Hare-Mustin (Eds.), *Women and psychotherapy* (pp. 245-265). New York: Guilford Press.

Gilbert, L. A. (1981). Toward mental health: The benefits of psychological androgyny. *Professional Psychology: Research and Practice, 12,* 29-38.

Gilbert, L. A. (1987a). Female and male emotional dependency and its implications for the therapist-client relationship. *Professional Psychology: Research and Practice, 18,* 555-561.

Gilbert, L. A. (Ed.). (1987b). Dual-career families in perspective. *The Counseling Psychologist, 15,* 3-145.

Gilligan, C. (1977). In a different voice: Women's conception of self and morality. *Harvard Educational Review, 47,* 481-517.

Gilligan, C. (1982). *In a different voice.* Cambridge, MA: Harvard University Press.

Gilligan, C., Lyons, N. P., and Hanmer, T. J. (1990). *Making connections.* Cambridge, MA: Harvard University Press.

Gilligan, C., Ward, J. V., and Taylor, J. M. (Eds.). (1988). *Mapping the moral domain.* Cambridge, MA: Harvard University Press.

Gilman, C. P. (1898). *Women and economics.* Boston: Small, Maynard, and Co.

Gilman, C. P. (1979). *Herland.* New York: Pantheon Books (Originally published in 1915).

Gilman, C. P. (1923). *His religion and hers: A study in the faith of our fathers and the work of our mothers.* New York: The Century Company.

Glaser, K. (1976). Women's self-help groups as an alternative to therapy. *Psychotherapy: Theory, Research, and Practice, 13,* 77-81.

Glenn, M. (1971). Introduction. In J. Agel (Eds.), *The radical therapist* (pp. ix-xxiii). New York: Ballantine Books.

Gluckstern, N. B. (1977). Beyond therapy: Personal and institutional change. In E. I. Rawlings and D. K. Carter (Eds.), *Psychotherapy for women* (pp. 429-444). Springfield, IL: Charles C Thomas.

Goldenberg. N. R. (1976). A feminist critique of Jung. *Signs: Journal of Women in Culture and Society, 2,* 443-449.

Goldman, E. (1969a). Marriage and love. In E. Goldman (Ed.), *Anarchism and other essays* (pp. 227-239). New York: Dover Publications, Inc (Originally published in 1917).

Goldman, E. (1969b). Woman suffrage. In E. Goldman (Ed.), *Anarchism and other essays* (pp. 195-211). New York: Dover Publications, Inc (Originally published in 1917).

Goldman, E. (1969c). The tragedy of woman's emancipation. In E. Goldman (Ed.), *Anarchism and other essays* (pp. 213-225). New York: Dover Publications, Inc (Originally published in 1917).

Goldman, N., and Ravid, R. (1980). Community surveys: Sex differences in mental illness. In M. Guttentag, S. Salasin, and D. Belle (Eds.), *The mental health of women* (pp. 32-55). New York: Academic Press.

Gonzalez, R. C., Biever, J. L., and Gardner, G. T. (1994). The multicultural perspective in therapy: A social constructionist approach. *Psychotherapy: Theory, Research, and Practice, 31,* 515-524.

Good, G., Gilbert, L., and Scher, M. (1990). Gender aware therapy: A synthesis of feminist therapy and knowledge about gender. *Journal of Counseling and Development, 68,* 376-380.

Good, G., and Mintz, L. M. (1990). Gender role conflict and depression in college: Evidence for compounded risk. *Journal of Counseling and Development, 69,* 17-21.

Goode, E. E. (December 7, 1992). Spiritual questing. *U.S. News and World Report, 113*(22), 64-68, 71.

Goodman, L. A., Koss, M. P., and Russo, N. R. (1993). Violence against women: Mental health effects. Part II. Conceptualizations of post-traumatic stress. *Applied and Preventive Psychology, 2,* 23-130.

Goodrich, T. J., Rampage, C., Ellman, B., and Halstead, K. (1988). *Feminist family therapy.* New York: Norton.

Gordon, S. (1991). *Prisoners of men's dreams.* Boston: Little, Brown, and Co.

Gordon, E. W., Miller, F., and Rollock, D. (1990). Coping with communicentric bias in knowledge production in the social sciences. *Educational Researcher, 19,* 4-19.

Gove, W. R., and Tudor, J. F. (1973). Adult sex roles and mental illness. *American Journal of Sociology, 78,* 50-73.

Greene, B. (1986). When the therapist is white and the patient is black: Considerations for psychotherapy in the feminist heterosexual and lesbian communities. In D. Howard (Ed.), *The dynamics of feminist therapy* (pp. 41- 65). Binghamton, NY: The Haworth Press.

Greene, B. (1990). What has gone before: The legacy of racism and sexism in the lives of black mothers and daughters. In L. Brown and M. P. Root (Eds.), *Diversity and complexity in feminist therapy* (pp. 207-230). Binghamton, NY: The Haworth Press.

Greene, B. (1992). Still here: A perspective on psychotherapy with African-American women. In J. C. Chrisler and D. Howard (Eds.), *New directions in feminist psychology: Practice, theory, and research* (pp. 13-25). New York: Springer Publishing Co.

Greene, B. (1994). African American women. In L. Comas-Díaz and B. Greene (Eds.), *Women of color: Integrating ethnic and gender identities in psychotherapy* (pp. 10-29). New York: Guilford Press.

Greene, B. (1995). An African American perspective on racism and anti-Semitism within feminist organizations. In J. Adleman and G. Enguídanos (Eds.),

Racism in the lives of women: Testimony, theory, and guides to antiracist practice (pp. 303-313). Binghamton, NY: The Haworth Press.

Greenspan, M. (1983). *A new approach to women and therapy.* New York: McGraw-Hill.

Greenspan, M. (1986). Should therapists be personal? Self-disclosure and therapeutic distance in feminist therapy. In D. Howard (Ed.), *The dynamics of feminist therapy* (pp. 5-17). Binghamton, NY: The Haworth Press.

Greenspan, M. (1995). On being a feminist and a psychotherapist. *Women and Therapy, 17*(1/2), 229-241.

Grimké, S. (1972). Letters on the equality of the sexes and the condition of woman. In M. Schneir (Ed.), *Feminism: The essential historical writings* (pp. 35-48). New York: Vantage Books (Originally published in 1838).

Gulanick, N. A., Howard, G. S., and Moreland, J. (1979). Evaluation of a group program designed to increase androgyny in feminine women. *Sex Roles, 5,* 811-827.

Gurko, M. (1976). *The ladies of Seneca Falls: The birth of the women's rights movement.* New York: Schocken Books.

Hackett, G., and Betz, N. E. (1981). A self-efficacy approach to the career development of women. *Journal of Vocational Behavior, 18,* 326-339.

Hackett, G., Enns, C. Z., and Zetzer, H. A. (1992). Reactions of women to nonsexist and feminist counseling: Effects of counselor orientation and mode of information delivery. *Journal of Counseling Psychology, 39,* 321-330.

Hackett, G., and Lonborg, S. D. (1994). Career assessment and counseling for women. In W. B. Walsh and S. H. Osipow (Eds.), *Career counseling for women* (pp. 43-85). Hillsdale, NJ: Erlbaum.

Halleck, S. L. (1971). *The politics of therapy.* New York: Science House Inc.

Hammond, V. W. (1987). "Conscious subjectivity" or use of one's self in therapeutic process. *Women and Therapy, 6*(4), 75-82.

Hanisch, C. (1971). The personal is political. In J. Agel (Ed.) *The radical therapist* (pp. 152-157). New York: Ballantine Books.

Harding, S. (1986). *The science question in feminism.* Ithaca, New York: Cornell University Press.

Harding, S. (1990). Feminism, science, and the anti-enlightenment critiques. In L. J. Nicholson (Ed.), *Feminism/Postmodernism* (pp. 83-106). New York: Routledge.

Harding, S. (1991). *Whose science? Whose knowledge? Thinking from women's lives.* Ithaca, NY: Cornell University Press.

Hare-Mustin, R. T. (1978). A feminist approach to family therapy. *Family Process, 17,* 181-194.

Hare-Mustin, R. T., and Marecek, J. (1986). Autonomy and gender: Some questions for therapists. *Psychotherapy: Theory, Research, and Practice, 23,* 205-212.

Hare-Mustin, R. T., and Marecek, J. (Eds.). (1990). *Making a difference: Psychology and the construction of gender.* New Haven, CT: Yale University Press.

Hare-Mustin, R. T., Marecek, J., Kaplan, A. G., and Liss-Levinson, N. (1979). Rights of clients, responsibilities of therapists. *American Psychologist, 34,* 3-16.

Harrison, M. I. (1987). *Diagnosing organizations: Methods, models, and processes.* Newbury Park, CA: Sage.

Hartman, S. (1987). Therapeutic self-help groups: A process of empowerment for women in abusive relationships. In C. Brody (Ed.), *Women's therapy groups: Paradigms of feminist treatment* (pp. 67-81). New York: Springer Publishing Co.

Hartmann, H. (1981). The unhappy marriage of Marxism and feminism: Toward a more progressive union. In L. Sargent (Ed.), *Women and revolution: A discussion of the unhappy marriage of Marxism and feminism* (pp. 1-41). Boston, MA: South End Press.

Hartsock, N. C. M. (1983). The feminist standpoint: Developing the ground for a specifically feminist historical materialism. In S. Harding and M. B. Hintikka (Eds.), *Discovering reality* (pp. 283-310). Dordrecht: D. Reidel Publishing Co.

Hartsock, N. (1984). Staying alive. In A. M. Jaggar and P. S. Rothenberg (Eds.), *Feminist frameworks* (pp. 266-276). New York: McGraw-Hill.

Hartsock, N. (1987). Rethinking modernism: Minority vs. majority theories. *Cultural Critique, 7,* 187-206.

Hawkesworth, M. E. (1989). Knowers, knowing, known: Feminist theory and claims of truth. *Signs: Journal of Women in Culture and Society, 14,* 533-557.

Hawxhurst, D. M., and Morrow, S. L. (1984). *Living our visions: Building feminist community.* Tempe, AZ: Fourth World.

Helms, J. E. (Ed.). (1990). *Black and white identity: Theory, research, and practice.* Westport, CT: Greenwood.

Hendricks, M. C. (1985). Feminist spirituality in Jewish and Christian traditions. In L. B. Rosewater and L. E. A. Walker (Eds.), *Handbook of feminist therapy* (pp. 135-146). New York: Springer Publishing Co.

Herman, J. (1981). *Father-daughter incest.* Cambridge, MA: Harvard University Press.

Herman, J. L. (1992). *Trauma and recovery: The aftermath of violence.* New York: Basic Books.

Hertzberg, J. F. (1990). Feminist psychotherapy and diversity: Treatment considerations from a self psychology perspective. *Women and Therapy, 9*(3), 275-297.

Hewlett, S. A. (1986). *A lesser life: The myth of women's liberation in America.* New York: William Morrow and Co., Inc.

Higgenbotham, E. B. (1992). African-American women's history and the meta-language of race. *Signs: Journal of Women in Culture and Society, 17,* 251-274.

Hill, M.A. (1980). *Charlotte Perkins Gilman: The making of a radical feminist 1860-1896.* Philadephia, PA: Temple University Press.

Hochschild, A. (1989). *The second shift.* New York: Viking.

Hoffman, L. (1981). *Foundations of family therapy.* New York: Basic Books.

Hole, J., and Levine, E. (1971). The first feminists. In A. Koedt, S. Firestone, A. Rapone, and E. Levine (Eds.), *Notes from the third year* (pp. 5- 10). New York: Quadrangle Books.

Holland, D. C., and Eisenhart, M. A. (1990). *Educated in romance: Women, achievement, and college culture.* Chicago, IL: University of Chicago Press.

Holroyd, J. (1976). Psychotherapy and women's liberation. *The Counseling Psychologist, 6,* 22-32.

hooks, b. (1981). *Ain't I a woman.* Boston: South End Press.

hooks, b. (1984). *Feminist theory: From margin to center.* Boston, MA: South End Press.

hooks, b. (1989). *Talking back: Thinking feminist, thinking black.* Boston. MA: South End Press.

hooks, b., Steinem, G., Vaid, U., and Wolf, N. (1993). Get real about feminism— The myths, the backlash, the movement. *Ms., 4*(2), 34-43.

Horner, M. S. (1970). Femininity and successful achievement: A basic inconsistency. In J. M. Bardwick, E. Couvan, M. S. Horner, and D. Gutman (Eds.), *Feminine personality and conflict* (pp. 45-74). Belmost, CA: Brooks/Cole.

Horney, K. (1939). *New ways in psychoanalysis.* New York: Norton.

Horney, K. (1945). *Our inner conflicts.* New York: Norton.

Horney, K. (1967). *Feminine psychology.* New York: Norton.

Horney, K. (1967). The flight from womanhood: The masculinity complex in women as viewed by men and women. In H. Kelman (Ed.), *Feminine psychology* (pp. 54-70). New York: Norton. (Originally published in 1926).

Horney, K. (1967). The dread of woman. In H. Kelman (Ed.), *Feminine psychology* (pp. 133-146). New York: Norton. (Originally published in 1932).

Horney, K. (1967). The denial of the vagina. In H. Kelman (Ed.), *Feminine psychology* (pp. 147-161). New York: Norton. (Originally published in 1933).

Horney, K. (1967). The overvaluation of love. In H. Kelman (Ed.), *Feminine psychology* (pp. 182-213). New York: Norton. (Originally published in 1934).

Hotelling, K. (1987). Curative factors in groups for women with bulimia. In C. Brody (Eds.), *Women's therapy groups: Paradigms of feminist treatment* (pp. 241-252). New York: Springer Publishing Co.

Hotelling, K. (1991). Sexual harassment: A problem shielded by silence. *Journal of Counseling and Development, 69,* 497-501.

Hurtado, A. (1989). Relating to privilege: Seduction and rejection in the subordination of white women and women of color. *Signs: Journal of Women in Culture and Society, 14,* 833-855.

Hurvitz, N. (1973). Psychotherapy as a means of social control. *Journal of Consulting and Clinical Psychology, 40,* 232-239.

Hutchinson, L. D. (1982). *Anna Cooper: A voice from the south.* Washington, DC: Smithsonian Institution Press.

Hyde, J. S. (1996). *Half the human experience: The psychology of women* (fifth edition). Lexington, MA: D. C. Heath and Company.

Jack, (1987). Self-in-relation theory. In R. Formanik and A. Gurian (Eds.), *Women and depression: A lifespan perspective* (pp. 41-45). New York: Springer.

Jack, D. (1991). *Silencing the self: Women and depression.* Cambridge, MA: Harvard University Press.

Jackson, A. P., and Sears, S. J. (1992). Implications of an Africentric worldview in reducing stress for African American women. *Journal of Counseling and Development, 71,* 184-190.

Jaggar, A. M. (1983). *Feminist politics and human nature.* Totowa, NJ: Rowman and Allenheld.

Jaggar, A. M., and Rothenberg, P. S. (Eds.). (1984). *Feminist frameworks.* New York: McGraw-Hill.

Jakubowski, P. A. (1977). Assertion training for women. In E. I. Rawlings and D. K. Carter (Eds.), *Psychotherapy for women* (pp. 147-190). Springfield, IL: Charles C Thomas.

Johnson, M. (1976). An approach to feminist therapy. *Psychotherapy: Theory, Research, and Practice, 13,* 72-76.

Johnson, M. (1987). Feminist therapy in groups: A decade of change. In C. Brody (Ed.), *Women's therapy groups: Paradigms of feminist treatment* (pp. 13-23). New York: Springer Publishing Co.

Jordan, J. V. (1991). The meaning of mutuality. In J. V. Jordan, A. G. Kaplan, J. B. Miller, I. P. Stiver, and J. L. Surrey (Eds.), *Women's growth in connection* (pp. 81-96). New York: Guilford Press.

Jordan, J. V., Kaplan, A. G., Miller, J. B., Stiver, I. P., and Surrey, J. L. (Eds.). (1991). *Women's growth in connection.* New York: Guilford Press.

Jordan, J. V., and Surrey, J. L. (1986). The self-in-relation: Empathy and the mother-daughter relationship. In. T. Bernay and D. W. Cantor (Eds.), *The psychology of today's woman: New psychoanalytic visions* (pp. 81-104). Hillsdale, NJ: Analytic Press.

Joreen. (1968, March). What in the hell is women's liberation anyway? *The Voice of The Women's Liberation Movement, 1*(1), 1.

Joreen. (1973). The tyranny of structurelessness. In A. Koedt, E. Levine, and A. Rapone (Eds.), *Radical feminism* (pp. 285-299). New York: Quadrangle Books.

Joseph, G. (1981). The incompatible ménage à trois: Marxism, feminism, and racism. In L. Sargent (Ed.), *Women and revolution* (pp. 91-107). Boston, MA: South End Press.

Josselson, R. (1987). *Finding herself: Pathways to identity development in women.* San Francisco, CA: Jossey-Bass.

Jung, C. G. (1953). The psychology of the unconscious. In S. H. Read, M. Fordham, and G. Adler (Eds.), and R. F. C. Hull (Trans.), *The collected works of C. G. Jung,* volume 7 (pp. 3-117). New York: Pantheon Books (Originally published in 1943).

Jung, C. G. (1954/1959). Psychological aspects of the mother archetype. In S. H. Read, M. Fordham, and G. Adler (Eds.), and R. F. C. Hull (Trans.), *The collected works of C. G. Jung,* volume 9, part 1 (pp. 3-41). New York: Pantheon Books.

Juntunen, C. L., Atkinson, D. R., Reyes, C., and Gutierrez, M. (1994). Feminist identity and feminist therapy behaviors of women psychotherapists. *Psychotherapy, 31,* 327-333.

Kahn, A. (1984). The power war: Male response to power loss under equality. *Psychology of Women Quarterly, 8,* 234-247.

Kaminer, W. (1992). *I'm dysfunctional, you're dysfunctional.* Reading, MA: Addison-Wesley.

Kanter, R. M. (1977). *Men and women of the corporation.* New York: Basic Books.

Kantrowitz, R. E., and Ballou, M. (1992). A feminist critique of cognitive-behavioral therapy. In L. S. Brown and M. Ballou (Eds.), *Personality and psychopathology: Feminist reappraisals* (pp. 70-87). New York: Guilford Press.

Kanuha, V. (1990). The need for an integrated analysis of oppression in feminist therapy ethics. In H. Lerman and N. Porter (Eds.), *Feminist ethics in psychotherapy* (pp. 24-35). New York: Springer Publishing Co.

Kaplan, A. G. (1976). Androgyny as a model of mental health for women: From theory to therapy. In A. G. Kaplan and J. P. Bean (Eds.), *Beyond sex-role stereotypes: Reading toward a psychology of androgyny* (pp. 353-362). Boston, MA: Little, Brown and Co.

Kaplan, A. G. (1979a). Introduction. *Psychology of Women Quarterly, 3,* 221-222.

Kaplan, A. G. (1979b). Clarifying the concept of androgyny: Implications for therapy. *Psychology of Women Quarterly, 3,* 223-230.

Kaplan, A. G. (1986). The "self-in-relation": Implications for depression in women. *Psychotherapy: Theory, Research, and Practice, 23,* 234-242.

Kaplan, A. G., and Surrey, J. L. (1984). The relational self in women: Developmental theory and public policy. In L. E. Walker (Ed.), *Women and mental health policy* (pp. 79-94). Beverly Hills, CA: Sage.

Kaplan, M. (1983). A woman's view of DSM-III. *American Psychologist, 38,* 786-792.

Kappeler, S. (1986). *The pornography of representation.* Minneapolis: University of Minnesota Press.

Kaschak, E. (1981). Feminist psychotherapy: The first decade. In S. Cox (Ed.), *Female psychology: The emerging self* (pp. 387-400). New York: St. Martin's Press.

Kaschak, E. (1992). *Engendered lives: A new psychology of women's experience.* New York: Basic Books.

Kashima, Y., Yamaguchi, S., Kim, U., San-Chin, C., Gelfand, M., and Yuki, M. (1995). Culture, gender, and self: A perspective from individualism-collectivism research. *Journal of Personality and Social Psychology, 69,* 925-937.

Kasl, C. D. (1992). *Many roads, one journey: Moving beyond the 12 steps.* New York: HarperCollins.

Katzman, M. A., Weiss, L., and Wolchik, S. A. (1986). Speak don't eat! Teaching women to express their feelings. *Women and Therapy, 5(2/3),* 143-158.

Keen, S. (1991). *Fire in the belly: On being a man.* New York: Bantam.

Kelly, J. A., Kern, J. M., Kirkley, B. G., Patterson, J. N., and Keane, T. M. (1980). Reactions to assertive versus unassertive behavior: Differential effects for males and females, and implications for assertive training. *Behavior Therapy, 11,* 670-682.

Kenworthy, J. A. (1979). Androgyny in psychotherapy: But will it sell in Peoria? *Psychology of Women Quarterly, 3,* 231-240.

Kerber, L. K. (1986). Some cautionary words for historians. *Signs: Journal of Women in Culture and Society, 11,* 304-310.

Kern, J. M. (1982). Predicting the impact of assertive, empathic-assertive, and nonassertive behavior: The assertiveness of the assertee. *Behavior Therapy, 13,* 486-498.

King, D. K. (1988). Multiple jeopardy, multiple consciousness: The context of a black feminist ideology. *Signs: Journal of Women in Culture and Society, 14,* 42-72.

King, Y. (1989). The ecology of feminism and the feminism of ecology. In J. Plant (Ed.), *Healing the wounds: The promise of ecofeminism* (pp. 18-28). Philadelphia, PA: New Society Publishers.

King, Y. (1990). Healing the wounds: Feminism, ecology, and the nature/culture dualism. In I. Diamond and G. F. Orenstein (Eds.), *Reweaving the world: The emergence of ecofeminism* (pp. 106-121). San Francisco, CA: Sierra Club Books.

Kingery, D. W. (1985). Are sex role attitudes useful in explaining male/female differences in rates of depression? *Sex Roles, 12,* 627-636.

Kingston, M. A. (1976). *The woman warrior.* New York: Knopf.

Kirk, S. (1983). The role of politics in feminist counseling. In J. H. Robbins and R. J. Siegel (Eds.), *Women changing therapy* (pp. 179-189). Binghamton, NY: The Haworth Press.

Kirsch, B. (1974). Consciousness-raising groups as therapy for women. In V. Franks and V. Burtle (Eds.), *Women in therapy* (pp. 326-354). New York: Brunner/Mazel.

Kirsch, B. (1987). Evolution of consciousness-raising groups. In C. Brody (Eds.), *Women's therapy groups* (pp. 43-54). New York: Springer Publishing Co.

Kitzinger, C. (1993). Depoliticising the personal: A feminist slogan in feminist therapy. *Women's Studies International Forum, 16,* 487-496.

Kitzinger, C., and Perkins, R. (1993). *Changing our minds: Lesbian feminism and psychology.* New York: New York University Press.

Klein, M. H. (1976). Feminist concepts of therapy outcome. *Psychotherapy: Theory, Research, and Practice, 13,* 89-95.

Klerman, G. L., and Weissman, M. M. (1980). Depressions among women: Their nature and causes. In M. Guttentag, S. Salasin, and D. Belle (Eds.), *The mental health of women* (pp. 57-92). New York: Academic Press.

Knox, K. (1985). Women's identity: Self psychology's new promise. *Women and Therapy, 4*(3), 57-69.

Koedt, A. (1973). Lesbianism and feminism. In A. Koedt, E. Levine, and A. Rapone (Eds.), *Radical feminism* (pp. 246-258). New York: Quadrangle Books.

Kohlberg, L. (1981). *The philosophy of moral development.* San Francisco, CA: Harper and Row.

Kohut, H. (1971). *The analysis of the self.* New York: International Universities Press.

Kohut, H. (1984). *How does analysis cure?* Chicago: University of Chicago Press.

Koss, M. (1993). Rape: Scope, impact, interventions, and public policy responses. *American Psychologist, 48,* 1062-1069.

Koss, M., and Harvey, M. (1991). *The rape victim: Clinical and community interventions.* Newbury Park, CA: Sage.

Kramarae, C., and Treichler, P. A. (1985). *A feminist dictionary.* Boston, MA: Pandora Press.

Kravetz, D. (1976). Consciousness-raising groups and group psychotherapy: Alternative mental health resources for women. *Psychotherapy: Theory, Research, and Practice, 13,* 66-71.

Kravetz, D. (1978). Consciousness-raising groups in the 1970s. *Psychology of Women Quarterly, 3,* 168-186.

Kravetz, D. (1980). Consciousness-raising and self-help. In A. Brodsky and R. T. Hare-Mustin (Eds.), *Women and psychotherapy* (pp. 267-284). New York: Guilford Press.

Kravetz, D. (1987). Benefits of consciousness-rasing groups for women. In C. Brody (Ed.), *Women's therapy groups: Paradigms of feminist treatment* (p. 55-66). New York: Springer Publishing Co.

Kravetz, D., Marecek, J., and Finn, S. E. (1983). Factors influencing women's participation in consciousness-raising groups. *Psychology of Women Quarterly, 7,* 257-271.

Kravetz, D., and Jones, L. E. (1991). Supporting practice in feminist service agencies. In M. Bricker-Jenkins, N. R. Hooyman, and N. Bottlieb (Eds.), *Feminist social work practice in clinical settings* (pp. 233-249). Newbury Park, CA: Sage.

Kreps, B. (1973). Radical feminism 1. In A. Koedt, E. Levine, and A. Rapone (Eds.), *Radical feminism* (pp. 234-239). New York: Quadrangle Books.

LaFromboise, T. C., Berman, J. S., and Sohi, B. K. (1994). In L. Comas-Díaz and B. Greene (Eds.), *Women of color: Integrating ethnic and gender identities in therapy* (pp. 30-71). New York: Guilford Press.

LaFromboise, T. D., Heyle, A. M., and Ozer, E. J. (1990). Changing and diverse roles of women in American Indian cultures. *Sex Roles, 22,* 455-476.

Laidlaw, T. A. (1990). Dispelling the myths: A workshop on compulsive eating and body image. In T. A. Laidlaw and C. Malmo (Eds.), *Healing voices* (pp. 15-32). San Francisco, CA: Jossey-Bass.

Laidlaw, T. A., and Malmo, C. (Eds.). (1990). *Healing voices.* San Francisco, CA: Jossey-Bass.

Lamb, L. (May-June, 1990). Is everyone codependent? *Utne Reader, 26,* 28.

Landrine, H. (1989). The politics of personality disorder. *Psychology of Women Quarterly, 13,* 325-339.

Landrine, H., Klonoff, E. A., and Brown-Collins, A. (1992). Cultural diversity and methodology in feminist psychology. *Psychology of Women Quarterly, 16,* 145-163.

Lane, A. J. (Ed.) (1980). The fictional world of Charlotte Perkins Gilman. In *The Charlotte Perkins Gilman reader* (pp. ix-xiii). New York: Panthen Books.

Lane, A. J. (1983). Charlotte Perkins Gilman: The personal is political. In D. Spender (Ed.), *Feminist theorists* (pp. 203-217). New York: Pantheon Books.

Lao, R. C., Upchurch, W. H., Corwin, G. J., and Groosnickle, W. F. (1975). Biased attitudes toward females as indicated by ratings of intelligence and likeability. *Psychological Reports, 37,* 1315-1320.

Larrington, C. (Ed.). (1992). *The feminist companion to mythology.* San Francisco, CA: HarperCollins.

LaRue, L. J. M. (1970, November-December). Black liberation and women's lib. *Trans-Action,* 61.

Lauter, E., and Rupprecht, C. S. (Eds.). (1985). *Feminist archetypal theory.* Knowville: University of Tennessee Press.

Lazarus, A. A. (1981). *The practice of multi-modal therapy.* New York: McGraw-Hill.

Leidig, M. W. (1977). "Feminist therapy." Unpublished manuscript.

Lerman, H. (1976). What happens in feminist therapy? In S. Cox (Ed.), *Female psychology: The emerging self* (pp. 378-384). Chicago, IL: Science Research Associates.

Lerman, H. (1986). *A mote in Freud's eye.* New York: Springer Publishing Co.

Lerman, H. (1987). Introduction. In C. Brody (Ed.), *Women's therapy groups* (pp. xxiii-xxviii). New York: Springer Publishing Co.

Lerman, H. (1992). The limits of phenomenology: A feminist critique of the humanistic personality theories. In L. S. Brown and M. Ballou (Eds.), *Personality and psychopathology: Feminist reappraisals* (pp. 8-19). New York: Guilford Press.

Lerman, H., and Porter, N. (Eds.). (1990). *Feminist ethics in psychotherapy.* New York: Springer Publishing Co.

Lerman, H., and Rigby, D. N. (1990). Boundary violations: Misuse of the power of the therapist. In H. Lerman and N. Porter (Eds.), *Feminist ethics in psychotherapy* (pp. 51-59). New York: Springer Publishing Co.

Lerner, G. (1971). *The Grimke sisters from South Carolina: Pioneers for women's rights and abolition.* New York: Schoken Books.

Lerner, G. (1979). *The majority finds its past: Placing women in history.* New York: Oxford Press.

Lerner, H. G. (1983). Female dependency in context: Some theoretical and technical considerations. *American Journal of Orthopsychiatry, 53,* 697-705.

Lerner, H. G. (1988). *Women in therapy.* Northvale, NJ: Aronson.

Lerner, H. G. (1990, April). Problems for profit? *Women's Review of Books, 7*(7), 15.

Levant, R. F. (1996). The new psychology of men. *Professional Psychology: Research and Practice, 27,* 259-265.

Levant, R. F., and Pollack, W. S. (Eds.). (1995). *A new psychology of men.* New York: Basic Books.

Levinson, D. (1978). *The seasons of a man's life.* New York: Knopf.

Lewin, M. (1984). The Victorians, the psychologists, and psychic birth control. In M. Lewin (Ed.), *In the shadow of the past: Psychology portrays the sexes* (pp. 39-76). New York: Columbia University Press.

Lewis, E. (1983). The group treatment of battered women. *Women and Therapy, 2*(1), 51-58.

Lewis, K. N., Davis, C. S., and Lesmeister, R. (1983). Pretherapy information: An investigation of client responses. *Journal of Counseling Psychology, 30,* 108-112.

Lewis, K. N., Epperson, D. L., and Foley, J. (1989). Informed entry into counseling: Clients' perceptions and preferences resulting from different types and amounts of pretherapy information. *Journal of Counseling Psychology, 36,* 279-285.

Libow, J. A., Raskin, P. A., and Caust, B. L. (1982). Feminist and family systems therapy: Are they irreconcilable? *American Journal of Family Therapy, 10,* 3-12.

Lieberman, M. A., and Bond, G. R. (1976). The problem of being a woman: A survey of 1,700 women in consciousness-raising groups. *Journal of Applied Behavior Science, 12,* 363-379.

Lieberman, M. A., Solow, N., Bond, G. R., and Reibstein, J. (1979). The psychotherapeutic impact of women's consciousness-raising groups. *Archives of General Psychiatry, 36,* 161-168.

Lindsey, K. (1974). On the need to develop a feminist therapy. *Rough Times: A Journal of Radical Therapy, 4,* 2-3.

Linehan, M., and Seifert, R. F. (1983). Sex and contextual differences in the appropriateness of assertive behavior. *Psychology of Women Quarterly, 8,* 79-88.

Lipman-Blumen, J. (1984). *Gender roles and power.* Englewood Cliffs, NJ: Prentice-Hall.

Longino, H. E. (1993). Feminist standpoint theory and the problems of knowledge. *Signs: Journal of Women in Culture and Society, 19,* 201-212

Longres, J., and McLeod, E. (1980). Consciousness raising and social work practice. *Social Casework, 61,* 267-277.

Lopez, S. R. (1983). The study of psychotherapy bias: Some conceptual issues and some concluding remarks. In J. Murray and P. R. Abramson (Eds.), *Bias in Psychotherapy* (pp. 353-365). New York: Praeger.

Lopez, S. R. (1989). Patient variable biases in clinical judgment: Conceptual overview and methodological considerations. *Psychological Bulletin, 106,* 184-203.

Lorde, A. (1983). An open letter to Mary Daly. In C. Moraga and G. Anzaldua (Eds.), *This bridge called my back* (p. 97). New York: Women of Color Press.

Lorde, A. (1984), *Sister outsider.* Trumansburg, NY: The Crossing Press.

Lott, B. (1981). A feminist critique of androgyny: Toward the elmination of gender attributions for learned behavior. In C. Mayo and N. M. Henley (Eds.), *Gender and nonverbal behavior* (pp. 171-180). New York: Springer-Verlag.

Lott, B. (1990). Dual natures of learned behavior: The challenge to feminist psychology. In R. T. Hare-Mustin and J. Marecek (Eds.), *Making a difference:*

Psychology and the construction of gender (pp. 65-101). New Haven, CT: Yale University Press.

Lovell, T. (Ed.). (1990). *British feminist thought.* Cambridge, MA: Basil Blackwell Ltd.

Luria, Z. (1986). A methodological critique. *Signs: Journal of Women in Culture and Society, 11,* 316-321.

Lyons, N. (1983). Two perspectives: On self, relationships and morality. *Harvard Educational Review, 53,* 125-145.

Maccoby, E. E. (1990). Gender and relationships: A developmental account. *American Psychologist, 45,* 513-520.

MacKinnon, C. A. (1989). *Toward a feminist theory of the state.* Cambridge, MA: Harvard University Press.

MacKinnon, C. A. (1993). Feminism, Marxism, method, and the State: Toward a feminist jurisprudence. In P. B. Bart and E. G. Moran (Eds.), *Violence against women: The bloody footprints* (pp. 201-227). Newbury Park, CA: Sage (Originally published in 1982).

Magolda, M B. (1989). Gender differences in cognitive development: An analysis of cognitive complexity and learning styles. *Journal of College Student Development, 30,* 213-220.

Mahler, M., Pine, F., and Bergman, A. (1975). *The psychological birth of the human infant: Symbiosis and individuation.* New York: Basic Books.

Major, B. (1993). Gender, entitlement, and distribution of family labor. *Journal of Social Issues, 49,* 141-159.

Mander, A. V., and Rush, A. K. (1974). *Feminism as therapy.* New York: Random House.

Manifesto (1971). In J. Agel (Ed.), *The radical therapist* (pp. xv-xxiii). New York: Ballantine Books.

Marcia, J. E. (1966). Development and validation of ego identity status. *Journal of Personality and Social Psychology, 3,* 551-558.

Marcia, J. E. (1980). Identity in adolescence. In J. Adelson (Ed.), *Handbook of adolescent psychology* (pp. 159-187). New York: Wiley.

Markus, H., and Kitayama, S. (1991). Culture and the self: Implications for cognition, emotion, and motivation. *Psychologyical Review, 98,* 224-253.

Marecek, J., and Kravetz, D. (1977). Women and mental health: A review of feminist change efforts. *Psychiatry, 40,* 323-329.

Marecek, J., Kravetz, D., and Finn, S. (1979). Comparison of women who enter feminist therapy and women who enter traditional therapy. *Journal of Consulting and Clinical Psychology, 4,* 734-742.

Margolies, L., Becker, M., and Jackson-Brewer, K. (1987). Internalized homophobia: Identifying and treating the oppressor within. In Boston Lesbian Psychologies Collective (Ed.), *Lesbian Psychologies* (pp. 229-241). Chicago, IL: University of Illinois Press.

Mark, C. G. (1990). The personal relationship between therapists and their theoretical orientation. In D. W. Cantor (Ed.), *Women as therapists: A multitheoretical casebook* (pp. 33-55). New York: Springer Publishing Co.

Markus, H., and Oyserman, D. (1989). Gender and thought: The role of the self-concept. In M. Crawford and M. Gentry (Eds.), *Gender and thought: Psychological perspectives* (pp. 100-127). New York: Springer Publishing Co.

Maslow, A. H. (1956). Self-actualizing people: A study of psychological health. In C. E. Moustakas (Ed.), *The self* (pp. 160-194). New York: Harper Colophon.

Matlin, M. W. (1996). *The psychology of women,* third edition. Fort Worth, TX: Harcourt Brace Jovanovich College Publishers.

Matthews, N. A. (1994). *Confronting rape: The feminist anti-rape movement and the state.* New York: Routledge.

McEvoy, M. (1990). Repairing personal boundaries: Group therapy with survivors of sexual abuse. In T. A. Laidlaw and C. Malmo (Eds.), *Healing voices* (pp. 62-79). San Francisco, CA: Jossey-Bass.

McGrath, E., Keita, G. P., Strickland, B. R., and Russo, N. F. (Eds.). (1990). *Women and depression.* Washington, DC: American Psychological Association.

McIntosh, P. (1989, July/August). White privilege: Unpacking the invisible knapsack. *Peace and Freedom,* 10-12.

McNair, L. D. (1992). African American women in therapy: An Afrocentric and feminist synthesis. *Women and Therapy, 12*(1/2), 5-19.

McShane, C., and Oliver, J. (1978). Women's groups as alternative human service agencies. *Journal of Sociology and Social Welfare, 5,* 615-626.

McWhirter, E. H. (1991). Empowerment in counseling. *Journal of Counseling and Development, 69,* 222-227.

Meara, N. M., and Harmon, L. W. (1989). Accomplishments and disappointments of the Division 17 Committee on Women, 1970-1987. *The Counseling Psychologist, 17,* 314-331.

Mednick, M. T. (1989). On the politics of psychological constructs: Stop the bandwagon, I want to get off. *American Psychologist, 44,* 1118-1123.

Mehrhof, B., and Kearon, P. (1971). Rape: An act of terror. In A. Koedt, A Rapone, and E. Levine (Eds.), *Notes from the third year: Women's liberation* (pp. 79-81). New York: Radical Feminists.

Miller, J. B. (1976). *Toward a new psychology of women.* Boston, MA: Beacon Press.

Miller, J. B. (1986). *Toward a new psychology of women,* second edition. Boston, MA: Beacon.

Miller, J. B. (1991). The development of women's sense of self. In J. V. Jordan, A. G. Kaplan, J. B. Miller, I. P. Stiver, and J. L. Surrey (Eds.), *Women's growth in connection* (pp. 11-26). New York: Guilford Press.

Millett, K. (1970). *Sexual politics.* Garden City, NY: Doubleday and Co.

Minuchin, S. (1974). *Families and family therapy.* Cambridge, MA: Harvard University Press.

Minuchin, S. (1984). *Family kaleidoscope.* Cambridge, MA: Harvard University Press.

Mitchell, J. (1969). The longest revolution. In B. Roszek and T. Roszak (Eds.), *Masculine/Feminine: Readings in sexual mythology and the liberation of women* (pp. 160-173). New York: Harper Colophon Books.

Mitchell, J. (1974). *Psychoanalysis and feminism.* New York: Vintage Books.

Mitchell, V. (1989). Using Kohut's self psychology in work with lesbian couples. *Women and Therapy, 8*(1/2), 157-166.

Moore, D. M. (1981). Assertiveness training: A review. In S. Cox (Ed.), *Female psychology: The emerging self,* second edition (pp. 402-416). New York: St. Martin's.

Moore, R., and Gillette, D. (1990). *King, warrior, magician, lover: Rediscovering the archetypes of the mature masculine.* San Francisco, CA: Harper.

Moore, R., and Gillette, D. (1992). *The king within.* New York: William Morrow.

Morawski, J. G. (1987). The troubled quest for masculinity, femininity, and androgyny. In P. Shaver and C. Hendrick (Eds.), *Sex and gender* (pp. 44-69). Newbury Park, CA: Sage.

Morawski, J. G. (1990). Toward the unimagined: Feminism and epistemology in psychology. In R. T. Hare-Mustin and J. Marecek (Eds.), *Making a difference* (pp. 150-183). New Haven, CT: Yale University Press.

Morawski, J. G., and Bayer, B. M. (1995). Stirring trouble and making theory. In H. Landrine (Ed.), *Bring cultural diversity to feminist psychology: Theory, research, and practice* (pp. 113-138). Washington, DC: American Psychological Association.

Morgan, R. (1980). Theory and practice: Pornography and rape. In L. Lederer (Ed.), *Take back the night: Women on pornography* (pp. 134-140). New York: William Morrow.

Morrison, T. (August 22, 1971). What the black woman thinks about women's lib. *The New York Times Magazine,* p. 15.

Moschkovich, J. (1983). "But I know you, American woman." In C. Moraga and G. Anzaldua (Eds.), *This bridge called my back,* second edition (pp. 79-84). New York: Kitchen Table, Women of Color Press.

Moss, L. E. (1985). Feminist body psychotherapy. In L. B. Rosewater and L. E. A. Walker (Eds.), *Handbook of feminist therapy* (pp. 80-90). New York: Springer Publishing Co.

Muehlenhard, C. L. (1983). Women's assertion and the feminine sex-role stereotype. In V. Franks and E. D. Rothblum (Eds.), *The stereotyping of women: Its effects on mental health* (pp. 153-171). New York: Springer Publishing Co.

Murray, H. A. (1938). *Explorations in personality.* New York: Oxford University Press.

Myron, N., and Bunch, C. (Eds.). (1975). *Lesbianism and the women's movement.* Baltimore, MD: Diana Press.

Naranjo, C. (1970). Present-centeredness: Technique, prescription, and ideal. In J. Fagan and I. L. Shepherd (Eds.), *Gestalt therapy now* (pp. 47-69). Palo Alto, CA: Science and Behavior Books.

National Organization for Women. (1967/1970). Bill of rights. In R. Morgan (Ed.), *Sisterhood is powerful* (pp. 512-514). New York: Random House.

Needleman, R., and Nelson, A. (1988). Policy implications: The worth of women's work. In A Statham, E. M. Miller, and H. O. Mauksch (Eds.), *The worth of women's work: A qualitative synthesis* (pp. 293-307). Albany: State University of New York Press.

Nelson, G. M. (1991). *Here all dwell free: Stories to heal the wounded feminine.* New York: Doubleday.

Nes, J. A., and Iadicola, P. (1989). Toward a definition of feminist social work: A comparison of liberal, radical, and socialist models. *Social Work, 34,* 12-22.

New York Radical Feminists. (1973). Politics of the ego: A manifesto for New York Radical Feminists. In A. Koedt, E. Levine, and A. Rapone (Eds.), *Radical feminism* (pp. 379-383). New York: Quadrangle Books.

Noddings, N. (1984). *Caring: A feminine approach to ethics and moral education.* Berkeley: University of California Press.

Norwood, R. (1985). *Women who love too much.* New York: Pocket Books.

Oakley, A. (1990). What is a housewife? In T. Lovell (Ed.), *British feminist thought* (pp. 71-76). Cambridge, MA: Basil Blackwell Ltd.

O'Connell, A. N. (1980). Karen Horney: Theorist in psychoanalysis and feminine psychology. *Psychology of Women Quarterly, 5,* 81-93.

Okun, B. F. (1992). Object relations and self psychology: Overview and feminist perspective. In L. S. Brown and M. Ballou (Eds.), *Personality and psychopathology: Feminist reappraisals* (pp. 20-45). New York: Guilford Press.

O'Neil, J. M. (1981). Patterns of gender role conflict and strain: Sexism and fear of femininity in men's lives. *Personnel and Guidance Journal, 60,* 203-210.

O'Neil, J. M., and Egan, J. (1993). Abuses of power against women: Sexism, gender role conflict, and psychological violence. In E. P. Cook (Ed.), *Women, relationships, and power: Implications for counseling* (pp. 49-78). Alexandria, VA: American Counseling Association.

O'Neill, W. (1971). *Everyone was brave: The rise and fall of feminism in America.* New York: Quadrangle Books.

O'Sullivan, E. (1976). What has happened to rape crisis centers? A look at their structures, members, and funding. *Victimology, 3*(1/2), 45-62.

Paludi, M. (Ed.). (1990a). *Ivory power: Sexual harassment on campus.* Albany: State University of New York Press.

Paludi, M. (Ed.). (1990b). *Exploring–teaching the psychology of women: A manual of resources.* Albany: State University of New York Press.

Parvin, R. A., and Biaggio, M. (1991). Paradoxes in the practice of feminist therapy. *Women and Therapy, 11*(2), 3-12.

Passons, W. R. (1975). *Gestalt approaches in counseling.* New York: Holt, Rinehart and Winston.

Payne, C. W. (1973). Consciousness raising: A dead end? In A. Koedt, E. Levine, and A. Rapone (Eds.), *Radical feminism* (pp. 282-284). New York: Quadrangle Books.

Pearson, C. S. (1986). *The hero within.* San Francisco, CA: Harper and Row.

Pearson, C. S. (1991). *Awakening the heroes within.* San Francisco, CA: HarperCollins.

Peplau, L. A., Cochran, S., Rook, K., and Padesky, C. (1978). Loving women: Attachment and autonomy in lesbian relationships. *Journal of Social Issues, 34,* 7-27.

Peplau, L. A., and Conrad, E. (1989). Beyond nonsexist research: The perils of feminist methods in psychology. *Psychology of Women Quarterly, 13,* 379- 400.

Peplau, L. A., and Gordon, S. L. (1983). The intimate relationships of lesbians and gay men. In E. R. Allgeier and N. G. McCormick (Eds.), *Changing boundaries: Gender roles and social behavior* (pp. 226-244). Palo Alto, CA: Mayfield.

Perkins, R. E. (1991a). Women with long-term mental health problems: Issues of power and powerlessness. *Feminism and Psychology, 1*(1), 131-139.

Perkins, R. E. (1991b). Therapy for lesbians?: The case against. *Feminism and Psychology, 1*(3), 325-338.

Perkins, R. E. (1992). Working with socially disabled clients. In. J. M. Ussher and P. Nicolson (Eds.), *Gender issues in clinical psychology* (pp. 171- 193). London: Routledge.

Perry, W. G. (1970). *Forms of intellectual and ethical development in the college years.* New York: Holt, Rinehart and Winston.

Phillips, F. B. (1990). NTU psychotherapy: An Afrocentric approach. *The Journal of Black Psychology, 17*(1), 55-74.

Phillips, R. D., and Gilroy, F. D. (1985). Sex-role stereotypes and clinical judgments of mental health: The Brovermans' findings reexamined. *Sex Roles, 12,* 179-193.

Plant, J. (Ed.). (1989). *Healing the wounds: The promise of ecofeminism.* Philadelphia, PA: New Society.

Pleck, J. (1984). Men's power with women, other men, and society: A men's movement analysis. In E. Carmen and P. P. Rieker (Eds.), *The gender gap in psychotherapy* (pp. 79-90). New York: Plenum.

Pleck, J. H. (1995). The gender role strain paradigm: An update. In R. F. Levant and W. S. Pollack (Eds.), *A new psychology of men* (pp. 11-32). New York: Basic Books.

Polster, M. (1974). Women in therapy: A Gestalt therapist's view. In V. Franks and V. Burtle (Eds.), *Women in therapy* (pp. 247-262). New York: Brunner/Mazel.

Pratt, A. V. (1985). Spinning among field: Jung, Frye, Levi-Strauss and feminist archetypal theory. In E. Lauter and C. S. Rupprecht (Eds.), *Feminist archetypal theory* (pp. 93-136). Knoxville: University of Tenessee Press.

Radicalesbians. (1973). The woman identified woman. In A. Koedt, E. Levine, and A. Rapone (Eds.), *Radical feminism* (pp. 240-245). New York: Quadrangle Books.

Rave, E. (1990). White feminist therapists and anti-racism. *Women and Therapy, 9*(3), 313-326.

Rave, E. J., and Larsen, C. C. (1990). Development of the code: The feminist process. In H. Lerman and N. Porter (Eds.), *Feminist ethics in psychotherapy* (pp. 49-76). Springfield, IL: Charles C Thomas.

Rawlings, E., and Carter, D. (1977). Feminist and nonsexist psychotherapy. In E. I. Rawlings and D. K. Carter (Eds.), *Psychotherapy for women* (pp. 49-76). Springfield, IL: Charles C Thomas.

Redstockings. (Eds.). (1975). *Feminist revolution.* New Paltz, NY: Redstockings, Inc.

Redstockings Manifesto. (1969). In B. Roszak and T. Roszak (Eds.), *Masculine/Feminine: Readings in sexual mythology and the liberation of women* (pp. 272-274). New York: Harper Colophon Books.

Reeser, L. C. (1988). Women and social work activism in the 1980s. *Affilia, 3*(3), 51-62.

Reid, P. T., and Comas-Diaz, L. (1990). Gender and ethnicity: Perspectives on dual status. *Sex Roles, 22,* 397-408.

Reid, P. T., and Kelly, E. (1994). Research on women of color: From ignorance to awareness. *Psychology of Women Quarterly, 18,* 477-486.

Reinelt, C. (1995). Moving onto the terrain of the state: The battered women's movement and the politics of engagement. In M. M. Ferree and P. Y. Yancey (Eds.), *Feminist organizations: Harvest of the new women's movement* (pp. 84-104). Philadelphia, PA: Temple University Press.

Rice, J. K., and Rice, D. G. (1973). Implications of the women's liberation movement for psychotherapy. *American Journal of Psychiatry, 130,* 191-196.

Rich, A. (1976). *Of woman born: Motherhood as experience and institution.* New York: Norton.

Rich, A. (1979). *On lies, secrets and silence.* New York: Norton.

Rich, A. (1989). Compulsory heterosexuality and lesbian existence. In L. Richardson and V. Taylor (Eds.), *Feminist frontiers II* (pp. 120-141). New York: McGraw-Hill (Originally published in 1980).

Richardson, M., and Johnson, M. (1984). Counseling women. In S. D. Brown and R. W. Lent (Eds.), *Handbook of counseling psychology* (pp. 832-877). New York: Wiley.

Riddiough, C. (1981). Socialism, feminism, and gay/lesbian liberation. In L. Sargent (Ed.), *Women and revolution* (pp. 71-90). Boston, MA: South End Press.

Ries, P., and Stone, A. J. (Ed.). (1992). *The American woman 1992-93: A status report.* New York: Norton.

Riger, S. (1992). Epistemological debates, feminist voices: Science, social values, and the study of women. *American Psychologist, 47,* 730-740.

Robertson, J., and Fitzgerald, L. F. (1990). The (mis)treatment of men: Effects of client gender role and life-style on diagnosis and attribution of pathology. *Journal of Counseling Psychology, 37,* 3-9.

Rogers, C. R. (1951). *Client-centered therapy: Its current practice, implications, and theory.* Boston, MA: Houghton Mifflin.

Rogers, C. R. (1956). What it means to become a person. In C. E. Moustakas (Ed.), *The self* (pp. 195-211). New York: Harper Colophon Books.

Rogers, C. R. (1961). *On becoming a person.* Boston, MA: Houghton Mifflin.

Roiphe, K. (1993). *The morning after: Sex, fear, and feminism on campus.* Boston, MA: Little, Brown and Co.

Romaniello, J. (1992). Beyond archetypes: A feminist perspective on Jungian therapy. In L. S. Brown and M. Ballou (Eds.), *Personality and psychopathology: Feminist reappraisals* (pp. 46-69). New York: Guilford Press.

Romney, P. (Fall, 1991). Perspectives on racism and the psychology of women. *Association for Women in Psychology Newsletter,* 1-2.

Rose, H. (1983). Hand, brain, and heart: A feminist epistemology for the natural sciences. *Signs: Journal of Women in Culture and Society, 9,* 73-90.

Rosewater, L. B. (1984). Feminist therapy: Implications for practitioners. In L. E. Walker (Ed.), *Women and mental health policy* (pp. 267-279). Beverly Hills, CA: Sage.

Rosewater, L. B. (1985). Feminist interpretation of traditional testing. In L. B. Rosewater and L. E. A. Walker (Eds.), *Feminist psychotherapies: Integration of therapeutic and feminist systems* (pp. 137-155). Norwood, NJ: Ablex.

Rosewater, L. B. (1990). Public advocacy. In H. Lerman and N. Porter (Eds.), *Feminist ethics in psychotherapy* (pp. 229-247). New York: Springer Publishing Co.

Ross, L. J. (1993). African-American women and abortion: 1800-1970. In S. M. James and A. P. A. Busia (Eds.), *Theorizing Black feminisms: The visionary pragmatism of Black women* (pp. 141-159). New York: Routledge.

Rossi, A. S. (Ed.). (1970). *Essays on sex equality.* Chicago: University of Chicago Press.

Rothblum, E. D. (1983). Sex-role stereotypes and depression in women. In V. Franks and E. D. Rothblum (Eds.), *The stereotyping of women* (pp. 83-111) New York: Springer Publishing Co.

Rubin, G. (1984). The traffic in women: Notes on the "political economy" of sex. In A. Jaggar and P. Rothenberg (Eds.), *Feminist frameworks* (pp. 155-171). New York: McGraw-Hill (Originally published in 1975).

Ruddick, S. (1989). *Maternal thinking: Toward a politics of peace.* New York: Ballantine Books.

Russell, D. (1986). Psychiatric diagnosis and the oppression of women. *Women and Therapy, 5*(4), 83-98.

Russell, D. E. H., and Lederer, L. (1980). Questions we get asked most often. In L. Lederer (Ed.), *Take back the night: Women on pornography* (pp. 23-29). New York: William Morrow and Co.

Russo, A. (1987). Conflicts and contradictions among feminists over issues of pornography and sexual freedom. *Women's Studies International Forum, 10*(2), 103-112.

Sadker, M., and Sadker, D. (1994). *Failing at fairness: How America's schools cheat girls.* New York: Scribners.

San Francisco Redstockings. (1969). Our politics begin with our feelings. In B. Roszak and R. Roszak (Eds.), *Masculine/feminine: Readings in sexual mythology and the liberation of women* (pp. 285-290). New York: Harper and Row.

Sanford, L. S., and Donovan, M. E. (1984). *Women and self-esteem.* New York: Penguin Books.

Sarachild, K. (1970). A program for feminist "consciousness raising." In S. Firestone and A. Koedt (Eds.), *Notes from the second year* (pp. 78-80). New York: Redstockings, Inc.

Sarachild, K. (1975a). The power of history. In Redstockings (Eds.), *Feminist revolution* (pp. 12-43). New York: Redstockings, Inc.

Sarachild, K. (1975b). Consciousness-raising: A radical weapon. In Redstockings (Eds.), *Feminist revolution* (pp. 144-150). New York: Redstockings, Inc.

Sargent, L. (1981). New Left women and men: The honeymoon is over. In L. Sargent (Ed.), *Women and revolution* (pp. xi-xxxi). Boston, MA: South End Press.

Schechter, S. (1982). *Women and male violence.* Boston, MA: South End Press.

Schneider, L. J. (1985). Feminist values in announcements of professional services. *Journal of Counseling Psychology, 32,* 637-640.

Schneir, M. (Ed.). (1972). *Feminism: The essential historical writings.* New York: Vantage Books.

Sedney, M. A. (1989). Conceptual and methodological sources of controversies about androgyny. In R. K. Unger (Ed.), *Representations: Social constructions of gender* (pp. 126-144). Amityville, NY: Baywood.

Segura, D. A., and Pierce, J. L. (1993). Chicana/o family structure and gender personality: Chodorow, familism, and psychoanalytic sociology revisited. *Signs: Journal of Women in Culture and Society, 19,* 62-91.

Sharpe, M. J., and Heppner, P. P. (1991). Gender role, gender-role conflict, and psychological well-being in men. *Journal of Counseling Psychology, 38,* 323-330.

Sherman, J. A. (1980). Therapist attitudes and sex-role stereotyping. In A. Brodsky and R. T. Hare-Mustin (Eds.). *Women and psychotherapy* (pp. 35-66). New York: Guilford Press.

Siegel, R. J. (1983). Accumulated inequalities: Problems in long-term marriages. In J. H. Robbins and R. J. Siegel (Eds.), *Women changing therapy* (pp. 171-178). Binghamton, NY: The Haworth Press.

Silverstein, L. B. (1991). Transforming the debate about child care and maternal employment. *American Psychologist, 46,* 1025-1032.

Silverstien, L. B. (1996). Fathering is a feminist issue. *Psychology of Women Quarterly, 20,* 3-37.

Singer, L. (1992). Feminism and postmodernism. In J. Butler and J. W. Scott (Eds.), *Feminist theorize the political* (pp. 464-475). New York: Routledge.

Smith, B. (Ed.). (1983). *Home girls: A Black feminist anthology.* New York: Kitchen Table, Women of Color Press.

Smith, M. (1980). Sex bias in counseling and psychotherapy. *Psychological Bulletin, 87,* 392-407.

Smith, A., and Douglas, M. A. (1990). Empowerment as an ethical imperative. In H. Lerman and N. Porter (Eds.), *Feminist ethics in psychotherapy* (pp. 43-50). New York: Springer Publishing Co.

Smith, A. J., and Siegel, R. F. (1985). Feminist therapy: Redefining power for the powerless. In L. B. Rosewater and L. E. A. Walker (Eds.), *Handbook of feminist therapy* (pp. 13-21). New York: Springer Publishing Co.

Snell, J. E., Rosenwald, R. J., and Robey, A. (1964). The wifebeater's wife: A study of family interaction. *Archives of General Psychiatry, 11,* 107-112.

Sochting, I., Skoe, E. E., and Marcia, J. E. (1994). Care-oriented moral reasoning and prosocial behavior: A question of gender or sex role orientation. *Sex Roles, 31,* 131-147.

Solomon, M. (1987). *Emma Goldman.* Boston: Twayne Publishers.

Solomon, L. J., Brehony, K. A., Rothblum, E. D., and Kelly, J. A. (1983). The relationship of verbal content in assertive responses to perceptions of the business-person. *Journal of Organizational Behavior Management, 4,* 49-63.

Solomon, L. J., and Rothblum, E. D. (1985). Social skills problems experienced by women. In L. L'Abate and M. A. Milan (Eds.), *Handbook of social skills training and research* (pp. 303-325). New York: Wiley.

Sophie, J. (1987). Internalized homophobia and lesbian identity. *Journal of Homosexuality, 14*(1/2), 53-65.

Spalter-Roth, R., and Schreiber, R. (1995). Outsider issues and insider tactics: Strategic tensions in the women's policy network during the 1980s. In M. M. Ferree and P. Y. Martin (Eds.), *Feminist organizations: Harvest of the new women's movement* (pp. 105-127). Philadelphia: Temple University Press.

Spelman, E. V. (1988). *Inessential woman.* Boston: Beacon Press.

Sprei, J. E. (1987). Group treatment of adult women incest survivors. In C. Brody (Eds.), *Women's therapy groups: Paradigms of feminist treatment* (pp. 198-216). New York: Springer Publishing Co.

Spretnak, C. (1990). Ecofemism: Our roots and flowering. In I. Diamond and G. F. Orenstein (Eds.), *Reweaving the world: The emergence of ecofeminism* (pp. 3-14). San Francisco, CA: Sierra Club Books.

Stanton, E. C. (1898). *The woman's bible.* New York: European Publishing Co (Originally published in 1895).

Stanton, E. C. (1965). Letter to the editor: "Year of the negro." In E. C. Stanton, S. B. Anthony, and M. J. Gage (Eds.), *History of woman suffrage, Vol. 2 (1861-1876)* (pp. 94-95). Rochester, NY: Charles Mann (Originally published in 1881).

Stanton, E. C. (1968). The matriarchate. In A. S. Kraditor (Ed.), *Up from the pedestal* (pp. 140-147). Chicago, IL: Quadrangle Books (Originally published in 1891).

Stanton, E. C. (1972). Address to the New York Legislature, 1960. In M. Schneir (Ed.), *Feminism: The essential historical writings* (pp. 117-121). New York: Vantage Press (Originally published in 1860).

Stanton, E. C. (1972). Solitude of self. In M. Schneir (Ed.), *Feminism: The essential historical writings* (pp. 157-159). New York: Vantage Books (Originally published in 1892).

Stanton, E. C., Anthony, S. B., and Gage, M. J. (Eds.), (1881). *History of woman suffrage, volume 2 (1861-1876).* Rochester, NY: Charles Mann.

Starhawk. (1989). Feminist, earth-based spirituality and ecofeminism. In J. Plant (Ed.), *Healing the wounds: The promise of ecofeminism* (pp. 174-185). Philadelphia, PA: New Society Publishers.

Starhawk. (1992). A men's movement I can trust. In K. L. Hagan (Ed.), *Women respond to the men's movement: A feminist collection* (pp. 27-38). San Francisco, CA: HarperCollins.

Steil, J. M., and Turetsky, B. A. (1987). Is equal better? The relationship between marital equality and psychological symptomatology. In S. Oskamp (Ed.), *Family processes and problems: Social psychological aspects* (pp. 73- 97). Beverly Hills, CA: Sage.

Steinem, G. (1992). *Revolution from within: A book of self-esteem.* Boston, MA: Little, Brown and Co.

Steiner, C. (1971). Radical psychiatry: Principles. In J. Agel (Ed.) *The radical therapist* (pp. 3-7). New York: Ballantine Books.

Stere, K. L. (1985). Feminist assertiveness training: Self-esteem groups and skill training for women. In L. B. Rosewater and L. E. A. Walker (Eds.), *Handbook of feminist therapy* (pp. 51-61). New York: Springer Publishing Co.

Stillson, R. W., O'Neil, J. M., and Owen, S. V. (1991). Predictors of adult men's gender-role conflict: Race, class, unemployment, age, instrumentality-expressiveness, and personal strain. *Journal of Counseling Psychology, 31,* 3- 12.

Stiver, I. P. (1991). The meanings of "dependency" in female-male relationships. In J. V. Jordan, A. G. Kaplan, J. B. Miller, I. P. Stiver, and J. L. Surrey (Eds.), *Women's growth in connection* (pp. 143-161). New York: Guilford Press.

Students for a Democratic Society. (1969). National resolution on women. In B. Roszak and T. Roszak (Eds.), *Masculine/Feminine: Readings in sexual mythology and the liberation of women* (pp. 254-258). New York: Harper and Row.

Sturdivant, S. (1980). *Therapy with women.* New York: Springer Publishing Co.

Sue, D. W. (1981). *Counseling the culturally different: Theory and practice.* New York: Wiley.

Sullivan, H. S. (1953). *The interpersonal theory of psychiatry.* New York: Norton.

Surrey, J. L. (1991). The relational self in women: Clinical implications. In J. V. Jordan, A. G. Kaplan, J. B. Miller, I. P. Stiver, and J. L. Surrey (Eds.), *Women's growth in connection* (pp. 35-43). New York: Guilford Press.

Taggart, M. (1985). The feminist critique in epistemological perspective: Questions of context in family therapy. *Journal of Marital and Family Therapy, 11,* 113-126.

Tallen, B. S. (January, 1990). Co-dependency: A feminist critique. *Sojourner, 15,* 20.

Tallen, B. S. (1992). Twelve step programs: A lesbian feminist critique. *National Women's Studies Association (NWSA) Journal, 2*(3), 390-407.

Tavris, C. (January-February, 1990). The politics of codependency. *The Family Therapy Networker,* 43.

Tavris, C. (1992). *The mismeasure of woman.* New York: Simon and Schuster.

Taylor, M. C., and Hall, J. A. (1982). Psychological androgyny: Theories, methods, and conclusions. *Psychological Bulletin, 92,* 347-366.

Taylor, V., and Whittier, N. (1993). The new feminist movement. In L. Richardson and V. Taylor (Eds.), *Feminist frontiers III* (pp. 533-548). New York: McGraw-Hill.

Tennov, D. (1973). Feminism, psychotherapy, and professionalism. *Journal of Contemporary Psychotherapy, 5,* 107-111.

Thomas, C. (1985). The age of androgyny: The new views of psychotherapists. *Sex Roles, 13,* 381-392.

Thomas, S. A. (1977). Theory and practice in feminist therapy. *Social Work, 22,* 447-454.

Thompson, C. (1971). *On women.* New York: New American Library.

Tinsley, E. G., Sullivan-Guest, S., and McGuire, J. (1984). Feminine sex role and depression in middle-aged women. *Sex Roles, 11,* 25-32.

Tolman, R. M., Mowry, D. D., Jones, L. E., and Brekke, J. (1986). Developing a profeminist commitment among men in social work. In N. Van Den Bergh and L. B. Cooper (Eds.), *Feminist visions for social work* (pp. 61-79). Silver-Spring, MD: National Association of Social Workers.

Tomm, W. (1992). Ethics and self-knowing: The satisfaction of desire. In E. B. Cole and S. Coultrap-McQuin (Eds.), *Explorations in feminist ethics* (pp. 125-130). Bloomington: Indiana University Press.

Tong, R. (1989). *Feminist thought: A comprehensive introduction.* Boulder, CO: Westview Press.

Triandis, H. C. (1989). The self and social behavior in differing cultural contexts. *Psychological Review, 96,* 506-520).

True, R. H. (1990). Psychotherapeutic issues with Asian American women. *Sex Roles, 22,* 477-486.

Truth Sojourner. (1972). Keeping the things going while things are stirring. In M. Schneir (Ed.), *Feminism: The essential historical writings* (pp. 128-131). New York: Vantage Press (Originally published in 1867).

Turner, J. (1990). Let my soul soar: Touch therapy. In T. A. Laidlaw and C. Malmo (Eds.), *Healing voices* (pp. 221-239). San Francisco, CA: Jossey Bass.

Turner, C. (1991). Feminist practice with women of color: A developmental perspective. In M. Bricker-Jenkins, N. R. Hooyman, and N. Gottlieb (Eds.), *Feminist social work practice in clinical settings* (pp. 108-127). Newbury Park, CA: Sage.

Unger, R. K. (1993). The personal is paradoxical: Feminists construct psychology. *Feminism and Psychology, 3,* 211-218.

Unger, R., and Crawford, M. (1996). *Women and gender: A feminist psychology* (2nd edition). New York: McGraw-Hill.

van Wormer, K. (1989). Co-dependency: Implications for women and therapy. *Women and Therapy, 8*(4), 51-63.

Vasquez, M. J. T. (1994). Latinas. In L. Comas-Díaz and B. Greene (Eds.), *Women of color: Integrating ethnic and gender identities in psychotherapy* (pp. 114-138). New York: Guilford Press.

Vaz, K. M. (1992). A course on research issues on women of color. *Women's Studies Quarterly, 20*(1/2), 70-85.

Vogel, S. R. (1979). Discussant's comments symposium: Applications of androgyny to the theory and practice of psychotherapy. *Psychology of Women Quarterly, 3,* 255-258.

Voss, J., and Gannon, L. (1978). Sexism in the theory and practice of clinical psychology. *Professional Psychology: Research and Practice, 7,* 623- 632.

Walker, A. (1983). *In search of our mothers' gardens: Womanist prose.* New York: Harcourt, Brace, Jovanovich.

Walker, L. (1979). *The battered woman.* New York: Harper and Row.

Walker, L. E. A. (1989). Psychology and violence against women. *American Psychologist, 44,* 695-702.

Walker, L. E. A. (1994). *Abused women and survivor therapy.* Washington, DC: American Psychological Association.

Walker, L. E. A., and Dutton-Douglas, M.A. (1988). Future directions: Development, application, and training of feminist therapies. In M. Douglas and L. E. Walker (Eds.), *Feminist psychotherapies: Integration of therapeutic and feminist systems* (pp. 276-300). Norwood, NJ: Ablex.

Walters, M. (1993). The codependent Cinderalla and Iron John. *Family Therapy Networker, 17*(2), 60-65.

Walters, M., Carter, B., Papp, P., and Silverman, O. (1988). *The invisible web: Gender patterns in family relationships.* New York: Guilford Press.

Warren, L. W. (1976). The therapeutic status of consciousness-raising groups. *Professional Psychology: Research and Practice, 7,* 132-140.

Waterhouse, R. L. (1993). "Wild women don't have the blues": A feminist critique of "person-centered" counseling and therapy. *Feminism and Psychology, 3,* 55-72.

Way, N. (1995). "Can't you see the courage, the strength that I have?" Listening to urban adolescent girls speak about their relationships. *Psychology of Women Quarterly, 19,* 107-128).

Wedenoja, M. (1991). Mothers are not to blame: Confronting cultural bias in the area of serious mental illness. In M. Bricker-Jenkins, N. R. Hooymen, and N. Gottlieb (Eds.), *Feminist social work practice in clinical settings* (pp. 179-196). Newbury Park, CA: Sage.

Wehr, D. S. (1987). *Jung and feminism: Liberating archetypes.* Boston: Beacon Press.

Weil, M. (1986). Women, community, and organizing. In N. Van Den Bergh and L. B. Cooper (Eds.), *Feminist visions for social work* (pp. 187-210). Silver Spring, MD: National Association of Social Workers.

Weiser, J. (1990). More than meets the eye: Using ordinary snapshots as tools for therapy. In T. A. Laidlaw and C. Malmo (Eds.), *Healing voices* (pp. 83-117). San Francisco, CA: Jossey-Bass.

Weissman, M. M. (1987). Advances in psychiatric epidemiology: Rates and risks for major depression. *American Journal of Public Health, 77,* 445-451.

Weissman, M., and Klerman, G. L. (1977). Sex differences and epidemiology of depression. *Archives of General Psychiatry, 34,* 98-111.

Weisstein, N. (1968/1993). Psychology constructs the female; or the fantasy life of the male psychologist. *Feminism and Psychology, 3,* 195-210.

Weitzman, L. (1985). *The diverse revolution.* New York: Free Press.

Weitzman, L. M. (1994). Multiple-role realism: A theoretical framework for the process of planning to combine career and family roles. *Applied and Preventive Psychology, 3,* 15-25.

West, C. M. (1995). Mammy, Sapphire, and Jezebel: Historical images of black women and their implications for psychotherapy. *Psychotherapy: Theory, Research, and Practice, 32,* 458-466.

Westkott, M. (1986). *The feminist legacy of Karen Horney.* New Haven, CT: Yale University Press.

Whitley, B. E. (1979). Sex roles and psychotherapy: A current appraisal. *Psychological Bulletin, 86,* 1309-1321.

Whitely, R. M., and Whitely, J. M. (1978). Sex bias in counseling theory. *Counseling and Human Development, 10,* 1-12.

Williams, E. F. (1976). *Notes of a feminist therapist.* New York: Praeger.

Willis, E. (1975). The conservatism of *Ms.* In Redstockings (Eds.), *Feminist Revolution* (pp. 170-171). New York: Random House.

Willis, E. (1984). Radical feminism and feminist radicalism. In S. Sayres, A. Stephanson, S. Aronowitz, and F. Jameson (Eds.), *The 60s without apology* (pp. 91-118). Minneapolis: University of Minnesota Press.

Wilson, E. (1990). Psychoanalysis: Psychic law and order? In T. Lovell (Ed.), *British feminist thought: A reader* (pp. 211-226). Cambridge, MA: Basil Blackwell Ltd.

Withorn, A. (October-November, 1977). The politics of serving the people. *Resist,* 1-6.

Withorn, A. (1980). Helping ourselves: The limits and potential of self help. *Radical America, 14*(3), 25-39.

Withorn, A. (1984). *Serving the people: Social services and social change.* New York: Columbia University Press.

Wolfe, J. L., and Fodor, I. G. (1975). A cognitive/behavioral approach to modifying assertive behavior in women. *The Counseling Psychologist, 5,* 45-59.

Wolfe, J. L., and Fodor, I. G. (1977). Modifying assertive behavior in women: A comparison of three approaches. *Behavior Therapy, 8,* 567-574.

Wollstonecraft, M. (1972). A vindication of the rights of woman. In M. Schneir (Ed.), *Feminism: The essential historical writings* (pp. 6-16). New York: Vantage Books (Originally published in 1792).

Wollstonecraft, M. (1792/1975) *A vindication of the rights of woman.* Baltimore, MD: Penguin.

Women's Liberation Collective. (1969). Towards a woman's revolutionary manifesto. In B. Roszak and T. Roszak (Eds.), *Masculine/Feminine: Readings in sexual mythology and the liberation of women* (pp. 269-272). New York: Harper and Row.

Wong, N. (1991). Socialist feminism: Our bridge to freedom. In C. T. Mohanty, A. Russo, and L. Torres (Eds.), *Third world women and the politics of feminism* (pp. 288-296). Bloomington: Indiana University Press.

Woo, M. (1983). Letter to Ma. In C. Moraga and G. Anzaldua (Eds.), *This bridge called my back* (pp. 140-147). New York: Kitchen Table, Women of Color Press.

Woolfolk, R. L., and Dever, S. (1979). Perceptions of assertion: An empirical analysis. *Behavior Therapy, 10,* 404-411.

Woolger, J. B., and Woolger, R. J. (1989). *The goddess within: A guide to the eternal myths that shape women's lives.* New York: Fawcett Columbine.

Worell, J., and Remer, P. (1992). *Feminist perspectives in therapy: An empowerment model for women.* New York: Wiley.

Wyche, K. F. (1993). Psychology and African-American women: Findings from applied research. *Applied and Preventive Psychology, 2,* 115-121.

Wyckoff, H. (1971). Radical psychiatry in women's groups. In J. Agel (Ed.), *The radical therapist* (pp. 181-187). New York: Ballantine Books.

Wyckoff, H. (1977a). Radical psychiatry for women. In E. I. Rawlings and D. K. Carter (Eds.), *Psychotherapy for women* (pp. 370-391). Springfield, IL: Charles C Thomas.

Wyckoff, H. (1977b). Radical psychiatry techniques for solving women's problems in groups. In E. I. Rawlings and D. K. Carter (Eds.), *Psychotherapy for women* (pp. 392-403). Springfield, IL: Charles C Thomas.

Yoder, J. D. (1985). An academic woman as a token: A case study. *Journal of Social Issues, 42,* 61-72.

Yoder, J. D., and Kahn, A. S. (1993). Working toward an inclusive psychology of women. *American Psychologist, 48,* 846-850.

Young, I. (1981). Beyond the unhappy marriage: A critique of the dual systems theory. In L. Sargent (Ed.), *Women and revolution* (pp. 43-69). Boston, MA: South End Press.

Young-Eisendrath, P. (1984). *Hags and heroes: A feminist approach to Jungian psychotherapy with couples.* Toronto, Canada: Inner City Books.

Young-Eisendrath, P., and Wiedemann, F. L. (1987). *Female authority.* New York: Guilford Press.

Zeldow, P. B. (1978). Sex differences in psychiatric evaluation and treatment: An empirical review. *Archives of General Psychiatry, 35,* 89-93.

Zeldow, P. B. (1984). Sex roles, psychological assessment, and patient management. In C. S. Widom (Ed.), *Sex roles and psychopathology* (pp. 355-374). New York: Plenum.

Zilber, S. (September, 1993). "Enhancing control while reducing blame." Paper presented at the Stop Rape on Campus conference. Ames, IA.

Zweig, M. (1971). Is women's liberation a therapy group? In J. Agel (Ed.), *The radical therapist* (pp. 160-163). New York: Ballantine Books.

Index

Order Your Own Copy of
This Important Book for Your Personal Library!

FEMINIST THEORIES AND FEMINIST PSYCHOTHERAPIES
Origins, Themes, and Variations

_____ in hardbound at $49.95 (ISBN: 1-56024-980-3)

_____ in softbound at $24.95 (ISBN: 1-56023-873-9)

COST OF BOOKS_____

OUTSIDE USA/CANADA/
MEXICO: ADD 20%_____

POSTAGE & HANDLING_____
*(US: $3.00 for first book & $1.25
for each additional book)*
*Outside US: $4.75 for first book
& $1.75 for each additional book)*

SUBTOTAL_____

IN CANADA: ADD 7% GST_____

STATE TAX_____
*(NY, OH & MN residents, please
add appropriate local sales tax)*

FINAL TOTAL_____
*(If paying in Canadian funds,
convert using the current
exchange rate. UNESCO
coupons welcome.)*

☐ **BILL ME LATER:** (\$5 service charge will be added)
(Bill-me option is good on US/Canada/Mexico orders only;
not good to jobbers, wholesalers, or subscription agencies.)

☐ Check here if billing address is different from
shipping address and attach purchase order and
billing address information.

Signature_____

☐ **PAYMENT ENCLOSED: $**_____

☐ **PLEASE CHARGE TO MY CREDIT CARD.**

☐ Visa ☐ MasterCard ☐ AmEx ☐ Discover
☐ Diner's Club

Account # _____

Exp. Date _____

Signature _____

Prices in US dollars and subject to change without notice.

NAME _____

INSTITUTION _____

ADDRESS _____

CITY _____

STATE/ZIP _____

COUNTRY _____ COUNTY (NY residents only) _____

TEL _____ FAX _____

E-MAIL_____
May we use your e-mail address for confirmations and other types of information? ☐ Yes ☐ No

Order From Your Local Bookstore or Directly From
The Haworth Press, Inc.
10 Alice Street, Binghamton, New York 13904-1580 • USA
TELEPHONE: 1-800-HAWORTH (1-800-429-6784) / Outside US/Canada: (607) 722-5857
FAX: 1-800-895-0582 / Outside US/Canada: (607) 772-6362
E-mail: getinfo@haworth.com
PLEASE PHOTOCOPY THIS FORM FOR YOUR PERSONAL USE.

BOF96

OVERSEAS DISTRIBUTORS OF HAWORTH PUBLICATIONS

AUSTRALIA
Edumedia
Level 1, 575 Pacific Highway
St. Leonards, Australia 2065
(mail only) PO Box 1201
Crows Nest, Australia 2065
Tel: (61) 2 9901–4217 / Fax: (61) 2 9906-8465

CANADA
Haworth/Canada
450 Tapscott Road, Unit 1
Scarborough, Ontario M1B 5W1
Canada
(Mail correspondence and orders only. No returns or
telephone inquiries. Canadian currency accepted.)

**DENMARK, FINLAND, ICELAND, NORWAY
& SWEDEN**
Knud Pilegaard
Knud Pilegaard Marketing
Mindevej 45
DK-2860 Soborg, Denmark
Tel: (45) 396 92100

ENGLAND & UNITED KINGDOM
Alan Goodworth
Roundhouse Publishing Group
62 Victoria Road
Oxford OX2 7QD, U.K.
Tel: 44–1865–521682 / Fax: 44–1865-559594
E-mail: 100637.3571@CompuServe.com

GERMANY, AUSTRIA & SWITZERLAND
Bernd Feldmann
Heinrich Roller Strasse 21
D–10405 Berlin, Germany
Tel: (49) 304–434–1621 / Fax: (49) 304–434–1623
E-mail: BFeldmann@t-online.de

JAPAN
Mrs. Masako Kitamura
MK International, Ltd.
1–50–7–203 Itabashi
Itabashi–ku
Tokyo 173, Japan

KOREA
Se–Yung Jun
Information & Culture Korea
Suite 1016, Life Combi Bldg.
61–4 Yoido–dong
Seoul, 150–010, Korea

MEXICO, CENTRAL AMERICA & THE CARIBBEAN
Mr. L.D. Clepper, Jr.
PMRA: Publishers Marketing & Research Association
P.O. Box 720489
Jackson Heights, NY 11372 USA
Tel/Fax: (718) 803–3465
E-mail: clepper@usa.pipeline.com

NEW ZEALAND
Brick Row Publishing Company, Ltd.
Attn: Ozwald Kraus
P.O. Box 100–057
Auckland 10, New Zealand
Tel/Fax: (64) 09–410–6993

PAKISTAN
Tahir M. Lodhi
Al-Rehman Bldg., 2nd Fl.
P.O. Box 2458
65–The Mall
Lahore 54000, Pakistan
Tel/Fax: (92) 42–724–5007

PEOPLE'S REPUBLIC OF CHINA & HONG KONG
Mr. Thomas V. Cassidy
Cassidy and Associates
470 West 24th Street
New York, NY 10011 USA
Tel: (212) 727–8943 / Fax: (212) 727–8539

**PHILIPPINES, GUAM & PACIFIC TRUST
TERRITORIES**
I.J. Sagun Enterprises, Inc.
Tony P. Sagun
2 Topaz Rd. Greenheights Village
Ortigas Ave. Extension Tatay, Rizal
Republic of the Philippines
P.O. Box 4322 (Mailing Address)
CPO Manila 1099
Tel/Fax: (63) 2–658–8466

SOUTH AMERICA
Mr. Julio Emõd
PMRA: Publishers Marketing & Research Assoc.
Rua Joauim Tavora 629
São Paulo, SP 04015001 Brazil
Tel: (55) 11 571–1122 / Fax: (55) 11 575-6876

**SOUTHEAST ASIA & THE SOUTH PACIFIC,
SOUTH ASIA, AFRICA & THE MIDDLE EAST**
The Haworth Press, Inc.
Margaret Tatich, Sales Manager
10 Alice Street
Binghamton, NY 13904–1580 USA
Tel: (607) 722–5857 ext. 321 / Fax: (607) 722–3487
E-mail: getinfo@haworth.com

RUSSIA & EASTERN EUROPE
International Publishing Associates
Michael Gladishev
International Publishing Associates
c/o Mazhdunarodnaya Kniga
Bolshaya Yakimanka 39
Moscow 117049 Russia
Fax: (095) 251–3338
E-mail: russbook@online. ru

LATVIA, LITHUANIA & ESTONIA
Andrea Hedgecock
c/o Iki Tareikalavimo
Kaunas 2042
Lithuania
Tel/Fax: (370) 777-0241 / E-mail: andrea@soften.ktu.lt

**SINGAPORE, TAIWAN, INDONESIA, THAILAND
& MALAYSIA**
Steven Goh
APAC Publishers
35 Tannery Rd.
#10–06, Tannery Block
Singapore, 1334
Tel: (65) 747–8662 / Fax: (65) 747–8916
E-mail: sgohapac@signet.com.sg